THE DIVINE GUIDE IN EARLY SHI'ISM

THE DIVINE GUIDE IN EARLY SHI'ISM

The Sources of Esotericism in Islam

by
Mohammad Ali Amir-Moezzi

translated by
David Streight

STATE UNIVERSITY OF NEW YORK PRESS

This work was originally published in French as *Le Guide Divin Dans Le Shi'isme Originel* by *Éditions Verdier.*

Published by
State University of New York Press, Albany

Printed in the United States of America

For information, address State University of New York Press,
State University Plaza, Albany, N.Y., 12246

Production by Christine Lynch
Marketing by Nancy Farrell

Library of Congress Cataloging-in-Publication Data
Amir-Moezzi, Mohammad Ali.
[Guide divin dans le shi'isme originel. English]
The Divine Guide in Early Shi'ism: The Sources of Esotericism in Islam / by Mohammad Ali Amir-Moezzi : translated by David Streight.
p. cm.
Includes bibliographical references and index.
ISBN 0–7914–2121–X (acid-free) : $54.50. — ISBN 0–7914–2122–8 (pb : acid-free) : $17.95
1. Imamate. 2. Shi'ah—Doctrines—History. I. Title.
BP194.M6413 1994
297'.24—dc20 93–42680
CIP

10 9 8 7 6 5 4 3 2 1

The author offers his heartfelt thanks to Professor Etan Kohlberg for his pertinent and valuable comments in the preparation of the English version of this work. Professor Kohlberg's careful reading of the French text, his erudition, and his encouragement have been of great assistance in bringing the present version up to date.

Contents

To my father Mostafa,
who so loved the imams
In memoriam

ABBREVIATIONS

AIUON = *Annali dell'Istituto Universitario Orientale di Napoli*, Naples
b. = ibn
BSOAS = *Bulletin of the School of Oriental and African Studies*, London
EI1, *EI2* = *Encyclopédie de l'Islam*, first edition, second edition
EPHE = Ecole Pratique des Hautes Etudes
GAL = *Geschichte der Arabischen Literatur* (Brockelmann)
IC = *Islamic Culture*, Heyderabad
IOS = *Israel Oriental Studies*, Tel Aviv
JA = *Journal Asiatique*, Paris
JAOS = *Journal of the American Oriental Society*, New Haven
JSAI = *Jerusalem Studies in Arabic and Islam*, Jerusalem
Md= Muhammad
MUSJ = *Mélanges de l'Université St Joseph*, Beirut
MW = *The Muslim World*, Hartford
REI = *Revue des Etudes Islamiques*, Paris
RHR = *Revue de l'Histoire des Religions*, Paris
RSO = *Rivista degli Studi Orientali*, Rome
SI = *Studia Islamica*, Paris
ZA = *Zeitschrift für Assyriologie und Vorasiatische Archäologie*, Berlin
ZDMG = *Zeitschrift der Deutschen Morganländischen Gesellschaft*, Leipzig-Wiesbaden

PREFACE

Between I. Goldziher's studies (*Beiträge zur Literaturgeschichte der Shiʿa und der sunnitischen Polemik*, Vienna, 1874) and H. Halm's work (*Die Schia*, Darmstadt, 1988), more than a century was dedicated to scholarly study of Shīʿism in general and of Imamism in particular. A number of Islamic scholars and orientalists have been interested in this most important "branch" of Islam, and the number of articles, works and monographs dedicated to the subject is impressive. Nevertheless, when it comes to early Imamism, that is, the doctrine supposedly professed by the historical imams of Shīʿism, later called Twelver Shīʿism, we must surprisingly admit that we still have no clear idea that has been corroborated by a coherent body of historical data. There is still no systematic, exhaustive study of this formative and early phase of the doctrine.

What most characterizes studies dedicated to Imamism is the constant confusion between the teachings of the imams reported by the oldest compilations of Imamite traditions and the ideas professed by later Imamite thinkers and scholars, not to mention the sudden historical and doctrinal evolution that Imamism has known since the occultation of the twelfth imam. We will certainly return to this confusion, which makes a clear understanding of early Imamism so difficult, as well as to the important evolution that Imamism has undergone.

The image, or rather the images, of Imamism reflected through these studies, once they are juxtaposed with the oldest texts, appear fragmentary, confused, even contradictory: ideological coherence and doctrinal logic are completely lacking. On closer examination, it appears impossible to have a global, synthetic understanding of the doctrine, an understanding indispensable for an analytic study of precise and fundamental details of early Imamism. Is it a revolutionary political-religious movement? Is it a mystical anthropomorphist doctrine? Is it a precocious political philosophy at the heart of Islam? Could it be a rationalizing theology of the Muʿtazilite kind, magnified by the irrational cult of the imams? Were the imams jurist theologians respectful of the *sunna* and respected by the entire Community? Were they frustrated men of ambition who developed messianic speculations? Were they enthusuastic enlightened individuals who justified their contradictions with the help of a body of incoherent and heretical ideas? Were they mystical philosophers who received their missions from the universe of archetypes? The reason for such disparate images is at the same time both complex and simple. It is complex because the early corpus of the imams constitutes a colossal survey of works in which cohesive logic and the normal order of discourse are often lacking. Some of this lack may have been voluntary, because of reasons inherent in a number of traditions which characterize themselves as esoteric. Restoring the doctrine to what was probably its original coherence entails a systematic examination of all available parts of this corpus. This has never been done, and such a lacuna has led to a simple problem that, despite its being apparent, has curiously escaped specialists in the field: we do not yet know the *Weltanschauung* of early Imamism. We know nothing, or next to nothing, about the vision that the imams had (and that they imparted to others) of the world, man, and history. In other words, Imamite cosmology, anthropology, and soteriology in their early phase have remained insufficiently studied and explored areas. Since we do not understand, or even know, what the "world vision" of the imams was, both general descriptions of it and analysis of its specific traits remain incomplete and fragmentary, if not also unintelligible.

Given this, we might divide the works dedicated to Imamism into four broad groups. Through this division, we are attempting only to underscore the insufficiency of these works to clarify a coherent historical and global vision of early Imamism:

1. Studies that are too "synthetic," since they are too general. These are general works about Shîʿism or Imamism. Because of their nature—most of them including fourteen centuries of history—these studies present one and the same doctrine regardless the time or the place. Doctrinal evolution, clashes of ideas, or semantic changes in technical terminology are often disregarded, to the benefit of that current that did not become dominant until after the occultation, and to the disadvantage of knowledge of the original teaching that became a minority view. Other works, besides their general nature, are marred by hurried overviews and hasty editing, primarily due to interest which arose from the Iranian revolution and recent events in Lebanon.
2. Studies that are too "analytic." These are works dedicated to precise points or particular aspects of Imamism. As a result of not being sufficiently precise about the "sense" of the early doctrine (that is, its direction, its purpose, as much as its deep meaning), these specific aspects are often considered outside the bounds of their global ideological context. This methodological shortcoming, combined with the confusion referred to above between the teachings of the imams

and the teachings of the theologians, ends up in extrapolations and contradictions. An analysis driven by parts of doctrine without taking into consideration the doctrine in its totality at a given point in time can result only in theses founded on part of the whole. These theses thus run the risk of being separated from other aspects of the doctrine, which remain forgotten or unnoticed. In order to arrive at a full understanding of fundamental details of doctrine, both their place and their interconnection must be analyzed. At the same time it must be recognized that in these details lies a whole which must be understood prior to understanding its constituent elements.

3. Studies that are too "exoteric." These are works that reduce Imamism to its sociopolitical or theological-judicial dimensions, and even these are not always defined or presented in accord with fundamental texts. Imamism is here frequently presented as a contentious political-religious "party" or a theological and judicial "school"; all dogmatic traits, all technical terms and ideas are seen through these lenses. This presentation is based on reductionist points of view, which, properly speaking, sidestep doctrine; without synthetic knowledge, understanding of historical events and theological characteristics can only remain partial—in both senses of the word.
4. Studies that are too "philosophical," where historical inquiry and critical study allow themselves to become absorbed in and annihilated by a certain philosophical vision that sees itself as beyond history. In this case we are faced with works written on the early texts, but whose reasoning and philosophical interpretations are justified only on the basis of hermeneutics from a much later time period. Among this last group of studies the original historical doctrine and its early "sense"—where "theosophy" is omnipresent and "philosophy" is nearly nonexistent—are almost completely absent.

The question thus remains open: what did the imams of the Twelvers profess? What was their teaching, not as it appears through the work of theologians, mystics, or Imamite philosophers, but in its original form that logically ought to be researched in the context of the entire early corpus, as it was collected in the very first compilations of Imamite traditions? It is only through a systematic examination and critical analysis of this corpus that the early doctrine of the imams has the possibility of being defined in a coherent and synthetic manner. This doctrine presents itself, as the imams proclaimed, as a "true religion" (*al-dîn al-ḥaqq*) or a "solid religion" (*al-dîn al-qayyim*); it shows itself to be complex, polyvalent, and presenting numerous interconnected and interdependent aspects. In this work it has been our attempt to discover a way to begin to untangle, albeit only a beginning, this bundle of ideas and practices.

Through our research, we have become aware that what has been called the Imamite "world vision" could be considered as the "center of emanation" from which the dark recesses of this labyrinthine doctrine might be clarified, and its goal and meaning understood. The true axis around which this world vision turns is the person of the Perfect Guide (the imam) in his ontological dimension (in this acceptation, it will be written with a capital "i": the Imam) as well as in his historical dimension (where "imam" will be written with a lowercase "i"). The two dimensions are inextricably bound to one another. Imamism's cosmology-cosmogony, its anthropology, its soteriology, and its eschatology all gravitate around its Imamology; these fields remain, as we have said, insufficiently studied and analyzed. This is why the essential part of our methodological procedure consists in separating out all the definitions and descriptions of the Imam given by the imams themselves through their voluminous corpus of works. The territory remains unexplored especially as regards a global definition of early Imamism through its world vision; only this definition can lead to a clear understanding of the structure. The definition should furnish us with a mode of understanding doctrinal traits as well as historical facts, if not also with some kind of satisfactory means of interpreting these facts and traits. The doctrinal history of early Imamism remains to be written; given the almost unknown character of the subject, our procedure voluntarily strays from being an erudite work, and attempts rather to work out a theoretical framework.

Throughout our research, the admirable lines of Josef Van Ess have served as a guide: "Given the state of underdevelopment that our research is in, it seems to me that *taqlîd* can only be disastrous, even more than normal. What we must do is proceed toward a critical analysis of all the information that the sources offer, an analysis accompanied by an imaginitive understanding of a time and problems which are not ours. To arrive at the reality of the events it is essential that we first destroy the interpretations to which the past has been subjected. We are aware that there is a danger of our doing nothing more than replacing one interpretation with another; but even failure is better than repetition" (*Une lecture à rebours de l'histoire du muʿtazilisme*, Avant propos). We believe strongly that a failure that opens perspectives for fruitful research is worth more than the repetition of the misinterpretations of the past. Our plan for the present study is thus to examine the data available and to form hypotheses based on these data; to outline the essential structures of early Imamism; to spend time with the fundamental, that is, with the unifying threads, with an aim to understanding both the unified and what is accessory to it; and to arrive as clearly as possible at the vision that the imams and, after them, a certain number of faithful Imamites had, and still have, of their own religious universe.

1

Introduction: Return to the Earliest Sources

> Our teaching is arduous;
> the only ones who can withstand it are
> a prophet sent to men, an angel of Proximity,
> or an initiated one whose heart has been tested by God for faith.

The entire doctrinal structure of Imamism is dominated by the fundamental figure of the Guide par excellence, the imam. It must however be immediately added that if this importance is well known in itself, its "why" and its "how," its nature, and its meaning, all founded on ideas that can be considered as original in early Islam, remain to be clarified. Our focus in this study will thus be Imamology and, within this framework, it seems essential to define "Imam" as well as can be done by using the words of the imams themselves. For reasons that will be examined in this introductory chapter, only the doctrine in its earliest formative phase will be considered (that is, the period covered by the lives of the historical imams); our study will take place by using the imams' own words (*aḥâdith*, *akhbâr*) pronounced theoretically between the middle of the first/seventh century and the beginning of the fourth/ninth century. In order to arrive at this strictly Imamite definition and to analyze its consequences, the themes studied will naturally be those that constitute so many "distinctive traits" of this early Imamism, traits that give it a certain originality within the early stages of Islamic thought. Our work is thus founded on doctrinal and dogmatic tradition, and not on the juridical tradition that differs little from the Sunni tradition;[1] the Sunni tradition will be of use to us only in an indirect and secondary manner.

The impressive dimensions of this corpus, its abstruseness, its lack of homogeneity and intrinsic logic, its need for systematic examination, and the complexity of the subject make the task a difficult one. These factors, in addition to the originality and the flagrant "heretical" character of a number of fundamental ideas, are undoubtedly the essential reasons for the absence of a synthetic and exhaustive study of this phase of Imamite doctrine. We have thus felt it necessary to pull together all the information available on this subject, less with a view to drawing definitive conclusions that would be impossible to formulate clearly given the present state of our knowledge, than to compiling an anthology of documents from which future research might draw.

Our first need was to recognize and catalogue sources, to identify their nature and their aims, and to set apart those texts that, too often, have been considered as belonging to the original doctrine that was thought be to homogenous and unchanged. We shall begin with an examination of the current point of view according to which Imamism is a "rational theology" of the Muʿtazilite type. Two facts are at the base of this idea that, to our view, immediately distorts any approach to the question. First of all, the imams have always said that *ʿaql* (often translated by "reason") is the "organ" through which their doctrine is understood. Secondly, quite early in the history of Imamism, a current that might be called "rationalist" became predominant. We shall thus first of all attempt to define *ʿaql* in the way that the imams meant it to be understood. This definition, far from dialectical and logical reason, tends to show that rational, or rather "rationalized," Imamism appeared, if not quite late, at least after the time of the imams. An outline of this evolution will help us to identify the sources belonging to the original current of Imamism, before its rationalization. Since the science of Imamite hadith and its criteriology of authenticity both appeared quite late, it would appear that only those criteria that have their genesis in doctrinal history could help us, first, to discern which sources arose out the early doctrine, and second, to prevent confusion between the early doctrine and later ideas. This methodological presentation thus entails four points: the idea of Imamite *ʿaql* in its original acceptation; the distinction of two Imamite traditions, each with its own nature and each with an entirely different vision of the world; the identification of those sources that belong to the original tradition; and finally the authority and the nature of Imamite hadith. These four points may be considered as epistemological elements constituting in themselves four different introductory criteria for understanding all that will be dealt with in the present study.

I-1. HIERO-INTELLIGENCE AND REASON

The *ʿaql* that is translated, depending on the context, by "reason," "intellect," "intelligence," or even "science" or "discernment" is a complex and delicate notion that covers a great semantic field, especially in the first centuries of Islam and previous to its conceptual quasi-stability after the systematization of Islamic dogmatic theology and philosophy. Islamologists and Arabists continue to research the precise early meaning of the word and to shed light on its many facets.[2] Before the advent of Islam, it seems that the term had no special importance; it merely meant "good sense." Etymologically, *ʿaql* was "what was tied to an animal's feet to restrain it"; its abstract meaning might thus be said to refer to that faculty that restrains human beings from foolishness. In pre-Islamic practical morality, *'aql* seems to have been eclipsed and even pushed into the background by the rich idea of *ḥilm*,[3] an attitude of tremendous importance in Arab tribal mentality that included numerous character traits "from serene justice and the measure of longanimity and indulgence to self control and dignity of demeanor."[4] It is important to point out here that it is *ḥilm* that stands in opposition to *jahl* and *safah*, that is, ignorance (not involuntary lack of knowledge, but "guilty ignorance"), the ignorance of one who believes himself to be free of faults and who makes no distinction between what is good for him and what is harmful. This is the *ḥilm* that gave those who possessed it, especially the tribal notables (the *sayyid*), unquestionable moral and social authority. This conceptual situation changes with the text of the Qur'an. Although the term *'aql* itself is absent from the Qur'an, the simple form *'aqala/ya'qilu* alone appears over fifty times, where it is used in the same syntagms of syntactical and stylistic structure as the verbs *tafakkara* (to think about God's Signs [*âyât*], to remember them, to meditate on them), *tadhakkara* (to keep God in one's memory), *sha'ara* (to grasp intuitively the meaning of God's signs), *faqiha* (to understand, to grasp especially the Word of God), and finally *'alima* (to be familiar with and to know how to recognize God's signs). Here *'aql* is opposed to *jahl*, the ignorance of the impious. From this point on the root covers a *religious* semantic field, and the idea is elevated to a sacred, transcendent dimension. It would be possible to think that the faculty of practical "good sense" before the time of Islam became, through the Qur'an, the faculty of religious "Good Direction" that to a certain extent takes the place of the *ḥilm* of the *jâhiliyya*.[5] The *'aql* found in the Qur'an may be considered a kind of consciousness or perception of the divine, simultaneously consisting of immediate meditative reflection, remembering, intuiting, and deep knowledge that imply assent and submission to divine authority.

Early Imamism, which will be defined later, exploits this religious domain of *'aql* to the extreme, going so far as to turn it into a capital aspect of its dogma in general, and of its Imamology in particular. According to the imams, *'aql* is the best if not the only way of approach to and understanding of their teachings;[6] in other words, without *'aql* the sayings of the imams remain incompletely understood, ineffective, or even incomprehensible. This is undoubtedly why Muḥammad b. Ya'qûb al-Kulaynî (d. 328–29/940–41) began the dogmatic part of his colossal *Kâfî* with the "kitâb al-'aql wa-l-jahl."[7] A thematic division of the traditions that make up this "book" will help us better to grasp the definition given by the imams of this important idea.

a) The Cosmogonic Dimension of *'aql*

In a famous tradition (attributed to the sixth imam, Ja'far al-Ṣâdiq) known as "the tradition of the armies of *'aql*" (*ḥadîth junûd al-'aql*), a number of fundamental aspects of the cosmogonic dimension of *'aql* are outlined. *'Aql*, proceeding from the God's Light, was the first of God's creations;[8] it is characterized by its submission and its will to be near God:

> God—may He be glorified and exalted—created *ʿaql* first among the spiritual entities; He drew it forth from the right of His throne (*ʿarsh*), making it proceed from His own Light. Then He commanded it to retreat, and it retreated, to advance, and it advanced; then God proclaimed: "I created you glorious, and I gave you pre-eminence over all my creatures."[9] Then Ignorance (*al-jahl*) was created; seeing its pride and its hesitation in approaching God, He damned it: "Then, from the briny ocean God created dark Ignorance; He ordered it to retreat and it retreated, to advance and it did not advance. Then God said to it 'Certainly you have grown proud,' and He damned it and chased it from His presence."[10] *ʿAql* and Ignorance then see themselves endowed with 75 Armies (*jund*) that are respectively the same number of moral and spiritual qualities and defects; they are elevated to the rank of cosmic powers and counter-powers, locked in combat from the origin of the universe. "Then God endowed *ʿaql* with 75 armies; when Ignorance saw God's generosity toward *ʿaql*, it became ferociously hostile and said to God: "O Lord, here is a creature similar to me [Ignorance is also a spiritual entity, a nonmatierial counter-power]; you have privileged it and made it powerful. I am its adversary and I have no power. Give me troops like those of *ʿaql*." And God replied, "So be it, but if you revolt again I shall banish you and your troops from my Mercy." Ignorance accepted this condition and God gave it 75 Armies.[11] The list of *ʿaql*'s Armies and their corresponding opposites from the Armies of Ignorance follows.[12]

Throughout this study it will be seen that Imamite doctrine constantly had recourse to parallelling, if not identifying, *ʿaql*, its Armies, and the Imam and his faithful, on one hand, and Ignorance, its Armies, and the enemies of the Imams on the other.[13] The cosmogonic dimension given to *ʿaql* and its Armies seems to be the result of a doctrinal development that breaks the mold of Qur'anic definitions and turns it into a kind of cosmic Morality, a metaphysical prototype of human morality, at war with cosmic Immorality.

b) The Ethical-Epistemological Dimension

On the human level, *ʿaql* is not just an acquired quality, but a gift from God. One might call it an innate faculty of transcendent knowledge, developed to a greater or lesser extent depending on the individual. On this level it is nevertheless different from *adab*, a good education, a kind of profane morality that is at the same time both the source and the result of secular knowledge: " *ʿAql* is a favor from God," says ʿAlî al-Riḍâ, the eighth imam, "whereas good education is a quality acquired with difficulty. He who works to achieve a good education can succeed, while he who works to attain *ʿaql* only increases his ignorance."[14] *ʿAql* cannot be acquired by human effort; man has no control over its presence. This aspect of *ʿaql* is illustrated by a dialogue between the sixth imam and one of his disciples.[15] The latter said, "one man knows the totality of my message [*kalâm*: perhaps some kind of doctrinal explanation?] after a few phrases; another does not understand me until my explanation is completed; a third, after having heard all that I had to say, asks me to explain again." Jaʿfar responds, "Do you know why that is? It is because the first is he whose embryo was kneaded with his *ʿaql* at the time of conception. The second is he whose *ʿaql* was instilled at the breast of his mother. The third is he whose *ʿaql* was composed in adulthood."[16] All man can do is to develop, to actualize *ʿaql*, this divine gift in the potential state; it is actualized with the aid of *ʿilm*, the initiatory knowledge taught by the imams in different fashions.[17] "Under the direction of his *ʿaql*," says Abû ʿAbdallâh Jaʿfar al-Ṣadiq, "which God has bestowed upon him as a support, an ornament, and a guide to salvation, the possessor of *ʿaql* (*al-ʿâqîl*) realizes that God is Truth, that God is his lord, that there are things that God loves and others that He does not love, that both obedience and disobedience toward God exist; and he also finds that by *ʿaql* alone one cannot grasp [the depth of] all this, that only sacred Knowledge (*ʿilm*) and its development can help man, and that without this Knowledge, *ʿaql* is of no assistance . . . "[18] Inversely, knowledge, or rather recognition of true Knowledge, that taught by the imams, is only possible through *ʿaql*.[19]

c) The Spiritual Dimension

In a long speech addressed to the famous Hishâm b. al-Ḥakam (who probably died shortly after 179/795–796),[20] the seventh imam, Mûsä al-Kâẓim outlines the different spiritual aspects of *ʿaql*.[21] He discusses almost all Qurʾanic references where the root *ʿaqala/yaʿqilu* appears, and presents *ʿaql* as a faculty for apprehending the divine, a faculty of metaphysical perception (identified with *baṣar*, interior vision), a "light" (*nûr*) located in the heart, and through which one can discern and recognize signs from God.[22] This presentation remains within the framework of definitions that differ from the Qurʾanic context, as we previously explained. One quite important point of doctrine is also mentioned: while the prophets and the imams constitute the "exterior proof" (*ḥujja ẓâhira*) of God, *ʿaql* is the "interior proof" (*ḥujja bâṭina*).[23] The highly spiritual and religious dimension of *ʿaql* stands apart from the constant parallels established between the imam (exterior *ʿaql*) and *ʿaql* (the interior imam).[24] The latter is a kind of "subtle organ" of religion, without which man is cut off from his relationship with the divine plan. Without *ʿaql*, man is without religion; that is, without that which can "tie" him back to God, man then forgets his condition as creature and falls into an impious selfishness. It is undoubtedly in this sense that ʿAlî's words, as they are reported by Jaʿfar al-Ṣadiq, must be understood: "Self infatuation is proof of the weakness of *'aql*."[25] According to a tradition attributed to the first imam, 'Alî b. Abî Ṭâlib, the angel Gabriel appeared to Adam and proposed, following a command from God, that Adam choose from among three things: *'aql*, modesty (*ḥayâ'*), and religion (*dîn*). Adam chose the first of these and the angel asked the other two to depart, abandoning Adam; they replied that they had received an order from God to remain always in the company of *'aql*, wherever it was.[26] "He who has *'aql*," says Ja'far, "has a religion, and he who has a religion wins Paradise."[27]

d) The Soteriological Dimension

The soteriological dimension was adumbrated in Ja'far's words cited previously. In the absence of *'aql*, the "organ" of religion, there can only be false religiousness, an appearance of piety, hypocrisy. When someone mentioned the *'aql* of a man obsessed by prayers and ablutions, Ja'far replied that such a man could not have *'aql*, since he was obeying Satan.[28] Later, responding to the question "What is *'aql*?" he said: "That by which the All Merciful is worshipped, and through which Paradise is won." Then he was asked, "Then what was it that Mu'âwiya had?[29] "It was trickery, a satanic attitude resembling *'aql*, but it was not *'aql*."[30] The quality of the religion of each thus depends on the quality of his *'aql*,[31] which is why it is the criterion by which men will be judged at the Last Judgment. According to a tradition reported by the fifth and eighth imams, Muhammad al-Bâqir and Abû al-Hasan 'Alî al-Ridâ, when God observes *'aql*'s submission and desire for proximity to Him, He will solemnly announce: "By My Glory and My Majesty, I have not created any creature dearer [or in another version, better] than you, and I offer you in your entirety only to him whom I love. It is taking only you into consideration that I command and that I forbid, that I punish and that I reward."[32] Al-Baqîr further says, "At the judgment on Resurrection Day, God judges His servants according to the degree of *'aql* that He has given them in this world."[33] As is known, in Imamite doctrine the coming of the resurrection is intimately tied to the "Return" of the hidden imam and to his final mission of definitively conquering the forces of Ignorance; one of the phases of this mission consists in completing and unifying the *'aql* of the handful of faithful who have resisted this period of spiritual darkness: "At the time of the Return, God will place the hand of our *qâ'im* on the head of the faithful; through this hand, they will have their *'aql* unified and their *ḥilm* completed."[34]

This *'aql* is thus a cosmic entity, the "imam" of the forces of Good in perpetual struggle against the forces of Evil directed by Ignorance. It is reflected in man as an intuition of the Sacred, as a light in the heart, making him a soldier of the "imam," of religion, and thus of God; it helps man to fight against the darkness of impious ignorance, and guarantees him salvation. "The beginning of all things," says Ja'far al-Sadiq, "their origin, their force and their prosperity, is that *ʿaql* without which one can profit from nothing. God created it to adorn His creatures, and as a light for them. It is through *ʿaql* that the servants recognize that God is their creator and that they themselves are created beings, that He is the director and they are the directed, that He is the eternal and they are the ephemeral; they are guided by their *ʿaql* when they observe God's creation, His heavens, His earth, His sun, His moon, His night and His day. . . . It is thanks to *ʿaql* that they can distinguish what is beautiful from what is ugly, that they realize that darkness is in ignorance and that light is in Knowledge."[35]

It is clearly seen that this *ʿaql*, which might be translated by "hiero-intelligence," is different in its definition as well as in its implications, from that *ʿaql* to which we are accustomed in theological texts. Depending on the context, the latter is translated by "reason," "intellect," "faculty of dialectical reasoning," "discernment," and so on. Although all these nuances may not be equal to one another, it might nevertheless be said that, to a general degree, the *ʿaql* of the theologians, even Imamite theologians, is the "organ" of the rational, while for the imams it is just as much the faculty of apprehending the rational as it is the "organ" for perceiving the suprarational, this second domain both including and superseding the first; it is the human counterpart to the cosmic entity, the first entity created by God.

The semantic slide from the Qur'anic idea of *ʿaql*, of which the early Imamite *ʿaql* appears to be a doctrinal development, to the logical *ʿaql* of the theologians appears to have taken place under the influence of Aristotelian texts translated into Arabic and the establishment of the dialectical methodology of *kalâm* (especially Muʿtazilite), from as early as the third/ninth century.[36] A look at the word in its philological context illustrates the rationalist evolution of the meaning of *ʿaql*. At the very beginnings of Islam, *ʿaql* was seen as the opposite of *jahl*, the impious ignorance of a person who is unconscious of the sacred, of God, of his Signs and his Mercies; by the beginning of the third/ninth century, its opposites, at least in popular language, were words like *junûn* (madness, lack of good sense) or one of its synonyms, or *safah* (in the sense of "lack of the facility of logical reasoning," the opposite of *safah* being *ḥikma*).[37] It must nevertheless be added that the new acceptation of *ʿaql* never goes so far as to be equivalent to the almost "profane" meaning that it had before Qur'anic revelation; the idea from that time on found itself in a religious universe and the term was used, with very few exceptions, in religious contexts. In Sunni hadith, such as it is recorded by the authoritative compilations, *ʿaql* almost always has the technical meaning of *fiqh*, as the equivalent to "price of blood" (*diya*). In the *kalâm*, the term is almost a synonym of *ʿilm*, in the sense of knowledge (religious or not) that comes either from sacred texts or from perception or our own knowledge of ourselves. Under the influence of a basically Neo-Platonic system of thought, with the first philosophers the idea wavers somewhere between theological concepts and a profane science of the soul. Among certain philosophers, it achieves the rank of a sacred cosmic entity having its potential counterpart in the human soul. Thus, *ʿaql* is not secularized, but rather rationalized and humanized, in a culture where reason and man cannot be conceived of except through their relation with God. In the Imamite milieu, al-shaykh al-Mufîd (d. 413/1022) seems to be the first great theologian to found his theological argumentation on *ʿaql* in its new acceptation, that is, as dialectical and logical reasoning.[38] Although in the definitions that he gives of the word he remains faithful to those of the imams,[39] he nevertheless feels forced to adopt the same usage as the Muʿtazilites in order to be able to confront them in theological polemics.[40] In his disciple al-Sharîf al-Murtaḍä (d. 436/1044), also a disciple of the famous Muʿtazilite thinker ʿAbd al-Jabbâr (415/1025), *ʿaql* appears to be completely devoid of its early meaning and becomes a synonym of "reasoning" (*istidlâl*)[41] and "faculty of dialectical speculation" (*naẓar*).[42] The intellectual influence of these thinkers in a particular doctrinal and historical context (cf. later discussion) was such that the rationalist tendency became, thereafter, the majority and dominant view within Imamism; this view has existed up to the present day. The new idea of *ʿaql* supplanted the previous one, and there remained between the two only a homonymous relationship open to confusion. The early *ʿaql* was defined as the axis of the religion of the imams, like an indispensable key for opening the mysteries of their teachings and for opening oneself to these teachings. The spiritual vision attained by virtue of this hiero-intelligence allowed one to distinguish the true from the false, light from darkness, Knowledge from Ignorance, in short, the doctrine of the imams from other doctrines. This doctrine, as will be seen in the present study, essentially consists of cosmogonic, mystic, esoteric, even magical and occult elements, that is, nonrational elements. It is through a kind of phenomenon of "resonance," of mystic synergy, that "the interior imam" or the *ʿaql* of the faithful believer (that is, the true Shiʿite [*al-mu'min*][43]), recognized and believed in the truth of the words, acts, and gestures, regardless of how incredible and nonrational they were, of the exterior *ʿaql* that the historical imams were. Through the "light" of hiero-intelligence, the religious consciousness of the faithful Imamite not only perceived cosmogonic data, inspired Knowledge, or the miraculous powers of the imams and other esoteric and occult elements that made up the essentials of basic Imamite doctrine as credible, but this light elevated these elements to the level of articles of faith. It happened this way because hiero-intelligence made all these elements look like so many Signs and gifts from God. The confusion between this hiero-intelligence and dialectical reasoning (both of which are referred to by the word *ʿaql*) is all the more serious here, since dialectical reasoning, which exists at a different epistemological, perceptual, and conceptual level, naturally rejects the nonrational; therefore religious consciousness is modified, since reasoning, even religious reasoning or reasoning evolving in a religious context, can neither perceive nor accept hiero-intelligence's intuitive and mystical "resonance" with the "miraculous," as a matter of faith. Al-Mufîd criticizes his master Ibn Bâbûye in the name of reason.[44] Al-Sharîf al-Murtaḍä, even more intransigent, goes so far as to censure al-Kulaynî and others, accusing them of having introduced into their compilations a great number of traditions which appear absurd in the light of reason.[45] Al-shaykh al-Ṭûsî (d. 460/1067) did likewise in his compilation of traditions about the hidden imam, by saying nothing about all the traditions of esoteric or occult character, traditions which he knew through one of his own sources, the *Kitâb al-ghayba* written by al-Nuʿmânî Ibn Abî Zaynab (d. circa 345/956). Because of the homonymy, these thinkers neglected the semantic slide in the idea, and believed they were working in the name of the *ʿaql* so lauded by the imams.[46] The imams were censured at the same time that their directives were believed to be followed.

The case of *ʿaql* shows first of all the need for paying particular attention to the technical terms of early Imamism: they must first be identified and recognized as such, since, given our mental habits, they can appear quite insignificant, with obvious meaning (as was seen in the case of *muʿmin* and *îmân*; the cases of terms such as *ʿilm*, *qalb*, *shîʿa*, and others will be seen later); and they must next be placed within the framework of a critical reading of all the references offered by the texts, and this within the larger framework of a doctrinal history of early Imamism without which semantic evolutions might go unnoticed, and the phases of the doctrine thus remain confused.

The early idea of *ʿaql* also shows the angle from which the imams wished the approach, the perception, and the manner of understanding their teachings to be undertaken. In its early acceptation, *ʿaql* as "hiero-intelligence" may be considered as the organ of early Imamism's "world vision"; it is in attributing to *ʿaql* the later meaning of "dialectical reasoning" that Imamism was looked upon as a "rational" doctrine, and thus the confusions and contradictions; this is why *ʿaql* was reserved the place of prominence, as an essential introductory criterion, at the head of this study.

I-2 ESOTERICISM AND RATIONALIZATION

What has just been said about *ʿaql* and its evolution may also be considered as a new piece to add to studies of the doctrinal history of the division of Imamites into what has now come to be called the Qumm School and the Baghdad School, or even the *akhbârî* (the traditionalists) and the *uṣûlî* (the rationalists).[47] Nevertheless, it must be explained that our nonrationalist/rationalist division which, as shall be seen, corresponds to the Imamite esotericists and exotericists, does not always coincide with the *akhbârî* and *uṣûlî* division, since the former were not always esotericists, and the latter were not always exotericists. In spite of what has often been said, the division of Imamites into partisans and adversaries of the use of dialectical reasoning in cases of sacred concepts does not date from the eleventh/seventeenth century;[48] on the contrary, its first traces can already be felt in the proto-Shiʿites of the second-third/eighth-ninth centuries.[49] Actually, one could go back as far as the entourage of the sixth imam, Jaʿfar al-Ṣâdiq (d. 148/765) and discover the first tendencies toward this opposition between the adversaries and the partisans of the use of dialectical theology, *kalâm*. Heresiological and biobibliographical sources count a certain number of Jaʿfar's disciples as the very first *mutakallimûn* of Imamism: Zurâra b. Aʿyan (d. 150/767), Hishâm b. Sâlim al-Jawâlîqî, Muhammad b. al-Nuʿmân *mu'min* (or, according to his adversaries, *shayṭân*) al-Ṭâq, Hishâm b. al-Ḥakam (d. circa 179/795–96).[50] The theological doctrines of these thinkers have come down to us in fragments only, most of the time related by their adversaries. Furthermore, their ideological language was still at the stage of lexical and conceptual "exploration." It is nevertheless undeniable that they became accustomed to these theological polemics, and what we do know of their thoughts and of the titles of the treatises attributed to them shows that they actively contributed to the formation of the budding science of *kalâm*.[51] On the basis of these facts, certain researchers have jumped to the conclusion that the imams, particularly the fifth and sixth imams, were themselves "theologians" who encouraged the study and use of *kalâm*.[52] The imams were far from being in agreement with all the intellectual ideas and methods of their theologian disciples.[53] The latter did not profess a unique doctrine, in this case that of the imams; not only did they enter into conflict among themselves,[54] but (though it was rare) they openly opposed, even affronted, their "guides."[55] Examination of the still extant fragments of the teachings of these disciples gives evidence of, among other things, a strong Dayṣânite influence in Hishâm b. al-Ḥakam[56] and ideas clearly colored by Murji'ism with a Jahmite tendency in Muḥammad b. Nuʿmân and Hishâm al-Jawâlîqî.[57] It appears as though the imams occasionally tolerated the study and use of *kalâm* for certain disciples, essentially for reasons of a "tactical" order, particularly to be able to affront their adversaries during public debates, but also to safeguard the unity of the Imamite community threatened by sometimes violent differences of opinion and quarrels over matters of theology.[58] But these cases would have been exceptional, and what characterized their teachings from this point of view is undoubtedly a position that is frankly hostile to *kalâm* and to the use of dialectical and logical reasoning, in whatever form (*qiyâs*, *ra'y*, *ijtihâd*), in the domain of sacred concepts. The first compilations of Imamite traditions give evidence of this in numerous cases. "The partisans of analogical reasoning (*aṣḥâb al-maqâ'îs*) were in search of [divine] knowledge, but their method resulted only in distracting them from the Truth; God's religion can not be acquired by analogical reasoning."[59]

Samâʿa b. Mihrân (Abû Muhammad al-Ḥaḍramî al-Kûfî, who died in Medina, a disciple of the sixth and seventh imams) said: "During our meetings we [the disciples] occasionally talk about something upon which, thanks to your blessed presence, we have a written document. But we also occasionally come upon something about which we have no idea; in this event we compare it to that case which is most similar to it, and about which we have information, with the use of analogical reasoning (*'indanâ mâ yushbihuh fa-naqîsu 'alâ aḥsanih*)." The seventh imam, Musä al-Kâẓim, said: "You have nothing to do with analogical reasoning (*wa mâ lakum wa li l-qiyâs*); those who came before you perished because of such reasoning. When it comes to a case about which you have received information, speak about it; otherwise, keep silent."[60]

Someone asked Ja'far: "What is your personal idea (*ra'y*) on such a subject?" The sixth imam replied, "Silence. All that we [the imams] say comes from the Prophet. We have no personal ideas."[61]

"He who knows and venerates God abstains from speaking about Him [or: abstains from using *kalâm*—literally, the word—in what concerns Him]."[62]

"Speak of God's creation and not of God Himself; using *kalâm* in what pertains to God only increases confusion (*taḥayyur*, or according to another tradition: going astray, *tîh*)."[63]

"Perdition is the lot of the partisans of *kalâm* (*yahliku aṣḥâb al-kalâm*), and salvation is that of the "submissive" (*wa yanjû l-musallimûn*). The submissive are the nobles [of this Community] (*nujabâ'*)."[64]

One of the principal effects of the rejection of *kalâm* and its methods of investigation by the imams was the predominance of the "traditionalist" tendency of traditionists from what is now called the "Qumm School." It is to be noted that this took place during the period of the presence of the imams, and during both the minor Occultation (260/284) and the major Occultation (which began in 329/941).[65] This predominance appears to have been almost absolute: the defenders of the "Intermediary School" (midway between "traditionalism" and "rationalism") and the "rationalists" were quite minor figures.[66] It was only in the second half of the fourth/tenth century that the "rationalist" tendency of theologians and jurists of the "Baghdad School" began to take the upper hand, with the impetus of the monumental work of Shaykh al-Mufîd (d. 413/1022) and his direct disciples.

To our knowledge, none of the scholars who dealt with this aspect of early Imamism asked the simple yet essential question, What was the effect of this passing from "traditionalism" to "rationalism," a transition that definitively (up to the present day) gives the predominant place to the "rationalists," on basic Imamite doctrine? What were the implications of the "rationalization" of Imamism (which began in the fourth/tenth century and continues up to the present day) for a very great majority of Twelver theologians, jurists and thinkers? What was the Imamite "worldview" before this change, and what did it become thereafter?

It would appear that a thematic comparison of the greatest early sources of Imamite traditions might open up a field of research and demonstrate a historical point of capital importance for the whole doctrinal evolution of

Imamism. We shall certainly compare the treatment of typical Imamite themes, and we shall do this through the most famous of the early sources, taken in chronological order. Three major themes in Imamite dogma will be used as guideposts: 1) cosmogonic data; 2) information on the miraculous and occult aspects of the imams, particularly where these concern their Knowledge and their supernatural powers; and 3) those data pertaining to what the imams thought of the Qur'an.[67] The oldest large compilation of Imamite dogmatic traditions known to us is that of Ṣaffâr al-Qummi (d. 290/903), the *Baṣâ'ir al-darajât* ; it will thus serve as the basic source for our comparison.[68] Other texts to be examined include the *Uṣûl min al-kâfî,* by al-Kulaynî (d. 329/940), some of the dogmatic works written by Ibn Bâbûye (d. 381/991), and some of the works of al-Mufîd (d. 413/1022) and of his disciple al-Sharîf al-Murtaḍä (d. 436/1044).

Ṣaffâr gives extensive details about cosmogony and the pre-existence of the imams, and he presents these details methodically: 1) the pre-eternal luminous entities of the imams; 2) the initiation of pure spiritual entities in the original worlds of the "shadows" (*ʿâlam al-aẓilla*) and the "particles" (*al-dharr*); 3) the pre-existential "Pacts" (*al-mîthâq*); 4) the creation of the spirits, the hearts and the bodies of the imams and their faithful, on the one hand, and of the "Enemies" of the imams and their partisans on the other; 5) the miraculous conception and birth of the imams; 6) the "clairvoyance" of the imams applied to men's "clay" in order to know their destiny and characteristics.[69] Al-Kulaynî will touch on all six of these subjects, but in a less-than-complete manner, as he deals with a smaller number of traditions.[70] Ibn Bâbûye transmits the first five series, taking care to "dilute" them among other categories of information.[71] Al-Mufîd and al-Murtaḍä transmitted only certain elements of the fifth series.[72]

Exactly the same situation can be seen in a number of details concerning the imams' Knowledge (*ʿilm*) and their supernatural powers (*aʿâjîb*), which, it might be added, are inextricably linked. On their Knowledge, for example: 1) knowledge of the Invisible World; 2) knowledge of the past, the present, and the future; 3) knowledge of the hermeneutic science (*ta'wîl*) of all previous sacred books; 4) knowledge of all languages, the language of the animals and the birds, of inanimate objects, and of the "metamorphosed" (*al-musûkh*); 5) the column of light (*ʿamud min nûr*) that the imam can visualize at will to see the answers to all his questions; 6) "the marking of the heart" (*al-nakt fî l-qalb*) and "the piercing of the eardrum" (*al-naqr fî l-udhn*), as occult means of the "transmission" of Knowledge.[73] On their supernatural powers: 1) possession of the supernatural power of the Supreme Name of God and of sacred objects that belonged to the prophets; 2) the power to bring the dead back to life, to communicate with the dead, to heal the sick; 3) the powers of clairvoyance, of "clairaudience," of physiognomy; 4) instantaneous deplacement in space and walking on clouds; 5) the practice of divination (*fa'l*) and magic (*siḥr*); 6) relations with the spirit of the Prophet Muhammad.[74]

As far as the problem of the Qur'an, the first compilations of Imamite traditions report quite a large number of statements according to which after the death of the Prophet, the only integral version of the Qur'an, containing all the mysteries of the heavens and the earth, of the past, the present, and the future, was in 'Alî's possession. According to the imams, the Vulgate compiled during 'Uthman's caliphate was a falsified, altered, and censured version that contained only a third of the integral Qur'an; this latter Qur'an is said to have been transmitted secretly from one imam to another up to the time of the hidden imam, who took it with him into his Occultation. Humanity will know the integral Qur'an only after the return of the Madhî.[75] But from Ibn Bâbûye's time on, not only are these traditions passed over in silence, but 'Uthman's Vulgate began to be considered as containing the integrality of the Divine Message revealed to the Prophet. It is further said that the words of the imams are aimed only at the suppression of 'Alî's commentaries (*tafsîr*) and hermeneutical glosses (*ta'wil*) by Sunni authorities.[76] These positions have been defended, with a few exceptions among the *akhbârîs*, by all the great Imamite thinkers up to the present day.[77]

Another great domain where this progressive silencing of certain kinds of traditions is felt is that of the hadith that deal with the twelfth imam, and more specifically with the twelfth imam's "companions"(*aṣḥâb*) or "troops" (*jaysh*, pl. *juyûsh*) at the time of his return and his last battle against the unjust. In our comparison, we will use as a basic source the *Kitâb al-ghayba*, by Ibn Abî Zaynab al-Nu'mânî (d. circa 345/956), the oldest great compilation on the subject extant. We will compare the presentation of certain themes from this work with those of Ibn Babûye's *Kamâl al-dîn wa tamâm al-ni'ma* and al-Ṭûsî's (i.e., Abû Ja'far al-Ṭûsî, d. 460/1067) *Kitâb al-ghayba*.

Al-Nu'manî, one of al-Kulaynî's disciples, reports a considerable number of traditions of a miraculous, esoteric, or occult nature, and he presents them in a quite coherent, well developed manner. As examples, let us take another look at the six series of traditions: 1) the conception, the birth, and the supernatural abilities of the twelfth imam; 2) the Mahdî will bring a new Sunna; 3) the length of his governance before the arrival of the final ressurection; and regarding his "companions": 4) they will be non-Arabs (*'ajam*) and will essentially do combat with Arabs and "Muslims" (because of their treachery in dealing with the imams); 5) they will be granted supernatural powers; and 6) they will be initiated to the esoteric teaching of the imams.[78]

Ibn Bâbûye deals with series 1, 3, 5, and 6 in a much less exhaustive fashion than al-Nu'mânî, and reports a considerably smaller number of traditions.[79] In al-Ṭûsî's work, only certain elements of the first series are treated.[80] Tables 1 and 2 present a schematic view of the preceding material.

	Ṣaffâr	Kulaynî	Bâbûye	Mufîd	Murtaḏâ
Cosmogony and "pre-existence"	1 to 6	1 to 6	1 to 5	5	5
The imams' Knowledge	1 to 6	1 to 4	1 to 3	3, 4	3, 4
The imams' Powers	1 to 6	1, 2, 3, 5	1, 2, 3, 5	1, 3	1, 3
The imams' "Qur'an"	+	+	—	—	—

Table 1.

	Nu'mânî	Bâbûye	Ṯûsî
"Non-rational" information about the hidden imam and his companions	1 to 6	1, 3, 5, 6	1

Table 2.

It must be repeated here that we have chosen only six of many representative themes in a few areas. The original Imamite doctrine, presented through the words of the imams and registered by the first compilers, of which Ibn Bâbûye represents the last great name, was clearly of "heterodox" esoteric and mystical—indeed, even magical and occult—character. As was stated at the outset in this introduction, we are here looking at only doctrinal and dogmatic tradition, not juridic tradition, which has few dissimilarities with the Sunni juridic tradition. The Occultation (minor as well as major) and the consequent absence of the Impeccable Guide (*ma'sûm*) to head the Imamite community constitute major events with diverse implications for the evolution of the history of Imamite doctrine. We shall return to this topic. From the time of the Occultation, around the middle of the fourth/tenth century, in a time profoundly marked by theological, and especially Mu'tazilite, rationalism, Imamite theologians and traditionists appear to have seen themselves confronted by "nonrational" teachings for which they had great difficulty finding theological as well as Qur'anic bases of justification. No longer having a "visible" imam to lead them, living in a socially hostile and politically unforeseen milieu,[81] and in a time that intellectually tended toward rationalism, Imamite thinkers appear to have felt forced to make a compromise between safeguarding the original doctrine and their concern for not brutally clashing with the dominant ideologies. Through shaykh Ṣaffâr al-Qummî, living during the period from the presence of the imams to Ibn Bâbûye, living at the time of the major Occultation and passing through al-Kulaynî, writing at the time of the minor Occultation, we are witnesses to a progressive silencing of a number of traditions. One result of this progressive silencing is that these essentially Imamological traditions, with a quite original metaphysical and mystical (and thus "heterodox") scope in Islam, take a turn toward rationalization and attempts at rapprochement with "orthodox" positions, attempts led by al-Mufîd and al-Murtaḍä. A second result is the generally open and violent condemnation of these same traditions in the name of "reason." The original tradition that might be called "esoteric nonrational Imamism"[82] is reported especially by the "traditionalist" traditionists of the "Qumm School"; this is the tradition that is meant when we refer to "early Imamism"; it is this tradition that is the object of the present study, and it is not to be confused, especially where Imamology is concerned, with the later tradition called "theological-juridical rational Imamism," influenced by Muʿtazilism and represented especially by the "rationalist" theologians and jurists of the "Baghdad School." It is the confusion between these two Imamite traditions of quite different natures and "visions of the world" that is in large part responsible for the incoherencies, extrapolations, and contradictions that can be seen in a great number of studies on Imamism. Recognition of the early suprarational esoteric tradition constitutes our second methodological criterion, since it is in relation to this tradition that we can measure the degree of fidelity of the sources to the original doctrine.

I-3. THE SOURCES

In order to identify the early Imamite doctrine with appropriate specificity and to define the Imamology that it encompasses, we will base our inquiry on the sources of "esoteric nonrational Imamism" of which Ibn Bâbûye's dogmatic work constitutes, from the early times, the last basically faithful representation. The sources upon which this study lays its foundation are, above all, the first great systematic compilations of Imamite traditions. The earlier writings, as far as we can judge from the rare manuscripts that are extant and from information furnished by biographical and biobibliographical works, were small collections of hadith, gathered by the followers of the imams, on specific themes belonging primarily to the field of jurisprudence.[83] A number of these collections appear to have been inserted into later works. Next, despite a certain "rationalist" reticence regarding certain traditions that they have contained ever since the time of shaykh al-Ṭûsî (d. 460/1067), these sources are considered to be an integral part of the patrimony inherent in Imamism. In effect, after al-Mufîd's attacks against the nonrational aspects of "traditionalist" Imamism and the censure of these aspects by al-Murtaḍä—measures that might have been most characteristic of early Imamism, but that simultaneously guaranteed the survival of the doctrine—a certain balance between "rationalism" and "traditionalism" was reestablished by al-Ṭûsî. Showing due respect to early Imamite scholars, and especially cognizant of the authority of the *âḥâd* traditions as useful sources for law and theology,[84] al-Ṭûsî managed to rehabilitate in a definitive and fairly complete manner the early compilations of the "traditionalist" kind.[85] But given the predominance of the "rationalist" current, the attitude of the majority of Imamite thinkers toward these compilations remained basically ambiguous: their authors continued to be respected, their works continued to be copied, but, with a few later exceptions, an almost absolute silence reigned regarding those traditions that "posed problems"; it was only the juridical sections of these compilations of the traditions that in no way conflicted with the "rationalist" convictions and ideas of the majority that were used, commentated, or meditated upon.[86]

The traditionists whose compilations constitute the basic sources for this work are, in chronological order:

al-shaykh al-Ṣaffâr al-Qummî, Abû Ja'far (or Abû l-Ḥasan) Md b. al-Ḥasan b. Farrûkh al-A'raj (d. 290/902–903), a contemporary of the tenth and eleventh imams; he was probably the disciple of the eleventh, and an acquaintance of his son, the hidden imam, the awaited Mahdî; he was the first systematic compiler of traditions about Imamite Imamology, constituting the basis of early Twelver metaphysics and mystical theology.[87] His greatest work, the only one extant,[88] is entitled *Baṣâ'ir al-darajât fî 'ulûm âl Muḥammad wa mâ khaṣṣahum Allâh bihi*,[89] better known under the abbreviated title *Baṣâ'ir al-darajât*, edited in Iran under the title *Baṣâ'ir al-darajât fî l-maqâmât wa faḍâ'il ahl al-bayt 'alayhim al-ṣalawât*.[90]

The famous al-Kulaynî, Abû Ja'far Md b. Ya'qûb al-Râzî (d. 329/940); there is no need to review his life, although it is little known, or his personality.[91] We will use the part of the *Uṣûl* from his *Kitâb al-kâfî fî 'ilm al-dîn*,[92] and the final volume of this work, entitled *Kitâb al-Rawḍa min al-kâfî*.[93]

Shaykh Ibn Abî Zaynab al-Nu'mânî, Abû 'AbdAllâh Md b. Ibrâhîm b. Ja'far "al-Kâtib" ("the scribe," because of the position he occupied especially with al-Kulaynî), who died around 345 or 360/956 or 971, a disciple of al-Kulaynî, among others. Of his life, we know only his teachers in Qur'anic science and hadith, and that he traveled in search of Imamite traditions.[94] He is also known as the compiler of the *Tafsîr* of the sixth imam, Ja'far al-Sâdiq.[95] His primary work, the *Kitâb al-ghayba*, is the first great systematic compilation of traditions about the twelfth imam, his Occultation, his Return, and, in a general sense, the principal ideas of Imamite eschatology in its early stage.[96]

Ibn Bâbûye (Arabized form: Ibn Bâbawayh), shaykh al-Ṣadûq, Abû Ja'far Md. b. Abî l-Ḥasan 'Alî b. Mûsä al-Qummî, born circa 311/923, and who died in Rayy in 381/991–92; he is too well known to be briefly dealt with here.[97] In the fifth/eleventh century, al-Najâshî and al-Ṭûsî attributed to him 193 and 43 works, respectively; except for about 20, the rest of these writings appear to be lost; in the last century, al-Khwânsârî drew up a list of 17 works, and more recently, F. Sezgin has counted 20.[98] As basic sources we will use his main doctrinal works, which abound in Imamological themes, although these are presented in a more "moderate" fashion than was the case for the works of his predecessors, like *'Ilal al-sharâ'i' wa al-aḥkâm wa al-asbâb* (a voluminous collection of traditions on the reasons and first causes of all things, from the time of the creation up to juridical details),[99] *Kamâl (ikmâl) al-dîn wa tamâm (itmâm) al-ni'ma fî ithbât al-ghayba wa kashf al-ḥayra*, about the Madhî, his two Occultations and his Return,[100] *Kitâb al-tawḥîd*, a book of hermeneutic, theological, and Imamological traditions,[101] *al-Amâlî (al-Majâlis)*, accounts of the author's hadith dictation sessions, containing traditions on diverse subjects, a number of which are esoteric and mystical in character,[102] *'Uyûn akhbâr al-Riḍâ*, a large monograph dedicated to the sayings, actions and other details of the eighth imam, 'Ali b. Mûsä al-Riḍâ,[103] *Ṣifât al-shî'a* and *Faḍâ'il al-shî'a*, two small collections of traditions on the qualities that the "true faithful" of the imam ought to have; a number of them are of "initiatory" character.[104] Other works by Ibn Bâbûye will be used as secondary sources, given the smaller number of esoteric, mystical, or Imamological traditions that they contain (for example, *Ma'anî al-akhbâr*, *Kitâb al-khiṣâl*, *al-Muqni' wa al-hidâya*, *Kitâb man lâ haḥḍuruhu l-faqîh*, *Risâlat al-i'tiqâdât* . . . [105]).

We have additionally made use of a certain number of other early sources for our work, sources that in our opinion, and given the perspective of the present work can be used only as secondary sources:

a) Works whose Imamological and esoteric aspects, two aspects that are inextricably interconnected and that constitute the nexus of the problem we are dealing with, are not immediately evident, perhaps intentionally, as will be seen in the final part of the present work. In this category, one might name the *Kitâb al-maḥâsin* by Abû Ja'far Aḥmad b. Md. al-Barqî (d. 274/887 or 280/893),[106] and especially the writings attributed to the imams themselves, writings whose authenticity, of course, is yet to be seriously called into question: *al-Ṣaḥîfat al-Sajjâdiyya*, by the fourth imam, 'Alî b. al-Ḥusayn al-Sajjâd (d. 92/711),[107] Ja'far al-Ṣâdiq, the sixth imam's *Tafsîr*,[108] and the *Tafsîr* by the eleventh imam, al-Ḥasan al-'Askarî (d. 260/874).[109]

b) Sources whose attachment to "esoteric nonrational Imamism," that is, to the original doctrine, is only partial: the *Tafsîr* of the early Imamite commentators like Furât b. Ibrâhîm al-Kûfî (d. 300/912),[110] 'Alî b. Ibrâhîm al-Qummî (d. 307/919),[111] and Md b. Mas'ûd al-'Ayyâshî (d. 320/932)[112] or three other early texts: the *Kâmil al-*

ziyârât by Jaʿfar b. Md b. Jaʿfar Ibn Qûlûye al-Qummî (d. 369/979), a collection of traditions about pilgrimage to holy places; the author, a traditionist and jurist, one of al-Mufîd's teachers, borrows frequently from al-Kulaynî and Ibn Bâbûye.[113] The *Kifâyat al-athar fî l-naṣṣ ʿalä l-aʾimmat al-ithnay ʿashar* by ʿAlî b. Md. b. ʿAlî al-Khazzâz al-Râzî (d. in the second half of the fourth/end of the tenth century), a collection of traditions that tend to prove the regular "investiture" of the twelve imams; the author was, among others, a follower of Ibn Bâbûye.[114] The *Muqtaḍab al-athar fî l-naṣṣ ʿalä ʿadad al-aʾimmat al-ithnay ʿashar* by Aḥmad b. Md b. ʿUbaydAllah Ibn ʿAyyâsh al-Jawharî (d. 401/1101), a collection of traditions aimed at showing that the number of imams was predestined.[115] Given the relatively small number of traditions that might be classified as "nonrational," the rather frequent use of dialectical reasoning, and at the same time the acceptance of a great number of *âḥâd* traditions, one might think that these authors considered themselves affiliates of the "Intermediary School" of Imamite traditionists and jurists.

c) Finally, early sources whose authenticity and integrality have not yet been established with certainty, for example, the *Nahj al-balâgha*, a collection of remarks, advice, letters and sermons attributed to the first imam, ʿAlî b. Abî Ṭâlib (d. 40/661), compiled by al-sharîf al-Raḍî (d. 406/1016; he was the elder brother of al-Murtaḍä),[116] or the *Ithhbât al-waṣiyya li l-imâm ʿAlî b. Abî Ṭâlib*, attributed, especially by the Shîʿites, to the famous al-Masʿûdî (d. 345/956), author of the *Murûj al-dhahab*; it is a treatise whose purpose is to prove the authenticity of the succession of the cycles of the Imamate as being an esoteric part of lawgiving prophecy, from the time of Adam up to Muhammad.[117]

To define the question before us with the greatest historical specificity possible, that is, the question of the definitions of the Imam given by the imams through the early doctrine of "esoteric nonrational Imamism," we cannot allow the use of secondary sources without the greatest of prudence, and then only when their statements corroborate or complete those of our primary basic sources.

I-4. THE NATURE AND AUTHORITY OF IMAMITE TRADITIONS

By "traditions" we are here translating the terms *sunna*, *ḥadîth*, *khabar*, *athar*, *riwâya*, which the early texts use indifferently to refer to sayings of the Prophet, of his daughter Fâṭima and the twelve imams, that is, the sayings of the "Fourteen Impeccables" (*maʿṣûm*). Let is be repeated that there are two distinct kinds of traditions in Imamism: there are first of all the juridical traditions like those found in juridical compilations such as the *Furû'* in al-Kulaynî's *Kâfî*, Ibn Bâbûye's *Kitâb man lâ yaḥḍuruhu l-faqîh*, Abû Ja'far al-Ṭûsî's *Tahdhîb al-aḥkâm*, or the summary of this last work by its author, al-*Istibṣâr fî mâ' khtulifa fîhi min al-akhbâr*.[118] It has of course been noticed that, with very few exceptions, this Imamite juridical tradition looks very much like the Sunni tradition, as a result of the absence of dogmatic traits that are properly speaking Shî'ite. As has already been said, the Imamite *fiqh* is not really distinguishable from the Sunni *fiqh* except on a small number of points, and in the essential chapters of both canon law and civil law the fundamentals are almost identical; the points of divergence from Imamite law generally do not differentiate it from Sunni law any more than do the four great schools.[119] On the other hand, the second category of Imamite traditions, those which might be called dogmatic or doctrinal traditions, is of a very different nature and tenor. Someone even vaguely familiar with the literature of Sunni hadith will no doubt have a clear sense of disorientation when approaching the Imamite doctrinal tradition. Although both categories of traditions may be called "Imamite traditions" because of their both being founded on the words of the imams, it is the second, to the extent that it is clearly distinctive in comparison with the Sunni tradition, that needs to be studied as Imamite tradition properly speaking; it is here that we find the truly original characteristics of the doctrine. The true axis around which Imamite doctrinal tradition revolves is that Imamology without the knowledge of which no other great chapter, as is the case with theology or prophetology, could be adequately studied. The Imam being in this case the center of everything, it is in relation to him that the nature and the authority of hadith can be considered.

According to the early writings of the imams, the Qur'an and the hadith (i.e., the prophetic traditions reported by the imams as well as the traditions of the imams themselves) constitute the only two authorities, absolute and complementary, to which the faithful should refer for all matters regarding their religion.[120] The Qur'an (in its integral version withheld by the imams, a subject to which we shall return at length) and the hadith are considered to contain all the answers to all the questions, be these on day-to-day matters or on matters of cosmic, metaphysical, or theological nature. "There is nothing with which a verse of the Qur'an or a tradition does not deal," says Ja'far.[121] Every thought, word, or deed should be based on hadith or the Qur'an, and preferably on the Qur'an, since it it supposed to be the basis of all hadith; hadith only explain and clarify what the Qur'an already contains in a manner that is more or less understandable to the common believer. "Everything should lead back to the Qur'an and Tradition," says the sixth imam. "A hadith that contradicts God's Book is nothing more than a well-disguised lie."[122] The Prophet, in his function as messenger of the Divine Word, and the imam, in his function as exegete initiated and inspired by this Word,[123] are the only persons capable of explicating the Qur'an by traditions. ʿAlî, the first imam, states: "The Qur'an contains the knowledge of the past and that of the future up to the Day of Resurrection; it serves as your arbiter, and it clarifies there where you may stray; ask me [for the science of the Qur'an] and I shall teach it to you."[124] Jaʿfar says: "The Prophet, God's messenger, engendered me, and I contain the Knowledge of the Qur'an, the Book that contains the beginning of creation as well as all that will take place up to the Day of Resurrection; it contains the account of the events of the heavens and the earth, those of Paradise and of Hell, those of the past and of the future, and I know all of this as clearly as if I saw it written on the palm of my hand. Yes, God has put a clear explanation of all things in the Qur'an."[125] The sayings of the imams are by nature as sacred as are those of the Prophet; indeed, they are even as holy as are the words of God; this is explicitly expressed in a tradition that goes back to Jaʿfar, a tradition the importance of which various commentators have emphasized: "My speech is identical to that of my father, his speech is identical to that of my grandfather, that of my grandfather identical to his father al-Ḥusayn, his identical to that of al-Ḥasan, his identical to that of the Prince of believers [*amîr al-mu'minîn*, i.e., the first imam, ʿAlî], his identical to that of the Prophet, and his identical to the Word of God."[126] Another important point of doctrine comes out of this tradition, that of the "unity" of the teachings of the imams. The imams have never ceased to reiterate that their teachings constitute an indissoluble whole that must be known in an integral manner.[127]

Taking as a foundation the words of the imams regarding the criteriology of hadith, one realizes that, on the basis of these words, it is difficult to find systematically applicable principles to verify the authenticity of traditions. It is true that at this time (the first three centuries after the *hijra*), even among traditional Sunni Muslims where the need for presenting guarantees of authenticity was becoming more and more important, the rules for critiquing hadith were only partially elaborated. Ibn Isḥâq (d. 150–51/767–68), in his *Sîra*, and even Mâlik b. Anas (d. 179/795) in his *Muwaṭṭâ* sometimes present complete chains of transmission (*isnâd*), and sometimes partial chains, but also sometimes no chains at all.[128] The first systematic treatises of the "science of hadith" were to be composed more than a century later: *The Kitâb al-jarḥ wa l-taʿdîl* by Ibn Abî Ḥâtim al-Râzî (d. 327/939), *al-Muḥaddith al-fâṣil bayn al-râwî wa l-wâʿî* by Abû Md al-Râmhurmuzî (d. 360/971), or the *Maʿrifa ʿulûm al-ḥadîth* by al-Ḥâkim al-Nîsâbûrî (d. 405/1014).[129] But this historical reason is not the only cause for the absence of a critical methodology of hadith in those around the imams; reasons of a purely doctrinal order have also played a role. The solidity of the chain of transmission in no way has the same importance in Sunni Islam. Actually, among the Sunnis, one of the fundamental criteria for the authenticity of a chain is the authority of the Companions of the Prophet. Among the Imamites, not only is the near-totality of these Companions looked upon with a lack of respect, but they are considered the worst enemies of the Prophet and his mission (we shall return to the Imamite idea of *sabb al-ṣaḥâba*); here, only the names of the imams can guarantees autenticity.[130] Moreover, the problem of direct or written authorization (*ijâza*) of the traditions is not so acutely raised as long as a living imam can guarantee the authenticity of the transmission and its contents. Furthermore, the idea of the fundamental identity of the teachings of the imams can further diminish the technical importance of the *isnâd* to the extent that an imam asks his disciples to transmit his traditions in the name of one of his predecessors.[131]

Another criterion proposed by the imams regarding the degree of veracity of traditions concerns the qualities required of the transmitter (*râwî*), who of course should have both perfect fidelity (*walâya*) and perfect submission (*taslîm*) to the imams, who should practice both asceticism (*zuhd*) and piety (*taqwä*), and who should be well-versed in the matter of religion (*faqîh*).[132] A way to categorize transmitters is likewise seen through a tradition that goes back to ʿAlî: there is first of all the hypocritical transmitter (*munâfiq*) who attempts to stir up trouble by making up or deliberately deforming traditions; then there is he who is in error without knowing so (*al-wâhim*), the unconscious one who in good faith does not know the reality of the teaching; thirdly, there is he who is not aware of different abrogations (*ḥâfiẓ al-mansûkh*); and finally there is the perfect transmitter, in this case the imam himself, knowing the "abrogater" and the "abrogated" (*nâsikh/mansûkh*), the "clear" and the "ambiguous" (*muḥkam/mutashâbih*), the "general" and the "particular" (*ʿâmm/khâṣṣ*), firmly believing in the cause of the imams, sincere and virtuous.[133] It is the absence of these qualities that is at the base of the hostility of the imams toward "professional transmitters" of traditions like preachers (*wuʿʿâẓ*), collectors of hadith (*kuttâb ruwât*), or public faultfinders (*quṣṣâṣ*).[134]

Contradicting the Sunni tradition appears to constitute another criterion for the degree of credibility of the traditions that the imams alluded to. In reply to a disciple who asked him about the sometimes difficult choice between two traditions, Jaʿfar stated:

> "Choose the tradition that is in accord with the Qur'an and the Sunna, and not in accord with the 'mass' [*al-ʿâmma*, i.e., the Sunnites; the Shîʿites are referred to as the 'elite,' *al-khâṣṣa*], and leave aside the one that is not in accord with the Qur'an and the Sunna, and which the 'mass' agrees with (meaning, the Sunnites run counter to the Qur'an and the Sunna). . . . The right direction is found in the tradition that contradicts the 'mass' (*wa mâ khâlafa l-ʿâmma fa-fîhi l-rashâd*)." "And if the two traditions are approved by two different groups of the 'mass,' what should one do?," asked the disciple. "Choose that which is least used by their arbiters and judges. . . . "[135]

It appears as though for the imams the decisive criterion for the authenticity of the tradition resides in its "deep meaning" (*maʿnä*, pl. *maʿânin*). Restitution of this meaning is of the highest priority and pushes to the background other criteria like chains of transmission, authority, or even the formal expression of the tradition (*matn*). Muhammad b. Muslim said to Jaʿfar: "I listen to the traditions, and when I want to report them sometimes I add to them or cut something out of them." "If you manage to restore their deep meaning," replied the sixth imam, "then there is no harm."[136] To Dâwûd b. Farqad, who confessed his inability always to transmit the words of the imams faithfully, the same Jaʿfar replied that that was not serious, provided that his actions were not intentional, and that he attempted to retain the meaning.[137]

A second place where Imamite methodology on hadith is strikingly original is that of "divergence of traditions" (*ikhtilâf al-ḥadîth*). Two ideas are at the base of *ikhtilâf*: the first is that of abrogation (*naskh*). According to the imams, one statement from the Qurʾan can abrogate another, as it can abrogate the Sunna; likewise, one prophetic tradition can be abrogated by another, or by the traditions of the imams; an existing imam (*lâḥiq*) can abrogate the words of an imam who preceded him (*sâbiq*), or even his own words, but in general, Tradition cannot contradict Qurʾanic text.[138] The second idea is that of *taqiyya*, sometimes too hastily and restrictively translated as "tactical dissimulation of that which pertains to doctrine," but in the early corpus actually meaning "the keeping or safeguarding of the secrets of the imams' teaching." "Divergence of traditions" is sometimes justified by the imams as a result of the need for using *taqiyya*: "He who is certain that we [the imams] proclaim only the truth (*ḥaqq*), may he be satisfied with our teaching," says Jaʿfar, "and if he hears us say something contradictory to what he heard earlier, he should know that we are acting only in his own interest."[139] To the difficulties in revealing the technical criteria of Imamite hadith we should add the fact that systematic recording of the traditions of the imams in writing appears to date only from the period of Jaʿfar al-Ṣâdiq's Imamate (circa 115/733–34). On the one hand, all the traditions according to which disciples are expressly asked to write down and vocalize the words of the imams come from Jaʿfar;[140] and on the other, almost all the authors of the famous "400 original books" (*al-uṣûl al-arbaʿumiʾa*)[141] were disciples of Jaʿfar and of the imams who followed him. According to Imamite traditionists, theologians, and chroniclers, from Jaʿfar's time on, and apparently in obedience to his exhortations, the disciples began to record the words of the imams systematically in writing, the result of this being the "400 books."[142] It might be thought that Jaʿfar al-Ṣadiq's appeals for the writing down of Tradition were motivated by his doctrinal and historical context. The fifth, and especially the sixth imams had taken advantage of the troubled period at the end of the Umayyad caliphate and the beginning of the Abbasids to formulate and put into place the foundations of Imamite doctrine.[143] At the time, hostility and repression were directed toward groups other than the Imamites; in fact, after the assassination of Yazid's son, Walid II, in 126/743, the Umayyads appear to have lost their cohesion, and their last reigns were spent in internal wars and palace intrigues. The beginning of the Abbasid caliphate—they had managed to take control of power with the aid of the Shî'ites—was likewise propitious for Ja'far, who had managed to keep his political neutrality during this whole period. The writing down of traditions appeared to be indispensable, since, on the one hand, the number of traditions had increased considerably during al-Bâqir and al-Ṣâdiq's Imamates, and on the other, armed revolts by other groups of Shi'ites engendered the threat of reprisals against all Shi'ites, including the moderate current led by Ja'far. As a matter of fact, it was during Ja'far's Imamate that the revolts led by his paternal uncle, Zayd b. 'Alî, and the uncle's son, Yaḥyä b. Zayd, broke out, as well as the revolts led by the Ḥasanid Zaydi Shî'ites Muhammad b. 'AbdAllâh (also called al-Nafs al-Zakiyya) and his brother, Ibrâhîm; all of the revolts were quelled via bloodshed.[144] Ja'far's alarmist tone exhorting the faithful to put traditions into writing is evidence of the unrest fomented by these violent tensions: "Write [our traditions] and communicate your knowledge to your brothers [the Imamites]; at the time of your death, leave your books to your sons, for the time of calamities (*zamân harj*) will fall upon those men who have no other companions but their books."[145] "Preciously guard your writings, for you will soon have great need of them."[146] As has just been stated, these pressing appeals were no doubt the reason for the composition of the "400 books." These works were especially guarded in two libraries in Baghdad under the Buyids. The first was the library of Shâpûr (in Arabic, Sâbûr), the son of Ardashîr, the vizier of the Buyid sultan Bahâ' al-Dawla (d. 403/1012), who was inaugurated in 383/993 in the Shî'ite quarter of Karkh, and who was called "Dâr al-'ilm" (the House of Knowledge). This library was intended more for the spread of Twelver Shî'ism than for objective teaching of knowledge.[147] The second was the personal library of Abû Aḥmad al-Mûsawî, a tremendously influential Imamite personality who was named in 394/1004 by Bahâ' al-Dawla as *emir* of the pilgrimage, presider over the courts of grievance (*maẓâlim*), head (*naqîb*) of the Imamites, and grand magistrate. According to the chroniclers, his library contained over eighty thousand works. He was the father of two great Imamite thinkers of the time, al-sharîf al-Raḍî (d. 406/1016), the compiler of the *Najh al-balâgha*, and the famous al-sharîf al-Murtaḍä, both of whom in turn inherited their father's functions, fortune, and library. It was at the time of shaykh al-Ṭûsî and during the life of al-Murtaḍä that these two libraries, as well as al-Ṭûsî's, were burned during anti-Shî'ite uprisings in Baghdad.[148] A number of the "400 books" were undoubtedly destroyed at that time.

The absence in the works of the imams of precise details allowing the identification of technical criteria for the degree of authenticity of hadith as well as the difficulties resulting from historical and doctrinal contexts seem to be the primary reasons for the late recognition of the authoritative "four books." The choice of these four to the exclusion of others is no doubt due especially to the predominance taken by the disciplines of jurisprudence over other branches of Imamite doctrine from the fifth-sixth/eleventh-twelfth centuries on.[149] On the other hand, the same reasons certainly explain the even later elaboration of the Imamite *ʿilm al-dirâya*, which is of course essentially due to Sunni methodology.

Within the framework of doctrinal history, we have endeavored to explain those criteria that allow us to identify to the greatest extent possible the corpus of Imamite doctrine in its earliest form. Taking as point of departure the different levels of meaning of the word *ʿaql* in its early phase and examining the thematic evolution of the first sources have shown two traditions of quite distinct nature and tenor within early Imamism. The first, what we have called "the early nonrational esoteric tradition," is that which prevailed up to the middle of the fourth/tenth century; it represents the pre-"kalamic" and pre-philosophical phase of the doctrine,[150] where language was still at what might be called its "mythic" stage, basically impermeable to dialectical reasoning. The second tradition, the "theological/juridical/rational tradition," a later development adopting a continually more "logical" language, became predominant at about that time and has remained to the present day. We feel that the sources belonging to the first tradition—or at least those that were close to it—more faithfully reflect the original teachings of the imams. These teachings are for the Imamite religious conscience of equally holy nature and equally high authority as are the prophetic traditions and the Qurʾan; they constitute an indissoluble whole each detail of which is incapable of finding its full meaning except in relation to the integrality of the doctrine. Likewise, no element can be considered without the function and place it occupies in the Imamite "world vision." This world vision is dominated by the omnipresent "Figure" of the Imam, who is the alpha and the omega of all doctrine. It would appear that searching for the definitions of the Imam within the early corpus attributed to the historical imams is the threshold through which one enters into the world vision of early Shîʿism. Out of concern for coherence and clarity, we shall attempt to identify these definitions in three different phases: the pre-existence, the existence, and the super-existence of the Imam. Thus the present study will look, via all ontological modalities, at the many characteristics that a synthetic definition of the Imam implies. Although space and time will not permit an in-depth look at all the implications of the problem, we shall at least attempt to formulate it correctly.

2

The Pre-Existence of the Imam

The Imam-Proof existed before the creatures.
Imam Jaʿfar al-Ṣâdiq

This section might best begin with a quick recall of a few basic facts covered in almost all studies of Imamism. First of all, Imamite doctrine is entirely dominated by the holy group assembled by the Prophet Muḥammad, his daughter Fâṭima and the twelve imams, referred to as the "Fourteen Impeccables" (*maʿṣum*), or the "Fourteen Proofs" (*ḥujja*). These individuals form a whole that alone faithfully reflects the two ways in which, according to Shîʿism, Divine Truth (*al-ḥaqq*) is manifested to humanity. One of these is obvious, apparent, exoteric (*ẓâhir*), and it envelops the other, which is secret, hidden, esoteric (*bâṭin*). The exoteric side of the Truth is manifested through lawgiving prophecy (*nubuwwa*), bringing to the mass of humanity (*ʿâmma*) a Sacred Book that "descended from Heaven" (*tanzîl*); Muḥammad is both the prototype and the end of this first aspect. The esoteric side of the Truth is revealed through the mission of the imams (*walâya*),[151] accompanying each prophetic mission, bringing to the elite believers (*khâṣṣa*) the only true interpretation (*ta'wîl*) of the Holy Book; together, the twelve imams, but in particular ʿAlî, who is considered the father of the eleven others, are the plenary manifestation of this second aspect. Fâṭima, called the "Confluence of the Two Lights" (*majmaʿ al-nûrayn*), reflects the "place" where the two aspects intersect.[152] Of course, the prophet (*nabî*) also has knowledge of the esoteric side of religion; he is thus also *walî*, but he reserves his esoteric teaching for his imam(s) exclusively; on the other hand, the imam is never considered the *nabî*. The specifics of this point are necessary, since in Imamite texts the terms *walî*, *ḥujja*, *ûlû l-amr*, and so forth, generally reserved for the imams, sometimes also apply to the prophets.[153]

II-1. THE WORLDS BEFORE THE WORLD. THE GUIDE-LIGHT

The Event took place a few thousand years before the creation of the world,[154] in an immaterial "place" called The Mother of the Book (*umm al-kitâb*).[155]

From his own light, God made a luminous ray spring forth, and from this ray he made a second ray proceed; the first was the light of Muḥammad, that of Prophecy (*nubuwwa*), that of the exoteric (*ẓâhir*); the second, of identical nature but subordinate to the first, was the light of 'Alî, that of the Imamate or of *walâya*, of the esoteric (*bâṭin*). "Two thousand years before creation, Muḥammad and 'Alî were one light before God . . . , light formed from one main trunk from which sprang a shining ray. . . . And God said: "Here is a light [drawn] from my Light; its trunk is prophecy and its branch is the Imamate; prophecy belongs to Muḥammad, my servant and messenger, and the Imamate belongs to 'Alî, my Proof and my Friend. Without them I would have created none of my creation. . . . " This is why 'Alî always said "I proceed from Muḥammad [or from Aḥmad] as one clarity proceeds from another . . . "[156]

Throughout the traditions of the imams, the Prophet himself frequently says that he was created with 'Alî, before the creation of the world, out of one and the same light.[157] The very names of these two archtypes of prophecy and the Imamate are forged from the Names of God. In a prophetic tradition, Muḥammad states: "In me God placed prophecy and benediction (*al-nubuwwa wa l-baraka*), and in 'Alî He placed the Imamate (var.: eloquence) and a chivalrous spirit (*al-imâma/al-faṣâḥa wa al-furûsiyya*); then He gave us names, having our names derive from His: from His name "The Praised Lord of the Throne" (*dhû l-'arsh maḥmûd*), He formed my name, Muḥammad, and from His name "The Supreme" (*al-a'lä*), He formed the name of 'Alî."[158] In a series of *hadith qudsî* reported by the Prophet or the imams, God proclaims that the name of Muḥammad is taken from His own name *al-Maḥmûd* (The Praised) and that of 'Alî from His name *al-'Alî al-A'lä* (The Supreme Superior).[159]

Other traditions relate that the primordial light that was drawn from the Divine Light was that of the *ahl al-bayt*, the "five of the cloak" (*ahl al-kisâ'*: Muḥammad , 'Alî, Fâṭima, al-Hasan and al-Husayn), or even that of the Fourteen Impeccables (the Prophet, his daughter, and the twelve imams); in this case, the light of *walâya* is represented by all the imams, that of Fâṭima being placed at the junction of the two lights of prophecy and the Imamate; sometimes, Fâṭima and her light are passed over in silence in favor of the light of the Prophet and the twleve imams.[160] Likewise, it is said that the names of the "five of the cloak" were derived from the Names of God and inscribed in the Divine Throne (*al-'arsh*). According to one hadith, when Adam was brought to life by the breath of God, he lifted his eyes toward the Throne and saw five inscriptions; asking God about this, he received the following reply: "First there is Muḥammad, for I am *al-maḥmûd* (The Praised One); second, there is 'Alî, for I am *al-'âlî* (The Most High); third, there is Fâṭima, for I am *al-fâṭir* (The Creator); fourth, there is al-Ḥasan, for I am *al-muḥsin* (The Benefactor); and fifth, there is al-Ḥusayn, for I am *dhû l-iḥsân* (The Lord of Kindness)."[161]

In his *Tafsîr*, commentating on verse 37 ("And Adam received words from his Lord . . . ") of the second sura of the Qur'an, sura *al-Baqara* , Ja'far said: "God was, and nothing of His creation existed; then He created five creatures from the light of His glory (*nûr 'azamatihi*) and He assigned to each of them a name derived from His own Names. Being the Praised One, He called His prophet Muḥammad; being The Most High, He called the prince of believers 'Alî; being the creator of the heavens and the earth, He created the name of Fâṭima; possessing the most beautiful names (*al-asmâ' al-ḥusnä*), He forged the names of al-Ḥasan and al-Ḥusayn; then He placed these names to the right side of His throne. . . . these were the five names that Adam received from his Lord."[162]

It might be useful here, parenthetically, to add some of the imams' definitions of the "Throne." According to these definitions, *al-'arsh* appears to be the name given to the Knowledge and the Power of God. While the Divine Seat (*al-kursî*) is the hermeneutic reference (*ta'wîl*) to the visible side, the exoteric part of the Invisible World (*ẓâhir min al-ghayb*), the Throne is, in the same way, its hidden esoteric face (*baṭin min al-ghayb*); the Seat is the source of the created world, the visible manifestation of the Invisible, while the Throne, marked by the essence of prophecy and of the Imamate, is Religion; it contains the esoteric mysteries of the Invisible and the explanations of the mysteries of the world:

" . . . The Throne is not God Himself," says the eighth imam. "The Throne is a name that denotes Knowledge and Power, and it contains all. . . . "[163]

According to a tradition of al-Bâqir reported by his son Ja'far, "the Throne is the Religion of Truth."[164] " . . . These two [the Seat and the Throne] are two of the greatest thresholds of the invisible worlds," says Ja'far. "They are themselves invisible, and intimately connected in the Invisible, for the Seat is the exoteric Threshold [var. hermeneutic; *ta'wîl*] of the Invisible; it is the place where those created beings from which all things proceed appear; the Throne is the esoteric Threshold that contains the Knowledge of how, of existence, of quantity, of limit, or where, of Volition, and of the attribute of Will; it contains also the Knowledge of words, of movements, and of immobility (?), as well as the Knowledge of the Return and of the Origin. . . . "[165]

As will be seen, initiatory Knowledge (*al-'ilm*) and to a certain extent the consequence of *'ilm*, miraculous powers (*al-qudra, al-a'âjîb*), constitute the two principles characteric of the existence of the imams. The imams say that their doctrine, which they often refer to as "the True Religion," contains all the esoteric mysteries of the universe as well as the answers to all questions about the domain of the Sacred. We know that each religion, according to the imams, has two indissoluble aspects, the exoteric, manifested by revelation and the teachings of the prophet of the religion, and the esoteric, manifested by the teachings of each prophet's imam. We also know that according to an early idea, one which belongs as much to the domain of the religious as it does to the domain of the magical, a "name" is not a simple appellation, but it is the sonorous representation of the essential reality of the named; the Throne, marked by the names of the Prophet and the Imam, carries in it the primordial essence of prophecy and the Imamate, that is, the essence of Religion, in this case that of the imams. This parallel between the Throne and Imamite doctrine is underscored by two successive traditions reported by al-Kulaynî. In the first, the *ḥujja* are the "bearers of the Throne";[166] in the second, God calls them "the bearers of my Knowledge and my Religion."[167] When it is known to what extent the content of Imamite doctrine is dominated by those individuals known as the Impeccables, the fact that the Throne can carry their names at the same time as it is being carried by them is easier to understand. Thus, one can ask whether *al-ʿarsh* does not, in an exclusively Imamological sense, refer to the archetype or the celestial counterpart of the Cause (*amr*) of the imams, a cause intimately linked to the Imam in the ontological acceptation of the word, as will be seen throughout the present work. If these facts are emphasized here, it is first of all because other aspects of the *ʿarsh* in relation to Imamology will be returned to, and second because a synoptic vision of dogmatic details in this domain seems indispensable.

As for the ontological modalities of the lights of the Impeccables, a number of traditions describe them as being "silhouettes of light" (*ashbâḥ nûr*). In reply to the question "What were you before the creation of Adam?" the third imam, al-Ḥusayn b. ʿAlî replied, "We were silhouettes of light revolving around the Throne of the All-Merciful."[168] In other traditions we see expressions like "spirits made of light" (*arwâḥ min nûr*),[169] or "shadows of light" (*aẓilla nûr*).[170] One might think of luminous entities of an extremely subtle substance: "Before his [material] creation, the imam . . . was a shadow made from breath, on the right side of the Divine Throne."[171] It must be emphasized that, according to certain (imprecise and allusive) details, this cosmogonic stage did not come about in the primordial "world" of the Mother of the Book, characterized by that original dart of light (light that is both unique and the double light of prophecy and *walâya*), but in a later world. Names like "the first world of the shadows" (*ʿâlam al-aẓillat al-awwal*) or "the first world of the particles" (*ʿalam al-dharr al-awwal*), used furtively in cosmogonic contexts, appear to have been applied to this second "world."[172] Passing from the Mother of the Book to the First World of the Shadows might thus mark the transformation of formless light into light having a human shape. In a hadith reported by al-Ḥusayn b. ʿAlî, the Prophet reports a story about the angel Gabriel. Having seen Muḥammad's name written on the material covering the Throne, Gabriel asked God to show him what the name contained, since it was certainly the most glorious of creatures. God led his angel into the First World of Particles, showed him twelve corporal silhouettes, and said: "Here is the light of ʿAlî b. Abî Ṭâlib, here is the light of al-Ḥasan and that of al-Ḥusayn . . . [and so on, up to the light of the twelfth imam, the *Qâʾim*]."[173] In a number of his ascensions into heaven, the Prophet reached the pre-existential World of the Shadows or Particles, and there looked upon the lights of the twelve Imams (or those of the Fourteen Impeccables).[174]

What do these subtle entities of light do? They float suspended[175] before the Throne of God, or float around it in an archetypal circumambulation, bearing witness to the Unicity of God and praising His Glory. Several different words are used to describe these activities, but it would appear that they can be divided into two principal categories: the first is Unification, witnessing the Unicity (*tahlîl, tawḥîd*); and the second is Glorification or Sanctification (*taḥmîd, tamjîd, tasbîḥ, taqdîs*). "Twelve silhouettes of light [suspended] between heaven and earth . . . , attesting to the Unicity of God and exalting His Glory."[176] "God created the light of His majesty, Muḥammad, ʿAlî, and the eleven other imams; He created them [like] spirits enveloped in the clarity of His light [so that] they might worship Him even before creation, glorifying and sanctifying Him. . . . "[177]

Then other shadows or particles surge forth from this same pre-existential world; there is no information about just "when" this new creation took place or "how much" time separated it from the formation of the luminous entities of the Imams; but these luminous bodies, as has been seen, were created and dedicated themselves to the worship of their creator at a time when nothing had yet been brought into being. The creation of new shadows thus constitutes a later stage. The shadows constitute the pre-existential entities of what might be called "pure beings." Actually, several kinds of shadows are presented in a great number of traditions from different compilations, with no regard for order or clarity. They might be divided into three categories:

1. The shadows of future spiritual and non-human inhabitants of heaven and earth (*al-rûḥâniyynû min ahl al-samâwât wa l-arḍ*), that is, the different categories of angels and the supernatural entities of the earth (including, perhaps, the *jinn*).[178]
2. The shadows of prophets, numbering 124,000, with particular emphasis on those prophets "endowed with firm resolution" (*ûlû l-ʿazm*); there are five of the latter, for Imamites: Noah, Abraham, Moses, Jesus, and Muḥammad; in this particular case it is of course the shadows of the first four that are being referred to.[179]
3. The shadows of the believers (*mu'minûn*) among the descendents of Adam, that is, the faithful of the imams of all times, those initiated into the esoteric dimension of all religions, as distinguished from simple practicers (*muslimûn*, lit. "the Muslims"), who are submissive to exoteric religion without understanding its deep meaning.[180]

Then came the time of the sacred pre-temporal Pact (*al-mîthâq*); the term is used more than twenty times in the Qur'an, where it most often has the technical meaning of an Alliance between God and humanity, and with the prophets in particular (*mîthâq al-nabiyyin*; cf. Qurʾan 3:81 and 33:7). Almost all Muslim commentators apply the term to the contract of faith between God and men, in a pre-existential "time" before their birth. The scriptural proof of this episode is found beginning with verse 172 in sura 7, *al-Aʿrâf,* although the term *mîthâq* itself is not there present: "When your Lord brought forth descendents from the loins of the sons of Adam, He had them bear witness against one another: 'Am I not your Lord?' They answered, 'Verily, we bear witness.' He did this lest, on the Day of the Resurrection, they say 'We were caught not expecting this.'"[181]

In Imamite traditions of a cosmogonic character, other developments have been elaborated around this central concept. The Pact takes place in the world of shadows or particles that for this reason is also called the World of the Pact (*ʿâlam al-mîthâq*). It is with the "pure beings" in the form of particles or shadows made "conscious" that God draws up the sacred pact.[182] This primordial Covenant entails a quadruple oath in the Imamite tradition, although all four parts of the oath are rarely mentioned together in a single hadith: an oath of worship (*ʿubûdiyya*) of God, oaths of love and fidelity (*walâya*) toward Muḥammad and his prophetic mission, toward the imams and their sacred Cause, and also toward the Mahdî as universal savior at the end of time:[183]

> Then God made the prophets take an oath, saying to them: "Am I not your Lord? Is not Muḥammad here My messenger, and is ʿAlî not the prince of believers? The prophets answered "yes," and prophetic status was firmly established for them (*fa-thabatat lahum al-nubuwwa*); and God made "those who are endowed with firm resolution" take an oath, saying: "I am your Lord, Muḥammad is My messenger, ʿAlî is the prince of believers, his heirs (*awṣiyâʾuhu*, i.e., the other imams) are, after him, the responsible directors of My Order (*wulât amrî*) and the guardians of the treasures of My Knowledge (*khuzzân ʿilmî*), and the *mahdî* is he through whom I will carry My religion to victory, through whom I will show My power, through whom I will take vengeance on My enemies, and through whom I will be worshipped whether they will so or not." [The prophets of firm resolution] answered: "We so affirm, Lord, and bear witness."[184]

Although there are no details afforded by the hadith, it would seem logical to place the "Primordial Initiation" after this Pact of the fourfold oath. In fact, it is said that in the world of shadows, the pre-existential entities of the Impeccables taught the sacred sciences to the shadows of "pure beings." These sciences being secret, the future initiate could receive them only after taking a solemn oath, according to a universal rule of all esoteric or initiatory doctrines. Jaʿfar said: "We were spirits of light, and we taught the secrets of the Science of Unification and Glorification to the shadows."[185] "... We were silhouettes of light revolving around the Throne of the All-Merciful," said Ḥusayn b. ʿAlî, "and we taught Praise, the formula for Unicity, and Glorification, to the angels."[186] The luminous entities of the Prophet and the Imams being the first created by God and the first to have recognized divine Unicity and Majesty, they initiate the other shadows of the World of the Pact to what they have known and to what they have spent their time doing since the origin of this World, namely Unification with and Glorification of the Lord. In a long hadith reported by the eighth imam, ʿAlî b. Mûsä al-Riḍâ, and the chain of transmission for which goes from imam to imam back as far as the Prophet, further details are brought to this Primordial Initiation; this is the tradition sometimes known by the title "the superiority of the Prophet and the Proofs [i.e., the imams] over the angels" (*ḥadîth faḍl al-nabî wa l-ḥujaj ʿalä l-malâʾika*):[187] the Prophet said:

> ʿAlî, how could we not be superior to the angels when we preceded them (*sabaqnâhum*) in the knowledge of the Lord as well as in praising Him, in witnessing His Unicity, and in glorifying Him. Certainly our spirits were the first of God's creations, and immediately thereafter He had us praise him and profess His Unicity. Then He created the angels, and when they contemplated our spirits in the form of a unique light, they recognized the grandeur of our Cause (*amr*); we began to praise [God] in order to teach the angels that we are created beings and that God is absolutely transcendent for us (*innahu munazzah ʿan ṣifâtinâ*). The angels, as they witnessed the divine transcendence, began to praise us. And when the angels saw the majesty of our rank (*shaʾn*), we began to profess divine Unicity so that they might learn that there is no god but God (*lâ ilâha illâ llâh*) and that we are not gods, but only worshipers. . . . And when the angels saw the elevation of our position (*maḥall*), we began to bear witness to the grandeur of God, so that they might know that God is the greatest (*Allâhu akbar*). . . . And when the angels were witness to the noble force and power (*al-ʿizza wa al-quwwa*) that God had placed in us, we began to recite: "There is no force nor power but through God (*lâ ḥawl wa lâ quwwa illâ biʾllâh*) so that the angels would know that we ourselves have no force or power but through God (*lâ ḥawl lanâ wa lâ quwwa illâ biʾllâh*)."[188] And when they saw that which God had so generously granted to us (*mâ anʿama ʾllâh bihi ʿalaynâ*) and how He had made obedience obligatory in our case, we said "Praise be to God" (*al-ḥamdu liʾllâh*), so that the angels might learn our gratitude to God for this gift. And they repeated "Praise be to God." It is thus thanks to us that the angels were guided toward knowledge of the Unicity of God and [knowledge of the words] of Unification and Glorification. . . . [189]

Another event is said to have taken place in the World of the shadows: the creation of Adam's descendents, in the form of particles, out of Earth and Water. The term "Second World of Particles" might be fitting for this stage, since, on the one hand, it would explain the name attributed to the First World of Particles, and on the other hand it would correspond to this progressive creation of less and less subtle, more and more material worlds. In a commentary on Qur'an 7:172 (cf. earlier discussion), the fifth imam, Muḥammad al-Bâqir, relates words that his father, the fourth imam, ʿAlî Zayn al-ʿÂbidîn, spoke in his presence:

> God took a handful of earth (*turâb*) from which he created Adam, and poured sweet, pleasant water into it, and left it for forty days; then he poured salty, brackish water[190] into it, and left it for another forty days; once the clay was ready to knead, he rubbed it vigorously, and out of it sprang the descendents of Adam, in the form of particles, from the right and left sides of this clay; God then ordered them into the fire. "The People of the Right" (*aṣḥâb al-yamîn*) obeyed and the Fire became cold and harmless for them; "The People of the Left" (*aṣḥâb al-shimâl*) disobeyed and refused to go into it.[191]

There is a whole series of cosmogonic traditions, both parallel and complementary, concerning the division of creatures into two opposite groups: there are the beings of light and knowledge on the one hand, and the beings of darkness and ignorance on the other; we have already seen the hadith concerning the Armies of Hiero-Intelligence and those of Ignorance, the "People of the Right" and those "of the Left," and we will soon have occasion to see the case of the "People of *ʿIlliyyîn*" and those of "*Sijjîn*." These terms refer of course to the Imams and their initiated faithful in the former case, and to the enemies of the Imams and their partisans on the other.

Adam's offspring likewise took an oath before God, but this oath covers only one point: the Unicity of the Creator. Two important details accompany this fact. First, it is said that after this oath the original human nature (*fiṭra*) was marked by recognition of Divine Unicity, a recognition called "*islâm*"; it is known that in Imamite terminology this term, the opposite of "*îmân*," technically refers to exoteric submission to religion. The second is that all the descendents of Adam, the believers (*mu'min*) as well as the infidels (*kâfir*), took this oath. The "believers" or the "People of the Right" are at this stage the subtle materialization of the human "pure beings" of the First World of the Shadows; thus, they have already taken oaths of *walâya*, the oaths of the esoteric part of religion. The "People of the Left," on the other hand, although monotheistic in their original nature, can only fall into "infidelity," forget their oath and disobey God, since they have failed to recognize *walâya*.[192]

What characterizes the Impeccables in this World of particles, besides their role as initiating masters of the "pure beings," is what might be called the faculty of "pre-voyance." What this means is that they "see" in the particles (*al-dharr*) or in the "clay" (*al-ṭîna*) of Adam's offspring (both the "pure" and the "impure") all his offspring's natures and their future destinies, down to the least of their thoughts, words, and deeds. The miraculous powers of the imams, relative to the reading of thoughts and to physiognomy during their existence in the sensible world, are sometimes presented as resulting from a remembrance of what they had "seen" in "the clay" of men in the World of particles.[193] We thus see a kind of archetype of the two main traits of the imams' existence in these two characteristics of the Impeccables, that is, Initiation and Pre-Voyance, the traits being their initiatory knowledge and their ability to perform miracles. Both of these will be returned to later.

As an overview of what has just been covered, Table 3 might be helpful in its attempt to sum up Twelver Shî'ism's cosmogony and anthropogony:

WORLDS	INHABITANTS AND THEIR FUNCTIONS
THE LIGHT OF GOD	
The Mother of the Book	The formless lights of the "Impeccables" (*'AQL*)
The First World of Particles or the World of Shadows or the World of the Pact	Lights formed from the Impeccables (Unification and Glorification) Initiation after oaths of recognition of the esoteric and the exoteric) (Pre-voyance)
	Shadows of pure beings (angels, prophets, believers=the Armies of *'aql*) (the four oaths on the esoteric and the exoteric, followed by learning the secrets of Unification and the Glorification)
The Second World of Particles	Particles of Adam's descendents made out of Clay (the People of the Right= the Armies of *'aql*= the believers) (the People of the Left= the Armies of *jahl*= the infidels) (the oath of recognition of the exoteric Unicity that characterizes original nature)
toward the creation of the material, sensible world	

Table 3.

II-2. ADAMIC HUMANITY. THE "VOYAGE" OF THE LIGHT

It is after this event that the creation of the material world takes place, and it is within this world that the capital event of the creation of spirits (*arwâḥ*), of hearts (*qulûb*), and of bodies (*abdân*) must be placed. Here again we are faced with the radical and omnipresent division of all beings into two opposing groups in the battle from the time of creation. On one side are the Guides and their faithful, and on the other are the Enemies and their partisans. A substantial number of traditions supply the following data regarding these strong parallels: the spirit and the heart (which is where the spirit is believed to reside) of the Impeccables were created out of a Clay located above the *ʿIlliyyin*, while their bodies were formed from the Clay of the *ʿIlliyyin* itself. The spirit and the heart of the faithful of the Imam, as well as the spirit and the heart of the prophets, were formed from the Clay of the body of the Imam, and the bodies of the faithful and of the prophet were formed from a Clay located beneath the *ʿIlliyyin*. On the other hand, the spirits, hearts, and bodies of the Enemies of the Imam were formed from the Clay of the *Sijjîn*; the spirits and hearts of their partisans were formed from this same Clay, while their bodies were formed from a clay located below the *Sijjîn*.[194]

[above the *ʿIlliyyin*] the spirits and hearts of the Impeccables	
[*ʿIlliyyin*] the bodies of the Impeccables	[*Sijjîn*] spirits, hearts, and bodies of the Enemies
spirits and hearts of their faithful and of the prophets	spirits and hearts of their partisans
[below the *ʿIlliyyin*] bodies of the faithful of the Impeccables, and that of the prophets	[below the *Sijjîn*] bodies of the partisans of the Enemies

Table 4.

The terms *ʿIlliyyûn* (*ʿIlliyyin* in the accusative) and *Sijjîn* are from the Qurʾan, and are seen, respectively, in verses 18–21 and 7–9 of Sura 83 (Sura al-muṭaffifîn):

> Surely, the Book of the Pure is in the *ʿIlliyyin*
> And what will have you know what the *ʿIlliyyûn* is?
> It is a Book covered with characters
> Those who are admitted into the Proximity of God will see it.[195]
>
> Surely, the Book of the impious is in the *Sijjîn*
> And what will have you know what the *Sijjîn* is?
> It is a Book covered with characters.[196]

The commentators have identified *ʿIlliyyin* and *Sijjîn*, respectively, as one of the highest levels of Paradise and one of the lowest levels of Hell; the root *ʿlw* or *ʿly* evokes the idea of elevation, of height, of domination, and the root *sjn* that of emprisonment, detention, and burying in the ground. Similarly, some authors have also seen, as the Qur'anic text appears to suggest, the naming of the two divine books as containing the "names" of the elect and those of the damned. In this sense, *ʿIlliyyûn* (the term also exists in Hebrew and in Chaldean, where it refers to something placed highly, or at a high elevation) may be compared to the "Book of Life" of Judeo-Christian tradition (cf. Exodus 32:32–33; Daniel 12:1; Psalms 49:29; Luke 10:20, Apocalypse XX:15; etc.). In Imamite tradition, the Qur'anic texts cited previously are almost always accompanied by the hadith concerning creation from *ʿIlliyyin* and *Sijjîn*, and even though copious details are not available on the subject,[197] it would appear as though the two concepts (the name of the place and the name of the Book) are equally present. It should be added that in early Imamism a cosmic Book could denote a metaphysical World, such as we saw in the case of the Original World of *umm al-kitâb*.[198] In one of Jaʿfar's traditions, *ʿIlliyyin* is replaced by Throne: "God created us [i.e. our entities of light or our spirits] from the light of His Majesty, then He gave form to our creation (*ṣawwara khalqanâ*) from a well-guarded secret Clay taken from under the Throne, and He had our light inhabit our form; we are thus luminous human creatures (*naḥnu khalqan wa basharan nûrâniyyîn*), endowed with that which God has not bestowed upon any other. And He created the spirits of our faithful from our Clay, and their bodies from another, well guarded and secret, but lower than ours. Other than our faithful and the prophets, God so endowed no other creatures. It is for this reason that only we and they [i.e., our initiated disciples, the pure human beings, the prophets, and the faithful of the imams] deserve to be called men, while the others are no more than gnats destined for the fires of Hell [lit. "this is why we and they have become men and the other men, gnats destined for the fires of Hell," *wa li-dhâlik ṣirnâ naḥnu wa hum al-nâs wa ṣâra sâʾiru l-nâs hamajan li l-nâr wa ilâ l-nâr*]."[199]

Two points from this series of traditions should be borne in mind. First of all, there is the fact of finding this equality of "level of being" between the faithful of the imams (that is, the "believers" who have been initiated into the esoteric dimension of religion) on the one hand, and the prophets on the other. This is an equality that implies the same spiritual status for both. These two groups of humans, like the angels (as we have seen), created simultaneously in the form of shadows in the First World of Particles, had together taken the four oaths of fidelity and had been initiated by the Impeccables into the secrets of the Sacred Sciences. According to Imamite tradition, those initiated into the esoteric dimension of religion have the same spiritual "weight" that the prophets do in the universal economy of the Sacred and in the battle against the Armies of Ignorance. The second point that should be taken into consideration is the consubstantiality of the heart of the faithful believer and the body of the imam. We shall return to this detail at length. This fact constitutes the cosmogonic and propositional basis for the most important spiritual practice in early Imamism, that of the practice of vision with (or in) the heart (*al-ru'ya bi'l-qalb*).[200]

At the time of the creation of the human race, the single and dual Light of prophecy [the Imamate], also called the Light of Muḥammad and 'Alî, was placed in Adam by God;[201] it was because of this light that the angels were commanded to prostrate themselves before Adam, which they all did with the exception of Iblîs, who was forever damned by God because of his haughty disobedience:[202] " . . . Then God created Adam and deposited us in his loins and commanded the angels to prostrate themselves before him so that we might be glorified (through Adam); their prostration was the proof of their adoration of God and their respect and obedience toward Adam because of our presence in his loins. . . . "[203]

Starting from Adam, this Light begins its "voyage" through the generations of humanity, covering the spaces and times of the sacred history of (the present?) humanity, to reach its predestined vehicles par excellence (that is, the historical Muḥammad and the historical 'Alî), and to be transmitted through them to the other imams. The Prophet said:

> We were silhouettes of light until God wanted to create our form; He transformed us into a column of light (*ṣayyaranâ 'amûda nûrin*) and hurled us into Adam's loins; then He made us be transmitted through the loins of fathers and the wombs of mothers without our being touched by the filth of associationism or any adultery due to infidelity (*akhrajanâ ilä aṣlâb al-âbâ' wa arḥâm al-ummahât wa lâ yuṣîbunâ najas al-shirk wa lâ sifâḥ al-kufr*); and when He had us reach the loins of 'Abd al-Muṭṭalib [the grandfather of both the Prophet and 'Alî], He divided the light in two and placed half in the loins of 'AbdAllâh [the Prophet's father] and the other half in the loins of Abû Ṭâlib [the Prophet's uncle and the father of 'Alî]; Âmina [the Prophet's mother] received in her breast the half that was for me, and she brought me into the world; likewise, Fâṭima, the daughter of Asad [the mother of 'Alî] received in her breast the half that was for 'Alî, and brought him into the world. Then God had the column [of light] come to me and I begot Fâṭima; likewise, He had it go to 'Alî, and he begot al-Ḥasan and al-Ḥusayn. . . . Thus, this light will be transmitted from imam to imam until the Day of Resurrection.[204]

This tradition and others—especially the terms used therein, particularly "loins" (*aṣlâb*) and "wombs" (*arḥâm*)—suggest that the transmission of the legacy of light takes place physically, via the seminal substance. This substance, containing the light of prophecy/Imamate (and for the majority of Sunni authors, the light of prophecy only), adorns the body, and particularly the forehead, of the individual that conveys it with a supernatural brilliance;[205] but according to another series of traditions, this transmission also takes place, this time by a spiritual route, along the initiatory chain of the prophets and their heirs (*waṣiyy*, pl. *awṣiyâ'*), that is, their imams. In contrast to the Sunni tradition, here all the ancestors of the Prophet, be they spiritual or physical, were illumined by the single light of Muḥammad and ʿAlî, a light that is divided, as we have seen, only when it reaches ʿAbd al-Muṭṭalib. The Prophet says, "ʿAlî and I were created from the same light. . . . When Adam reached Paradise, we were in him [literally: "in his loins"]. . . . When Noah boarded the ark, we were in him; when Abraham was thrown into the fire, we were in him. . . . God never ceased transmitting us from pure loins to pure wombs [*wa lam yazal yanqulunâ'llâhu ʿazza wa jall min aṣlâb ṭâhira ilä arḥâm ṭâhira*] to the moment we arrived at ʿAbd al-Muṭṭalib; there, he divided our light in two. . . . "[206]

In effect, Imamite tradition recognizes two distinct genealogies for the Prophet and the imams; the first, which might be called "natural ascendence," corresponds basically, although there have been the inevitable alterations in certain names, to one or another of the classical genealogies of the Prophet in Sunni literature. The second, "spiritual ascendence," which composed the uninterrupted chain of the prophets and their imams since the time of Adam, is typically Imamite.[207] We have used our classical sources in constructing these two lists (Ibn Bâbûye and Ibn ʿAyyâsh al-Jawharî in particular); they have been completed and checked, on the one hand using the details available in the *Ithbât al-waṣiyya*, an Imamite work attributed to al-Masʿûdî (d. 345/956) and dedicated entirely to the idea of Imamite *waṣiyya*,[208] and on the other hand with the Biblical surnames; some names, nevertheless, remain unidentifiable:

1) Natural genealogy, in ascending order: Muḥammad-ʿAbdAllâh (or Abû Ṭâlib) — ʿAbd al-Muṭṭalib-Hâshim — ʿAbd Manâf — Quṣayy (or Fihr) — Kilâb — Murra — Kaʿb — Lu'ayy — Ghâlib — (Fihr) —Mâlik-al-Naḍr (or Quraysh) — Kinâna — Khuzayma-Mudrika — Ilyâs — Muḍar — Nizâr — Maʿadd — ʿAdnân-Ûdd — Udad-al-Yasaʿ — al-Hamaysaʿ — Salâmân — Nabt — Ḥaml — Qaydâ — Ishmaël (the father of the Arabs), and from there, we pass on the the non-Arabs: Abraham, Tharé (Târiḥ) — Nachor (Nâḥûr) — Sarug (Sarûgh) — Réü (Arʿû) — Phaleg (Fâlij) — Héber (Hâbir) — Salé (Shâliḥ) —Arphaxad (Arfahshad) — Shem — Noah — Lameck (Lâmak) —Methuselah (Mattûshalaḥ) — Enoch (Ukhnûkh)/Idris — Jared (Yârad) — Malaléel (Mahlâ'îl) — Caïnan (Qaynân) — Enos (Anûsh) — Seth (Shîth) — Adam.[209]

2) Spiritual genealogy, in descending order: Adam, Seth (Shîth/Hibatu'llâh) — Caïnan — MkhLT (alteration of Mahlâ'îl/Malaleel ?) — Maḥûq (?) — Ghathmîshâ (or Ghanmîshâ, or Ghathmîthâ ?) — Hénoch/Idrîs — Noah — Shem — Ghâthâs (or ʿAthâmir ?) — Barghîshâsâ (or Barʿîthâshâ ?) — Japhet (Yâfith) — BRH (alteration of Târih/Tharé ?) — JFNH (or JFSH or JFÎSH ?) —ʿImrân — Abraham — Ishmael — Isaac — Jacob/Israel — Joseph —Bithriyâ (?) — Shuʿayb — Moses — Joshua (Yûshaʿ) — David —Salomon — Âṣaf b. Barakhiyâ — Zachary — Jesus — Simeon (Shamʿûn) — John (Yaḥyâ) — Mundhir b. Shamʿûn — Salama (or Salîma) — Barda (or Barza or Bâliṭ or Abî, this last name referring perhaps to a "father" of the church?) — Muḥammad-ʿAlî — the eleven imams.[210]

A few of the Biblical prophets (especially the *ûlû l-ʿazm*) and their imams are common to the two lists; what gives them this high religious rank is the presence in them of the light of Muḥammad and ʿAlî (and thus, of the eleven other imams, since ʿAlî represents all of them). This is why, throughout the Imamite tradition, the imams are constantly compared to the prophets and saints of Israel, although they are superior to them, since, through the light of the imams, they have acquired their sacred status. Muḥammad said: "I am the master of the prophets; my heir [ʿAlî] is the master of the *waṣiyyûn*, and his *awṣiyâ'* [the other imams] the masters of the other *awṣiyâ'*" [*waṣiyyûn* and *awsiyâ*, lit. "heirs" ; is there a difference between these terms? Why use two different terms?]; the sages [we will see that in early Imamite terminology *ʿâlim*, pl. *ʿulamâ'*, refers to the imam as spiritual initiator] are the heirs of the prophets; the sages of my Community are like the prophets of the people of Israel."[211]

The transmission of light constitutes perhaps the most important element of the capital idea of *waṣiyya*.[212] In the texts, this transmission is referred to as *naql* (transport, transferral), *taqallub* (return, an allusion to the "return trip" that the Light takes back to Muḥammad and ʿAlî, its first source; or derived from the term *qâlab*, the "carnal envelope" here inhabited by the Light), or *tanâsukh*, which is usually translated as "metempsychosis" in the context of certain Islamic transmigrationist currents,[213] but which must here be translated rather as "metemphotosis" (lit. "the displacement of light"). In one of his sermons, ʿAlî states: "God deposited them [i.e., the light of the Impeccables carried by the seminal substance] in the most noble places they could be placed, and had them rest in the best of resting places; the glorious loins assured their transmission to the purified wombs."[214] The Shîʿite poet Kumayt b. Zayd al-Asadî (d. 125/742), singing the light of glory of the prophet, uses the same term: "The long branches of your tree run through your lineage from Eve to Âmina, /From generation to generation you were sent by the brilliance of silver and gold."[215]

It appears as though the term, in the technical sense of "metemphotosis," is of Imamite origin, and that from there is gradually passed on, probably via "extremist" (*ghulât*) circles with greater or lesser connections to Shîʿism, to transmigrationist milieux, taking on the meaning of "metempsychosis."

A number of studies have heretofore been dedicated to the concept of *waṣiyya* in Islam in general and in Shîʿism in particular;[216] the majority of them (Hodgson, Watt, Sharon, Momen) have reduced *waṣiyya* to nothing more than its political aspect. The double "natural" and "spiritual" ascendence has been considered the proof of the "Arabo-Persian conflict" (Goldziher) or that of an opposion between the "Arab Shîʿites of the North and the Arab Shîʿites of the South" (Rubin). Great erudition and rigor of argumentation have not kept some from holding an extremely reductionist point of view or others from arriving at conclusions that are at least moot; the question of ethnic and cultural mixing in Islam's early years is far from being clearly outlined, a similarity of ideas does not necessarily prove cultural influence, especially since similar forms may have different contents and different forms may have analogous contents; one word is not tantamount to a demonstration, and we cannot conclude that there is influence because there is analogy. Within the framework of the history of ideas, the question of the vitality of an early belief having the possibility of influencing the form or the content of a new belief remains open; neither tribal affiliation nor geographical proximity can necessarily demonstrate the adoption or the assimilation of complex ideas. It is evident that this complex network of problems cannot be solved in the space of a chapter or an article. In the present work we shall be more prudent and remain faithful to the limits that we imposed upon ourselves in the beginning; we shall examine the problem only from within Imamism and within the framework of Imamism's own worldview. It is clear that the idea of the "Sacred Legacy," giving a legitimacy to unquestionable "inheritors," has political implications, but the idea appears more than anything to be an illustration and an application of two important doctrinal "axioms" of Imamism: first, the dogma according to which the earth can never be without living Proof of God, or else it would be annihilated (*"inna l-arḍ lâ takhlû min al-ḥujja," "law baqiyat al-arḍ bi-ghayr imâm la-sâkhat," "law lam yabqa fî l-arḍ illâʾthnân la-kâna aḥaduhumâ al-ḥujja,"* etc.); the Shîʿite imams constitute the continuation of an uninterrupted chain of imams since the origin of our humanity, a chain that guarantees universal Salvation, and whose last link is the twelfth imam, the Mahdî, who is present but hidden until the end of the time of this cycle of humanity. The second "axiom" is that according to which all reality is composed of a *ẓâhir* (an apparent, exoteric aspect) and a *bâṭin* (a hidden, esoteric aspect); from this point of view, the "natural ascendence" would be the *ẓâhir* of the transmission of prophetic/imamic light, that which is brought about through the seminal substance, while the "spiritual ascendence" constitutes the *bâṭin*, the transmission that occurs through initiation.

II-3. EXCURSUS: "VISION WITH THE HEART"

"*Al-ru'ya bi'l-qalb*," which might be translated as "vision with the heart" or "vision in the heart," appears to be a spiritual application of facts relating to the Imam's pre-existential luminous entity, its doctrinal foundation being found in cosmogonic elements of Imamology and in certain aspects of Imamite theology.[217] This idea, unnoticed up to now, founded on what might be called "subtle anatomy," leads into an anthropological dimension of Imamism and reveals another little-studied subject, that of the early practices of Imamite spirituality. Before entering into the subject, we need to remember a few fundamental points of Imamite theology; these points have been studied in detail elsewhere, although in most cases they have been separated from their general doctrinal context and looked at independently of cosmogonic data. In this brief introduction to the subject we do no more than offer an appendix to those studies that have been carried out.[218]

According to the theology of the imams, the Divine Being absolutely transcends all intelligence, imagination, or thought; in His Absolute Being, God remains the inconceivable Transcendent who can be described or apprehended only in the terms with which He has described Himself in His revelations. This is why the term "thing" (*shay'*), with the greatest possible neutrality, can be applied to God; in reply to the question "Is it permitted to say that God is a thing?" al-Bâqir said, "Yes, since [this term] places God outside the two limits of agnosticism (*taʿṭîl*) and assimilationism (*tashbîh*)."[219] Jaʿfar said, "God is a thing different from things; by *thing* we mean the deep meaning, that is, the reality of "thingness" without body or form."[220] ʿAbd al-Raḥmân b. Abî Najrân asked Abû Jaʿfar II (Muḥammad al-Jawâd, the ninth imam), "Can one imagine God as a thing?" "Yes," was the reply, "[but as a thing] unintelligible and indefinite; He is different from everything that can fall into the field of your imagination as a thing. No thing is like Him and no imagination can apprehend Him; and how would imaginations apprehend Him when he is something other than that which is intelligible, other than all that imaginations can conceive ? One cannot imagine Him other than something that is unintelligible and indefinite."[221]

God is *the* thing on the subject of which man cannot speak but negatively by refusing everything that might give a conceivable representation. Actually, in the traditions of a purely theological character, there is a whole series of negations in the words of imams on the subject of God: negation of a conception of body or form (*jism*, *ṣûra*),[222] negation of space (*makân*), of time (*zamân*), of immobility and movement (*sukûn*/*ḥaraka*), of descent and ascent (*nuzûl*/*ṣuʿûd*), of qualification and representation (*tawṣîf*/*tamthîl*), and so on.[223] God, however, in His infinite mercy, wanted His creatures to be able to know Him, and gave Himself a certain number of names, or attributes; some of these attributes concern God's Essence (*dhât*), while others are attributes of His Act (*fiʿl*). The attributes of Essence are those that God has given Himself for all eternity, absolutely without the presence of their opposites: God is always living (*ḥayy*) and He can never be otherwise; He was always been knowing (*'alîm*) and can absolutely not be unknowing; likewise, He is just, powerful, seeing, and so forth. The attributes of Act did not become necessary until after creation; they are those whose opposites can also qualify God: He is indulgent (*'afuww*) but also vengeful (*muntaqim*), He can be satisfied (*râḍî*) but also angry (*sâkhiṭ*), and so forth.[224] These attributes, revealed to humanity by the Most Beautiful Names of God, have places of manifestation, "vehicles," "organs," so that they can be applied to the entirety of creation and to humanity in particular, "organs" thanks to which they become efficient and act upon the created plan. These "vehicles of attributes," these "active organs" of God are the Imams. Throughout the traditions, the Imams unceasingly and indefatigably repeat that "we are the eye (*'ayn*) of God, we are the hand (*yad*) of God, we are His face (*wajh*), His heart (*qalb*), His side (*janb*) His tongue (*lisân*), His ear (*udhn*). . . . We are the Most Beautiful Names of God."[225] It is through these "organs" that the creatures and men in particular are led to know the attributes of God. Thus, two ontological plans of the Divine Being can be distinguished: the first is the plan of Essence, indescribable, inconceivable, beyond all intelligence, intuition, or thought; this is the plan of the Unknowable, of God in His vertiginous, unmanifested concealment. The other is the plan of Acts performed by the organs of God, the Imams, instruments capable of making known to the creatures what can be known of God; this is the plan of the manifest God, of the unknown aspiring to be known. It is also to support this sense that the Imam is described as being the "Proof of God" (*ḥujjat Allâh*), the "Vicar of God" (*khalîfat Allâh*), the "Path of God" (*ṣirâṭ Allâh*), the "Threshold of God" (*bâb Allâh*), or described by such Qur'anic expressions as "the Supreme Sign" (*al-âyat al-kubrä*, Qur'an 79:20), "the August Symbol" (*al-mathal al-a'lä*, Qur'an 16:60), "the Most Solid Handle (*al-'urwat al-wuthqä*, Qur'an 2:256 and 31:22).[226] One might wonder whether in this division between Essence and Organ there is a transposition, on the divine level, of the omnipresent division of all reality into *bâṭin* and *ẓâhir*. The esoteric, the hidden aspect not manifested by God would thus become His Essence, eternally inaccessible; His Organs, that is, His exoteric, His revealed aspect, would be the Imam in his ontological sense, including His historical manifestations, that is, the imams of all ages. Thus, knowledge of the reality of the Imam is the equivalent to knowledge of that which can be known of God. In the words of al-Ḥusayn b. 'Alî:

> "God created His servants so that they might know Him, for when they know Him they worship Him and thus free themselves from the worship of anything that is not Him." Someone then asked: "What is knowledge of God?" "It is, for the people of each age, knowledge of the imam to whom they owe obeisance."[227]

The goal of creation is thus knowledge of the creator by the creatures; the Imam, being the supreme symbol of that which can be known of God, that is, His manifested aspect, thus constituted the reason and goal of creation. "He who knows us knows God, and he who does not know us does not know God," repeat the imams.[228] "It is because of us that God is known," says Jaʿfar al-Ṣâdiq, "and because of us that He is worshipped."[229] The same imam also said, "Without God, we would not be known, and without us, God would not be known."[230] " . . . God made us His Eye among his worshippers, His speaking Tongue among his creatures, His Hand of kindness and mercy stretched out to his servants, His Face by which one is led to Him, His Threshold that leads to Him, His Treasure in heaven and on earth. . . . It is by our service that God is served. Without us, God would not be worshipped."[231]

Let us return to the question of the vision of God. This problem, its possiblity or impossibility, its modalities, its realization on earth or in the other world, its relationship to the more general problem of the manifestation of God and the discussions and polemics related to them, occupy countless pages of Muslim theology and constitute important chapters of it.[232] The Imamite position is marked by two complementary ideas, and its originality is due to the place it accords here again to the Imam, on the one hand, and going beyond speculative theological reasoning to arrive at a lived, contemplative, and direct interior experience on the other. Imamites thus believe that they avoid the two "traps" of *tashbîh* and *taʿṭîl*: assimilationism that tends to anthropomorphize or materialize the Divine Being, and agnosticism that tends to strip God of any ontological consistency.

1) First, the impossibility of ocular vision of God, in this world as well as in the other, is professed; in one of Jaʿfar's stories, which he claims comes from his "fathers," the earlier imams, it is reported that at one point the Prophet Muḥammad encountered a man who was praying with his eyes raised to sky. He said to the man: "Lower your eyes, for you will not see Him."[233] Brought by a disciple to the house of the eighth imam, the traditionist Abû Qurra said to the imam:

> It is said that God divided Hearing [*kalâm*, lit. "the Word," although here it is a case of hearing the Divine Word] and Vision between two prophets; Hearing went to Moses, and Vision went to Muḥammad. Al-Riḍâ replied: "But who was it that preached divine revelation to the *jinn* and to men: 'Looks can not reach Him, but He can reach looks' (Qur'an 6:103), 'they do not encompass Him at all with their science' (Qur'an 20:110), 'Nothing is of resemblance to Him' (Qur'an 42:11)? Was it not Muḥammad? . . . Then how could he have said that I have seen God with my eyes, that I have encompassed Him with my knowledge, or that God has a human form? Are you not ashamed? No, the heretics [*zanâdiqa*] cannot accuse the Prophet of contradiction."[234]

Aḥmad b. Isḥâq said:

> I have questioned [imam] Abû l-Ḥasan III[235] in writing on the subject of seeing God and of the different teachings of people who report it; he wrote in reply: "Visibility [lit. vision] is only possible when there is transparent air between the subject seeing and the object seen [lit. when between the seer and the seen there is an air that can penetrate the look]; without this air and without a light between the subject and the object, there can be no visibility. Now, the existence of a common cause of the act between the subject and the object implies a similarity of nature between the two [lit. for when the seer shares with the seen the cause of the act of vision, this act implies similarity of nature], which is nothing other than assimilationism."[236]

2) Second, the imams state insistently that God can be seen with the heart; Ya'qub b. Isḥaq said: "I questioned [imam] Abû Muḥammad (the eleventh imam, al-Ḥasan al-'Askarî) in writing: 'How can a servant, not seeing his Lord, worship the Lord?' A letter by his own hand replied: 'Abû Yûsuf! My master and lord, he whose benefits have honored my ancestors and myself is too transcendent to be seen.' I then asked: 'And the Prophet? Has he seen the Lord?' He replied in writing: 'God—may He be glorified and exulted—has made visible to the heart of his Messenger what He has wanted to show of the light of his majesty.'"[237]

One of the Khawârij asked the fifth imam, Abû Ja'far al-Bâqir:

> "O Abû Ja'far, what do you worship?"
>
> "[I worship] God Most High."
>
> "Have you seen Him?"
>
> "He can not be seen with the eyes, but hearts can see Him through the realities of faith; God cannot be known by analogy or apprehended by the senses or compared to humans; He is described by signs, recognized by indices."[238]

This vision with the heart is presented not only as possible, but necessary, constituting one of the indispensable conditions of true faith. A religious scholar (*ḥibr*, perhaps a rabbi?) asked 'Alî b. Abî Ṭâlib:

> "O prince of believers! Do you see the Lord when you devote yourself to worship?"
>
> 'Alî replied, "Beware! I would not worship a God that I could not see."
>
> "Then how did you see Him?," asked the scholar.
>
> 'Alî said "Beware! the eyes cannot see Him with the glance; it is rather hearts that see Him through the realities of faith."[239]

The Imamite vision of God entails two distinct times. In compilations of Imamite traditions there are chapters dedicated to the first of these, the impossibility of ocular vision; this is perhaps the reason why this first aspect has already been studied.[240] But studying the first "phase" of the theory and omitting the second result in destroying the equilibrium, neglecting the theological fundamentals, and finally suppressing the practical and initiatory implications that, to our mind, constitute its finality. It is true that the details concerning vision with (or in) the heart, its contents, its modalities, its initiatory function, and its results are quite fragmentary, allusive, and dispersed throughout an impressive mass of traditions;[241] a relatively clear idea is possible only through systematic examination of the compilations.[242]

As has been seen, vision is possible only when there is similarity of nature between the seeing subject and the seen object; God, in his Essence, remains a "thing" absolutely different from other things; what remains forever invisible is the divine Essence, since it transcends absolutely everything, including vision. But at the same time, God, in his manifested aspect (the "signs," the "indices," said the fifth imam) is visible to the heart of the "believer." The two "phases" of the theory of the vision of God are illustrated by two speeches of Jaʿfar al-Ṣâdiq; the first comes in a commentary on chapter 7 of the Qur'an, verse 143, concerning Moses' request to see God: "In relation to the Lord, three things are impossible for servants: manifestation (*al-tajallî*, "theophany"), access (*al-waṣla*), and knowledge (*maʿrifa*); for no eye can see Him, no heart can reach Him, no intellect can know Him."[243] Elsewhere, the same imam gives this reply to a disciple who asked him about the raptures (*ghashya*) that the Prophet was in when revelation "descended upon" him: "It was when there was no longer anyone [to be understood as the absence of the angel of revelation] between God and him; it was when God showed Himself to him."[244] The first speech concerns the divine Essence, not manifested and not manifestable, eternally unattainable, unknowable, inconceivable; the second looks toward the revealed God, His sign, His symbol, that is to say, His "organ," one might also say, the Imam.

What can be revealed through fragments concerning vision with the heart goes in the same direction. What is seen with "the eye of the heart"[245] is a light (*nûr*), or more precisely several modalities of light (*anwâr*).[246] It is located at the center of the heart and is sometimes identified with Hiero-Intelligence (*al-ʿaql*): "Hiero-Intelligence in the heart is like a lamp in the center of the house."[247] *ʿAql* is the means of vision with the heart and in this case it is a synonym of *îmân*, faith,[248] but at the same time its reality (*ḥaqîqa*) constitutes the object of vision. It is known that the reality of *ʿaql* is identical to the Imam: *ʿaql* is the interior Imam of the believer, the Armies of *ʿaql* are identical to the "pure beings" initiated by the Imam, the first thing created by God was either *ʿaql*, or the pre-existential light of the Imam, and so on. This is why we also find furtive allusions attempting to prove the presence of the light of the Imam in the heart, even the identity of the Imam and the heart: "The light of the Imam in the hearts of the faithful is more brilliant than that of the brilliant day star";[249] "the rank of the heart within the body is the same as the rank of the imam among those who owe their obedience to him."[250] The object of vision with the heart and in the heart is thus the light of the Imam, the Supreme Symbol (*al-mathal al-aʿlä*) and the Greatest Sign (*al-âyat al-kubrä*) of the revealed God. The Imam *is* the Light of God,[251] whence the evocations of the vision of God with (or in) the heart. The *sine qua non* condition of this vision is faith, *îmân*; God does not make Himself visible to the heart of the faithful believer (*mu'min*) except throught "the realities of faith," his light: that is, the light of the Imam is found only in the hearts of the faithful; we know that in Imamite technical terminology "faith" means Imamite "religion" in the sense of the esoteric (*bâṭin*) part of the prophetic message, particularly love (*walâya-maḥabba*) and submission (*taslîm*) to the ontological Imam and his terrestrial manifestations, the historical imams. In the same way, by "faithful" is meant "true Shîʿites," that is, those initiated by the imams.

This possibility of vision flows logically, it might be said, both from Imamite cosmogony and from its theory of vision founded on theology. We have seen that the heart of the faithful believer is consubstantial with the body of the Imam, a body identical in pre-existence with the luminous form of the Imam. The heart of the faithful Imamite and the luminous form of he Imam are thus essentially identical, which makes the act of vision possible where the seeing subject is the "heart of the initiated" and the object seen is the "Imam's body of light." The light of the Imam as the greatest evidence of what can be manifested by God appears to have several modalities; various remarks by the imams allude to the complexity of these modalities:

ʿAlî b. Abî Ṭalib states: "God created the Throne from four lights: Red, which reddens all that is red; Green, which makes green all that is green; Yellow, which yellows all that is yellow; and White, which whitens all that is white. [The Throne] is the Knowledge that God ordained the Carriers [of the Throne] to carry, and this light is [drawn] from his Grandeur. It is by his Grandeur and his Light that God gives sight to the hearts of his believers. . . . "[252] A sentence from Jaʿfar adds other details about these lights: "The sun is one seventieth of the light of the Seat (*kursî*), this Seat being one seventieth of the light of the Throne (*ʿarsh*), with the Throne being one seventieth of the Light of the Veil (*ḥijâb*), and the Veil being one seventieth of the light of the Curtain (*sitr*); thus if [those who claim the possibility of ocular vision of God] are sincere, let them stare at the sun (lit. "let them fill their eyes with the sun) when it is not hidden by clouds."[253] Finally, in the words of the eighth imam, ʿAlî al-Riḍâ, these elements appear to find a certain "synthesis," being placed in a visionary experience: " . . . When Muḥammad directed the glance of his heart to his Lord, he placed Him [*jaʿalahu*, perhaps meaning "he visualized Him"?] in a light similar to that of the Veils (*al-ḥujub*) until that which is in [*sic*] the Veils showed itself to him; in fact, it is from the Light of God that all which is green turns green, all that is red becomes red, all that is white turns white, and so forth."[254] These divine lights or these modalities of divine light are thus not visible by sight with the eyes, but they are by "the eye of the heart." These traditions remain cryptic, and early Imamite literature will not be of great help to us in penetrating them. Although the principle of "vision with the heart" was also professed by certain theologians, the Muʿtazilites in particular, the "technical details" that the imams allude to (modalities of lights and colors, identification of the Light of the heart with the Imam, the terminology employed) nevertheless invite us to search for the keys to the mysteries by looking at the mystics. Given the lack of information on this subject in Islamic texts of the time, we are obliged, in this excursus, to look for links between these texts and later Islamic sources, essentially sufi sources. We are not attempting to find easy comparisons to make, since the details that underlie these ideas differ according to the context; but we do wish to demonstrate the technical, practical, experiential aspect of vision with the heart where elements common to a visionary experience can be found in one group or another. This will help us to discover other initiatory roles of the Imam.

1) Although it had a whole "science of the heart," early Sunni sufism made only quite furtive allusions to vision with the heart.[255] Things seem to take form and be conceptualized starting with Najm al-Dîn al-Kubrä (d. 617/1220–21) and his School. In his *Rawâʾiḥ al-jamâl wa fawâtiḥ al-jalâl*,[256] the Master of Khawârazm provides lengthy explanations on the "subtle centers" (*laṭîfa*, pl. *laṭâʾif*), and in particular "the subtle center of the heart," the seat of the pacified soul (*al-nafs al-muṭmaʾinna*; cf. Qurʾan 89:27–30), its lights (chapter 7), and the colors that characterize these lights (chapter 13). The Sun of the heart (*al-shams al-qalb*) is called the Master of the Invisible (*shaykh al-ghayb*) (chapter 66), the Guide (*muqaddam*) or the Scale (*mîzân*) of the Invisible, elevating the mystic from the station of the heart up to Heaven (chapter 69). Najm al-Dîn "Dâyeh" al-Râzî (d. 654/1256), classifies the colored lights visualized in the heart according to their seven ascending degrees of depth: white, yellow, blue-gray, green, sky blue, red, and black.[257] For ʿAlâʾ al-Dawla al-Simnânî (d. 736/1336), another Kubrâwî master, the order of the subtle centers and the hierarchy of colored lights are different;[258] the subtle center of the physical body (lit. the subtle center of the mold, *laṭîfa qâlabiyya*) is black or dark gray, and that of the carnal soul (*nafs ammâra*) is blue-gray; the other five *laṭâʾif* are located in the heart: the subtle center of the heart or of the Self (*qalbiyya/anâʾiyya*) being red; that of the "Secret" (*sirriyya*) being white; that of the Spirit (*rûḥiyya*), yellow; that of the "Hidden" (*khafiyya*), shining black, and that of the "Truth" (*ḥaqqiyya*) being green. Of course, at each degree the mystic comes closer and closer to Divine Reality.

In contrast to the Indian yogis, Muslim mystics appear to have little interest in the subtle centers of energy in the chest, the neck, or the head; they appear to have their attention fixed on the subtle centers of the heart, differentiated by their colored lights.[259] The Naqshbandi sufis also distinguish five *laṭâʾif* at the level of the heart; Muḥammad Amîn al-Kurdî al-Shâfiʿî al-Naqshbandî (d. 1324/1914), in his important work entitled *The Illumination of Hearts*, describes them thus:[260] the "heart," located two fingers below the left nipple, toward the outside, yellow; the "spirit," two fingers below the right nipple toward the middle of the chest, red; "the Secret," two fingers above the left nipple, toward the middle, white; "the Hidden," two fingers above the right nipple, toward the middle, black; and finally "the most Hidden" (*akhfä*), in the center of the chest, green. The author then gives the description of concentration in each level, and particularly the corresponding *dhikr* for each of them. Can one not suppose that the five kinds of light in the enigmatic words of Jaʿfar, that is, the Sun, the Seat, the Throne, the Veil, and the Curtain, each a seventieth of the following, might be an "archaic" allusion to the sufi's five levels of light in the heart?[261] Likewise, would not the colored lights in the speech of ʿAlî and al-Riḍâ refer to the photisms of suprasensible colors visualized by mystics at the level of the heart?

2) Vision with the heart appears to be practiced by all the principal schools of Imamite mystics, schools organized as such essentially after the sixteenth century and the declaration of Imamism as the state religion of Iran by the Safavid dynasty. The practice is based on techniques of concentration and recitation of prayers that the masters claim to have received by oral transmission through chains of initiated that go back to the historical imams. The subject constitutes one of the greatest secrets of the schools, and in written sources there is typically the greatest discretion about anything that concerns the technical aspects of the practice, or else things are explained using language and expressions that only initiated disciples are supposed to understand. There are, however, some allusions to it, and although they are rare in the texts, they are sufficiently telling to be helpful in our understanding. Among the masters of the Niʿmatullâhiyya brotherhood, Muẓaffar ʿAlî Shâh (d. 1215/1801), writes in his Persian treatise entitled *The Red Sulfur*: "The real spiritual heart is the place of manifestation of the Light of God and the Mirror of the epiphanies of the Presence of the Imam (*mawlä*); we are here speaking of a subtle divine entity, an immaterial spiritual entity. And the physical form of this real heart is the carnal organ in the pineal shape located on the left side of the chest cavity, and which is like a window that faces the subtle spiritual entity like the vicar of this immaterial entity. Any abstract epiphany that takes place in the spiritual heart is manifested in a form or a concrete representation in the physical heart. The perfect form, the representation of the perfect Epiphany . . . is the form of Man."[262] *Ṣâliḥiyya*, a work by Nûr ʿAlî Shâh the Second (d. 1337/1918), another master of the same brotherhood, also contains a number of allusions:[263] "The Light that is manifested in the heart is that of the Imam, a Light in the heart of the faithful believer, more brilliant than that

of the sun. . . . In fact, there is no common measure, the Light of the Iman is the manifestation of the Light of God [or of Truth, *ḥaqq*] and that of the sun is only darkness and dust. . . . [ʿAlî said (in Arabic in the text):] "To know me as Light is to know God and the knowledge of God is the knowledge of me as Light; he who knows me as Light is a believer whose heart has been tested for faith by God."[264] "The heart has two faces: its apparent face (exoteric, *ẓâhir*) represents life, guaranteeing the life of organic forces and that of the body; this face is the seat of Light. Its hidden face (esoteric, *bâṭin*), whose place of manifestation is found in the chest, is the place of reunion and of the epiphany of the Divine Attributes and Names, which is why this face is called the Throne. . . . This is why ʿAlî [as the archetypal Imam] is the Throne, for through his esoteric Face he is God, he is the confluence of Secrets."[265] Elsewhere, the author enumerates[266] with no great attention to detail the five or seven luminous "levels" of the heart (*qalb/fuʾâd/sirr/khafiyy/akhfä*, or else *ṣadr/qalb/rûḥ/ʿaql/sirr/khafiyy/akhfä*), their colors (green, blue-gray, combined colors, *alwnâ-e âmîkhteh*, red, white, colorlessness, *bî lawn*, or yellow, and black), and finally the prayers or *dhikr* corresponding to each of them.[267]

The sufis of the Oveysî (Uwaysî) Order made vision with the heart the fundamental practice of all their teaching; the watchword of the brotherhood, which according to the masters contained and summarized the alpha and the omega of the mystic Path, was "*ʿalayka bi-qalbika*," a lapidary phrase attributed to Uways al-Qaranî, the famous mystic and ascetic of the time of the Prophet from whom the order takes its name; the phrase is roughly translated as "It is up to you to watch over your heart." While remaining quite discreet on the technical aspects, the brotherhood recently judged it necessary to publish a book, prepared by a follower, on the references to vision with the heart, or on references said to refer to the practice, in the Old and New Testaments, the Qurʾan, the hadith of both the Prophet and the imams, as well as the writings of the masters of the Oveysî Order; the Light of the heart is there considered like the interior Imam of the mystic; it is consciousness and vision of this Imam as well as obedience in his regard that guarantee progress on the spiritual path.[268]

In doctrinal sources from the Dhahabiyya brotherhood, we often find expressions like "interior vision of the heart" (*baṣîrat-e qalbiyye*) or "contemplation of the lights of the heart" (*mushâhadât-e anwâr-e qalbiyye*), with no further concrete details on this vision, except in a few cases where the mystic is said to be able to see his imam.[269] Among the sources we have been able to consult, there is only one case where significant and detailed elements have been found; this is the fourth of the twelve responses of Master Mîrzâ Abû l-Qâsim Râz-e Shîrâzî (d. 1286/1869) to his disciple Râʾiḍ al-Dîn Zanjânî:[270]

> The disciple: Why do we call the eighth imam the seventh *qibla* [it is to be noted that the initiatory chain of the Dhahabis goes back to the eighth imam, ʿAlî b. Mûsä al-Riḍâ]?

> The master: Know, my dear noble son, that this serious question leads to one of the greatest secrets of the heart (*asrâr-e qalbiyye*) that the simple curious should never discover . . . for their understanding depends on the unveiling of the heart from which only the lords of these hearts can profit. . . . The reason for the name of the holy imam, as is the case with that of the other appellations like "the Confidant of Souls" (*anîs al-nufûs*) or "the Sun of suns" (*shams al-shumûs*) is the shining of the Light of his Love (*nûr-e walâyat*) in the heart of faithful believers (*mu'minân*). This holy Light does not belong to him alone; all the imams are, in fact, the Divine Light sent down for the creatures . . . but since the initiatory chain of [our] school begins with the eighth imam, it is his blessed form (*ṣûrat-e mubârak*) that is manifested in [the subtle center called] "the Black Hidden" center of the heart of his Friends (*dar sirr-e suwaydâ'-e qalb-e awliyâ'ash*); this [center] is the seventh Mountain of the heart (*ṭûr-e haftom-e qalb*). . . . Know that the septuple Mountains of the heart of the holy Friends refer to the manifestations of the seven Lights of varied colors and the seventh manifestation, that is, the black Light that shows itself for us under the blessed form of this holy imam; this Light is of a magnificent, shining, transparent black color of extreme intensity; it is "the Confidant of souls" and "the *qibla* of the seventh Mountain of the heart"; the great [mystics] consider directing their true prayer in the direction of this *qibla* to be obligatory . . . this is why we call this imam "the seventh *qibla*." . . . Those for whom the secrets of the heart are not disclosed cannot fathom this profound meaning. . . . My son, grasp the true value of unveiling the secrets of the hearts of the holy Friends and hide them from those who are not worthy.[271]

There are a number of common elements in the visionary experiences of Sunni and Shî'ite mystics: Light, the fact that at a certain point of the experience the Light is manifested in a human form, and that this form is identified, perceived, and experienced as being the luminous form of the Divine Master, and the fact that, thanks to this Master of Light, the mystic attains Knowledge.[272] These sufis also share the perception of several levels of colored lights. All these elements are further found, scattered, in allusive, often fragmented sentences, in the oldest compilations of the traditions of the imams. Vision with (or in) the heart might have been the spiritual practice par excellence of early Imamism; the imams presented it as being the condition of authentic worship and undoubtedly initiated their closest disciples to it. Does the consecrated expression "the faithful believer whose heart has been tested by God for faith" (*al-mu'min imtaḥana'llâhu qalbahu li l-îmân*), often used by the imams, not refer to the disciple who has passed the test of initiation into the "technique" of vision with the heart? Is this not because such a faithful servant has had the vision of the Light of the Imam, the manifestation of God, and attained the source of Knowledge, that he is always placed by the imams on a level of equality with a prophet (*nabî mursal*) sent by God and an angel of Proximity (*malak muqarrab*)? The practice probably entailed a particular kind of concentration[273] and repetition of sacred phrases,[274] but to our knowledge there is nothing in the early corpus on the subject of a required posture. What is seen in the heart are different modalities or colors of the Light of hiero-intelligence or of the Imam, that is, the luminous form of the Imam, which is sometimes identified with God himself, since the Imam is ontologically the Supreme Symbol, the Sign, and the Proof par excellence, the Manifestation of what can be manifested by God.

One cannot help but think at this point about remarks by two of the companions of the imams, the "two Hishâm" (*Hishâmayn*), Hishâm b. al-Ḥakam and Hishâm b. Sâlim al-Jawâlîqî, avouched "assimilationist" and "anthropomorphist" remarks, with variations, in both Imamite texts and in heresiological sources;[275] it is reported that according to the first of them, God had a body of extreme luminosity, a compact body with parts and dimensions that were fitting for him; the knowledge of this divine body is indispensable. It is reported that the second believed God to have a human form, a body of light whose upper part was hollow and whose lower part was compact, with senses, organs, and a "mane" composed of black light. These remarks, fragmentary and deformed though they might be, appear to give more evidence of the visionary experiences of their authors than of their theological speculations. Actually, they contain neither anything theologically convincing nor anything with any particular aesthetic sense. Did the "two Hishâms" not relate, rather, what they had perceived in their vision with the heart, to which the imam had initiated them? Nevertheless, the imams have categorically refuted the two Hishâms' remarks, without ever going as far as banishing them from their entourages. Would this refutation be perhaps due to the fact that "speaking" (*kalâm*) about the Reality of God is something vain, as the imams have taught, since such discourse would have no grasp of this Reality, and thus would inevitably deform it?[276] Did the two companions speak about secrets that should have remained secret, and were they thus criticized not so much for what they said as for the fact that they said it? Should they have spoken about the Imam instead of God, to remain within the respectable bounds of Imamite theological dogma? It was perhaps a certain equivocation regarding the words of the imams, perhaps even voluntary, that led them to this mixup?[277]

Supernatural powers and the kind of Knowledge that leads to salvation are the fruits of the discovery of the Light of the interior Divine Guide, as has been emphasized by mystics from several different schools. Vision with the heart is experienced and described as a spiritual practice of the mystical and magical kind, developing the wisdom and the occult powers of the practitioner; once again, we here find the ubiquitous "pair" in all levels of early Imamology, (initiatory) Knowledge and (supernatural) Power.[278]

We have seen the extremely reticent and critical position of the imams vis-à-vis exclusively speculative theology. It appears as though according the the imams proximity to and the knowledge of the divine plan do not happen by theological speculations, methods of dialectical reasoning, or personal attempts at rationalization (*kalâm*, *qiyâs*, *ra'y*, *ijtihâd*), but through direct living experience, that interior experience of what can be seen and known of God, that is to say, of his manifestation, the Imam. It is through this experience, where love for the Imam (*al-walâya*) plays a fundamental role, that, according to the imams, true faith is realized, a faith beyond assimilationism (*tashbîh*, we are not here speaking of God but of His manifestation) and agnosticism (*taʿṭîl*, the knowledge of God is not dismissed in the name of an absolute apophatic theology). Vision with the heart appears to be the means par excellence of bringing about this experience: the vision of the Imam of Light of whom the ontological Imam is the archetype and the historical imam is the manifestation available to the senses. Thus, the initiatory practice, quite probably accompanied by prayers with sacred phrases, becomes an actualization, a repetition of the primordial event of the pre-existential Initiation where the shadows of the "pure beings" learned secret phrases from the luminous form of the Imam and repeated them in his presence. The imams present their doctrine as being that of the Secret, enclosing well-guarded secrets: "Our doctrine is a secret contained within a secret, a well-protected secret, a secret that is of advantage only to a secret, a secret veiled by a secret";[279] "our doctrine is hidden, sealed by the pretemporal Pact. God will make him who reveals it despicable";[280] "our doctrine is the Truth, the Truth of the Truth, it is the exoteric and the esoteric and the esoteric of the esoteric; it is the secret and the secret of the secret, a well-protected secret, hidden by a secret."[281] As regards vision with the heart, undoubtedly one of the greatest secrets of the teaching, one might think that the ontological Imam is the contents of the Secret, contents seen in the secret of the heart, and the historical imam its container and he who initiates the faithful believer.[282] Only the faithful believer, the beneficiary of the Light of the Imam of his heart, is said to be able to penetrate, for the same reason as a prophet or an archangel, the secrets of the teaching: "Our teaching is arduous, very difficult; the only ones who can stand it [var: "can add their faith to it"] are a prophet sent from God, an angel of Proximity, or a faithful believer whose heart has been tested by God for faith."[283] According to our hypothesis, the technical "allusions" to vision with the heart in the early corpus of the imams would be the earliest attestation of a spiritual practice in Islam, practice which would later be in widespread use among mystics in both Sunnism and Shîʿism; at the same time it demonstrates, within Imamite doctrine, the experiential aspect of an interiorized Imamology.

II-4. CONCEPTION AND BIRTH

The information related to the conception and birth of the imam constitutes one of the privileged domains of the "marvelous" in Imamism, but here again we must be conscious of the fact that we are dealing with a "theosophic" doctrine where the marvelous only serves as an introduction to the occult and leads to a certain vision of the sacred. What we are studying here finds its natural place at the juncture of the pre-existence and the existence of the imam, and guides us toward the latter.

In a long hadith, Jaʿfar al-Ṣâdiq describes the circumstances of the conception and birth of an imam for a group of his disciples who accompanied him on a pilgrimage to Mecca. The speech took place on the occasion of the birth of Jaʿfar's son, Mûsä al-Kâẓim.[284] According to this hadith, the night that the seed of an imam is foreseen to be conceived, a mysterious being (*âtin*, lit. "an arriver") appears before his father, the present imam, and has him drink something "finer than water, softer than butter, sweeter than honey, colder than snow, and whiter than milk," and commands him to unite with his spouse; thus the seed of the future imam is conceived. After four months, "the spirit is produced in the seed,"[285] then God sends a celestial entity called Ḥayawân ("the Living," lit. "the Animated") to inscribe on the embryo's right arm the phrase "And the Word of Your Lord is accomplished in all truth and justice. No one can change His Words, He it is who hears and knows" (Qurʾan 6:115).[286] Once born, the child places his hands on the earth, for "he receives all the Science of God come down from Heaven on earth," and raises his head toward the sky, for "from the interior of the Throne and on behalf of the Lord of Magnificence, a Herald calls him by name and by the name of his father, and this from the Supreme Horizon (*al-ufuq al-aʿlä*)"[287] and says: "You are my chosen one among my creatures, the place of my Secret, the repository of my Science, my confidant in my Revelation, my vicar on my earth. I have reserved my Mercy, offered my Paradise, and allowed my Proximity to you and to those who love you with a holy love (*li-man tawallâka*, i.e., all those who feel *walâya* for you and believe in your *walâya*, that is, the "true Shîʿites") and by my Glory and my Majesty I shall consume with my worst punishments him who rises up as an enemy against you, even if in the lower world I allow him to profit from an easy life (lit: "even if I provide for him in this lower world which is mine, the riches of my provisions")." Once the celestial Herald stops speaking, the newborn imam answers: "God has given this testimony, and with him the angels and those who are endowed with wisdom: there is no other god than He, He who maintains justice, there is no other god than He, the powerful, the wise (Qurʾan 3:18)." After this word, God gives him the "First Knowledge and the Last Knowledge" (*al-ʿilm al-awwal wa l-ʿilm al-âkhir*), and he [the imam] becomes worthy of the visit of the celestial entity al-Rûḥ (lit. "the Spirit") during the night of the Decree (*laylat al-qadr*). At this point in the story, Abû Baṣîr[288] asks whether al-Rûḥ is not the angel Gabriel, to which Ja'far replies: "Al-Rûḥ is greater than Gabriel, for Gabriel is one of the angels, while al-Rûḥ is a creature superior to the angels"; and then, to mark this difference, he refers to the Qur'anic verse "In that night (the Night of the Decree), the angels and the spirit (al-Rûḥ) descend with God's decree for all matters (Qur'an 97:4)." The details of this story of Ja'far's are found, with some variations, in other traditions from the same chapter; for example, the mysterious being who brings "the drink" to the imam-father is said to be the same as the one who inscribes the sacred phrase on the body of the embryo, that is, Ḥayawân; "the drink" itself is drawn from "the Water beneath the Throne" (*min mâ' taḥta al-'arsh*; cf. Qur'an 11:7)[289] and the inscription is written between the eyes of the embryo (or between his shoulder blades).[290] It is also reported by Ja'far that at the moment that the seed of an imam is conceived in the womb of his mother, she falls into a kind of rapturous stupor (*aṣâbahâ fatra shibh al-ghashya*) that will last a whole day or a whole night;[291] she will then be visited in a dream by "a man" (*rajulan*, an angel who has taken a human form?) who will tell her the good news;[292] upon waking, she will hear a voice announcing the same news coming from her right side. During the pregnancy, she feels light, and she has no pain with the birth. When the moment of the imam's birth arrives, a strange noise (*ḥiss*) fills the room and a light, that only the parents can see, is visible in the house.

The seed of Fâṭima is also of celestial origin. In a hadith, Muḥammad says that his seminal fluid (lit. "the water of my loins," *mâ' fî ṣulbî*) from which his daughter was conceived came from the absorption of an apple from the Garden of Paradise that the angel Gabriel had brought him, "which is why, thanks to her, I can smell the perfume of Paradise."[293] In another hadith, the Prophet recounts that at the time of one of his celestial ascensions, as he reached the Veils, beyond the sixth heaven, he saw before him "some dates, softer than butter, more perfumed than musk and sweeter than honey," and he ate one of them that became the future seed of Fâṭima.[294]

From the time of their birth, the imams have a certain number of extraordinary physical characteristics:[295] they have their umbilical cord cut (*masrûr*), they are clean and circumcised (*makhtûn*), they are conscious even in sleep (lit. "their eyes sleep but their hearts do not sleep," *tanâm 'aynuhum wa lâ hanâm qalbuhum*). Fâṭima has the particularity of never having a menstrual period.[296]

These elements constitute so many "signs of recognition" (*sumbolon*/symbol) for the Twelver religious conscience, and they reveal other facets of the sacred, other outpourings of the divine in the sensible world. The Impeccables, "Supreme Symbols," are above all divine lights marrying the human form of the prophets and of their imams in each introductory period in the history of the sacred; they are perceived by the faithful as being the miracle par excellence and their miraculous conception, birth, and particularities are only corollaries of this propositional miracle that is their being. These accounts are the first examples in Islam of a hagiography of marvelous character, a genre frequently used later especially by popular mystical literature in accounts of the lives of saints; the idea according to which the seed of a man can be of celestial origin seems to be totally unknown in the Islamic milieu of the time. The case of Jesus Christ was of course known by the Arabs, but it constituted an exception, a miracle that justly proved the prophetic mission of Jesus and his selection as the Word of God. Imamite tradition, in taking up the basic elements of a Christology known by the Arabs, introduces this doctrine, well known by several previous religious traditions, into the heart of Islam: namely, that the bodies of the great universal teachers are the results of causes with celestial origins. These facts tend also, and once again, to support the Imamite teaching of the prophetic character of the Cause (*ʿamr*) of the imams, while emphasizing their superiority as regards the prophets, with the exception of Muḥammad, from whose primordial Light they come: an ontological superiority (cf. earlier discussion) and a theological superiority. While the prophets are inspired by the angel Gabriel, the Imams can also benefit from the ministry of al-Rûḥ, a celestial entity superior to the angels; moreover, the imams are inspired from the moment of their birth.

Another supernatural phenomenon accompanies the birth of the imam: the appearance of the "column of light" (*ʿamûd min nûr*). This "column," its description, its characteristics, and the use that the imam makes of it, are all the more interesting in that they present striking analogies with the details concerning a known phenomenon in the occult sciences and magic. According to a whole series of traditions,[297] from the moment an imam is born, God makes a light appear for him; this light is described in several ways: the most frequent description is that of a column of light or a column made of light,[298] but it has also been called a "minaret of light,"[299] "a lamp made of light,"[300] or even "a light like a gold ingot."[301] At the moment of its appeareance, the column of light fills all of space, linking the divine Throne with the earth or, according to another version, linking God with the imam.[302] The imam draws his Knowledge from it, since he "sees" in it all that he wants to know. Jaʿfar says: "God establishes a column made of light between Himself and the imam. . . . When [the imam] wants to know something, he looks into this light and acquires the knowledge of it."[303] From the moment of his birth, and throughout his whole life, the imam has the ability to visualize this column of light at will, and it is one of the numerous sources of his "initiatory Knowledge." Our traditions especially emphasize two kinds of knowledge acquired by "vision" through this supernatural light. First, there is the vision of the thoughts, intentions, and actions of created beings: " . . . For [the imam] a "lamp of light" is established by which he knows hidden thoughts (*al-ḍamîr*) and sees the actions of the creatures (*aʿmâl al-khalâʿiq*)."[304] Then there is the vision of all that he wants to see throughout the world; this is the occult ability of seeing at a distance: " . . . For him is raised a Column of light in which he sees all that is between the east and the west"; " . . . For him, at the place where he is, is established a Column that allows him to see other places."[305]

The "Column" is thus a light made manifest by God, filling all of space, stretching between the earth and the sky, and with which or in which the imam "sees," from the moment of his birth, all that he wants to see.[306]

3

The Existence of the Imam

> It is because of us, the initiated Guides
> That the sky does not come crashing down to earth,
> That the beneficent rain falls from the sky
> That mercy is spread . . .
> The earth will engulf its inhabitants
> If one of us is not upon it.
>
> Imam ʿAlî b. al-Ḥusayn

III-1. COMMENTS ON THE "POLITICAL" LIFE OF THE IMAMS

Given the image proffered by both most scholarly studies and recent events in Iran and Lebanon, the dominant view of Imamite Shîʿism is that it is, at base, a political, theological, and juridical movement, "subversive" if not revolutionary. This view is shared by both scholars and the public at large. However, when Shîʿism's early direct sources are carefully examined, such a view finds itself at variance with scientific objectivity. Three incoherencies of a methodological order appear to be at the base of the errors:

a) The image is founded almost exclusively on two indirect sources: either information furnished by heresiographs and Sunni propagandists from the classical age (which of course skews the view), or the opinions of the great Imamite theologians, a view that vitiates the important doctrinal difference between early suprarational esoteric Imamism and a later, theological-juridical-rational Imamism.
b) There is confusion among the different forms of Shîʿism; actually, among the principal branches of Shîʿism, militant activism is encountered most often among the Zaydis and later among the Ismâʾîlis, and also among the descendents of imam al-Ḥasan. Our focus in the present work is more concerned with Twelver Shîʿism, Imamism from the line of al-Ḥusayn.
c) There is neglect of the fact that the politicization of Imamism, even if it has its roots in the theological-juridical-rational tradition, is the

result of a long doctrinal and historical process lasting several centuries, a process that did not begin to concretize until the sixteenth century and the declaration of Imamism as the state religion in Iran by the Safavids.

The result of these methodological incoherencies has generally been to reduce the historical existence of the imams to the theological and political roles that they played, thus making Imamism a doctrine identical to itself in all times and in all places, reduced further to theological-juridical or sociopolitical dimensions exclusively. At the other extreme, there is another conception, admittedly less common, that sees Imamism as a gnostic and premature kind of "philosophy," outside any historical context. We will attempt here, through our research, to help catch the study of early Imamite doctrine up with its historical evolution, and thus avoid considering the two as separate epiphenomena. We have already had occasion to look closely at the extremely critical attitude of the imams toward *kalâm*, which is perceived as being a purely speculative theological dialectic, and thus unable to bring the faithful effectively to God. According to early Imamite "theology" (which the imams called *tawḥîd* or *'ilm al-tawḥîd* and never *kalâm*), only knowledge of the reality of the Imam is equivalent to knowledge of what can be knowable in God; "theology" is here subordinate to Imamology; neglecting Imamology or paying insufficient attention to it will lead to reducing Imamism to a theological doctrine in the "kalâmic" sense of the term, as is the case with Mu'tazilism or Ash'arism, for example, which is an aberration if one checks the basic texts. As far as the relationship of early Imamism with politics goes, it may be interesting to examine briefly the attitude of the imams toward temporal power, in order to see to what extent Imamism can be presented as a political and revolutionary movement; this will not be an attempt to deal comprehensively with the question, but rather to see what the importance of the political dimension in the existence of the imams has been.

On the basis of their political life, the imams can be divided into four categories: a) those who were directly and positively involved with politics; b) those to whom no political activity has been attributed; c) the particular case of the third imam, al-Ḥusayn b. 'Alî; and d) the particular case of the twelfth imam, the Mahdî.

a) Three imams may be placed in the first of these categories: the first, the second, and the eighth.

—The first imam, 'Alî b. Abî Ṭâlib (assassinated in 40/661),[307] was separated from power after the death of the Prophet. During the twenty-five years of the reign of his predecessors (Abû Bakr, 'Umar, and 'Uthmân), he had no political activity properly speaking, and according to the Shî'ite traditon, he dedicated the better part of his time to teaching his disciples and to compiling a recension of the Qur'an. His relations with the power structure during these twenty-five years amount to a few incidents where he criticized details of the religious life of the caliphs. This attitude was dictated especially by the canonical prescriptions to "institute good" and "prevent evil"; 'Alî was far from being the only one to have this attitude toward the caliph. His own caliphate began in one of the most troubled periods in the early history of the Muslim community. His two predecessors had met with violent deaths, and the ephemeral coalition that brought him to power was a quite heterogeneous group. The approximately five years of his reign (35–40/656–661) saw a series of battles in a society torn by unceasing intrigues. The great conquests that took place during 'Umar's caliphate stimulated a veritable sociocultural revolution. Besides fantastic riches, in the space of a few years a tribal Bedouin community had firsthand experience with the complications of an almost urbanized society. A half century after the death of the Prophet, the political-religious model that he had managed to set up was outmoded by further events. In a nutshell, it might be said that at this time, the ascetic spirit of 'Alî and some of his companions like 'Ammâr b. Yâsir, Abû Dharr al-Ghifârî, Ḥudhayfa, and others, with the religious politics of the Prophet as a model, clashed violently with the new Umayyad aristocracy formed in a society that was beginning to taste the advantages of riches and urbanization.

—The political life of the second imam, al-Ḥasan b. 'Alî (d. 49/669) is known for the conflict that opposed him to the Umayyad Mu'âwiya I. This conflict, which led to the imam's abdication in favor of Mu'âwiya's caliphate, has been interpreted in a variety of ways. Examination of Shî'ite and Sunni sources[308] leads to the following conclusions: it appears as though it was Mu'âwiya, hostile to the Shî'ites since the battle of Ṣiffîn, who started the struggle for power. Al-Ḥasan, who undoubtedly found the battle too unequal, consented to abdicate, under certain conditions: that the Umayyad religious authorities cease their public cursing of 'Alî, that Mu'âwiya abstain from mistreating the Shi'ites, and that al-Ḥasan be given a subvention from the public treasury. It is interesting to note that none of these conditions was either particularly political or very demanding (receiving a subvention from the public treasury was a legitimate right of any Muslim, and especially of a close relative of the Prophet). Sunni sources call this year (41/680) "the year of the [reconciliation or unification of the] Community" (*sanat al-jamâ'a*). According to the Shî'ite version, a few years after the negotiations, in 49/669, Mu'âwiya had the imam poisoned, considering him an eventual danger at the time of his son Yazîd I's enthronement. There was some Shî'ite agitation at the time, stirred up by a former partisan of 'Alî named Ḥujr b. 'Adî, who was upset over al-Ḥasan's abdication. For a short time, he managed to have part of Iraq on his side, but the revolt was quickly, and bloodily, quelled by the Umayyad authorities.[309]

—The eighth imam, 'Alî al-Riḍâ (203/818) had no contact with political life until the time when the Abbasid al-Ma'mûn, adopting a pro-Shî'ite political stance, named him his designated heir in 201/817.[310] According to Shî'ite sources, al-Riḍâ rejected the proposal for a while, but under pressure from his partisans, who represented a variety of interests, he left for Marw in Transoxiania, where Ma'mûn was stationed. There was strong opposition on the part of Iraqi Sunnites; it appears as though it was at this time that powerful members of the Abbasid family informed Ma'mûn that they would facilitate his route to a universally recognized caliphate, provided he abandon his pro-Shî'ite political stance. After some hesitation, al-Ma'mûn set out for Iraq. On the way, his pro-Shî'ite vizier Faḍl b. Sahl al-Barmakî was assassinated (202/818). A few months later, in 203/818, again on the road to Iraq, imam al-Riḍâ died in Ṭûs under what remained mysterious circumstances. Once in Iraq, al-Ma'mûn had absolute power and abandoned his pro-Shî'ite politics. The "political" attitude of the eighth imam is characterized as one of moving passivity; according to Shî'ite sources, for the some fifteen months that he was officially declared "inheritor of the caliphate" he never ceased repeating that the only reason he accepted going to Marw was under pressure, and to ensure that the Shî'ites and, at their head, the imam, should remain far from the temptations of power under all circumstances, in order that they might be "the witnesses of the Beyond" (*shuhadâ' al-âkhira*).[311]

b) Historiographical and biographical sources attribute no positive political activity to seven of the imams:

—The fourth imam, 'Alî Zayn al-'Âbidîn (92 or 95/711 or 714), was one of the rare survivors of the massacre of Karbalâ.[312] In Medina, he led a life of piety and retreat, and seemingly caused not even the least discomfort to the Umayyad powers. Sunni sources describe him with the same veneration that Shî'ite sources do. The historical information available about him is meager, with sources limiting themselves to accounts of his pious words, or to praising his exemplary piety and asceticism. He nonetheless appears to have attempted to calm the Shî'ites, undoubtedly in revolt after Karbalâ, and to appease their adversaries to a certain extent, by citing as his sources Sunni personalities like 'AbdAllâh b. 'Abbâs and even 'Â'isha, his grandfather 'Alî's bitter enemy in the Battle of the Camel (36/656), and the woman "damned" by the Shî'ites.

—The fifth imam, Muḥammad al-Bâqir (d. circa 119/737), is known for his piousness, his religious knowledge, and his basically esoteric teachings; he engaged in no political activities. Although it was toward the end of his Imamate that the revolt of his half-brother Zayd (whence the name "Zaydis") broke out, he was in no way involved with the undertaking.[313]

—The sixth imam, Ja'far al-Ṣâdiq (d. 148/765), is known as one of the most brilliant, if not the most brilliant scholar of his time in the Muslim tradition. He is known for his "traditional knowledge" (*tafsîr*, *ḥadîth*, *fiqh*, etc.) as well as for his esoteric and occult wisdom (mystical knowledge, alchemy and astrology, the occult science of letters . . .). He lived in a time marked by the violent passing of power from the Umayyads to the Abbasids, a time of almost general armed insurrection in which Ja'far engaged in no political activity and was never bothered by the powers that be. It has never been suggested that he had a desire for power.[314] His reply to the famous messenger from Abû Muslim, one of the leaders of the anti-Umayyad coalition who had requested his assistance, was notable: In burning Abû Muslim's letter he said, "This man is not one of my men, this time is not mine."[315] He had the same negative, passive attitude toward the Zaydi Shî'ite insurgents led by is paternal uncle Zayd b. 'Alî in 122/740 and by his cousin Yaḥyâ b. Zayd in 125/743, and finally in 145/762 by the Ḥasanid Shî'ite al-Nafs al-Zakiyya and his brother Ibrâhîm.[316]

—The seventh imam Mûsä al-Kâẓim (183/799) was another to have no political involvement. However, the anti-Shî'ite repression begun during al-Manṣûr's caliphate, especially because of al-Nafs al-Zakiyya's armed revolt, began to weigh even on the Imamites. Mûsä was arrested a first time by the caliph al-Mahdî, who had him taken to Baghdad in order to better keep him under control. Once his apolitical stance was proved, he was allowed to return to Medina. Zaydi revolts continued to break out in a number of regions, and the following caliph, Harûn al-Rashîd, who saw a possible source of subversion in all Shî'ites, had Mûsä taken to Baghdad once again; he died there under house arrest. The Sunnites deeply revere Mûsä, and he is considered a reliable source for hadith.[317]

—The ninth imam, Muḥammad al-Taqî (220/835) lived only to the age of twenty-five, and was involved in no political activity; he married al-Ma'mûn's daughter, probably under pressure from her father, in order to calm some of the faithful who were revolting because of the mysterious death of the eighth imam.[318]

—The tenth imam, 'Alî al-Naqî (254/868) lived peacefully in Medina under the caliphates of al-Mu'taṣim and al-Wâthiq. Things changed under al-Mutawakkil (232–47/847–61) and his successors. Their politics of severe repression of the Shî'ites were due especially to renewed activity on the part of the Zaydis; al-Mutawakkil's unjustified hatred of any kind of Shî'ism is noted even in Sunni sources. Around 250/864, the imam was suspected of engaging in subversive activities in Medina. A representative of the caliph searched his house and, according to the story, found nothing more than a few copies of the Qur'an, some collections of prayers, and a few other religious books. Although the caliph appears to have been convinced of the inoffensive piety of the imam, he nevertheless kept him under house arrest in the military camp of Sâmarra, not far from Baghdad; it is there that the tenth imam died, at the age of forty-two.[319]

—The eleventh imam was al-Ḥasan b. 'Alî al-'Askarî (260/874). No source attributes activities of a political nature to him. He did, however, suffer from the politics of Shî'ite repression of al-Mutawakkil's successors. Like his father, he lived almost his entire life under house arrest in the military camp (thus his nickname "al-ʿAskarî") in Sâmarra. He died at about the age of thirty, during the caliphate of al-Muʿtamid.[320]

c) The particular case of the third imam.

Al-Ḥusayn b. ʿAlî refused, after the death of his brother, al-Ḥasan, to pledge allegiance to Yazîd I; he then retired to Mecca. In 61/680, at the invitation of a number of his partisans, he started out for Kûfa, in Iraq. He was accompanied only by his family and a small escort. Great methodological care must be taken in a truly objective study of the historical circumstances that led to the tragedy at Karbalâ. Given the seriousness and the delicate nature of the subject—less than fifty years after the death of the Prophet, his grandson and the grandson's entire family had been massacred by their own community—we are forced to choose from the information available, to confront both Shîʿite and Sunni sources systematically, and to decide on the basis of both emotional accounts and accounts filtered through the eyes of the ideological positions of their authors.[321] For the present, we must limit ourselves to the following brief conclusions. From a historical point of view, nothing suggests that al-Ḥusayn planned an armed combat with the Iraqi Umayyad authorities. It appears as though it was his cousin Muslim b. ʿAqîl who opened the hostilities. Having left with the vanguard, Muslim stirred up the beginnings of an armed insurrection among the Shîʿite population of Kûfa. The insurrection was quickly quelled by bloodshed, and it is there that Muslim lost his life. Almost a week later, a carefully watched imam al-Ḥusayn arrived in Iraq. For reasons that have never been fully explained, attempts at negotiation and bargaining were in vain. Finally, on the tenth of Muḥarram in 61 (October 10, 680), in the land of al-Ṭaff, in Karbalâ, al-Ḥusayn and his companions were hit by forces that greatly outnumbered them. The imam and nearly all his family were killed with no regard for the age of the victims. When the early Imamite corpus is examined, the phenomenological view that the reader is left with shows that the case of the third imam is doctrinally more complex than it might appear when the imam is looked at as no more than an insurgent against Umayyad power. In fact, according to the teachings of the imams, their corpus constitutes an indissoluble whole; when taken together, unified and coherent, each "present" (*lâḥiq*) imam is the exegete of his predecessors (*sâbiq*), unveiling the true meaning and the true intentions of their acts and words. As far as al-Ḥusayn's case is concerned, to our knowledge none of his successors interpreted his presence in Karbalâ as being a "political" act aimed at upsetting the powers that be. According to his own successors, the act of the imam was that of a Friend of God (*walî*) fulfilling his destiny according to the will of the Beloved (*mawlä*). Al-Ḥusayn's grandson, imam Muḥammad al-Baqir, said: "[At the time of the battle of Karbalâ] God Most High had Victory (here, a celestial entity) descend upon al-Ḥusayn such that Victory filled up [the space] between the sky and the earth; then the imam was placed before his choice: victory or meeting God; he chose to meet God Most High."[322] The eighth imam, ʿAlî al-Riḍâ, in reference to Qur'an 38:107 and the act of Abraham, who was willing to sacrifice his son in order to fulfill divine will, defines al-Ḥusayn's act as "the Grandiose Sacrifice" (*al-dhibḥ al-aẓîm*) of messianic dimensions.[323] The battle and the massacre at Karbalâ were predestined, both so that the imam could completely fulfill his destiny as martyr and so that his enemies could be revealed, abhorred, and forever damned.[324] According to a tradition attributed to Jaʿfar, the Prophet received a sealed Book called the Legacy (*al-waṣiyya*) from heaven; this Book, the only one received as such by Muhammad, contained twelve sealed messages regarding the mission of each of the imams. The imams inherit the *waṣiyya*, each in turn opening the seal intended for him so that he can accomplish what the Divine Will has intended for him. In al-Ḥusayn's seal, the third, was written: "Do battle, kill, and be killed! Rise up in a group for martyrdom, for they will know martyrdom only with you."[325] These words give a view of the matter that is far from that of a revolt concerning political or social demands. Even up to the present day militant Shîʿism has continued to justify its activities religiously by the case of imam al-Ḥusayn and the battle of Karbalâ with out-of-context use, as ideological necessities suggest, of some of al-Ḥusayn's words and actions. It is interesting to note that modern political texts refer almost exclusively to the words and actions of ʿAlî (especially those reported in the *Nahj al-balâgha*) and al-Ḥusayn with no attention paid to the explanations and exegeses of the other imams; the early religious doctrine is thus transformed into a political ideology. What is more serious is the fact that, as a result of insufficient examination of the basic texts, the majority of specialists have not distinguished between "doctrine" and "ideology." They have thus defined Imamism as an essentially political and subversive ideology and have everywhere seen political reasons for each point of doctrine, even where these do not exist.[326]

d) The special case of the twelfth imam.

The entire fourth part of the present study will be dedicated to the hidden imam. For the present it must be said that the specifically political and demanding attitude of early Imamism is crystallized around the Figure of this imam and the idea of his triumphal Return at the End of our Time, militant combat against oppressors, avenging the oppressed of all time, and particularly vengeance for the murder of al-Ḥusayn and the foundation of a world of knowledge and justice. All of these tasks await the twelfth imam, and him alone, upon his final Return. According to the imams, not only is any Shîʿite attempt politically to reestablish good between now and then ineluctably doomed to fail, but any power is by nature oppressive and usurping regardless the doctrine upon which it is founded.[327]

These details of doctrine, far from being subversive, rather invite the faithful to adopt a radically "apolitical" attitude. Mûsä b. Jaʿfar said, "Shîʿites, do not obey [those who invite] disobedience to your sovereign; if he is just, ask God to give him longevity, and if he is unjust pray God that he be reformed. Your well-being resides in the well-being of your sovereign. A just sovereign is like a benevolent father; love for him that which you love for yourselves, and reject for him that which you reject for yourselves."[328] There is a series of traditions attributed to the fifth, sixth, and eighth imams gathered by al-Kulaynî in a subchapter entitled "The Will to Command,"[329] where the following statements are found.

> Jaʿfar: "He who seeks to command is lost"; "He who wishes to command is lost."[330] "Beware of those who command and who consider themselves leaders; as God is my witness, the man behind whom the sound of sandals [of his partisans] is raised will only perish and cause [others to] perish."[331] "He who believes himself to be chief is damned, he who tries to become one is damned, he who proclaims himself to be one is damned."[332] "Avoid leading people and avoid following people [who lead]."[333]

> Al-Bâqir: "Beware, o Abû l-Rabîʿ, of seeking to command in any way; do not be [as] a wolf devouring people in our [the imams'] name, for God will make you miserable; do not say about us what we have not said about ourselves [i.e., probably "Do not say that we demand temporal power"] for you should know that you will ultimately be held to make an account; if you have been truthful we will confirm you, and if you have lied, we will deny you."[334]

The presence of such details in the early corpus of the imams invites at least the consideration of nuances in the *idée fixe* that reduces the existence of the imams to a political and militant role and their doctrine to an ideology of subversion.[335] It is true that the group that will later be called the *shîʿa ʿAlî* (the partisans of ʿAlî) formed under the political conditions of the famous arbitration of the Battle of Ṣiffîn (37/657), and that according to an exclusively historical point of view Imamite "opposition" appears to have led to the battle of the third imam against the Umayyad authorities at Karbalâ (61/680); but it must be noted that from that date on the imams abandoned all activity that could be considered as positively political and they retained only a kind of "intellectual" opposition to the Umayyad and Abbasid powers. Imamite doctrine properly speaking was formulated and structured at the time of the fifth and sixth imams, in a period that could be called that of the "radical apoliticalism" of the early history of Imamism. The drama of Karbalâ seems to have been a decisive turning point in the political stance of early Imamism. All the information suggests that the imams realized and were trying to persuade their faithful that the age of "understanding" between "temporal" and "spiritual" powers, as was the case in the time of the Prophet, had come to an end. They seem to have deduced that the True Religion (*al-dîn al-ḥaqq*, i.e., the esoteric doctrine of the imams) as they understood it, and politics had become two poles, *forever* irreconcilable. We emphasize "forever," that is, until the "End of Time" (*âkhir al-zamân*) since, according to the imams, "The Ideal City," administered by an "Impeccable," is unrealizable until the Return of the Resurrector; thus, the political, which leads to perdition, must be abandoned in order to safeguard the religious.[336]

The Imamological traditions of the early compilations of hadith, despite their multiplicity and their lack of cohesive logic, may be divided into two quite strongly interdependent categories: those that give definitions of the Imam, and those that present his functions. The definition of the Imam is what the present study is attempting to tease out; as far as his functions are concerned, the imam is the Master and the Thaumaturge par excellence. In fact, what characterizes the existence of the imam is not his political role but his initiatory and esoteric kind of Knowledge (*ʿilm*), and his occult and supernatural Powers (*aʿâjîb*), which are extensions on the plane of sensation of his two main pre-existential functions. One can get an idea of these categories by a simple look through the tables of contents—when they exist—of the early compilations.

III-2. THE SACRED SCIENCE

To our knowledge no monograph has yet dealt in depth with the early Imamite idea of *ʿilm*. The reason for this has been the tendency to ascribe to *ʿilm* the meaning it had taken on in early Sunnism, or in later "rationalist" Shîʿism, that is, the science of the Qur'an and the hadith.[337] However, this is in no way the case in the view of the early corpus of the imams. In this corpus, *ʿilm* occupies a fundamental place; the idea appears quite complex, with a number of different levels and properties. *Al-ʿâlim* is one of the most common names for the imam, his disciple being referred to as *al-mutaʿallim*. The object of *ʿilm* is comprehension of the deep or hidden meaning (*maʿnä, bâṭin*) of everything, both the general and the particular. In early Imamism *ʿilm* certainly referred to the religious sciences, but also and especially to the esoteric part of these sciences and other secret sciences; this is why it often has an initiatory, possibly even magical, connotation in the words of the imams. In a word, this is the doctrinal specificity of the idea; the traditions that refer to it are numerous, dense, disordered, and classed according to a "logic" the purpose of which is to say the most about the multiple aspects of the question. None of this is help to the researcher in search of doctrinal coherence. By way of example, al-Ṣaffâr al-Qummî's *Baṣâ'ir al-darajât* deals with the different facets of Imamite *ʿilm*; the commentator begins his book with the famous hadith "The search for science is a canonical duty for every Muslim; God loves those who ardently search for science."[338] While for the exoteric Muslim this hadith deals with the duty to learn the exoteric religious sciences, the rest of the traditons in the work, presented with no logical order and with no concern for clarity, show that for the "true Shîʿite" this duty concerns the esoteric and initiatory knowledge of the secrets taught by the imams. In order to see this more clearly, we might present the different facets of the problem in three parts: a) the sources of the "Initiatory Knowledge" of the imams,[339] b) the modes of transmission of this Knowledge, and c) the nature of the Knowledge.

a) Sources

By his ontological status, the imam is the Gate or the Threshold that allows the passage into Divine Knowledge, the Knowledge contained in the messages brought by the lawgiving prophets. The Prophet said, "I am the City of Science [var: of Wisdom] and ʿAlî is its threshold."[340] The stakes for "passing over this Threshold" are presented as being enormous, namely the knowledge of God and the secrets of creation. According to Jaʿfar, "God has things run only through causes, and for each cause he has created an explanation, for each explanation a Key, for each Key a science, and for each science a Speaking Gate (*bâban nâṭiqan*); he who knows this Gate knows God, and he who does not know it does not know God; the Messenger of God and we ourselves [the imams] are [this Speaking Gate]."[341] The imam is "the mine of the Knowledge of God" (*maʿdin ʿilm Allâh*),[342] "the treasure-keeper of Divine Knowledge" (*khâzin ʿilm Allâh*);[343] each time that the Qur'an refers, in different ways, to "those who have Knowledge," it is alluding to the prophets and their imams in general, or else to the Fourteen Impeccables in particular.[344] The sources of this Knowledge may be divided into four categories.

1) Celestial sources: the imam receives celestial inspiration; the typically Imamite terms in this case are *al-taḥdîth* (lit. the fact of speaking to someone) and *al-tafhîm* (lit. the fact of making someone understand something). The imam is thus called *al-muḥaddath* (he to whom the celestial beings speak) and *al-mufahham* (he who receives understanding from heaven).[345] According to a number of traditions, *al-muḥaddath* can only hear the voice of the celestial beings that inspire him without seeing their forms,[346] which is at the base of the classical point of view according to which the imam hears the angel without seeing it, as opposed to the prophet who both hears and sees the angel; but other traditions tell of the visit paid by the angels to the imams and the fact that the latter preciously guard "the feathers that fell from the angels" (*zaghab al-malâʾika*).[347] Might there then be two kinds of angels, the "angels of *al-taḥdîth*" of whom the imams could only hear voices, and other angels, whose forms they might also see? There is a certain (perhaps voluntary?) ambiguity on this subject, namely, that the underlying implication may be of sizable religious importance. On the basis of certain dialogues between the imams and

their disciples, it appears as though the word *muḥaddath* was a synonym, for the disciples, for "prophet" (*nabî*);[348] moreover, we have accounts according to which the imams were in effect considered by some people as being the "prophets" or "messengers" (*rasûl*) of God.[349]

In the eyes of Muslim "orthodoxy," such ideas were intolerable, and at the risk of attracting the wrath of the authorities, the imams could not logically not react. It is perhaps from this situation that comes the importance of distinguishing, especially in regard to rapport with an angel, the difference between a prophet/lawgiving messenger (*rasûl*), a non-lawgiving prophet (*nabî*) and the imam-*muḥaddath*. The imam hears but does not see the angel, the *nabî* sees and hears the angel only when asleep, and the *rasûl* sees and hears the angel when both awake and asleep;[350] thus there is both a clear distinction made between the imam and the prophet, and the exoteric doctrine of the religious superiority of the prophet is safeguarded.[350bis]

But other details perhaps reduce the scope of these remarks. First, there is an ambiguous attitude on the part of Jaʿfar, when faced with a disciple's question "Do the angels show themselves to you?" The sixth imam avoided a direct answer, and instead patted one of his sons' heads, saying, "Toward our children the angels are kinder than we ourselves are."[351] Then, as we have seen, the Impeccables receive, in addition to inspiration from angels, inspiration from a celestial being called al-Rûḥ, a being superior to the angels, including the angel Gabriel, the angel of prophetic revelations.[352] In addition to that, as we have also seen, the Impeccables are ontologically superior to the prophets since they were created from a more noble "matter," which implies, among other things, that they have a more important role than the prophets in the sacred universal economy.

According to a whole series of traditions, the imam also receives celestial inspiration throughout the Night of the Decree (*laylat al-qadr*).[353] Two kinds of revelations are received during this night: first, information concerning the events that will take place during the year between one Night of the Decree and another, and then the deep meaning (*maʿânin*) and the detailed explanation (*tafâsîr*) of what the imam already knows in a "condensed" form (*mujmal*).[354]

Thus, heaven comes down to the imam. Inversely, the imam is capable of a spiritual celestial ascension to renew and increase his Knowledge. This is a Knowledge acquired (*ʿilm mustafâd*) each Friday night. The sixth imam states, "Through God, each night that begins Friday our spirits, in company with those of the prophets, make the pilgrimage of the Divine Throne; they do not return to our bodies until they are filled with all of the Knowledge."[355] The same imam says, "During the night that begins Friday . . . the spirits of deceased prophets, those of the deceased Heirs [i.e., the former imams], and the spirit of the Heir who is among you [the present imam] are permitted to make a celestial ascension to the Throne of the Lord; there, they go seven times around the Throne, while performing two *rakʿa* at the foot of each of its pillars. Then the spirits return to their bodies; this is why the prophets and the Heirs awaken on [Friday] morning filled with joy, and the Heir who is among you awakens, since his Knowledge has been completely increased."[356] On another occasion Abû ʿAbd Allâh Jaʿfar al-Ṣâdiq says, "During Friday's night, the Prophet messenger of God [i.e., Muḥammad] and the imams make the pilgrimage of the Divine Throne, and I am there also, in their company; I do not return until a [new] Science is acquired; without it, the Knowledge that I already have would disappear."[357]

Although our texts have not attempted to draw an explicit parallel, we might nevertheless have reason to think that the imam, the same as the prophet, possesses the ability to receive celestial revelation because of the five-faceted constitution of his spirit in general, and of his "first spirit" in particular, that is, the holy spirit (*rûḥ al-quds*, cf. note 285); the descriptions that the imams give of this spirit appear to justify the comparison, for it is the holy spirit that procures for the prophets and the imams "the Knowledge of all things," "the Knowledge of what is found below the Throne and above the earth"; it is thanks to the holy spirit that they can "carry the repository of prophecy."[358]

2) Occult sources: We have already had occasion to encounter the "Column of Light" (*ʿamûd min nûr*), one of the sources of the imam's Knowledge, as the imam can "visualize" the answers to all his questions in the column.

Two other supernatural "forces" are sources of Knowledge for the imam; the first of these marks his heart, and the second pierces his eardrum.[359] It is said that by undergoing these two operations the imam is able to hear the voices of angels and acquire, especially, Knowledge of the future.[360] Although the nature of these "forces" remains mysterious,[361] the traditions freely use such words as *waḥy* (classically, "revelation received by the prophets") and *ilhâm* (classically, "inspiration of celestial origin") to refer to them.[362] The fifth imam, Abû Jaʿfar Muḥammad al-Bâqir, adds an experiential detail to the phenomenon. In defining *al-muḥaddath*, he says, "The *muḥaddath* sometimes has his eardrum pierced, and he then hears something like drumming on a bowl, or sometimes his heart is marked and he then hears something like the sound of a heavy chain falling on a bowl."[363]

The imams might also acquire Knowledge by having recourse to divination. In this case, it is divination by the "throwing of stones" (*rajm*), although the imams give no details on the practice.[364] It is simply said that when faced with "difficult cases" (*muʿḍilât*) about which there is no information available in either the Qur'an or in the hadith, the imam practices "the throwing of stones" and arrives at the solution needed.[365]

Finally, the imams are able to communicate with the prophets, and previous imams and sages; this is the phenomenon that might be called "visiting with the deceased" (*anna l-aʾimma yazûrûn al-mawtä wa anna l-mawtä yazûrûnahum*). Here, the imam receives information on a specific subject or Knowledge of a general order.[366] According to ʿAlî, "among us [prophets and the imams of all ages], he who dies is not dead";[367] thus, each living imam can have ocular vision of the deceased, especially vision of the prophets (Adam, Noah, Abraham)[368] and the previous imams,[369] and in most cases that of Muḥammad himself. The imam can also have others see "the deceased"; Mûsä al-Kâẓim shows Jaʿfar, who had been dead for a number of years, seated in the entryway to his house, to his disciple Samâʿa b. Mihrân;[370] ʿAlî takes the first caliph, Abû Bakr, to the mosque of Qubâ so that he can see the Prophet, and hears him say that he had been unjust (*ẓâlim*) in usurping the power that by divine right should have gone to ʿAlî.[371]

Perhaps the most interesting information of all concerns Muḥammad's last order to ʿAlî and the posthumous teaching that he offered to him. According to a series of ten traditions,[372] just before his death the Prophet said to ʿAlî: "After I die, wash and perfume my body and wrap me in my shroud; then put me in a seated position, place your hand on my breast, ask me all that you wish to ask, and through God I shall answer all your questions."[373] In several traditions the Prophet also orders ʿAlî to put down in writing what he is going to hear,[374] and in the last tradition of the series, ʿAlî states that the Prophet will likewise reveal to him all that is going to happen up to the Day of Resurrection.[375] This is a typical case of "spiritualistic initiation" as found in a number of esoteric and magical traditions.

3) Written sources: The imams possess all the revealed Books of the previous prophets, and can read and understand them despite the number of languages in which they were written.[376] This is part of the prophetic Heritage (*mîrâth al-nubuwwa*). The imams also possess the original and integral version of the Qurʾan, three times the size of the Vulgate compiled during ʿUthman's caliphate; according to the imams, this Vulgate was composed from a damaged, deformed, and censured version shortly after the death of the Prophet and ʿAlî's separation from power (cf. later discussion).

In addition to the Books of the prophets, the imams also have a number of secret books, which are also revealed and thus sacred; here, details are numerous, confusing, disordered; apparently a number of titles are ascribed to a single Book, or, inversely, one title is given to a number of different Books. A careful perusal of the information[377] available, in an attempt to find some order and coherence, suggests the following conclusions:

There appear to be seven of these Secret Books:

—*Al-Ṣaḥîfa* (lit. "the page"), also called *al-Muṣḥaf* ("the book") or *al-Ṣaḥîfa al-jâmiʿa* ("the enclosing page") or simply *al-Jâmiʿa* ("the encloser"). This revealed Book, dictated by Muḥammad and copied by ʿAlî on a role seventy cubits long, contains all Knowledge of what is licit and what is illicit.

—*Al-Jafr*, divided into the white *Jafr* and the red *Jafr*; the first is a leather role containing the Books of David (*Zabûr*), Moses (*Tawra*), Jesus (*Injîl*), and Abraham (*Ṣuḥuf*), the sacred writings of the previous imams and ancient sages, Knowledge of what is licit and what is illicit, Knowledge of Fortune and Misfortune (*ʿilm al-manâyâ wa l-balâyâ*), Knowledge of the past and the future, as well as Fâṭima's Book (*Muṣḥaf*, see later discussion). The red *Jafr* is a Weapon (*silâḥ*) that will only be used by the hidden imam at the time of his final return.

—*Muṣḥaf Fâṭima*, or *Kitâb Fâṭima* (The Book of Fâṭima) is the Book revealed by the Angel Gabriel to the Prophet's daughter during the seventy five days that followed her father's death and preceded hers; it contains the account of the posthumous states of Muḥammad as well as that of the future of Fâṭima's descendents. She dictated these revelations to her husband, ʿAlî, who wrote them down.

—*Kitâb ʿAlî* (The Book of ʿAlî); this title refers either to the recension of the Qurʾan done by ʿAlî, the only complete recension, according to the imams (cf. Part III-3), or to the writing down of the posthumous remarks made by the Prophet to ʿAlî; in the latter case, the Book contains, as we have seen, the account of "all that will take place up to the Day of the Resurrection."

—The Book (or the Books; *kitâb/kutub*) containing the list of all the sovereigns of the earth; it is also called The Book of ʿAlî, or The Book of Fâṭima (cf. note 316).

—The Book containing the list of the faithful of the twelve imams, the "true Shîʿites" and their genealogy.

—The Page (*al-Ṣaḥifa*), or the two volumes containing the list of the people of Paradise and those of Hell, and their genealogies. In this case it refers to the faithful who are initiated by the imams of all times and their adversaries, the partisans of the "guides of darkness," since such technical expressions as "People of the Right" (*aṣḥâb al-yamîn*) and "People of the Left" (*aṣḥâb al-shimâl*) are encountered here.

Among the written sources for the imams' Knowledge, mention should also be made of Fâṭima's two tablets (*lawḥ*). The first is a "page" (*ṣaḥifa*) of white pearl (*durra bayḍâʾ*) upon which are inscribed the names and *kunya* of the twelve imams and those of their relatives.[378] The second is an emerald tablet (*lawḥ min zumurrud*) brought to Fâṭima by the Angel Gabriel (or brought to the Prophet and given by him to his daughter) and bearing in lines of luminous writing the names and the missions of the Prophet and each of the twelve imams. Fâṭima allows one of the Companions of the Prophet, the long-lived Jâbir b. ʿAbd Allâh al-Anṣârî, to make a copy of it; according to the account from the famous tradition of the [emerald] tablet (*ḥadîth al-lawḥ*), al-Bâqir, the fifth imam, attested to the authenticity of Jâbir's copy.[379] Finally, let us mention the Sealed Book (*kitâb al-makhtûm*) called *al-Waṣiyya* that the Prophet received from Heaven and that contains twelve Seals upon which were inscribed the missions of each of the imams.[380] It is through these written "proofs" of celestial origin that the identity of the historical imams was known before their birth; their "written investiture" (*naṣṣ*, pl. *nuṣûṣ*), which each imam effected for his successor, was no more than human ratification of a divine investiture.

4) Oral Sources: Oral sources include the teaching that each imam receives from his predecessor, beginning with ʿAlî, who was initiated by the Prophet himself. All the traditions reported by an imam under the authority of his father, grandfather, or ancestors, make up this teaching, and it is normal that there is no one chapter that is specifically dedicated to this subject. There are nevertheless two allusions to this initiation. The first is the expression that is unceasingly repeated by the imams: "The Prophet taught ʿAlî a thousand chapters (or "a thousand sayings" or "a thousand words"), each of which gave access to a thousand others."[381] We know that ʿAlî is the prototypical imam, and what is said about his initiatory status concerns all the imams.[382]

Then there is the "hadith of the two pomegranates" (*rummânatayn*); the angel Gabriel brings the Prophet two fruits from the pomegranate tree of Paradise; Muḥammad eats the first pomegranate, divides the second in half, eats one half and gives the second to ʿAlî to eat, saying: "O my brother, do you know what these two pomegranates were? The first was prophecy (*nubuwwa*) that is not of your concern; the second was Knowledge, and it I share with you." Imam al-Bâqir, in reporting the tradition, adds: "There is nothing that God taught to Muḥammad that He did not order him to teach to ʿAlî."[383]

b) Modes of Transmission

Initiatory Knowledge is "hereditary"; it is called "the heritage of the prophets" (*mîrâth al-nabiyyîn*) or the "heritage of prophecy" (*mîrâth al-nubuwwa*).[384] Let us here remember the spiritual genealogy of the Impeccables, where, among others, figure such names as Adam, Enoch, Noah, Abraham, Moses, Jesus, and the imams initiated by each of them; the same names are encountered in the traditions dealing with the heritage of Initiatory Knowledge; likewise, let us remember that the names of these prophets, and no longer those of their imams, are found in the natural genealogy of the Impeccables, and that, from our point of view, this double genealogy represented the esoteric (*bâṭin*) and the exoteric (*ẓâhir*) aspects of the transmission of prophetic/Imamic Light, respectively. The twelve imams, superior to the imams that preceded them, thus share along with the great prophets the privilege of uniting within themselves the esoteric and the exoteric of the primordial Light, a Light whose most essential element seems to be precisely Initiatory Knowledge. This Knowledge existed before the creation of the physical world, and it is to this Knowledge that the "shadows" and the "pure beings" were initiated by the pre-existential entities of the Impeccables. Since the creation of the world, thanks to the transmission of prophetic/Imamic Light, this Knowledge has been transmitted from Adam through the line of prophets and Heirs all the way to the original Repositories, the Impeccables. The heritage of the Knowledge passes from one imam to another. Al-Bâqir said: "The Knowledge is hereditary; no initiated Sage [*ʿâlim*, i.e., imam] from among us dies without having initiated his successor to the Knowledge."[385] Thus, the Knowledge will exist until the end of our time, thanks to the occultation of the last imam. This is the reason why the imams are called "the repositories of God on earth,"[386] and their "breast" (*ṣadr*) is said to be the Repository of Divine Knowledge.[387] It is said that just before his death, the imam places one of his hands on his own chest and the other hand on that of his successor, thus transmitting his Knowledge to him.[388] It may also be that the successor places his hand on the breast of his predecessor in order to "receive" his Knowledge.[389] As in other esoteric teachings, Knowledge here is not, of course, intellectual and theoretical knowledge; the imam's Knowledge is an integral part of his being, it is ontologically inherent in him, and in its transmission organic factors of the physical body play a role.

Magic, theurgic as well as goetic, teaches that the "liquids" of the body can serve as "vehicles" for spiritual influences; we have already seen that the transmission of prophetic/Imamic Light can take place via seminal fluid. It is also true that, in certain traditions directly or indirectly concerning the Knowledge of the imams, furtive hints show that the Prophet and the imams transmitted their Knowledge to their successor by introducing their saliva or their sweat "into" his body, through the pores of his skin, his mouth, or his eyes. When the Prophet was initiating ʿAlî into the "thousand chapters" of Knowledge, the two men were perspiring, and the perspiration of each flowed over the body of the other.[390] ʿAlî also recounts that the Prophet spit into his eyes, and that thereafter no harm could come to his eyes, and that he acquired the ability to "see" men as they are, as well as the power to discern his friends from his enemies just by seeing them.[391] According to another account, the Prophet placed his saliva into ʿAlî's mouth and passed his hand over his breast just prior to investing him.[392] Upon his accession to the caliphate, wearing the Prophet's turbin, his shirt, sandals, and sword, ʿAlî began his enthronement sermon with the words "O people! Question me before you lose me! Here is the basket of Knowledge! Here is the saliva of the Prophet, which he had me drink drop by drop! Ask me, for I hold the Knowledge of the Beginnings and the Ends (or the Knowledge of the old [sages] and the new)."[393] There are likewise a number of traditions in which an imam is reported to slip his tongue into the mouth of his newborn son, the future imam, who begins eagerly to suck his father's tongue, or else the father makes "passes" over the body of his newborn son.[394]

Imamite sources are apparently the only ones, at the time, to employ these practices in an initiatory or esoteric sense. Sunni literature includes these details, but in it their meaning and scope appear to be different; in his *Sîra*, Ibn Isḥâq (d. 150–51/760–61) reports that a woman took her seven-year-old son to the Prophet. The child was suffering from epileptic fits twice a day. The Prophet spat into his mouth and said: "Come out, enemy of God! I am the Prophet sent by God"; this is a question of exorcism rather than an initiatory practice. Elsewhere, the same author reports examples of this practice where the father puts his tongue into the mouth of his child in order to transmit personal qualities to the child; in all probabilty this was an educational tradition with its origin in magic.[395] Imamism appears to be the first current of ideas in Islam to have applied these aspects of the transmission of initiatory Knowledge. This transmission via "bodily fluids" still exists, but it seems that in order to be able to speak of other examples we would need to rely on oral traditions or rituals coming out of esotericism or occultism. An English researcher claims to have attended an initiation ceremony in Sikkim in which a tantric master spat saliva into the mouth of his disciple.[396] In 1973, the author of the present study witnessed a transmission of the *baraka* and of Wisdom by means of saliva among the Qâdirî dervishes of Iranian Beluchistan; according to these dervishes, the *baraka* carries with it a "practice" (*'amal*), essentially, supernormal powers and Wisdom (*'ilm*), that is, esoteric Knowledge. There is not much more that we can say about the subject.

c) Nature

According to the imams, divine Knowledge may be divided into two parts. The first is a particular Science (*'ilm khâṣṣ*) reserved for God and contained in the "Mother of the Book," out of the reach of the creatures. This Knowledge is hidden (*maknûn*), sealed (*makhzûn*), veiled (*makfûf*). The second is a general Knowledge (*'ilm 'âmm*) that God teaches to his angels, his prophets, and his imams; this is why it is called the lavished Knowledge (*mabdhûl*).[397] A parallel may be established between these two kinds of Knowledge and the two ontological planes of the Divine Being, according to Imamite metaphysics: the "Hidden Knowledge" would be that of the Divine Essence, of the Unknowable, forever inaccessible to the creatures, while the "Lavished Knowledge" is that of the manifestation of God, of Creation, of the Unknown aspiring to be known. Via the "Lavished Knowledge" the secrets of the world and of man, of the Beginning and the End may be known. Pushing the comparison further, we might say that the Imam, the manifestation of God par excellence, the "Organ" and the "Symbol" of God, the "Lavished Knowledge" is therefore that science whose ultimate goal is the ontological Imam, the knowledge of whom is tantamount to the knowledge of God, or more precisely, of what can be knowable in God.[398]

Let us look at the characteristics of the imams' Knowledge, beginning with its constitutition. Although there are no details given,[399] in a whole series of traditions, the Knowledge is said to be made up of three parts: the Supreme Name of God (*al-ism al-akbar/al-ism al-aʿẓam*) with occult powers (to which we shall return), the Heritage of Science (*mîrâth al-ʿilm*), and the Marks of the Science of prophecy (*âthâr ʿilm al-nubuwwa*).[400] Then there is the "domain" or the "field" (lit. its "range"—*mablagh al-ʿilm*); the imams' Knowledge encompasses the past, the present, and the future (*mâḍin wa ḥâdith wa ghâbir*); the imams aphoristically state "The past is what is explained, the future is what is written, the present is the marking of hearts and the piercing of eardrums,"[401] by which should be understood: "Knowledge of the past" and of its events "is explained" by the Sacred Books of the Ancients, certain Sacred Books of the imams (the *Jafr*, the Book of Sovereigns, the *Jâmiʿa*, the Books of Genealogies) or by the Master, the preceding Impeccable; "Knowledge of the future" and of its events "is written" in the secret Books (again, like the *Jafr*, the *Kitâb ʿAlî*, the Book of Sovereigns, the *Muṣḥaf Fâṭima*, the two Books of Genealogies, or Fâṭima's two tablets); and "Knowledge of the present" and of its events is obtained through two occult forces of inspiration, the first of which "marks the heart" of the imam, and the second "pierces his eardrum."

Initiatory Knowledge is the constituent element of the imam's being. The imam is what he is because he has this Knowledge. The surnames and the descriptive phrases of the imam are, in a large majority of cases, linked to their Knowledge: "Treasurer of the Knowledge of God," "Mine of the Knowledge of God," "Knower of the Qur'an," "he who is solid in Knowledge," "Inheritor of the Knowledge," and so on.[402] This Initiatory Knowledge is so essential that the imams radically divide humanity into three groups: "There are three categories of men: the Initiating Sage, the initiated disciple, and the froth carried off by the wave; we are the Initiating Sages, our faithful are the initiated disciples, and the others are the froth carried off by the wave."[403]

The imam initiates his disciple to the arcane elements of the Knowledge and, as will be seen later, to supernatural powers (probably by having him pass the "test of the heart"—*imtiḥân al-qalb*—that is, to our understanding, initiating him to the "technique" of vision with the heart). Although the disciple will never attain the status of Imam,[404] he nevertheless acquires the same merit as his initiating Master, and attains the same soteriological "degree" (*daraja*); Abû Jaʿfar al-Bâqir said: "The initiated Sage and the disciple who can be initiated will be similarly rewarded; on the Day of the Resurrection they will step forward together, shoulder to shoulder like two race horses."[405] The long tradition about the "75 Armies of Hiero-Intelligence" (cf. earlier discussion) ends with the words " . . . and all of these [75] qualities that make up the Armies of Hiero-Intelligence are united only in a prophet, an Heir, or faithful believer whose heart has been tested by God for faith; he from among our faithful friends [*mawâlînâ*] who does not yet possess all of them is continually perfecting himself and purifying himself of the Armies of Ignorance until he reaches the Supreme Degree [*al-darajat al-ʿulyâ*] that the prophets and Heirs occupy; this degree is not reached but by the Knowledge of Hiero-Intelligence and of its Armies, and by separation from Ignorance and its Armies."[406]

III-3. NOTES ON "THE INTEGRAL QUR'AN"

The Qur'an, as we have seen, is one of the written sources of the imams' Knowledge. The imams state unceasingly that all their doctrine, all their teachings, and everything they say are based on the Qur'anic text.[407] Jaʿfar goes so far as to say, " . . . Any hadith that contradicts the Qur'ân is a grand lie."[408] The Imam, master par excellence of spiritual hermeneutics, interpreter of the esoteric part of Revelation, is called "the speaking Qur'an" (*al-qur'an al-nâṭiq*), while the Qur'an, a hermetic text, is called "the Silent Guide" (*al-imâm al-ṣâmit*). It is difficult to find Qur'anic foundations for almost all of the specific details of early Immamite doctrine—from cosmogonic developments to the conception of the Imam to eschatological details—at least in the text that we know today. Even the imams' spiritual interpretations (*ta'wîlât*), which are quite few in number, are far from able to justify the impressive number of "differences" as regards the revealed Text; or such is at least the case if we consider that the totality of the doctrine is the esoteric interpretation of the Qur'an, but the "keys" to the interpretation are not presented, nor is the procedure explained.

Jaʿfar stated: "I am engendered by the Messenger of God (*qad waladanî rasûl Allâh*—that is, "I am a descendent of the Prophet" and or "the prophetic/Imamic Light is in me"), and I know God's Book ["I have the *ʿilm*, the initiatory Knowledge, of the Qur'an"]: it contains [the account of] the origin of creation as well as all that will take place until the Day of Resurrection; it contains the account of the events of the heavens and the earth, those of Paradise and those of Hell, those of the past and those of the future; I know all of this as clearly as if I saw [it in] the palm of my hand."[409] We can guess what an imam might mean by these phrases: the emanation of the original Light and the formation of the pre-existential luminous entities of the Impeccables, the formation of the "shadows" of other creatures, the events of the pre-existential worlds of "the Mother of the Book," of the "Pact," or of the "Second World of the Particles"; the account of the lives of the earlier prophets and imams and their struggles against their adversaries; the identity and the destiny of the imams' initiated faithful, that is, the people of Paradise, and those of their adversaries, the partisans of the "guides of darkness," the forces of counter-initiation, that is, the people of Hell; and finally, the events of the future, essentially meaning those connected with the hidden presence and the final Return of the Mahdî. The Qur'anic text that we know is far from containing all of this. Could there be another version known to the imams alone?

In May 1842, Garcin de Tassy published for the first time in the West, in *Journal Asiatique*, the text and translation of an "unknown chapter of the Qur'an."[410] It was the sura "of the two Lights" (*sûrat al-nûrayn*), that is, the spiritual Lights of Muḥammad and ʿAlî, explicitly mentioned. Of course this sura is not part of the Qur'anic Vulgate. The text is taken from a Persian work of the seventeenth century, the *Dabestân-e madhâhib*, written by a Zoroastrian of Iranian origin and living in India.[411] One year later, in December 1843, in the same *Journal Asiatique*, Mirzâ Alexandre Kazem-Beg established the text in a much more satisfactory manner via reliance on another manuscript, by vocalizing it and dividing it into 43 verses, and giving it a more precise translation than Garcin de Tassy had. Curiously, Kazem-Beg remained silent regarding the manuscript he used.[412] In July 1913, St Clair Tisdall, in an article published in *The Moslem World*,[413] reproduced the text of another unknown sura of the Qur'an, the *sûrat al-walâya*. The author claimed to have discovered the text in a manuscript of the Qur'an dating from the sixteenth or seventeenth century, in Bankipore, India. Besides the integral text of this sura, divided into 7 verses, the manuscript contains the previously cited sura of "the two Lights," as well as 37 verses that are supposed to belong to different suras of the Qur'an, but which do not appear in the official recension. As in the case of the sura of "the two Lights," the sura of the *walâya* also explicitly mentions ʿAlî, and presents him as being the Friend (*walî*) of God par excellence, as well as the spiritual Heir of the Prophet. We shall return to this subject.

These publications encouraged a few erudite researchers to study the problem of the Imamite conception of the Qur'anic text: to what extent, according to the Imamites, is the text of the official Qur'anic Vulgate that was compiled during the caliphate of ʿUthmân b. ʿAffân (24–35/644–56), faithful to the original Revelation made to Muḥammad? The question is of the utmost seriousness, since the entire dogmatic system of Islam and all Muslim religious consciousness are crystallized around this central sacred kernel of the Qur'an in its official form; belief in the integrity and the fidelity of this version as regards the Divine Revelation made to the Prophet constitutes one of the most inalienable articles of faith in Islam. If Christianity can be considered the religion of God made Man, Islam would be the religion of God made Word and of this Word made Book.

It would seem fastidious to delve into all the erudite details and polemics of the studies dedicated to the problem, but it might be said that, on the whole, the studies lead to three kinds of conclusions:

a) Doubt about the integrity of the Qur'anic Vulgate on the part of Imamites is without historical foundation; the doubt comes purely from dogmatic and political views. Once ʿAlî was separated from power, it was natural that his partisans declare his version to be the most complete, in order to demonstrate his superiority in relationship to the other Companions of the Prophet;[414] this thesis has the fault of reducing Imamism to a movement in search of temporal power; moreover, it in no way bases itself on the information available in the corpus attributed to the imams. To our view, the problem lends itself to a historical study only with great difficulty, given the fragmentary state of the texts and the sacred duty of "keeping the secret" (*taqiyya, kitmân*) among the Imamites. On the other hand, it is both possible and more prudent to examine it from a phenomenological point of view and to estimate its religious and esoteric significance.

b) Imamite critics of the Qur'anic Vulgate do not fault its integrity or the authenticity of its content, but only the omission of a few words or expressions and the mixing up of the order of verses and suras; according to the Imamites the Vulgate contains the totality of Revelation, and 'Uthmân's "crime" was that of having rejected 'Alî's commentaries, commentaries that appeared in the margin of his own copy and that were indispensable for a complete understanding of the Sacred Text.[415] This conclusion typically reflects the confusion between the ideas of the great Imamite theologians and the teachings of the imams themselves, a confusion fatal to any understanding of early Imamism, and to which we have alluded at a number of points previously. As will be seen in what follows, Ibn Bâbûye appears to have been the first to support this thesis, which contradicts the words of the imams.

c) The imams have placed serious doubt on 'Uthmân's Vulgate;[416] this thesis is effectively corroborated by the early corpus of the imams, although the researchers who have supported it, probably because of a lack of systematic examination of the basic texts, have been able neither to cite all the information about the integral Qur'an of the imams nor to examine the dogmatic implications of the subject. Our contribution thus aims at this third category of studies, with the modest hope of adding to what they have begun. We thus hope, at the same time, to fill in some of the methodological gaps that exist in studies that belong to the first two categories.

The basic question comes down to the following: which is the Qur'an that the imams are dealing with in their early corpus? Within this corpus their are suggestions that the Qur'an to which the imams are referring is not the text known to all. These suggestions are of two kinds.

1) Direct indications: We know that the Qur'anic Vulgate compiled during the reign of the third caliph was essentially based on the recension by a

committee presided over by Zayd b. Thâbit, and that a certain amount of time was needed before this version was universally recognized. We know also that there were other recensions: that of ʿAbd Allâh b. Masʿûd, that of Ubayy b. Kaʿb and others, and that of ʿAlî b. Abî Ṭâlib. Although the differences between these copies amounted to basically unimportant variations, ʿAlî's recension, according to the imams, was of a different order, first, since it was the only one to be absolutely faithful to Revelation because of the privileged relationship that linked the Prophet to ʿAlî, and second, because it was nearly three times as long as the version that was made official. "No one can pretend to have assembled the totality of the Qur'an as it was revealed by God, unless the person is a liar. Only ʿAlî b. Abî Ṭâlib and after him the imams have assembled and preserved the Qur'an as it was revealed by God Most High."[417] "No one, with the exception of the Heirs [the imams], can pretend to have at his disposition the totality of the Qur'an in either its exoteric or its esoteric aspect."[418] "The Qur'an that the angel Gabriel brought to Muḥammad contained 17,000 verses."[419] According to classical numbering, the number of verses in the Qur'an varies from 6000 to 7000; the original whole Qur'an transmitted by the Prophet to ʿAlî is thus nearly three times as voluminous as the official recension. According to a tradition ascribed to Jaʿfar:

> When ʿAlî finished copying the Book, he showed it to the people and said: "Here is the Book of God, may He be exalted and glorified, such as it was revealed to Muḥammad; I have compiled it from two tablets." And the people answered him, saying: We already have a complete version of the Qur'an, and we have no need [of your version]." And ʿAlî replied: "By God, from today on you shall see it no more; my only mission was to inform you of your duty to read what I had compiled."[420]

A document that comes from the library of ʿAlî's sanctuary in Najaf, and dating from the seventh/thirteenth century, adds other details to this episode; the text is reproduced by Majlisî in his *Biḥâr al-anwâr* (vol. 13, pp. 146–47). The document is actually the account of a trip of an Imamite shaykh named ʿAlî b. Fâḍil al-Mâzandarânî to the "Land" of the hidden imam. Corbin cites it in his *En Islam iranien* (vol. 4, pp. 346–47), and in our paraphrase of it we rely on Corbin's beautiful translation. At a certain moment the hero of the account asks his teacher of Qur'anic sciences, shaykh Zayn al-Dîn ʿAlî al-Maghribî:

> "O master, I notice that certain verses of the Qur'an have no connection with what precedes or what follows them. My inadequate intelligence is incapable of knowing why." To which the teacher replied: "Such is truly the case. The reason is that when the Prophet was

> transferred from this perishable abode to the permanent Abode, and the two Qurayshites (that is, the first two caliphs, Abû Bakr and 'Umar) committed what they did in forcefully grabbing hold of the public, exoteric caliphate, the Prince of Believers ['Alî] assembled the totality of the Qur'an (*jamî' al-Qur'ân*) in a leather pouch and brought it to them, while the people of the Quraysh were assembled in the mosque. Then 'Alî said to them: 'This is the Book of God that the Prophet God's Messenger commanded me to present to you so that on the Day of Resurrection a witness for you might stand up before God.' But the Pharaoh and the Nimrod of this Community [that is, 'Umar, known and detested by the Imamites for, among other things, the pride with which he opposed the commandments of God and the Prophet] replied, 'We have no need of your Qur'an,' to which the imam said, 'The Messenger of God who was my dear friend told me that you would answer in such a manner, but in acting thus I have sought to have evidence burst out against you.' He then retired to his home, saying 'There is no God but you, you alone. None is associated with you. There is no one who can reject what is already known to your Mind, nor who can oppose what your Wisdom requires. Let it thus be you who is my witness against them on Resurrection Day.' At that, Ibn Abî Qaḥâfa (i.e., Abû Bakr) called the Muslims together [*muslimîn*, the exoteric "Sunnite" Muslims, as opposed to the *mu'minîn*, the esoteric believers of the imams] and said to them: 'Let him who has a verse or a sura of the Qur'an at his home bring it here.' Then Abû 'Ubayd Allâh, and 'Uthmân, and Mu'âwiya . . . came, each with a verse or a sura, and they thus compiled *this* Qur'an. But they rejected all that might have hurt their interests or demonstrated their evil actions after the Prophet's death. That is why the verses are without connection to one another. But the Qur'an that the Prince of Believers had compiled with his own hand is preserved with the Lord of the Cause (*ṣâḥib al-amr*, that is, the hidden imam). It contains all, absolutely everything.'"

The entire Qur'an thus passed secretely from imam to imam until it was taken into occultation with the hidden imam. It is he and he alone who will bring it back when he returns at the end of our time, and he will make it known to all: "When our Resurrector has risen up, he will recite the Book of God—may He be exalted and glorified—as it should be recited, and he will unveil the Volume written by 'Alî."[421]

Other descriptions of the integral Qur'an are also given by the imams. Ḥusayn b. Khâlid asked Ja'far, "In how many 'parts' (*juz'*) should I do a complete reading of the Qur'an?" Ja'far replied: "Read it in five or in seven 'parts'; however, I have in my possession a sacred Volume divided in fourteen 'parts' (that is, 'it can be finished only in fourteen parts')."[422] Aḥmad b. Md b. Abî Naṣr recounts: "[Imam] Abû'l-Ḥasan (that is, the eighth imam, 'Alî al-Riḍâ) lent me a Volume of the Qur'an, but asked me not to look inside. However, I opened the book and came upon the verse, "those who became impious . . . [*lam yakun alladhîna karafû*]," and I saw in what followed of the verse the names of 70 men from the Quraysh tribe and the names of their fathers. The imam then sent someone to tell me to return the Volume."[423] The Qur'anic reference is deliberately imprecise, since the phrase is used more than 30 times, but it is nevertheless sufficiently explicit to condemn the Qurayshites of impiety. On the other hand, the imams state that the Qur'an is divided into four parts: a first part dedicated to the Impeccables, a second to their enemies, a third to sayings and parables, and a fourth to canonical duties and the precepts pertaining to worship.[424]

Among the direct indications we should include certain Qur'anic citations of the imams, citations different from the passages of the Qur'an that we presently know. We will here outline but a few flagrant examples. The differences or those things added to the text of 'Uthmânic Vulgate are in italics:

> Qur'an 2:102: "And they approved, *by fidelity to the demons*, what the demons told them about the kingdom of Solomon."[425]
>
> Qur'an 2:205: "As soon as he turns his back, he attempts to corrupt what he finds upon the earth, he destroys the harvest and the livestock *by his injustice and wickedness*, God does not like corruption."[426]
>
> Qur'an 2:211: "Ask the Sons of Israel how many irrefutable proofs we have given them, *some of them had faith in them, some denied them, some recognized them, and others deformed them*, but for him who deforms the gift of God after receiving it, God prepares a terrible punishment."[427]
>
> Qur'an 2:255: "All that is in the heavens and upon the earth belongs to Him, *and all that is between the heavens and the earth, or under the earth, the Invisible World and the visible world; He is gracious and merciful*; who can intercede with Him without his permission?"[428]
>
> Qur'an 3:103: "You were on the edge of an abyss of fire, and He saved you *through Muḥammad*."[429]
>
> Qur'an 4:63: "God knows what is in their hearts, keep away from them *for the Word of Wretchedness is destined to them, as is torment* [here the words "exhort them" are missing]; address them in convincing words, that apply to their situation."[430]
>
> Qur'an 4:65–66: "Then they will not find in themselves the possibility of escaping what you have decided *about the cause of the Divine Friend* [i.e., the imam] and they will submit *to God to obey* totally/If we had told

them: "Have yourselves put to death and *submit totally to the imam*," or else "leave your houses *for him*," they would not have done so, except for a small number of them. If *those who oppose* [instead of: If they] followed the exhortations they received, it would truly have been better for them and more conducive to greater strength."[431]

Qur'an 9:40: "God had His "Sakîna" descend upon *His Prophet* [instead of: him] and sustained him with invisible Armies."[432]

Qur'an 9:128: "A Prophet, taken from among *us* [instead of: you] has come to *us* [instead of: you]; the evil that weighs upon *us* (instead of: you) is heavy upon him; he ardently desires *our* (instead of: your) welfare; he is good and merciful toward believers."[433]

Qur'an 20:115: "In the past we confided to Adam *words about Muḥammad, 'Alî, Fâṭima, al-Ḥasan, al-Ḥusayn, and the imams of their descendents*, but he forgot."[434]

Qur'an 22:52: "Before you We sent neither a lawgiving prophet nor a non-lawgiving prophet, *nor one inspired by angels*, without Satan intervening in his desires."[435]

Qur'an 33:71: "Whoever obeys God and His Prophet *regarding the holy power of 'Alî and the imams after him* will enjoy great happiness."[436]

Qur'an 42:13: "He has established for you, *o Family of Muḥammad*, that which he prescribed to Noah in religion, and what We reveal to you, *o Muḥammad*, and what We had prescribed to Abraham, to Moses, and to Jesus: "Establish the religion *of the family of Muḥammad*, do not divide yourselves in it, and be united; how hard for the associationists, *those who associate other powers with the holy power of 'Alî*, does that to which you are calling them *through the holy power of 'Alî* seem. Certainly God *guides* toward this religion, *o Muḥammad*, him who repents, *him who accepts your call toward the holy power of 'Alî*" [instead of: God chooses and calls to this Religion whomever He chooses; He guides toward it him who repents]."[437]

Qur'an 70:1–3: "A questioner clamored for ineluctable punishment/For those who do not believe *in the holy power of 'Alî*, and no one can reject this punishment/That comes from God, the Master of Degrees."[438]

There are other examples in the early compilations where differences with the official Vulgate are less marked.[439]

2) Let us now pass on to indications that might be called "indirect." Although mentions throughout the early corpus are sparsely scattered, the Impeccables face the question of the official recension of the Qur'an using

such words as falsification (*taḥrîf*), alteration (*taghyîr*), or change (*tabdîl*). In a long hadith reported by Jaʿfar, who heard it from "his fathers," the imams, and ultimately from the Prophet, Muḥammad tells the Community to beware:

> You will be asked to give an account of what you have done to the Two Precious Objects [*thaqalayn*] that I leave to you, that is, the Book and my family.[440] Beware! As for the Book, do not say we have altered and falsified it [*ghayyarnâ wa ḥarrafnâ*]; and as for my Family, do not say we have abandoned it and massacred it."[441] In one of his sermons, ʿAlî says: " . . . Know that after me will come a time where nothing will be hidden more than the truth [*al-ḥaqq*] and nothing will be more manifest than falsity [*al-bâṭil*], nothing will be more prolific than lies attributed to God and His Messenger, and nothing will be more despised than God's Book . . . whose composition has been falsified [*idhâ ḥurrifa ʿan mawâḍiʿihi*]. . . . Those who know the Qur'an reject it and those who have memorized it are forgetting it. They are ruled by their passions and return to the habits of their ancestors; through lies and deceit they are attempting to falsify the Book [*wa ʿamalû bi-taḥrif al-kitâb kidhban wa takdhîban*], they sell it for a vile price, so indifferent are they to it."[442]

The same accusations are found in the confidential letters of some of the imams to their closest disciples, letters reproduced by al-Kulaynî in his *Rawḍa*.[443] Al-Bâqir says: "God takes the Knowledge out of the Book for every Community that rejects His Book, *and He has this Community ruled by* its own enemies. . . . Rejecting the Book is when the people, by their own will, establish its words and set up its divisions . . . and thus alter the pillars [lit. "the handles"] of religion. . . . Know how to recognize those who [in this Community] look like the religious authorities of the Jews and the Christians who hid their [true] Book and falsified it; verily, know how to recognize their like within the Community, those who, through their own will, established the words of the Book and falsified it. . . . "[444]

Imam Mûsä wrote: "Do not seek to embrace the religion of those who are not Shîʿites [that is, "the Sunnis"]; do not love their religion, for they are traitors who have betrayed God and the Prophet, and who have betrayed their Repositories. Do you know how they betrayed the Repositories? God's Book was given to them, and they falsified and changed it; their [true] leaders [ʿAlî and the imams] were shown to them, but they turned away from them."[445]

The writings of the classical heresiologists on the subject can also be counted as indirect indications. Al-Ashʿarî (324/935), from a point of view that we find disconcerting, divides the Shîʿites into three groups: those who believe that parts of the revealed text were censured, those who maintain that there have been deliberate additions, and those who accept the integrity of the official Vulgate.[446] Ibn Ḥazm (456/1054) makes no distinction, maintaining that one of the doctrinal particularities of all Shî'ites is their rejection of the integrity of the 'Uthmânic Vulgate; he nevertheless adds that al-sharîf al-Murtaḍä and two of his disciples did not share this opinion of their fellow believers.[447]

Al-Isfarâ'inî (471/1078–79) also writes that, according to all sects of Shî'ism, the original text of Revelation, which contains numerous references to the Imamate of 'Alî and his descendents, was altered and censured by the Companions.[448]

In the letters that were alluded to previously, and in a number of other traditions of the imams, the Companions of the Prophet, and especially the first two caliphs, Abû Bakr and 'Umar, are presented as those primarily responsible for "betrayal" of the divine Text. The two companions are attacked with special vehemence, certainly because they are accused of having separated from power, both by trickery and by force, the true and only successor to the Prophet, 'Alî, but also and especially because they are accused of rejecting 'Alî's version of the Qur'an, and of having altered, falsified, and censured the original and integral text of Revelation in their own interests and in the interests of the most powerful of the Quraysh.[449] Thus, the questions of the imams' Qur'an, the Qur'an's rejection by the Companions, and the Companions' falsification of the original Qur'an appear to throw a new light of the contents and the reasons for certain of the imams' ideas or technical terms. There is first the idea of *sabb al-ṣaḥâba* (lit. insulting the Companions); up to the present, researchers have only managed to isolate the political reasons for the idea: the imams' violent diatribes against the main Companions of the Prophet are based on the fact that they took power from 'Alî[450] ; but a careful reading of the early corpus of the imams shows that the religious reason, that is, the falsification and censure of the integral Qur'an, is, if not more so, at least as important as the political reason. In the eyes of the imams, the main Companions of the Prophet were, because of this "betrayal," those truly responsible for the rapid moral and religious decline of the Muslim community, a decline that took place after the Prophet's death. The texts reported by al-Kulaynî, in his *Rawḍa*, show the imams afflicted by the violence and the ignorance of a community that, after a few decades, has completely forgotten the teachings and directives of its Prophet and his God, and the fault for this lies incontestably on those who permitted the falsification of the Divine Message, and who deceitfully and forcefully made the majority of Muslims accept their falsification. It is perhaps in this context that we should take the Prophet's words as reported by a number of imams: "In the beginning, Islam was unknown, and it will again become unknown; happy are the unknown."[451]

The idea of *sabb al-ṣaḥâba* should moreover be placed in a larger context, that of *al-barâ'a*, or *al-tabarrî* (lit. renunciation).[452] For the imams, *barâ'a* (or *tabarrî*) is the indispensable complement to, and opposite of, *walâya* (or *tawallî*). If we translate *walâya* (or *tawallî*) by "faithful, tender love" of the Imam, then *barâ'a* (or *tabarrî*) would be "wild, implacable hatred" of the Enemy of the Imam. We should be simultaneously mindful of everything that involves this opposition of "Imam/Enemy of the Imam" or "the imams' faithful believers/the partisans of the imams' adversaries," as well as all the other corresponding pairs of opposites: the Armies of Hiero-Intelligence and those of the counterpower of Ignorance, the battle waged between the two since before the creation of the physical world, the People of the Right and those of the Left, the People of Paradise and those of Hell, the continuation of the universal battle throughout the cycles of sacred history between the imams and their faithful, on the one side, and the adversaries of the imams and their partisans on the other, the Guides of Justice and the Guides of Injustice (*a'immat al-ʿadl/a'immat al-jawr*), the Guides of Good and those of Evil (*a'immat al-khayr/a'immat al-sharr*), the Guides of Light and those of Darkness (*a'immat al-nûr/a'immat al-ẓalâm*), the initiated Masters and their disciples as opposed to the counter-initiated and their masters, the People of the exoteric *and* the esoteric as opposed to those of the exoteric alone, and so on.[453] According to the imams, one cannot fully love the Imam and his Cause without simultaneiously hating the Enemy opposed to him and to his Cause since the time of creation; the "believer" who is faithful to the imams should pledge Love and Obedience to the Master who initiates him into the divine Sciences, and Hatred and Disobedience to him who stands for the opposite of this Initiation. If the world is the way it is, invaded by evil and darkness that will only increase until the triumphal return of the Mahdî, it is because the Masters of Injustice and the mass majority (*ʿâmma*) that follows them are dominant, condemning the Sages and the chosen minority (*khâṣṣa*) that follows them to isolation and suffering. As we have seen, the imams have forbidden their faithful to show their Hatred or their Disobedience in the form of revolt or open insurrection; *barâ'a* should thus remain interiorized (just as is the case for *walâya*, because of the danger of death for the person who professes it) until the Return of the hidden imam, even if on the outside obedience to the unjust is forced; this is one of the facets of the Battle that has forever opposed the initiated and the counterinitiated; *sabb al-ṣaḥâba* is one way of upholding it.[454]

The question of the imams' Qur'an and the imams' doubting of the ʿUthmânic version also enter into the Imamite idea of "keeping the secret" (*al-taqiyya*); keeping the secret of course applies to a number of points of doctrine (cf. later discussion), but also to the problems connected with the true text of Revelation, and applying *taqiyya* in this manner has never been pointed out. In their confidential letters to disciples, the imams repeat, and emphasize, on numerous occasions that the secret of the falsification of the Qur'an by the Companions must be kept.[455] Moreover, they invite their disciples to read the Qur'an like everyone else, and to be satisfied with the official version until the

Mahdî's return. Hearing a disciple read the Qur'an, probably according to his own instructions, Ja'far interrupted the disciple and said: "Stop that reading, and read as [other] people do, until our Resurrector rises up; he will read the Book of God Most High as it should be read, and he will unveil the Volume copied by 'Alî."[456] "Sufyân b. al-Samṭ said: 'I asked Abû 'AbdAllâh (i.e. Ja'-far) about the revelation of the Qur'an; he replied by saying 'Read it as you learned to (before you knew of our teaching).'"[457]

Let us resume. According to the imams, the original integral Qur'an is nearly three times the length of the official Vulgate. True Revelation contained "everything" regarding the past, the present, and the future. Only 'Alî, the only true initiate and inheritor designated by God and the Prophet, had a copy of this Qur'an.[458] The principal Companions of the Prophet and the most powerful members of the Quraysh, with Abû Bakr and 'Umar at their head, rejected and falsified the original Text, since it contained a number of verses that spoke disparagingly of them or that specifically named 'Alî and Muḥammad's family as the models and leaders of the Community. Rejected, the integral Qur'an was hidden by 'Alî; it was secretly passed from imam to imam until the twelfth imam took it with him into Occultation. No one other than the hidden imam knows its contents, the totality of which will be revealed only at the time of his Return. Between now and then, Muslims are to make do with the censured, falsified, and deformed version of the 'Uthmânic Vulgate that resulted from the treasonous behavior of the Companions who, through their impious pride, are responsible for the decline of the great majority of the Community.

Ibn Bâbûye al-shaykh al-Ṣadûq (d. 381/991) is apparently the first great Imamite author not only to let these details pass in silence, but to adopt a position identical to that of the Sunnites: "According to us [Imamites], the Qur'an revealed by God to the Prophet Muḥammad is identical to the one between these two covers [*mâ bayna al-daffatayn*; i.e. the official version]. . . . Whoever suggests that the revealed text was larger than the text established here is only a liar." The author makes no mention of those traditions that deal with falsification and alteration (*taḥrîf/tabdîl/taghyîr*), and is content to speak of a change (*ta'lîf*) that took place in the order of certain verses or suras, or in the elimination, by the Companions, of 'Alî's commentaries on the Qur'an that were written in the margins of the first imam's recension; it is the Mahdî who will unveil the original order of verses and suras of the Qur'an, as well as 'Alî's precious interpretations.[460] However, less that a few decades before Ibn Bâbûye, al-Nu'mânî was still speaking about the censure and falsification of the original Qur'an by the Sunnites.[461] The "turn" seems again to have been the Occultation of the last imam, and the isolation and persecution that threatened a minority that was left without a charismatic leader. The integrity of the Qur'an was and remains an extremely delicate problem, and even an Ibn Bâbûye, even though he is more "traditionalist" than "rationalist," could no longer continue to sow doubt about the integrity and authenticity of a Vulgate that had since become universally recognized. After the domination of the "theological-juridical-rational" current in Imamism that began with al-Mufîd, the great Imamite theologians continued to take Ibn Bâbûye's points of view, in one way or another.[462] While continuing to respect, to a greater or lesser degree, authors like al-Ṣaffâr al-Qummî, al-Kulaynî, or al-Nu'mânî, these theologians did not hesitate, despite the resistence of the minority "traditionalists," to refer to as dubious the authenticity of those traditions where the integrity of the Vulgate is doubted. This is one of the rare cases where the competence of the early Imamite compilers regarding the authenticity of traditions is called into question.[463] This procedure continues to the present day,[464] and we can say that from the middle of the fourth century of the Hegira up to the present, almost all Imamites have accepted the integrity and the authenticity of the 'Uthmânic Vulgate, just as the Sunnites do.

Let us now return to the two "unknown chapters" of the Qur'an, the sura of the Two Lights, and that of *walâya*. Garcin de Tassy tends to believe in their authenticity, although he presents no proof to support his belief. Mirza Kazem Beg, who relies essentially on literary and stylistic criteria, refutes the authenticity of the first of the two. St Clair Tisdall does likewise with the second of the suras, although he admits the possible authenticity of the first;[465] Schwally, using historical methodology, considers the date for the appearance of the sura of the Two Lights to be late;[466] Blanchère agrees in this regard,[467] and although neither knows the edition of the sura of the *walâya*, their argument may be the same, since the manuscript discovered by St Clair Tisdall dates only from the seventeenth or eighteenth century.

The question of the authenticity of these two suras remains complex; it is tied to the question of the authenticity of the "integral Qur'an" of the imams; an impressive number of Imamite sources are still in manuscript form, and await publication in order to be better known. The majority of those that have been edited have yet to be systematically analyzed in a scholarly fashion. Once the early sources are edited, the late date of the appearance of the two "unknown" suras may be revised; for example, Ibn Shahrâshûb al-Mâzandarânî, who died in 588/1192, writes in his *Mathâlib al-nawâṣib* that the enemies of the imams (*nâṣibî*, pl. *nawâṣib*) suppressed from the Qur'an all of the sura of the *walâya* (*asqaṭû sûrat al-walâya kullahâ*);[468] the title of the sura is thus announced by a sixth/twelfth century author, although nothing is said about its contents; is this the same sura edited by St Clair Tisdall? In *al-Dharî'a* there are six works mentioned entitled *al-Tabdîl wa l-taḥrîf*, or *al-Taḥrîf wa l-tabdîl*, or even *al-Tanzîl min al-Qur'ân wa l-taḥrîf*, four of which date from the third/ninth and fourth/tenth centuries and were already mentioned by al-Najâshî, and al-Ṭûsî in his *Fihrist*. All but one are apparently lost; did these perhaps contain mentions of the two suras?[469] The only manuscript extant is housed at the University of Tehran; it is that of the *Kitâb al-Tanzîl wa l-taḥrîf*, by Abû ʿAbdAllâh Aḥmad b. Md al-Sayyârî, one of al-Kulaynî's teachers; the work, in 54 folios, lists the verses "censured" or "falsified," going from the first to the last sura of the Qur'an. It was clearly used by al-Kulaynî, although it makes no mention of the two "unknown chapters."[470] There is, additionally, supportive information to be found in early Imamite doctrine. There is no historical proof of the imams' Qurʾan, but there are a number of pieces of concordant information. These details do not appear to be theoretical, as was the case in Khârijite criticism of the Vulgate. The seriousness of the matter and the unimaginable implications that it might carry in its wake, the Shîʿite duty of keeping the secret about all that touches upon fundamental points of doctrine, and finally the complex relationships (a mixture of respect and suspicion) that Sunni authors had with the imams from the Prophet's family, all tend to explain, at least in part, the paucity of historical information in both Imamite and Sunni sources. For the moment we can take it for granted that according to basic Imamite doctrine, that is the original "esoteric-magical-suprarational" tradition that predominated before the Occultation of the twelfth imam, the integral Qurʾan copied by ʿAlî and the altered and falsified character of the ʿUthmânic version were seen as undeniable "historical" realities, except that, according to the imams, they were the only ones to know the integral Qur'an; moreover, its contents will not be revealed except by the awaited Mahdî. Would the imams perhaps mean by that that before the End of Time and the Return of the Resurrector, any text supposedly belonging to the integral Qurʾan would be a forged text? As we have seen, the imams cited verses from this Qur'an for their disciples, while firmly demanding that they respect the "guarding of the secret"; we might suppose that they also mentioned the titles of certain suras, although the early corpus contains no citation for an entire sura, and, for dogmatic reasons, we might find it difficult to imagine that the imams revealed entire suras to disciples who might at some point slip in their promise of discretion. Thus, there are also doctrinal reasons for doubting the authenticity of our two suras.[471]

III-4. SACRED POWER

The miraculous powers of the imams are presented as the results of their initiatory Knowledge, in accord with the old esoteric saying "Knowledge Is Power." The early Imamite writings abound not only in information about the imams' Knowledge, but in accounts of the wonders they work. These included technical words like *aʿâjîb* (the plural of *uʿjûba*, lit. "something amazing," or "extraordinary," or "marvelous") or *qudra* ("ability," "power"; in this case, the phrase is often "the Power that God gives them"—*al-qudrat allatî aʿṭâhum Allâh*). The word *karâma* (pl. *karâmât*), used later to refer to the wonders worked by saints, particularly the sufis, is not used, to our knowledge. Once again, it is only Ṣaffâr al-Qummî who, in his *Baṣâʾir al-darajât*, presents the subject methodically by grouping details in independent chapters; it is for this reason that we have felt his work to serve as the best basic source here. In the works of the other compilers, details regarding the powers of the imams are sparse, fragmentary, or diluted among the mass of traditions. This fact of the imams' lives could not be simply passed over without comment, since it is an integral part of doctrine; nevertheless, an attempt has been made to hide it as much as possible from the eyes of a majority who would not admit that miracles are systematically worked by people other than the Prophet.[472]

As has been said, the powers of the imams devolve from their Knowledge. As will be seen, most of these powers are shown to be associated with the knowledge of magic. This characteristic, once again, shows the initiatory, esoteric and occultist nature of early Imamism. The imams teach their secrets, part of their *'ilm*, to a restricted number of their closest disciples, and these individuals in turn are able to perform wonders. However, a certain number of things remain the exclusive property of the imams, mainly "elements of power" that the imams inherited from earlier prophets, and from the Prophet Muḥammad in particular, that they transmit to one another exclusively. These "elements of power," which are also part of the "prophetic heritage" (*mîrâth al-nubuwwa*), may be divided into two categories:

The first "element of power" is the Supreme Name of God (*al-ism al-a'ẓam/al-ism al-akbar*); this Name, with its thaumaturgic powers, is composed of 73 letters, one of which is known to God alone. According to a series of traditions attributed to the fifth, sixth, and eleventh imams,[473] two letters from the Name were given to Jesus, who performed his miracles through them; Moses received four, Abraham eight, Noah fifteen, and Adam twenty-five; it is also said that Solomon taught only one letter to his initiate Âṣaf b. Barkhiyâ, who by its virtue was able to get a glimpse of the throne of Bilqîs, the queen of Saba'. Only Muḥammad was privileged to receive 72 letters that were transferred to the imams; the last letter is reserved by God for Himself, in His secret Knowledge of hidden things.[474] According to words ascribed via several chains of transmission to Juwayria b. Mus-hir, a companion of 'Alî,[475] the Supreme Name appears to be a magical phrase in Syriac or in Hebrew: 'Alî and his companions are in Babylonia (*arḍ Bâbil*); the sun is about to set and it is time for evening prayer; 'Alî then says that the land of Babylonia is damned because it was the first region where idols were worshipped, and that it is forbidden for the prophets and the Heirs of the prophets to perform prayer in this land. The companions are worried because the sun is setting and they are going to miss the best time for evening prayer; but 'Alî calmly continues his travel until the group leaves the region; then, when the sun has completely disappeared over the horizon, he asks that his companions prepare for evening prayer. Juwayria reports that the imam, withdrawing from the group, began to whisper a phrase in Syriac or Hebrew (*suryânî aw 'ibrânî*); then the sun began to reappear from behind the mountains, and the people could say their prayer. When Juwayria asked about it, 'Alî replied that he had spoken the Supreme

Name, and that through the power of this Name he was able to reverse the course of the sun.[476]

The power of the Supreme Name seems terrifying, and only the prophets and the imams are able to stand such power; such is what we might conclude from a tradition reported by al-Ṣaffâr: ʿUmar b. Ḥanẓala, a close disciple of al-Bâqir,[477] asked his master to teach him the Supreme Name. "Can you stand it?" asked the fifth imam, to which the disciple replied affirmatively. They then went to the imam's abode, where his hand was placed on the earth as he began to say the Name; the house was plunged into the greatest darkness, and ʿUmar's entire body began to tremble. He nevertheless heard the first part of the phrase and the imam ordered him to not divulge it; al-Bâqir raised his hand off the ground, and things became normal again.[478]

Besides the Supreme Name of God, the imams have other "elements of power" capable of working magic, referring to ritual and/or personal objects that belonged to the prophets: Adam's cloak (*qamîṣ*),[479] Solomon's Seal (*khâtim*),[480] Joseph's coat that had belonged to Abraham,[481] the Staff (*ʿaṣä*), the sacrificial bowl (*ṭast*), the Ark of the Covenant (*tâbût*) and Moses' tablets (*alwâḥ*),[482] the ring (*khâtim*), the armor (*durʿ*), and the weapon (*silâḥ*) of Muḥammad. Muḥammad's weapon was none other than Dhû al-faqâr, the famous double-edged saber brought from heaven by the angel Gabriel.[483] These sacred objects are also signs of the Imamate, and thus remain the exclusive property of the imams; they were taken by the hidden imam into his Occultation.

Other prodigious powers based on occult knowledge are also attributed to the imams. We will limit ourselves here to those most frequently mentioned in the early compilations, and those that are well known in the magical aspects of other esoteric traditions. The imams know the events and the mysteries of the sky and the earth, of Paradise and Hell, of the past and the future.[484] They possess the Knowledge of Happiness and Misfortunes, and the genealogy of the nations (*ʿilm al-manâyâ wa l-balâya wa l-ansâb*).[485] They know the *faṣl al-khiṭâb*.[486] Consciences and souls hold no secrets from them (*ʿilm al-aḍmâr wa l-anfus*),[487] and they have the power of both physiognomy (*firâsa/tafarrus/tawassum*) and mind reading.[488] The imams know not only all human languages and all those of the Sacred Books of the past,[489] but also the languages of the birds (*manṭiq al-ṭayr)*, of the animals (*al-bahâʾim*), and of the "metamorphosized" (*al-musûkh*), that is, of human beings who have died and been reincarnated in the form of a harmful or malefic animal.[490] The imams have the *jinn* at their service, and give religious instruction to them.[491] It is also reported that inanimate objects (*ghayr al-ḥayawânât*) obey the imams and communicate with them.[492] We have already seen that the imams had the power to see the dead and to communicate with them.[493] They can similarly make themselves invisible.[493bis]

Resuscitating the dead (*iḥyâ al-mawtä*), healing the sick (the most frequently cited are lepers—*abraṣ*—and the blind—*akmah*) and walking on water (*al-mashy ʿalä al-mâʾ*) are also among the powers of the imams,[494] such powers (except for the last) being reminiscent of the miracles that the Qurʾan attributes to Jesus. The imams themselves declare that God has given them all the miraculous powers that He had already given to the earlier prophets, most notably to Jesus, who is often mentioned as the prophet with the most powerful miracles. As far as "healing the blind" is concerned, it should be noted that in the traditions blindness refers to both physical and spiritual blindness; besides the traditions relating to the healing of congenital blindness, there are others where the imam opens "the spiritual eye" (*baṣar*) of his disciple; Jaʿfar al-Ṣâdiq touches Abû Baṣîr's eyes and allows him to contemplate the mysteries of heaven; on another occasion, during the pilgrimage to Mecca, the imam performs the same gesture on the same disciple and makes him able to "see" the true natures of the great majority of the pilgrims: monkeys and pigs.[495]

Another of the imams' powers is the phenomenon called "the magical voyage" in the occult traditions, especially in shamanism. Our texts refer to it as "the power of displacement" (*qudrat al-sayr*).[496] It appears as though the power was known in Arabia, and from what we can infer from one of Jaʿfar's traditions, it was practiced in Yemen: a Yemenite appeared at Jaʿfar's house, and the imam asked him: "Do you have any initiated (*ʿulamâʾ*) among you?" "Yes," replied the visitor. "How much Knowledge do your initiated possess?" "In a single night they can travel the distance that normally takes two months, and they practice divination based on the behavior of the birds [ornithomancy] and on signs marked on the earth [a kind of geomancy] (*yazjur al-ṭayr wa yaqîfu l-âthâr*)";[497] then Jaʿfar said: "The Initiated One from Medina [i.e., Jaʿfar himself] is even more knowledgeable than your initiated . . . for in one hour of the day[498] he can travel the distance that the sun does in a year . . . and he can visit twelve suns and twelve moons, twelve Easts and twelve Wests, twelve Earths, twelve Seas, and twelve Worlds. . . . "[499]

In the same manner, the imams are able to "displace" their disciples; here again, as we have seen in the case of blindness, "the magical voyage" has two aspects; the imam can take his disciple through the physical world to specific places on the earth, or into suprasensible places like the land of Darkness (*ẓulumât*, where Dhû l-qarnayn, "the man with two horns," the legendary early sage alluded to in Qurʾan 18:83–98 was), the Fountain of Life (*ʿayn al-ḥayât*, where the famous and mysterious Khiḍr drank), the Kingdom of the Skies (*malakût al-samâwât*, composed of twelve Worlds), or the spiritual World where tents of silver are set up for the deceased Impeccables to live in.[500]

There is also the power to stride over the clouds and to climb into the sky (*rukûb al-saḥâb wa l-taraqqî fî l-samâwât*).[501] The traditions that deal with this subject attribute this power to the first and the last of the imams, ʿAlî and *al-Qâ'im*. The imams further maintain that they themselves are not all equal in their abilities to perform supernatural acts.[502] According to these traditions, two kinds of clouds may be walked upon, thus allowing access to the heavens: *al-dhalûl* (the docile), a white cloud, and *al-ṣa'b* (the indocile), a cloud swollen with rain, thunder, and lightning. Striding upon the first of these clouds was reserved for Dhû l-qarnayn, the man-with-two-horns,[503] while the second was reserved for 'Alî and the hidden imam;[504] this is the explanation for how 'Alî was able to visit the seven heavens and the seven earths, five of which were inhabited and five uninhabited.

The imams had what might be called a "spiritual eye" (*al-baṣar/al-'ayn*)[505] through which they could both "see" in all directions at the same time and remain awake, even when sleeping. This is perhaps the same "subtle organ" as the Hindu Eye of Shiva, the Third Eye of the Tibetans, or the Astral Eye in occult traditions; however, whereas in these cases the eye is usually located in the subtle center between the eyebrows, for the imams it is located in the heart.[506] There is a hadith on this subject that is of particular interest, as it appears canonically to justify the practice of a certain kind of magic (*siḥr*). The tradition is attributed to Ja'far, of whom it is asked why the Prophet gave the name "truthful" (*ṣiddîq*) to Abû Bakr.[507] The sixth imam then tells the famous story of the cave where the Prophet and Abû Bakr were hiding; at a certain moment, God's Messenger says: I see Ja'far b. Abî Ṭâlib's boat lost at sea." Abû Bakr asks him whether he could make him "see" also. The Prophet tells his companion to come closer, and he rubs his eyes with his hands (*masaḥa 'alä 'aynayhi*); then Abû Bakr sees the boat being tossed by the waves, as well as other scenes; and he says to himself: "Now I am convinced that you are a magician [*al'âna ṣadaqtu annaka sâḥir*]"; the Prophet, reading his thoughts, replies: "You are the truthful one [*al-ṣiddîq anta*]."

There are acts of magic attributed to the imams. The fourth imam, 'Alî b. al-Ḥusayn, with a wave of his hand (var., with prayer), returns youth to a hundred-year-old woman, the wâlibiyya.[509] The sixth imam, Ja'far al-Ṣâdiq, eats a date and plants the seed, which begins to grow immediately, becoming a large tree full of fruit.[510] Challenged by a magician from the court of Hârûn al-Rashîd, who was attempting to humiliate him, the seventh imam, Mûsä al-Kâẓim, brought a lion to life that was painted on a palace curtain; the huge animal swallowed the magician before the eyes of the caliph and the courtisans.[511] A few indirect details or fragmentary pieces of information suggest that some of the special powers of the imams were based on their knowledge of traditional occult sciences. There is first of all the science of letters, or magical and divinatory application of the numerical value of the letters of the alphabet (*'ilm al-ḥurûf/ḥisâb al-jummal*); some disciples, namely the "representatives" of the hidden imam during the period of the minor Occultation, knew this science (cf. Part IV), and we might reasonably conclude from this that they were ititiated by the imam.

There is also astrology (*al-nujûm*); the efficiency of this divinatory "art" is recognized by the imams. Mu'allä b. Khunays[412] asks Ja'far whether astrology is true, to which the imam replies affirmatively.[513] In a conversation about astrological calculations, the same imam states: " . . . This calculation is actually true, but only he who has the Knowledge of the horoscope of all creatures [that is, the imam] can know it."[514] And Ja'far al-Ṣadiq also says: "Only one family from among the Arabs [*ahl baytin min al-'arab*—that is, the family of the Prophet, the imams] and one family from among the Hindus [*ahl baytin min al-hind*] know the Science of astrology."[515] 'Abd al-Raḥmân b. Siyâba[516] says to Ja'far: "People [*al-nâs*, that is, the Sunnites] have said that astrology is illicit, but I am attracted to it; is it prejudicial to my religion? If so, I will give up my study, but if this is not the case, I wish to learn it." The imam replies, "It is not as they say; astrology does no harm to religion. However, you are studying something about which you know very little, and the least amount that you grasp will do you no good, since your calculations are based only on the trajectory [*ṭâli'*] of the moon; do you know how many minutes there are between Jupiter [*al-mushtarî*] and Venus [*al-zuhra*]?" "No." "How many minutes there are between Venus and the moon? Between the sun and Virgo [*al-sunbula*]? . . . Between Virgo and the Well-Guarded Tablet [*al-lawḥ al-maḥfûẓ*]?" "No, for heaven's sake, for no astrologist has spoken of these things." "In each case there are 70 minutes. 'Abd al-Raḥmân, who knows these calculations thoroughly, could tell you exactly how many reeds there are in a field of rushes."[518]

There are, however, other statements where the imams appear to wish to warn their disciples against purely magical applications of astrology, astrology that has been "profaned," separated from a Science that has been acquired through divine intervention, since it would otherwise tend toward "black magic." 'Alî says: "O people [*ayyuhâ l-nâs*, although we are not sure whether he is speaking with disciples or with "ordinary" people], beware of learning astrology, except where it assists you in finding your way over land or sea.[519] Astrology leads you to divination; the astrologist is like the diviner, the diviner like the magician, the magician like the impious, and the impious are destined for Fire. Undertake your actions [by relying] on the Name of God."[520] Elsewhere the same imam, after rejecting the predictions of an astrologist, finishes his statement with the words "My God, there is no divination other than Your divination [*al-ṭayr*, lit. "ornithomancy," although the word here means techniques of divination in general, including astrology], there is no bad omen other than Your bad omen, there is no good omen other than Your good omen, and no god other than You."[521]

Imamite occultism is thus presented as a kind of theurgy; the imams' magic is founded on Knowledge and Power that are granted by God. But, what is called "natural magic," is rejected. Divine human beings, in this case, the imams, are the only ones to have been given these powers, and they are, by virtue of this, the only ones who can initiate their faithful into the Sacred Knowledge that opens the door to Sacred Power. From the time of his pre-existence, the imam is characterized by his initiatory Knowledge and his occult Power; his existence, the manifestation of his pre-existential entity in the sensible world, is thus marked by these same characteristics.[522]

4

The Super-Existence of the Imam

> You are like the stars of the sky;
> as soon as one star sets, another rises,
> up until the Day of Resurrection.
>
> The Prophet

After the pre-existence and the existence of the imam, it is logical to expect his post-existence; the imam actually continues to live even after he leaves the physical world. 'Alî says: "He among us who dies is not dead."[523] The deceased Impeccables are transported to a supersensible world where, living under their "tent of silver," they can be visited by their faithful initiates.[524] Every Thursday evening (or in other versions, "every morning" or "every day") the acts of the faithful are exposed to the Impeccables in their celestial abodes.[525] But the idea of the triumph of the Imam over death is entirely dominated by the figure of the hidden imam, the savior of the End of Time. The twelfth imam is not immortal, and such an idea would be inconceivable, since only God is immortal, but he has been granted a hidden and marvelously long existence by God so that he can fulfill his eschatological mission. It is for this reason that the fourth part of this work is entitled "the super-existence of the imam." Imamite and Shî'ite messianism, the Occultation and its historical implications, the Figure of the hidden imam and certain facets of his personality have already been studied in a number of works.[526] In order to avoid repetition and to remain faithful to the problem as outlined, we will limit ourselves to the "theosophical" (in the sense of "esoteric" or "occult") aspects of the superexistence of the hidden imam, aspects that up to the present have remained almost unknown.[527] Before that, however, it may be useful to look at a point of doctrinal history that has not yet garnered the attention it deserves.

IV-1. IMAMITE POINTS OF VIEW ON THE ANCIENTNESS OF THE INFORMATION

As is known, according to Imamite sources, Muḥammad b. al-Ḥasan al-'Askarî (*al-Mahdî*) had a first occultation when he was no more than a small child. This occultation, in 260/874, lasted nearly 70 years. During his occultation the imam communicated with his faithful via four Representatives (*safîr/nâ'ib/wakîl*). This was what is referred to as "the first Occultation" (*al-ghaybat al-ûlä*), or "the minor Occultation" (*al-ghaybat al-sughrä*). Then, around 329/941, came the beginning of "the second Occultation" (*al-ghaybat al-thâniya*), or "the major Occultation" (*al-ghaybat al-kubrä*). This occultation is still in effect, and will not end until the End of Time (*âkhir al-zamân*) when the Mahdî comes back to reestablish Justice on earth.[528] Information concerning the Mahdî of the Imamites, his identity, his name, and the fact that he is the son of the eleventh imam, and thus that he is the twelfth imam, as well as information regarding his Occultations, are reported by sources later than the first Occultation. Historically, we might conclude that the old idea of *ghayba* (existing at least since the time of the Kaysâniyya, who applied it to the son of ʿAlî, Muḥammad b. al-Ḥanafiyya) was taken over by the Imamites relatively late. These Imamites applied it to the twelfth imam and thus became, since the fourth/tenth century, Twelvers.[529] The difficult situation created by the Occultation in effect led the Imamites to profess, only a posteriori, the ideas connected to the number of imams and to the fate of the last of the imams. But what for historians constitutes the proof of an a posteriori invention is for the faithful a demonstration of the predestined characteristic of the number of imams and the identity of the Mahdî. Our purpose here is to analyze how the Imamites prove how old the information concerning the twelfth imam is. Seen from this angle, things may look more complex than they already appear to be. Doubt about the doctrinal authenticity of the Occultation and the number of imams is not recent. The mysterious fate of the son of the eleventh imam divided the early Shîʿite family into a number of factions; some maintained that this son died at a very early age; others, that he had lived and that he died in old age; still others denied his existence altogether, choosing to think that al-Ḥasan al-ʿAskarî had never had a son, and so forth.[530] Only a small minority defended the idea according to which the son of the eleventh imam was alive, that he was the hidden Mahdî, and that he would return at the End of Time, an idea adopted later by all Imamites, essentially as a result of the efforts of al-Nuʿmânî and Ibn Bâbûye; we shall return to this subject.

In the first place, the technical name for the doctrine is undoubtedly of a later date than the Occultation. The imams themselves speak only of their "partisans" (*shîʿatunâ*) or "the believers" (*al-muʿminûn*). Abû'l-Ḥasan al-Ashʿarî (d. 324/935–36) uses the word Qaṭʿiyya to refer to those who affirmed the death of the seventh imam (as opposed to the Wâqifiyya), and he extends this term to those who, from that time on, continued the chain of imams up to Muḥammad b. al-Ḥasan. He further refers to this latter group with the general term Râfiḍa, pl. Rawâfiḍ, of whom only the first subsect (still called the Qaṭʿiyya) and the twenty-fourth believed in the Occultation. The term Imâmiyya (the Imamites) is used only exceptionally by al-Ashʿarî.[531] Prior to him, pseudo-Nâshi' al-Akbar[532] already referred to those who "categorically affirmed the death of Mûsä b. Ja'far" as "Qaṭ'iyya."[533] The expression *Ithnâ 'ashariyya* (Twelver) is not yet found in Ibn al-Nadîm's (d. 380/990) *Fihrist*, although 'Abd al-Qâhir al-Baghdâdî (d. 429/1037) used it to refer to a subdivision of the Imâmiyya; by "Twelvers" he specifically meant the Qaṭ'iyya who continued the chain of imams up to Muḥammad b. al-Ḥasan.[534] The synonymy between *imâmiyya* and *ithnâ 'ashariyya* was thus progressive.[535]

Next, imformation concerning the number of imams, the twelfth imam, his two Occultations, and his final triumphal Return is furnished only by sources posterior to the first Occultation. Among the great authors of the "esoteric non-rational" tradition, let us cite al-Kulaynî, who died in 329/940, the same year as the beginning of the major Occultation, and who wrote his *Uṣûl min al-kâfî* during the period of the minor Occultation. Al-Nu'mânî Ibn Abî Zaynab (d. circa 345 or 360/956 or 971), was the author of the *Kitâb al-ghayba*. Ja'far b. Md Ibn Qûlûye al-Qummî (d. 369/979), authored the *Kamîl al-ziyârât*. 'Alî b. Md al-Khazzâz al-Râzî al-Qummî (d. in the second half of the fourth/tenth century), was the author of the *Kifâyat al-athar fî l-naṣṣ 'alä l-a'immat al-ithay 'ashar*. Ibn Bâbûye (d. 381/991) especially in his *Kamâl* (*Ikmâl*) *al-dîn*, seems to have collected the essentials of the information from his predecessors. And finally, there was Aḥmad b. Md Ibn 'Ayyâsh al-Jawharî (d. 401/1101), who composed the *Muqtaḍab al-athar fî l-naṣṣ 'alä 'adad al-a'immat al-ithay 'ashar*.[536] It appears as though these authors have used the early data, in a number of ways, to prove the ancientness and then the authenticity of their information. The two greatest compilers from before the Occultation, al-Ṣaffâr al-Qummî (d. 290/903) in his *Baṣâ'ir al-darajât*, and one of his teachers in hadith, Abû Ja'far Aḥmad b. Md al-Barqî (d. 274/887 or 280/893), in his *Kitâb al-maḥâsin*, have provided almost no information about the subject that is our concern here.[537] Nevertheless, as will be seen, later authors did make use of their names.

The theme of the *ghayba* was well known in the imams' entourage. Shî'ite bibliographical works list a number of writings about the Occultation of the Mahdî composed by members of the imams' entourage. Almost all of these writings have been lost, although sections of their contents were collected and reported by later authors, such as al-Kulaynî, al-Nu'mânî, and Ibn Bâbûye. Among the very first compilers, there were first of all Wâqifite Shî'ites (claiming that such and such imam is the Mahdî, that he is not dead but hidden, and that he will later manifest himself as the *qâ'im*):

Ibrâhîm b. Ṣâliḥ al-Anmâṭî al-Kûfî, a partisan of the fifth imam al-Bâqir (d. circa 115/733–34), who considered al-Bâqir to be the hidden Mahdî, and who authored a *Kitâb al-ghayba*.[538]

'Alî b. al-Ḥasan al-Ṭâṭârî al-Ṭâ'î, a partisan of the seventh imam, Mûsä (d. 183/799), also the author of a *Kitâb al-ghayba*.[539]

Al-Ḥasan b. Md b. Sumâ'a, a disciple of 'Alî b. al-Ḥasan al-Ṭâṭârî al-Ṭâ'î, and who believed, like his teacher, in the Occultation of the seventh imam. He was also the author of a *Kitâb al-ghayba*, and was one of the sources used by al-Kulaynî.[540]

Al-Ḥasan b. 'Alî al-Baṭâ'inî al-Kûfî, a partisan of the eighth imam al-Riḍâ (d. 203/808) and propably a Wâqifite as regards this imam, as was his father, 'Alî al-Baṭâ'inî; his work was likewise entitled *Kitâb al-ghayba*.[541]

Apparently originally a Zaydi, before his conversion to Imamism, Abû Sa'îd 'Abbâd b. Ya'qûb al-'Uṣfurî (d. 250/864) was a contemporary of the tenth and eleventh imams, and the author of a *Kitâb* that formed part of the "400 original books" of the Imamites (*al-Uṣûl al-arba'umi'a*); he speaks of eleven [*sic*] imams, with no mention of their names, with the eleventh being the Resurrector. His name appears in chains of transmission (*isnâd*) for al-Kulaynî, al-Nu'mânî, and Ibn Bâbûye.[542]

Among the Qaṭ'iyya who later became Imâmiyya were:

Al-Ḥasan b. Maḥbûb al-Sarrâd al-Kûfî (d. 224/838), a disciple of the eighth imam and author of a *Kitâb al-ghayba* also called *al-Mashyakha*. This was one of the sources most extensively used by later authors on the subject of the Occultation of the Mahdî.[543]

Md b. al-Muthannä al-Ḥaḍramî (third/ninth century), the author of a *Kitâb* that became part of the *Uṣûl arba'umi'a*, reports in his work one of Ja'far's traditions according to which, after the Prophet, there would be seven imams, the last of which would be the Mahdî.[544]

'Alî b. Mahizyâr al-Ahwâzî, a companion of the ninth and tenth imams (d. in 220/835 and 254/868, respectively), the author of a *Kitâb al-malâḥim* ("Book of Prophecies") and a *Kitâb al-qâ'im* ; his name appears in numerous chains of transmission (for traditions of a "messianic" character) in the works of al-Kulaynî and Ibn Bâbûye.[545]

Al-Faḍl b. Shâdhân al-Nîsâbûrî (d. 260/873), a disciple of the eleventh imam and a famous Imamite scholar, the author of a *Kitâb al-ghayba*; he was one of the main references for later authors.[546]

Finally, let us mention Ibrâhîm b. Isḥâq al-Aḥmarî al-Nahâwandî (late third/ninth century), a contemporary of the eleventh imam, author of a *Kitâb al-ghayba* that was one of al-Nu'mânî's sources.[547]

An examination of the *isnâd* of the great compilations from the time after the Occultation turns out to be a fruitful endeavor. For example, we are able to see that fragments, sometimes even entire treatises, have been collected and inserted into systematic compilations. Such is the case, for example, of the *Kitâb al-nuṣra* by the Wâqifite ʿAlî b. Aḥmad al-ʿAlawî (d. circa 200/815), incorporated into al-shaykh al-Ṭûsî's *Kitâb al-ghayba*; the author includes some forty "messianic" traditions in which the number of imams stops at seven, as would be expected for one of Mûsä's Wâqifites.[548] There is also the *Kitâb al-ḥujja fî ibṭâʾ al-qâʾim* by Md b. Baḥr al-Ruhnî al-Shaybânî (second half of third/ninth century to the beginning of the following century, thus after 260/874), inserted by Ibn Bâbûye into his *Kamâl al-dîn*, and by al-Ṭûsî into his *Kitâb al-ghayba*. Al-Ruhnî, a familiar visitor of the tenth imam, alludes to the fact that there would be twelve imams, and he announces that the Mahdî would be the grandson of his teacher.[549] This proves, according to Ibn Bâbûye and al-Ṭûsî, that the tenth imam had revealed to his disciples the number of imams and the identity of the Mahdî. A careful examination of the chains of transmission of "messianic" traditions shows something else. We have seen that in the compilations prepared by Abû Jaʿfar al-Barqî and al-Ṣaffâr al-Qummî very few traditions were reported concerning the number of imams or the identity or destiny of the hidden imam. However, their two names appear repeatedly in the chain of transmission for several traditions that refer to these subjects, in al-Kulaynî, al-Nuʿmânî, or Ibn Bâbûye's works.

The way the compilations are organized suggests that their authors were attempting to resolve these contradictions by recourse to the Imamite duty of "keeping the secret" (*al-taqiyya*, see later discussion), one of the main purposes of which is presented as being precisely that of protecting the identity of the Mahdî. In al-Kulaynî and Ibn Bâbûye, numerous traditions concerning the number of imams or the identity of the *Qâʾim* contain appeals for discretion. The works of al-Nuʿmânî and Ibn ʿAyyâsh begin with a whole chapter on *taqiyya*, apparently in attempt to convince the reader that all matters concerning the twelfth imam should be marked by the seal of secrecy. It is interesting to note that none of the traditions from the first chapter of al-Nuʿmânî's work contains mention of the Mahdî, but rather general traditions on the sacred nature of the idea of *taqiyya*; but given this chapter's location at the beginning of the book, and after a long introduction to the subject by the author, the reader is subconsciously led to make the connection between the Mahdî, his Occultations, and "keeping of secret." The figure of the Islamic "Savior" and the sayings concerning his awesome role in the bloody purification of the world and the reestablishment of justice were known by all. The disquiet that these accounts of Shîʿite origin caused to the Umayyad, and especially to the Abbasid powers, is known. All of the "Mahdist" movements were persecuted, and all rebellions were quelled with bloodshed. The Shîʿites, with the imams at their head, despite their political passivity (especially since the time of the fourth imam), were carefully watched. According to Imamite logic, in order to save the life of the Mahdî who at the same time would be the last of the imams, it was imperative to keep secret both the number of imams and anything that might reveal the identity of the Mahdî until he made his way to absolute safety, that is, until he found his way into Occultation. Seen in this way, the contradictory elements are presented as being so many "tactics" to hide tracks, and are used as needed by the cause. Everything that tends to show that a certain historical reality forced the a posteriori adoption of these teachings is used by Imamism and presented as one of so many different facets of *taqiyya* regarding the number of imams and the identity of the Mahdî who is to be the last of them. Earlier authors, Wâqifites of one of the preceding imams, are thus taken over, since one of the first tactics to be adopted would be to confuse the facts. The imams gave different numbers to say how many of them there would be: five (al-Anmâṭî's *Kitâb al-ghayba*), seven (the *Kitâb al-ghayba* of al-Ḥasan b. Md b. Sumâ'a; the *Kitâb* by Md b. al-Muthannä al-Ḥaḍramî), eight (according to the two al-Baṭâ'inî), eleven (al-'Uṣfurî's *Kitâb*), twelve (?; according to the *Kitâb Sulaym b. Qays*, of doubtful authenticity, and al-Ṣaffâr's *Baṣâ'ir*).

On the other hand, and for the same reasons, the imams would have declared that each of them could be the Mahdî, the *Qâ'im* (the Resurrector; he who rises up [to reestablish Truth]).[550] At the same time, it is said that the Mahdî is he whose birth takes place in a hidden manner,[551] which might serve as further obfuscation, since a number of imams who were supposed to be the Mahdî did not have hidden births. The phenomenon is not attested to except in the case of the twelfth imam. In a long account, Ḥakîma bint Muḥammad b. 'Alî, the tenth imam's sister, tells about her nephew (the eleventh imam)'s wife not showing any signs of pregnancy until the day she gave birth, further saying that the night of the birth and up to the very moment that it took place, the mother was calmly asleep, with no feeling of pain whatsoever.[552] The father showed his newborn son to only about forty of his closest disciples,[553] and then the child was hidden. According to a number of accounts,[554] the eleventh imam, al-Ḥasan al-'Askarî, adopted a double tactic to guarantee the safety of his son. There were rumors among the Shî'ites that identified the Mahdî as the twelfth imam, and the rumors had reached the ears of the agents of the Abbasids in power; this is why, according to Imamite authors, none of the previous imams had been spied upon as had the eleventh. In the beginning, Al-Ḥasan al-'Askarî attempted to hide the fact of the birth from everyone but his closest friends. He named his mother, Ḥudayth, his sole inheritor. It is known that according to Imamite law (codified for the most part in the time of Ja'far al-Ṣâdiq), an inheritance naturally goes to the mother of the deceased when no children have been born.[555] Next, al-'Askarî tried to cover up the evidence by distracting attention. Just before his death (in 260/874), he is supposed to have had the rumor started that one of his servants, Ṣaqîl, was pregnant by him. The caliph al-Mu'tamid's spies had been following the life of the eleventh imam closely, which is why he was under house arrest in the military camp of Sâmarrâ (Surra-man-ra'ä) in Iraq. When, after a serious illness, the imam's death seemed inevitable, the caliph dispatched to the place five of his confidants, a number of doctors, and the grand judge al-Ḥasan b. Abî l-Shawârib, known for his violently anti-Shî'ite positions. Immediately after the imam's death, Ṣaqîl was arrested and declared herself to be pregnant by the imam. For almost a year she remained under the surveillance of the caliph's and the grand judge's servants; a vain operation, since she showed no signs of pregnancy. Since she was deemed no longer to be in need of being watched, she was released and forgotten. The caliph and his entourage were now convinced that the eleventh imam had passed away without leaving any progeny. According to Imamite authors, Divine Providence had been accomplished and the young hidden imam was theretofore secure in his Occultation. The majority of the partisans of the imams were also led to share the Abbasid convictions.[556] Only a small minority continued to believe in the version that thereafter became the official belief of the Imamites.[557]

Another aspect of the "rule of the arcane" concerning the identity of the Mahdî is the prohibition, promulgated by the imams, against pronouncing the latter's name (*al-nahy 'an al-ism, al-man' 'an al-tasmiya*).[558] Here again, the authors appear to distinguish between two phases in the application of this prohibition. There is first of all the whole series of traditions in which the imams categorically refuse to identify the name of the future Mahdî. Ja'far al-Ṣâdiq says, "No one but an infidel pronounces the name of the Lord of this Cause (that is, the hidden imam)."[559] The eighth imam said, in speaking about the *Qâ'im*: "His body is not seen and his name is not pronounced."[560] Dâwûd b. al-Qâsim al-Ja'farî reports:

> I heard Abû l-Ḥasan al-'Askarî (the tenth imam) say, "My successor will be al-Ḥasan; but what will be your attitude toward my successor's successor?"
>
> I replied: "May God sacrifice me for you, why [this question]?"
>
> He answered: "Because you will not see him and you are not allowed to pronounce his name."
>
> "Then how shall we refer to him?"
>
> Say, "The Proof among the descendents of Muḥammad (*al-ḥujja min âl Muḥammad*)."[561]

According to the authors, this interdiction was in effect at least up to the beginning of the minor Occultation, if we judge by a written response by the twelfth imam dating from this period: " . . . If I tell [the partisans] the name, they will reveal it, and if they know the place [of hiding of the hidden imam], they will tell it [to others]."[562]

On the other hand, there are traditions in which the name of the hidden imam is given, but most often with the letters separated, M Ḥ M D

(Muḥammad).[563] This seems to involve a second phase, and the prohibition in this phase is not against pronouncing the name of the Mahdî, but against pronouncing it aloud (*al-man' 'an al-tanwîh*).[564] The passage into this second phase appears additionally to be attested to by an autograph (*tawqî'a*) of the hidden imam, where the interdiction is not aimed at the pronunciation of the name, but only at revealing it in public.[565] A look at the details suggests a distinction between two phases in everything that concerns the definite number of imams and the Mahdî: the lack of information, or confused and contradictory information prior to the Occultation followed by precise information after the fact. The almost complete silence of authors like al-Barqî and al-Ṣaffâr on the subject in their own compilations, and then the presence of their names in the *isnâd* of traditions on the subject; the interdiction against pronouncing the name of the Mahdî followed by that of pronouncing it aloud; the non-existence of a specific name for the doctrine prior to the Occultation followed by the name "Twelver" immediately thereafter. The turning point is once again the Occultation.

These data suggest that the early Imamite corpus, which belonged to a primitive esoteric tradition, is attempting to posit the following: the imams passed on two kinds of traditions concerning the Mahdî and how many imams there would be; the first category contained confusing information, and was aimed at that large group of disciples who were writing down traditions. In this category, the name of the Mahdî is not specified. As long as the specific number of imams was not known, which imam was the Mahdî remained a secret, and thus the rule of the arcane concerning the Mahdî was observed. A second kind of tradition, aimed only at the closest of disciples, contained specific information about the number of imams, as well as the identity and the fate of the Mahdî. His name was included in this group of traditions except that, in order to guarantee the safety of his life, this category of traditions was only to be transmitted orally until after the beginning of the Occultation; it could be put into writing only after the life of the son of the eleventh imam was out of danger. Using the cases of al-Barqî and al-Ṣâffar in this regard is revealing.[566] There was no longer a need for the rule of the arcane to be applied to the Madhî. Ibn 'Ayyâsh says expressly that this is the real meaning of the division of Knowledge by the imams into a "lavished Knowledge" (*'ilm mabdhûl*) and a "hidden Knowledge" (*'ilm maknûn*).[567]

There is another hypothesis, this one of a more esoteric nature. In the texts that have come to us, the number twelve is made sacred by the support of numerous traditions, to the extent that it legitimizes a fact.[568] The application of the rule of the arcane to the case of the Mahdî and the hypothesis of "two categories of traditions" are presented as justifying this fact. The hadith "After me, there will be twelve vicars, all from the tribe of Quraysh" was in circulation for a long time before the Occultation, since it is reported by Ibn Ḥanbal (d. 241/855) and al-Bukhârî (256/870).[569] The Muslims were well aware of

Jewish, Christian, and Judeo-Christian traditions, especially because of the oral and written literature of the *Isrâ'îliyyât*.[570] It is known that for the Biblical authors, the number 12 is the number of Election, that of the men chosen by God. Israel-Jacob had twelve sons, ancestors named for the twelve tribes of the chosen people (Genesis 35:23f.). The Tree of Life had twelve fruits and the priests twelve jewels. In the Christian tradition, Jesus, in choosing his twelve apostles, proclaimed his decision to choose a new people (Matt. 10:1f., and parallels). The heavenly Jerusalem of the Apocalypse has twelve Doors upon which are written the names of the twelve tribes of Israel, and its rampart has twelve seats, with the names of the twelve apostles (Apocalypse 21:12). The faithful at the End of Time number 144,000, or 12,000 faithful for each of the twelve tribes (Apocalypse 7:4–8; 14:1), which is why this number represents the number of chosen faithful (although it must be said that there are just as many arguments in favor of the number 4 or 7, especially when Apocalypse is the source). The number 12 thus has, for Imamite authors, a particular value in the universal economy of the Sacred (just as the number 7 has for the Mûsawite Wâqifites or the Ismâ'îlis). The imams knew a substantial amount of this information.[571] According to the imams, as has been seen, creation begins with a luminous emanation that immediately thereafter divides into twelve lights (the pre-existential luminous entities of the imams). The number thus has a sacred and cosmic value. On the other hand, according to the imams, it is because of this first creation and its duodecimal structure that all that constitutes order and harmony in the universe has such a structure: the twelve houses of the zodiac, the twelve months of the year, the twelve hours of the day and the night.[572] According to an Imamite point of view, because the Imam is the axis of the cosmic order, the number of imams could be no other than twelve, and because of the rule of the arcane, they could not reveal this secret to everyone.

There are two suggestions of an esoteric kind left by these authors that suggest that the imams wanted to make the secret known to some of their initiates, through the use of a practice well known in esoteric traditions. We have already spoken of arithmomancy or gematry (*ḥisâb al-jummal*) in the teaching of the imams, and the importance of the secret science of numbers and the numeric value of letters for Shî'ites has been known since early on.[573] For Imamites, the three sacred phrases par excellence[574] are all composed of twelve letters: LÂ IL(a) H(a) IL(l)A ALL(â)H (There is no god but God), M(u) H(a) M(m) (a) D R(a) SÛL ALL(â)H (Muḥammad is God's Messenger), and W(a) HD(a) H(u) LÂ SH(a) RÎK(a) L(a) H(u) (He is One, none is associated with him).[575]

Moreover, we have also seen that the name of the future Mahdî is sometimes given in separate letters: M Ḥ M D. In one of the ways of calculating the numeric values of letters, using what is called the "Eastern" method,[576] the number that is repeated an even number of times is not counted; it is said that two identical letters in a word cancel one another out (*khâlî al-zawjayn*).[577] According to this procedure, in the word MḤMD, the two Ms are thus not counted and the sum of the remaining letters, Ḥ and D, is 8 + 4 = 12. The faithful believer initiated into the science of letters would thus be invited to ask himself whether, in giving the name of the Mahdî in this uncustomary manner, the imams were not attempting to say that the Mahdî would be the twelfth of them. These are only suppositions, although to our thinking they correspond quite well to the practices that must have taken place within a doctrine that claimed to be esoteric and that had recourse to arithmomantic and gematric procedures. Our aim has been simply to point out a methodologically quite different way of proceeding, since we are dealing with esoteric teachings, and early Imamism was unquestionably esoteric. The Imamite authors appear to have been wanting to demonstrate that within such a doctrine silence about a subject (in this case everything that has to do with the identity of the twelfth imam), or making it abstruse, does not necessarily prove the non-existence or lack of knowledge about the subject; and all the more so, since keeping the secret (*al-taqiyya*) and the deliberate and discreet dispersion of information (*tabdîd al-'ilm*) have remained two constants in the doctrine.

IV-2. THE IMAM AND HIS OCCULTATION: ESOTERIC ASPECTS

The future arrival of the Mahdî constitutes the most frequent of the imams' predictions. Al-Kulaynî and al-Nu'mânî each dedicated an entire chapter to it, and Ibn Bâbûye devoted thirteen chapters to the predictions of the Prophet, Fâtima, and the eleven imams regarding the twelfth imam.[578] The twelfth imam is said to have been born under conditions the description of which is imbued with mysticism and the miraculous. Imamite sources have given the hidden imam's mother a number of names; the name seen most often is Narjis (narcissus), but she has also been called Rayḥâna (basil), Sawsan (lily) and Maryam (Mary).[579] According to some accounts, she was a black slave, probably from Nubia;[580] other accounts present her as the granddaughter of the Byzantine emperor, himself a descendent of the Apostle Simon.[581] According to this version, the Byzantine princess was captured by Muslim armies and sold as a slave to Baghdad, to a man in the entourage of the tenth imam, a certain Bishr b. Sulaymân al-Nakhkhâs. The latter went to Sâmarrâ, and gave the slave to Ḥakîma, his teacher's sister. Just before being captured, the princess, whose name at the time was Malîka bint Yashû'â, had seen Mary, the mother of Jesus, and Fâṭima in a dream; they both asked her to convert to Islam and to allow herself to be captured by the Muslim troops, since she was destined for a glorious life. The legendary and hagiographical nature of this version seems patent.[582] What does seem certain is that the mother of the twelfth imam had been a slave; in the first place, the names that have been given for her are almost all the names of flowers or plants, as was the case for female slaves.

Next, in several traditions there is a parallel established between Fâṭima, "the mother of the imams," and Narjis, "the mother of the *Qâ'im*"; the former is called "the Great Lady of free women" (*sayyidat al-nisâ'*) or "the best of free women" (*khiyarat al-ḥarâ'ir*), and the latter "the Great Lady (or "the best") of slaves" (*sayyida/khiyarat al-imâ'*).[583] The tenth imam, who through clairvoyance recognized in her the future mother of the Mahdî, gave her in marriage to his son, al-Ḥasan, the future eleventh imam.[584] Her signs of pregnancy, as has been mentioned, were miraculously hidden. Still according to the account of Ḥakîma (the eleventh imam's aunt, who was present at the birth), just before the child's birth, a kind of torpor fell over both women;[585] or, according to another version, a kind of veil hid the mother from the eyes of the other woman present.[586] The actual moment of birth was thus seen by no one. Once the child was born, Ḥakîma, now in full possession of her senses, realized that the birth clothing of the mother was not stained by a single drop of blood, as is the case with all the mothers of the imams, she added.[587] As we have seen, "the hidden birth" is one of the distinctive signs of the Mahdî, according to he imams. Furthermore, let it be remembered that the conception of any imam—and such is the case with the twelfth, also—is accompanied by a number of mystical or magical signs: the supernatural abilities of the newborn imam and the occult phenomena that take place at the time of his birth or thereafter; the seed of the imam coming from a mysterious beverage that a celestial Messenger has his father drink; the Qur'anic phrase "And the Verb of your Lord was accomplished in all truth and justice" written by the angel al-Ḥayawân on the child's body; the appearance of the "Column of Light" before the newborn's eyes, thus bestowing the power of clairvoyance upon him; the fact that the imam is born clean and circumcised and receives inspiration beginning at the moment of his birth, and so forth. The twelfth imam enjoys the same providential privileges. Ibn Bâbûye adds further details to the moment of the Mahdî's birth.[588] The child was born in the position of prostration; the father took his newborn son in his arms and put his tongue into his mouth, an occult way of transmitting the Knowledge of the imams, as we have seen.

A light shot forth from the top of the child's head and went up to the heights of the sky. The father commanded his son to speak. The son then said: "I bear witness that there is no god but God, He is alone and there is none associated with Him, Muḥammad is the Messenger of God," the three sacred phrases, each containing twelve letters. The child then greeted each of the eleven preceding imams one by one, finishing with the Qur'anic verses "We have wanted to show favor to the weak upon the earth, and to make them imams, and to make them inheritors/We have wanted to establish them on earth, and to show Pharaoh and Hâmân [Pharaoh's minister, according to the Qur'an] and their armies that which they feared."[589] Ḥakîma continues to recount that then a bird came and unfolded its wings over the head of the child, and in turn put his tongue into the mouth of the newborn child. Other birds arrived, fluttering over the holy family. Then the father addressed the first bird, "Take him, protect him, and bring him back to us every forty days."[590] The bird took the child and flew off, followed by the other birds. Then the father exclaimed: "God entrusted you to the one to whom the mother of Moses entrusted her son."[591] Then, in reply to Ḥakîma's question, he said that the bird is actually the Holy Spirit whose duty it is to look after the imams, to help and guide them, and to confer Knowledge to them [var: "and adorn them with Science]."[592] After forty days, the great aunt returned to the eleventh imam's house; she saw a child walking. She was so astounded that she could not help saying that the child was at least two years old. The father replied: "The children of the prophets and the Inheritors, when they are imams themselves, grow differently from other children. Our son had the same growth in one month that others have in one year; our son began to speak, to recite the Qur'an, and to worship his Lord when he was still in his mother's womb. . . . "[593]

The great compilers collected numerous statements about the childhood of the twelfth imam from the disciples of the eleventh imam who claimed to have seen the child before his first Occultation.[594] During some of these encounters a miracle was performed, most often in the form of an incisive remark from the young imam that erased any doubt from the mind of the disciple. We offer one typical example. Aḥmad b. Isḥâq al-Ash'arî[595] recounts that he was at the eleventh imam's house to ask him about his successor. Before his question was even formulated, the imam, "reading his mind" [*fa-qâla lî mubtadi'an*, lit. "he said to me first," that is, "before I had even worded my question"], told him that the earth can never remain devoid of an imam, and that thanks to this last one, life on earth can go on. He then went into a room and came out with a child who looked about three years old upon his shoulders. The imam addressed the disciple again, explaining that because of his fidelity to the cause of the imams he was being allowed to see the child; he told him that the child had the same name and the same *kunya* as the Prophet, that he was the Mahdî, "he who will fill the earth with equity and justice, just as it is now filled with oppression and injustice [or darkness]."[596] He said also that the case of this child would be similar to those of Khiḍr and Dhû'l-qarnayn, who were hidden from the eyes of men, and that no one would believe in him other than his faithful whose faith had been strengthened by God. Al-Ash'arî asked for a convincing sign (*'alâma*). Then the child began to speak in eloquent Arabic: "I am the Remainder of God on his earth,[597] I am God's vengeance against his enemies, and you, o Aḥmad b. Isḥâq, demand no more signs after having seen with your eyes."

The disciple left full of joy. The following day, again at his master's house, he learned from him that the Mahdî would have a long Occultation. Finally, the eleventh imam finished his explanation with the following words: " . . . Aḥmad b. Isḥâq! Here is a Cause that is part of God's Cause, a Secret of

God's Secret, a Mystery of God's Mystery; receive what I have offered you, conceal it and be thankful, for tomorrow you shall be with us, in Paradise Most High."[598]

According to the tradition, the twelfth imam entered into his first Occultation as a child, at the time of his father's death in 260/874.[599] During the minor Occultation, the hidden imam communicated with his faithful via four representatives (*nâ 'ib/wakîl /safîr*):

1) Abû ʿAmr ʿUthmân b. Saʿîd al-ʿUmarî (or al-ʿAmrî), "representative" from 260/874 to 267/880 (although this latter date is uncertain).

2) Abû Jaʿfar Md b. ʿUthmân al-ʿUmarî (al-ʿAmrî), the son of the above, from 267/880 (uncertain date) until 305/917.

3) Abû l-Qâsim al-Ḥusayn b. Rawḥ al-Nawbakhtî, from 305/917 to 326/937.

4) Abû l-Ḥasan ʿAlî b. Md al-Sumirrî, from 326/937 to 329/941.

There is no need to go over the life and personalities of the four "representatives"; much has been written about them,[600] but as usual, such writing tends to be from a "rationalist" kind of hagiographical perspective (the learned Imamites) or from the never-ceasing "sociopolitical" view (of scholars who write in Western languages). A closer look at the early texts brings to light the fact that the essential activities of the "representatives" consisted in making sure that the canonical precepts were respected by the faithful, in collecting and distributing legal taxes; in taking the faithful's questions of a religious order to the hidden imam, then making public the imam's responses; and finally, in convincing the faithful who were prone to perplexity and confusion (during the period called the *ḥayra*) by performing "miracles."

To our knowledge, no one has yet written about the "supernatural powers" of the "representatives," even though these powers were considered to result from the teaching of the hidden imam, and were perceived as irrefutable proofs of the veracity of both the sayings of the earlier imams, and of the "representatives" when talking about the hidden imam. At the same time, the powers were assurance for skeptics who doubted the authenticity of the "representatives." Through accounts collected primarily by Ibn Bâbûye in his *Kamâl al-dîn*, the following details about the occult powers of the "representatives" may be gleaned; these details are most often found in long and sometimes boring accounts of an encounter between the faithful and one of the "representatives." The faithful bring gifts for the hidden imam, or problems of a religious order to be solved. They are thus forced to pass through the "representative" as an intermediary. By looking at these details we are able to see several miraculous powers attributed to the "representatives." The subject is of particular interest because it gives us an idea of what early Imamism considered to be the result of initiation by the imams; moreover, we find in them a number of the imams' miraculous powers (*aʿâjîb*) that we have already had occasion to examine. We thus still find ourselves within the boundaries of Imamology. Once again, we are dealing with well-known phenomena in occult traditions.

—*Powers of divination and clairvoyance*: A faithful Muslim who had collected the *zakât* from the people of his region realized, even before arriving at the home of the first "representative," ʿUthmân b. Saʿîd, that some of the money was missing; he secretly added the difference out of his own pocket. The *safîr* took the money, but returned the sum added to its owner.[601] The second "representative," Ibn ʿUthmân, knew the exact contents of a hermetically sealed box brought from a faraway place.[602] One of the faithful brought the same *safîr* what he legally owed. The *safîr*, instead of collecting it, asked the man to take the whole sum to Wâsiṭ and to give it to the first person he met along the bank of the river. Perplexed, the man carried out the order. The first person he met when he got out of the boat in Wâsiṭ told him that he needed a certain amount of money, which corresponded exactly to the amount being carried, for the funeral services of a faithful believer.[603] A believer wanted to take the third *safîr*, al-Ḥusayn b. Rawḥ, his legal taxes in the form of gold ingots. A resident of Balkh, in Transoxiania, he set out; when he reached Sarakhs, in Khurâsân, he stopped in the desert. In Hamadân, in western Iran, he realized that he had lost one of his ingots; he bought a new one, and presented all of them to the "representative" in Medina. The *safîr* returned the ingot purchased in Hamadân, and said that the lost gold could be found in a certain place in the Sarakhs desert, and that it was safely covered by sand. On the return trip the believer found the ingot at the place specified, and later gave it to the fourth "representative."[604]

—*The knowledge of languages*: The "representatives" speak with the faithful from different regions, or even different countries, in their own languages or dialects.[605]

—*Mindreading, and writing at a distance*: A faithful believer had a religious question to ask the second "representative." Before he sent the question he had written down, he received a letter with the answer to the question. After he read the letter, another question came to mind; he immediately saw the answer appear on the same paper.[606]

—*Materialization*: An Imamite woman who had doubts about the authenticity of the status of the third *safîr* went to his house to test him. She asked him whether he could tell her what she was carrying. The "representative" told her to go to the bank of the Tigris and to throw what she was carrying into it. The woman did so, and returned. Al-Nawbakhtî then asked one of his servants to bring a package. He opened it and the woman saw that the package contained the small box closed with a key that she had just thrown into the river. The *safîr* then began to list in detail all the contents of the still-closed box. The woman opened it, and everyone present saw that the "representative" had not made the slightest error.[607]

—*Knowledge of the "Science of letters."*[608]

—*Supersensual communication with the hidden imam*: The faithful asked their questions through the third "representative." One of them began to doubt and wondered to himself whether he should trust the *safîr*'s responses, and whether the responses were approved by the hidden imam. The "representative," reading his thoughts, told him that none of the responses came from either him or his personal opinions, but that being in communication with the hidden imam, all he did was repeat what he heard.[609]

The "miraculous powers" of the *safîr* were perceived by the Imamite religious conscience, not as exploits or individual merits, but as the result of the direct teaching of the imam; this would corroborate the idea that we have already stated, according to which the imams initiated their particularly intimate disciples into the sacred Knowledge that made the "miracles" possible.

Around 329/941, the fourth "representative" received a last autograph note from the hidden imam:

> In the name of God, the Compassionate, the Merciful; 'Alî b. Muḥammad al-Simarrî, may God increase, through you, the reward of your brothers [in religion; that is, the Shî'ites]; yes, your death will take place in six days. Prepare yourself, and name no one as your successor [as "representative"] after your death. Here is the advent of the second Occultation [var. the complete Occultation] in which there will be no more manifestation, except if it be with divine permission, and that will not take place but after a long time, when hearts will be hardened and the earth filled with violence. Among my partisans, some will claim to having seen [me] with their eyes [as was the case with the "representatives"]. Beware! He who claims to have seen [me] with his eyes before the raising of al-Sufyânî and [the sounding of] the Cry [two signs, precursors to the End of Time and the Return of the Mahdî; cf. later discussion] is a liar and an impostor. Greatness and Power belong to God alone.

Six days later al-Simarrî, on his death bed, was asked, "Who will be your successor?" He replied, "From this point on the matter is in God's hands; He will conduct it Himself." Those were his last words.[610] This letter is of the utmost importance to the historical and doctrinal destiny of Imamism. It signals the beginning of the major Occultation that will last until the Return of the Mahdî, "the Lord of Time" (*ṣâḥib al-zamân*). The axis around which all Imamite "religion" revolves was hidden, and the faithful no longer had at their head either a physical Guide or a "representative" who could put them in contact with him.

At this juncture, it might be useful to introduce the reasons that Imamite tradition gives for the Occultation; they fall into four categories:[611]

1. Safeguarding the life of the twelfth imam; a whole series of traditions, some of which are attributed to the Prophet, maintain the necessity of the *Qâʾim*'s Occultation, as his life was in danger.[612]
2. Independence vis-à-vis temporal powers. It is said that through his Occultation the Mahdî will owe allegiance to no temporal power.[613] In a letter from his own hand (*tawqîʿa*), the hidden imam wrote: " . . . Regarding the reason for the Occultation, know that God, may He be exalted and glorified, said: 'O you who believe! Do not ask about things that would do you harm if they were unveiled' [Qurʾan 5:102]; none of my ancestors [the preceding imams] was able to avoid pledging allegiance to some oppressor of his time [*ṭâghiya zamânih*], but when I rise up I will have no allegiance to oppressors. . . . "[614]
3. Putting "believers," that is, Imamites, to the test. The Occultation is a long period of trial, a challenge to their faith. The seventh imam, Mûsä, said: "The Occultation of the Lord of this Cause is inevitable so that those who profess this cause may withdraw from it. This is a painful test that God has given to His creatures."[615] Jaʿfar, the sixth imam, said: "The Lord of the Cause will inevitably have an Occultation, and during it all who are frivolous will experience overbearing doubt."[616]
4. Finally, there is a hidden reason for the Occultation, a reason that is said to be the most important of all, although it will not be revealed until the Return of the Mahdî at the End of Time. ʿAbdAllâh b. al-Faḍl[617] asked Jaʿfar the deep reason (lit. "the aspect of wisdom" *wajh al-ḥikma*) for the Occultation. The imam replied: "The deep reason is the same as the reason for God's Tests and the Occultations that came before. The deep reason will not be unveiled until after [the Mahdî's] manifestation, exactly in the same way that the deep reason for the sabotage of the ship, for the murder of the young man, and for the construction of the wall by al-Khiḍr was not revealed to Moses until later, after their separation. Son of al-Faḍl, this is a Cause that is

part of God's Cause, a Secret of God's Secret, a Mystery of God's Mystery; when we know that God is Wise, we are certain that all His acts contain wisdom, even if this wisdom remains hidden."[618]

IV-3. THE RETURN AND THE RISING: ESOTERIC ASPECTS

According to Twelver tradition from as early as the fourth/tenth century, the hidden imam is living in his physical body, providentially endowed with a long life. The compilations of al-Kulaynî, al-Nu'mânî, and Ibn Bâbûye, to name only the oldest and the best known, contain a number of eyewitness accounts from people who were able to meet the twelfth imam; the imam appeared as a young man, and his resemblance to Jesus Christ, in both appearance and manner, has been noted more than once.[619] To support the physical aspect of the existence and presence of the hidden imam, Ibn Bâbûye dedicates six chapters of his *Kamâl al-dîn* to those known for their extraordinarily long lives in the Arabic tradition, and he reports words from the imams to the effect that a number of earlier prophets had lived incredibly long lives.[620] There was undoubtedly also a "spiritualistic" aspect of the imam's situation at the time, although it appears to have been of significantly less importance and was quickly forgotten.[621]

As has been stated, accounts of encounters with the hidden imam have been numerous. The general tone of these accounts might best be conveyed by the following, "typical" story: two Imamites were making the annual pilgrimage to Mecca. Upon their arrival at al-Mawqif [in 'Arafât], they met a young man sitting down, finely dressed and with no evidence of having made a long trip. A beggar happened by, and was quickly chased away by the two men. He then went over to the young man, who bent over, picked up a handful of earth, and gave it to the beggar. While the beggar was involved in long and touching thanksgiving, the young man stood up and disappeared. Intrigued, the two Imamites went over to the beggar, who showed them the large piece of gold that he had just received. The two pilgrims then realized that they had met the hidden imam without recognizing him. They quickly began to search for him, but in vain. They asked people in the vicinity about him, but were told that the young man was an 'Alid who came to the pilgrimage on foot every year.[622] In the traditions of the imams, it is also said that the hidden Mahdî attends the annual pilgrimage to Mecca, and that he sees people even if they cannot see him.[623] This might be thought of as an invisible presence, although according to other traditions, the hidden imam is visibly present, but incognito.[624] In this latter case, he is compared to Joseph (Qur'an, sura 12, Yûsuf), seen but not recognized by his brothers; it is added that, as in Joseph's case, God can allow him to be recognized by some people. Invisible or incognito, the presence of the hidden imam has a beneficent effect on the faithful; his influence is compared to an illumination, or to rays of light; the Prophet is said to have stated:

" . . . His faithful are illumined by his Light; they profit from his *walâya* during his Occultation, just as one profits from the sun even when it is covered by clouds."[625] In one of his letters, the twelfth imam wrote: " . . . Regarding how to benefit from my presence [lit. "benefit from me"] during my Occultation, it is like the benefit that one draws from the sun when it is hidden from view by the clouds."[626] It seems that this radiant effusion of the hidden imam takes place in an occult and mysterious fashion, since, after its presentation, it is added that the effusion of light is a Sealed Secret and a Hidden Treasure of God's Knowledge, and that it must be hidden from those who are not worthy.[627] The occult presence of the Mahdî dominates the entire religious consciousness of Imamism during the period of the Occultation, and will do so until the Return of the Awaited Savior.

Let us now look at the circumstances and reasons for this Return. The return, as well as the Rising of the Qâ'im, will be preceded by signs. The theme of "signs of the Return" is one of the most developed of those that occur in collections of hadith, in both Sunni and Shî'ite literature.[628] Moreover, it happens that when an important historical event takes place (a revolt, a far-reaching insurrection, the beginning of a dynasty, the enthronement of a caliph after a troubled period), traditions concerning "signs of the Return" are forged; these traditions correspond to certain events, and tend to identify, in the public's mind, the Mahdî promised by the Prophet as the main protagonist. At any rate, in the flurry of details, certain constant "signs" can be seen, and these signs fall generally into two categories: "signs of general or universal order" and "signs about specific events or details."

1) The universal sign of the Return consists in the generalized invasion of the earth by Evil, the victory of the forces of Evil over those of Good, thus requiring in some way the manifestation of the eschatological Savior, for if he does not come, all of humanity will be engulfed in darkness.[629] This general theme is a constant; what changes according to doctrines, ideologies, or historical events, are the faces of the Evil, the events that accompany it. The imams in turn have numerous comments on the different aspects of the Evil that will envelop the earth at the End of Time. What follows is parts of a long sermon by 'Alî b. Abî Ṭâlib who, we believe, both summarizes and incorporates into his words the early Imamite data on this subject:

> The Sign [of the Return] consists of the following: people will be neglectful of prayer, they will squander what has been left to them, they will make untruthfulness lawful, they will practice usury, they will accept bribes, construct tall buildings, sell religion in order to win this lower world; they will employ idiots, consult women, break family ties, obey passions, and consider bloodshed insignificant. Magnanimity will be considered a weakness, and injustice will be gloried in; princes will live in debauchery, and ministers will be

> oppressors; the scholars will be traitors, and readers [of the Qur'an] will live in vice. Bearing false witness will take place openly, and immoralities will be proclaimed aloud. Speech will be calumny, sin, and exaggeration. Sacred volumes will be decorated, mosques will be ornate, and minarets elongated; criminals will be boasted of, lines of combat will be close, hearts will be in discord, and pacts will be broken. . . . Women, covetous of the riches of this world, will go into business with their husbands; the voices of vile men will be loud, and they will be harkened. Those least noble will be the leaders of the people; the debauched will be feared because of the harm they may cause, the liar taken as telling the truth, and the traitor as one's confidant. Singing women and musical instruments will be common . . . and women will ride upon horseback; they will look like men, and men will look like women. . . . People will prefer the activities of this world to the World Beyond, and they will cover hearts of wolves with the skins of sheep. . . . [630]

Obviously, what characterizes the world just prior to the coming of the Mahdî is the loss of the meaning of the sacred, the obliteration of all that connects man to God and to his neighbor, general failure in the observance of religious precepts and moral duties, turning human values upside down. In this somewhat somber picture Shî'ites are not necessarily any better off than others. Only a small minority of them, the "true Shî'ites"—that is, those who have been initiated to the teaching of the imams—will be spared from the clutches of Evil, but even the "true Shî'ites" will experience the persecution that their coreligionists will experience.

We have already noted that one of the reasons for the Occultation was precisely that of testing the faithful Imamites. Ja'far said: "This event [that is, the Return of the imam] will not take place until some of you spit in the faces of others, until some of you damn others and treat them as liars."[631] And al-Bâqir said: "O partisans of the Prophet's family, you will be erased like kohl is wiped off eyelids. You know when kohl is applied to your eyes, but you do not know when it will be wiped off. Likewise, man will rise up by being faithful to a teaching of our Cause, and will go to bed abandoning it, or he will go to bed being faithful and will wake up a negator."[632] The sixth imam summons his partisans with these words: "By God, you will be shattered like glass [*al-zujâj*], but since glass is treated, it rebecomes what it was. By God, you will be shattered like dry clay [*al-fakhkhâr*], and clay, once shattered, never again becomes what it was. By God, you will be severely sifted, and clearly distinguished one from another. By God, you will be completely purified until there is nothing left of you but a minority."[633] As has been seen, this minority consists of those "whose hearts have been tested by God for faith," those who are held up by the strength of their *walâya*, their Certitude, and their Knowledge.

2) The "universal signs" aside, the compilations listed a great number of "particular signs" that announced the manifestation of the Mahdî. Five of these occur with such frequency that they were referred to as "the five signs" (*al-ʿalâmât al-khams*). We do no more than outline them here, as they have been studied at length.[634]

1. The "revolt of the Sufyânite" (*khurûj al-Sufyânî*); probably a descendent of Abû Sufyân, the father of the Umayyad caliph Muʿâwiya, who will head an army formed by the "enemies of the imams."
2. The "counter-revolt of the Yemenite" (*khurûj al-Yamânî*); the Yemenite will oppose the Sufyânite.
3. "The Cry" (*al-ṣayḥa/al-nidâʾ*); it appears as though there will actually be two "cries" of supernatural origin that will be heard before the coming of the Mahdî. One cry will come from the sky, calling men to defend the Cause of the imam, and the other will come from the depths of the earth (sometimes this is seen as the voice of Iblîs), inviting people to join the ranks of the Enemy of the Imam; these cries will be heard during the month of Ramaḍân.
4. "The assassination of the Pure Soul" (*qatl al-nafs al-zakiyya*); might this be, as some have believed, the assassination of the Ḥasanid Muḥammad b. ʿAbdAllâh, who is called al-Nafs al-Zakiyya, killed in 145/762 in an armed revolt against the Abbasids?[635] Did the imams foresee the Return as being imminent? This is not probable, especially since in some traditions al-Nafs al-Zakiyya is not spoken of, but merely al-Nafs.[636]
5. "The swallowing up of the army" (*khasf al-jaysh*); an army composed of the adversaries of the Mahdî will be swallowed up by the earth (according to some traditions, this will take place on the plain between Mecca and Medina).

The Mahdî will thus return to combat and eradicate the Evil that has invaded the earth at the End of Time. When the traditions concerning the mission of the Mahdî are examined, it can be seen that the final Combat takes place for three principal reasons. Here again we must keep in mind different elements of the early Imamite doctrine and adopt a synoptic view of the doctrine in order to see it coherently. In the pages that follow, these elements will be pointed out as they arise.

1) There is first of all what might be called the "historical" reason. The Qâʾim returns to avenge the death of al-Ḥusayn. In a number of traditions, it is said that after the massacre at Karbalâʾ the angels broke out in sobs and went to wail before God, asking Him whether He was going to let the assassination

of "His Chosen One," "The Son of his Messenger," go unpunished. God replied that the revenge would take place when the Qâ'im had his triumphal return.[637] In other traditions, it is the angel Gabriel who informs the Prophet of the tragic fate of his grandson, adding that al-Ḥusayn will be avenged by his own ninth descendent, the Qâ'im.[638] According to the imams, the fact of separating ʿAlî, the only true initiate of the Prophet, from power, and rejecting his version of the Qur'an, the only complete version, struck a fatal blow to Islam as a community religion for the salvation of humanity; but the real coup de grace was the assassination of al-Ḥusayn. The Muslim Community, with the exception of the small minority that remained faithful to the teachings of the imams, was thenceforth a Community composed of "enemies" of the imams and their partisans. With the assassination of a divine initiate, especially one who was the grandson and inheritor of the Prophet, "official Islam" condemned itself to flounder in violence, corruption, and oppression. This is why, in order to reestablish order and justice, one of the aspects of the final mission of the Mahdî consists in avenging al-Ḥusayn's death; in this way, majority Islam can be purged of the most despicable crime that it has ever committed.

2) The second reason is of a religious order. The Qâ'im returns to reestablish the lost meaning of the sacred. First, he will reestablish Islam in its original purity and integrity. Since the rejection of ʿAlî's integral version of the Qur'an, Muslims have "lost the sacred Word." We have seen that this version will be brought back by the Mahdî at the time of his Return; he will thus return to Islam its abandoned, forgotten Word.[639] This is where the famous prophetic tradition reported by the imams comes into play: "In the beginning, Islam was unknown, and it will again become unknown. Happy are the unknown," to which the imams add: "At the time of his Rising, our Qâ'im will again start a Call, as the Prophet God's Messenger did."[640] The Mahdî will also restore other religions, likewise abandoned and disfigured, to their original truth; in effect, it is said that he will take out of his cave, where they are hidden, all the holy Books of the earlier prophets, and that he will have their principles followed by their faithful.[641] Thus, he will repair the Evil caused by religious degeneration.

3) The third is a reason of a spiritual order: the Mahdî returns to bring Wisdom (*al-ḥikma*) and the hidden spiritual meaning of the celestial Books (*al-ta'wîl/al-tafsîr*; both words are used) to humanity.[642] Let us remember also that, because of the Mahdî, human beings will recover their Hiero-Intelligence, their *ʿaql*, that "interior imam" that resides within human beings, the luminous organ of sacred apperception seated in the heart. This third reason completes the second in the sense that the religions reestablished by the Mahdî will no longer be mere exoteric dogmas, but they will be spiritual esoteric teachings at the same time. This is the universal initiation by the imam of all human beings into the secrets of existence and those of their own religion, and it is undoubtedly in this sense that that we are supposed to take the defini-

tion of the word Mahdî given by the fifth imam, al-Bâqir: "The Mahdî ["the Guided One"] is so called because he will lead (*yahdî*) to a secret Teaching."[643] Thus, the awaited Imam (*al-muntaẓar*) will be the Instrument of both divine Vengeance and divine Wisdom, preparing the earth for the final court of the Resurrection.

Other details of an esoteric nature also mark the Return of the twelfth imam. These details are seen especially in traditions concerning the "companions" of the Qâʾim at the time of his Rising. Let it be said at the outset that according to Imamite doctrine a certain number of individuals will come back to life to assist the Mahdî in his mission at the time of his Return. The names of a number of great religious personalities are seen in the traditions, although three names are found much more commonly than others: al-Ḥusayn b. ʿAlî, Jesus Christ, and Ishmael "faithful to his promises" (*Ismâʿîl ṣâdiq al-waʿd*).[644] According to the Imamite view, these three divine figures have in common the fact that they were the victims of impiety and the violence of their people; they are all in some way symbols of the crime of a Community against God. Besides them, the Qâʾim will be accompanied by an Army (*jund*). Careful examination of the relevant traditions shows that the Qâʾim's army is composed of three kinds of "aides":

—The angels. Al-Bâqir said: "At the time of the Rising of the Qâʾim, God will have him assisted by "Angels-who-mark" (*al-musawwimîn*; cf. Qurʾan 3:125, regarding the Battle of Badr), the "Angels-one-after-another" (*al-murdifîn*; cf. Qurʾan 8:9, still about the Battle of Badr), the "Angels-descended-from-on-High" (*al-munzalîn*; cf. Qurʾan 3:124), and "the Cherubim" (*al-karrubiyyîn*). Gabriel will stand before him, Michael at his right, and Seraphiel at his left."[645] In a long account of a vision that he had of the coming of the Mahdî, Jaʿfar said at one point: " . . . 9000 angels descend [from the sky], and another 313 angels . . . [the first] are those that accompanied Noah in the Ark, and Abraham when he was thrown into the fire, and Moses when the waters of the sea were parted for him, and Jesus when God raised him up to Him. There are also the 4000 'Angels-who-mark' [or, in Qurʾan 3:125, it is 5000 *musawwimîn*] who were with the Prophet and the 313 angels that accompanied him the day of the Battle of Badr [one angel per combattant? Under these circumstances Qurʾan 8:9 would be talking about 1000 angels]. . . . "[646] Just like the great prophets at the time of the big tests of their missions, the Mahdî will be assisted by angels at the time of his Battle. As will be seen, the similarity with the Battle of Badr is constant. Badr is seen as being the first great victory of Muslims led by the Prophet against unbelievers. In a way, it represents the beginning of the establishment of Islam. The battle of the Qâʾim will mark the final victory of the "believers" against their "enemies" and the definitive and universal establishment of the "religion" of the imams. The first universally founded exotericism, and the second will universally establish esotericism.

—Next, there is "the Terror" (*al-ruʿb*). Although the traditions remain discreet, this nevertheless appears to be a terrifying celestial entity who aids the Mahdî in his mission by "marching" with his Army.[647]

—The third is "the believers" (*al-mu'minûn*) who constitute "the troops" (*jaysh*) of the Mahdî. In comparison to the two other categories of "companions of the Qâ'im's Army," the early corpus of the imams provides significantly more information about these troops. The men who make them up are called "Companions of the Qâ'im" (*aṣḥab al-qâ'im*), "people of sincerity" (*ahl al-ikhlâṣ*), "the sincerely devoted" (*al-khullaṣ*), or sometimes "the troops of anger" (*jaysh al-ghaḍab*). In number they are the same as the combattants of Badr, 313, and it is said that, just like the troops at Badr, "they will not be killed, nor will they die" before winning victory.[648] None, or very few, of them are Arabs.[649] In fact, a number of the eschatological traditions of the imams have a pronounced anti-Arab flavor; one is certainly led to think that, according to the Imamite vision, those who are truly responsible for the decline of religion, from the separation of ʿAlî from power to the persecution and even assassination of the imams and their faithful, were the Arabs. In the descriptions of the coming of the Mahdî and the battle against the "enemies" there are frequent phrases like "unhappiness for the Arabs," "unhappiness for the Arabs from the Evil that is coming," "Our Qâ'im will have no pity for the Arabs," "Between the Qâ'im and the Arabs there will be only the sword," "Between us and the Arabs there will be nothing but slaughter."[650] Nearly all, if not all, of the Companions of the Mahdî are "non-Arabs" or "Persians" (according to both meanings of the word *ʿajam* at the time).[651] Jaʿfar is even supposed to have claimed that "they are like sun worshippers and moon worshippers (*shibh ʿabadat al-shams wa l-qamar*)," and according to a tradition attributed to al-Bâqir, they originally came from the Orient (*al-mashriq*).[652] The Mahdî's troops are made up of initiated warriors, at least according to the information in which each of the 313 Companions bears a sword inscribed with "a thousand words, each of which gives access to a thousand others"; we know that this is the usual expression referring to Imamite initiation.[653] Other information, of a magical order, confirms this, and we now know to what extent the initiatory and the magical are linked in early Imamism. At the time of his Rising, the 313 men will be dispersed to all parts of the world; the Qâ'im will bring them instantly together in Mecca through the power of God's "Hebrew name," that is, the "Supreme Name." Regarding this, Jaʿfar says: "After receiving permission [to manifest himself], the [hidden] imam will pronounce the Hebrew name of God; then his Companions,

313 in all, will gather around him in Mecca, in the same way that small clouds come together in the autumn."[654] Commentating on the Qur'anic verse "Vie with one another to do good works; wherever you are, God will join you all together" (Qur'an 2:148), the fifth imam said: "The 'good works' (*al-khayrât*) are faithful Love for the imam (*al-walâya*); "wherever you are, God will join you all together" refers to the Companions of the Qâ'im, the 313 who will gather together in an hour like clouds bank together in the autumn."[655] The comparison with clouds is not insignificant. The "displacement" of the Companions of the Troops is reminiscent in many ways of the "magic flight" in occult traditions. 'Alî Zayn al-'Âbidîn says: "313 men, the number of those who fought at Badr, will disappear from their beds and awaken in Mecca; this is the meaning of the divine words 'wherever you are, God will join you all together'; they are the companions of the Qâ'im."[656] Speaking about the same verse, Ja'far al-Ṣâdiq said: "This verse refers to the Companions of the Qâ'im. . . . Some of those who will disappear from their beds during the night and wake up in Mecca in the morning will march upon the clouds. Their names and their fathers' names, their qualities (*ḥilya*) and their ancestorship (*nasab*) are known [to us]."[657] We have seen that "magic displacement" and "walking upon clouds" were some of the supernatural powers of the imams, and we may assume that the 313 Companions were initiated to these powers. Other prodigious gifts are also attributed to them: once gathered in Mecca, their swords will descend from the sky marked with their names and the names of their fathers.[658] All or part of them [depending on the tradition] will be sent by the imam to different parts of the earth, where they will rule over absolutely everything, where even the birds and the wild animals will obey them.[659] When they have difficult decisions to make, the imam will give them instructions and directions that will appear written on the palms of their hands; they will only have to look and carry out the order.[660] Writing "something" on their feet, they will acquire the power to walk on water, and it is said that, seeing this miracle, the inhabitants of Constantinople (Qusṭanṭîniyya) will open the gates to the city.[661] The Mahdî's Army can only win. Let us remember that the hidden imam also has what he inherited from his predecessors, the objects with the magical powers that belonged to the prophets: Adam's cloak, the Seal of Solomon, the Staff and the Ark of the Covenant from Moses . . . and especially Muḥammad's invincible weapon.[662] When they see the triumphal march of the Army of Salvation, thousands of faithful will rejoin its ranks.[663] The Ememy will be exterminated once and for all, the earth will be embellished with Justice, man will be resuscitated by the light of Initiation. And what will happen then? We know that the Mahdî will prepare the world for the Resurrection, and that according to different versions current in different doctrines, a more

or less short time will pass between the victory of the Mahdî and the Last Judgment. In early Imamite tradition it is reported that the Qâ'im will reign for 19 years and some months, after which he will die.[664] However, according to a long *ḥadîth qudsî* reported a number of different times by Ibn Bâbûye, the power will remain in the hands of the Friends (*awliyâ'*), that is, the initiates in the Imamite sense of the word, until the Day of Resurrection.[665] And, according to a curious tradition from al-Bâqir, the reign of these "men of the imams" (*rijâl minnâ ahl al-bayt*, lit. "the men who from among us people of the House of the Prophet") will last "313 years and 9 years more."[666]

From now until that End of Time, during the increasingly more gloomy period of the Occultation, the faithful Imamite is invited to arm himself with unshakable patience. Numerous are the invitations to "wait for the joyous Deliverance" (*intiẓar al-faraj*) and the injunctions against "haste" (*isti'jâl*) or the "determination of the time" (*tawqît*) on the part of the faithful. In the imams' traditions of a more eschatological nature, phrases like "the hurried [lit. "the race horses"] are condemned to perdition" (*halakat al-maḥâḍîr*), "those who state a time [for the Return] are liars" (*kadhaba l-waqqâtûn*), "those who are in a hurry are lost and those who are submissive [to God's Will] are saved" (*halaka l-musta'jilûn wa najâ l-musallimûn*).[667] The tenor of these traditions suggests that what is demanded of the faithful involves three things: a religious level, submission to the Divine Will; an esoteric level, keeping the secret regarding the date of the Return of the hidden imam;[668] and finally a "political level," taking an apolitical, passive stance.[669]

The faithful Imamite should thus wait patiently, but this wait should be accompanied, as we have seen, by the strength of his faithul Love (*walâya*), supported by the search for Certitude (*yaqîn*) and for Knowledge (*ma'rifa*), so that he can know his Imam, for "the advancement or the delay of this matter [that is, the Return] brings no prejudgment upon him who knows his Imam," for "he who knows his Imam is already under the tent of the awaited imam,"[670] for such a faithful believer is already "resuscitated" by the Knowledge of his Imam. It is undoubtedly in this eschatological and soteriological context that these words —unfailingly repeated throughout their teachings— should be taken. They are words that warn against the danger of perdition for those who do not know their Divine Guide: "He who dies without an Imam [or "without having known his Imam] dies the death of the "ignorant pagans."[671]

Conclusions

> The People of my Family
> are like Noah's Ark;
> Whoever boards the Ark is saved,
> Whoever stays away is carried off by the waves.
> The Prophet

"The Imam-Proof existed before the creatures, he exists with them, and he will exist after them."[672] The Imam, the Divine Guide, in both his cosmic, ontological aspect and his historical aspect, dominates and determines the Imamite "world vision." Here, religious conscience perceives creation through the "filter" that the Imam is, in a dizzying vision that goes from a cosmogonic pre-existence to an eschatological superexistence. Without the Imam, the universe would crumble, since he is the Proof, the Manifestation, and the Organ of God, and he is the Means by which human beings can attain, if not knowledge of God, at least what is knowable in God. Without the Perfect Man, without a Sacred Guide, there is no access to the divine, and the world could only be engulfed in darkness. The Imam is the Threshold through which God and the creatures communicate. He is thus a cosmic necessity, the key and the center of the universal economy of the sacred: "The earth cannot be devoid of an imam; without him, it could not last an hour."[673] "If there were only two men left in the world, one of them would be the imam."[674] The universal Order is maintained through the presence of the divine Man: "It is because of us," say the imams, "that the heavens and the earth are maintained"; it is because of the imams "that God keeps the sky from crashing into the earth, and the earth from shaking up its inhabitants."[675] Without an Imam, there is no religion; without esotericism, exotericism loses its direction, its purpose, its goal, as well as its meaning; without *walâya* toward the Imam and *barâ'a* toward his Enemy, no duty or obligation in matters of worship can be approved by God.[676] Early Imamism, what from the beginning of this study was called "the early esoteric suprarational tradition," is not a theological-political doctrine *with* a "theory of the Imamate"; on the contrary, this Imamism *is* a "theory of the Imamate" in which, and in regard to which, all other aspects of the doctrine are developed: theology, cosmogony, ethics, politics, the practical aspects of worship, mysticism, law, eschatology, and so forth.[677] Let it be remembered that it is *walâya*—a term that denotes the ontological-theological status of the Imam as well as faith in this status—that the imams call "the Religion" (*al-dîn*), "the true Religion," or "the Religion of Truth" (*al-dîn al-ḥaqq/dîn al-ḥaqq*), or even "the solid Religion" (*al-dîn al-qayyim*); the aspects mentioned previously are only the components, the derivatives, the secondary applications of the *walâya*.

Every facet of early Imamism studied throughout the course of this work confirms that early Imamism is an esoteric doctrine, and there should be no need of further attempting to make the point. But it must be made specific here that, in contrast to certain Bâṭinite currents derived from Shîʿism, exotericism is presented as being equally as important as esotericism. It might be said, in effect, that if without esotericism exotericism loses its meaning, then in just the same way without exotericism, esotericism has no ground in which to reside. It is when the "apparent" (*ẓâhir*) is deepened that the "hidden" (*bâṭin*) can be reached. The *ẓâhir* constitutes the foundation and the indispensable support of the *bâṭin*. From this point on, and by using the information presented throughout this study, we are able to distinguish at least three complementary and increasingly more "secret" levels in the Teaching attributed to the imams:

1. An exoteric level. This refers to the teaching of traditional disciplines (Qur' anic sciences, exoteric hadith, canon law), with a few exceptions, identical to Sunni teaching.[678] The references to the words of the imams in Sunni works and the presence of their names in the chains of transmission of some of the more "orthodox" works of hadith or of *fiqh* might be thought of as corresponding to this level of Teaching. Of course, all kinds of faithful Imamites and even the Sunnites have had access to this level.

2. A level that might be referred to as mesoteric, a level for the closest of the disciples and dealing with cosmogony, the sacred history of the prophets and earlier imams, as well as with the fight that opposes them to their "enemies," information about the divine privileges of the imam, his ontological status, his intiatory role, his Qur'an and other secret Books, his miraculous powers, his soteriological and eschatological role, in short, Imamology and its basic theoretical facts.

3. A strictly esoteric, very secret level lavished upon an elite number of the particularly devoted disciples. We might distinguish between two different categories of information here. The first is information whose secret nature is, according to Imamite "logic," provisionary: information about the number of imams and the identity of the Qâ'im. The second is information whose secret must be forever safe-

guarded: the date of the hidden imam's Return, or the occult sciences and spiritual teachings whose magical character leads into supernormal powers.

We realize that the essential part of the imams' doctrine does not address *'aql* in the sense of "logical reasoning," but it supposes an investment, a total commitment of this *'aql* that they define as the interior Imam, and that we have translated as "Hiero-Intelligence" or "intuition of the sacred." The very method that they adopted to explain their doctrine goes in the same direction; it is well known in a number of esoteric traditions, and we shall refer to it, as the Shî'ite occultists of the Jâbirian corpus have, as the method of "dispersion of information."[679] Actually, although to our knowledge the expression itself is never used in the early Imamite corpus, the method is widely applied: the chapters of compilations are divided according to a supposedly thematic classification system, but if the doctrine is looked at globally, it quickly becomes clear that this classification system is purely superficial. In fact, the fundamental traits of the Teaching, the cosmogonic details, the initiatory ideas, the esoteric and occult information, the eschatological details, are split up and scattered through chapters that most often have no evident logical connection with them. Thus, in cases similar to what we just saw in Jâbir's text (cited in the note), a speech about prayer leads into an expose on the World of Shadows, comments about the Companions of the Mahdî are inserted in an expose on divine Unicity, remarks about political power in office end with a description of the secret Books and rolled Manuscripts of the imams, and so forth. The reason for this is not only the interdependence and interpenetration of ideas, all of which are connected by Imamology, but also the esoteric process by which the doctrine is exposed in the form of a real "puzzle," which essentially appears to aim at two goals: first, safeguarding the secret of the Sacred Knowledge that by nature must be difficult to access, since it cannot be passed on to those who are not worthy; and second, putting to the test the perseverence of the faithful believer, who is thus invited to reconstitute the whole from its "scattered" parts progressively, through *'aql*.

The doctrine of the imams revolves around two central, "polarized" axes. The first is "vertical"; it may be characterized by the two complementary poles defined by pairs such as *ẓâhir/bâṭin* (apparent/hidden; exoteric/esoteric), *nabî/walî* (prophet/imam), *tanzîl/ta'wîl* (literal revelation/spiritual interpretation), Muḥammad/'Alî (the first of whom represents lawgiving prophecy, the exoteric part of religion, while the second represents the Imamite mission that consists in unveiling the esoteric part of the religion), *islâm/îmân* (submission to exoteric religion/initiation to esoteric religion), and so forth. This axis is "vertical," since the passage from exotericism to esotericism is done in the sense of a progressive approach to the divine and an ever greater knowledge of the secrets of the universe. The second axis is "horizontal," being characterized by the two "opposite poles" that are defined by "pairs" like *imâm/'aduww al-imâm* (imam, enemy of the imam), *'aql/jahl* (Hiero-Intelligence/Ignorance), *aṣḥâb al-yamîn/aṣḥâb al-shimâl* (People of the Right/People of the Left), *a' immat al-nûr/a' immat al-ẓalâm* (Guides of the Light/Guides of the Darkness), *walâya/barâ' a* (Sacred Love of the imams/Sacred Hatred of their Enemies), and so on. This second axis is "horizontal," since it determines the history of humanity, a history marked by the opposition between the imams and their faithful, on the one hand, and the "enemies" of the imams and their partisans on the other. In other words, one might say that the "vertical" axis is the axis of Initiation, running through all phases of creation from the initiation of the shadows of the "pure beings" in the World of Particles, by the pre-existential luminous entities of the imams up to the universal initiation of the Mahdî at the End of Time, passing through the initiation of the disciples by the imam or imams of each religion. Thus, the "vertical" axis begins at the beginning of creation and ends at the End of Time, where the difference between exotericism and esotericism is annihilated, where through universal unveiling of the Secret, that which is "apparent" becomes "hidden," and the "hidden" becomes "apparent."

In like fashion, the "horizontal" axis is that of the perpetual Combat: all the way from the pre-existential and cosmic Combat between the Armies of Hiero-Intelligence and those of Ignorance, to the final Battle of the Mahdî against the forces of Evil, passing through the battle that has forever opposed the imams to their enemies. The horizontal axis, with what the stakes are (the combat between the initiated and the counterinitiated, Light and Darkness), also runs through all the phases of creation from pre-existence to the End of Time; it stops at the End of Time, since after the definitive destruction of the Enemy by the Mahdî, it will no longer have any reason for its existence: the Adversary, the dominant and persecuting force throughout history, is conquered, obliterated, once and for all. Any obstacle to full revelation of the Truth is taken away.

Continual Initiation and perpetual Combat are the two fundamental constants of the "religion" of the imams; by their nature and movement, these two axes are inextricably and perpetually connected to one another. The faithful Imamite is invited to remain constantly at their point of intersection.

Historically, then, at the beginnings of esotericism in Islam we find an initiatory, mystical, and occultist doctrine. Just as in other esoteric traditions, the process of the spread of teachings obeys the rules of a complex game; without ever having the appearance of being divulged or popularized, Imamism has destined itself for an elite minority; its development has simultaneously both unveiled and disguised the secret Science. Via allusive statements, technical terms, and the tactic of "dispersion," the Secret has remained hidden "except for those who are worthy of it." Many things have been said, but it is reasonable to assume that, according to a rule inherent in all esotericism, a fairly complete silence has been kept about many others; in this case, such is probably the case for details regarding the "second and third levels of the Teaching," using our classification. This idea is supported by the fact that "keeping the Secret" (*taqiyya/kitmân*) is elevated by the imams to the level of being an article of faith and a sacred obligation.[680] "Nine tenths of the Religion (that is, the religion of the imams) consists of keeping the Secret; whoever does not practice this has no Religion."[681] "Keeping the Secret is part of my Religion and that of my ancestors [the preceding imams]; whoever does not keep the Secret is devoid of Faith [that is, does not practice the doctrine of the imams]."[682] "He who divulges our teaching is like him who denies it."[683] "God's Rule is keeping the Secret."[684] "Supporting our Cause is not [only] knowing it and admitting it; it is protecting it and keeping it hidden from those who are not worthy of it."[685] Finally, let it be added that keeping the Secret is part of the Armies of Hiero-Intelligence, and that it is thus elevated to the rank of a virtue of cosmic dimension.

The reason invoked is that the mass, "the majority," led by the "guides of Darkness," ignorant and fanatical in its blind obedience to exotericism alone, becomes violent when esoteric truths are exposed to them, and they threaten the lives of those who profess these views. The history of humanity is ruled by two kinds of government (*dawla*): the government of Adam and the government of Iblîs. Under the government of Adam, divine Religion can be practiced openly (*'alâniyatan*), while under that of Iblîs, as is the case with humanity today, the True Religion can only be practiced in secret (*sirran*).[686] In the corpus of the imams, certain subjects appear to constitute the main objects of *taqiyya*: information relating to the "Qur' an of the imams," the *barâ' a* toward the Companions of the Prophet and in particular toward the first three caliphs, or the identity of the Qâ'im; but in a general sense, the whole doctrine is presented as being that of the Secret, the esoteric Secret of Islam.[687]

If we have emphasized the concept of keeping the Secret and its sacred character to such an extent here, it is because some particularly sensitive points of doctrine appear to have deliberately been left in the shadows. But we do believe that there are areas of research that may ultimately help to discover them. One that should be particularly important, for example, is following "extremist" Shî'ite currents, the *ghulât*. It is true that the imams vigorously chased the "extremists" from their entourage, even going so far as to condemn them publicly; from very early times a clear distinction was made between the Imamites, considered as "moderates,"and the "extremists"; but when we take a closer look, this distinction appears artificial. Among ideas and theses attributed to the *ghulât*[688] are the following: symbolic and esoteric interpretation of the Qur' an; reincarnation, particularly that of adversaries in animal form (*al-maskh*); the possiblilty of miracles being worked by individuals other than prophets; the idea of inherence of the divine in the creature (*al-ḥulûl*); or what we have referred to as "metemphotosis," that is, the transmission of the prophetic/Imamic Light (*al-tanâsukh*). We have seen all these themes in the corpus of the imams; although their development may be different depending on whether it is a development by imams or "extremists," the basic thought nevertheless remains analogous.

Then there are the different forms of anthropomorphism attributed to the "extremists." Is this not a deformation caused by "extremists" or heresiographers of the idea that underpins all early Imamite doctrine, according to which the Imam is the Manifestation of the Science and Power of God, or even more so, although the idea is less frequently expressed, that the Imam *is* God, manifested in human form?[689] On the other hand, almost all of the most remarkable individuals of the *ghuluww* were disciples of the imams, mostly those of Muḥammad al-Bâqir and Jaʿfar al-Ṣâdiq: Jâbir b. Yazîd al-Juʿfî, Abû Ḥamza al-Thumâlî, Ḥamza al-Buraydî, Saʿîd al-Nahdî, Bayân b. Samʿân, Abû l-Khaṭṭâb, Mughîra b. Saʿîd al-ʿIjlî, Muʿâdh b. Farra al-Naḥwî, and others. The authors of the earliest Imamite biographical works, like al-Najâshî, al-Kashshî, or al-Ṭûsî, list a number of other "extremist" disciples of the imams. Let us take the example of al-Ṭûsî's *Rijâl*, where the chapters are placed in the order of the disciples of the imams, from ʿAlî to al-ʿAskarî; there are numerous items that finish with the lapidary phrase *fa-yurmä bi l-ghuluww* (" . . . and he was accused of extremism"), or *ghâlin malʿûn* ("condemned extremist," that is, condemned by his master, the imam). It is interesting to note that, in a number of cases, an "extremist" disciple condemned by an imam is listed among the disciples of the following imam or imams, thus showing that, despite "public condemnation," he continued to follow the teaching of the imams.[690] The act of condemning does not necessarily prove a divergence from doctrine, especially since certain remarks by the imams tend to suggest that the imams did not curse some of their disciples for what they said, but rather because they said it, in other words, because they did not respect the rule of the Secret. Jaʿfar said: "I sometimes teach a tradition to someone, and then he leaves me and reports the tradition exactly as he heard it from my mouth; because of this, I declare that it is licit to condemn and to hate him."[691] There is thus not a clear doctrinal distinction between "Imamite moderates" and "Shîʿite extremists" made among the "esoteric nonrational" Imamites. We know that "extremist" ideas were to a great extent foundational to Bâṭinism and Ismâʿîlism, and that, through these movements, they infiltrated into certain sufi, as well as Sunni and Shîʿite currents, and also into milieux where occult Islamic sciences were practiced. All these may provide fields of research for those seeking traces of the "hidden teachings" of the imams, and those who thus seek to eventually follow the later evolutions of these teachings.[692] Such a study could not help but be at least as long as the present work. As was stated in the beginning of this book, the present study, whose focus was an almost unexplored field, willingly eschewed being a work of erudition that might have only increased the confusion that already exists; its purpose was rather to establish a theoretical framework. It is our hope that such a method will allow a global definition of early Imamism through its vision of the world, a vision that revolves around the axial idea of the Imam. This "definition," based as it is on that of the Imam, will lead to an understanding of some essential structures, some fundamental details, some "glue," and provide a way of understanding that "hangs together," a "schematic framework" to aid in the reading and interpretation of points of doctrine and historical facts. From this, a new approach to the different facets of Imamism seems possible, an approach that provides directions for further research: its cultural antecedents, its mythology, its anthropology, its gnoseology, its angelology, its ethics, its late philosophical form, its mysticism, its occultism, and so forth.

Appendix

SOME IMPLICATIONS OF THE OCCULTATION: INDIVIDUAL RELIGION AND COLLECTIVE RELIGION

The imam is omnipresent in Imamite religious life. Given the capital role that this presence plays, it is obvious why there were such substantial modifications in Imamite religious life after the final Occultation. One question inevitably comes to mind when we examine the evolution of Imamite doctrine: after the Occultation, is Imamite religious life deprived of all collective characteristics, of all community practice, of all social application? This question is at first glance provocative; it nevertheless appears to find a partial answer in certain "distinctive characteristics" of the doctrine. Although our work here has been a study of early Imamism, we might do well at this point to outline the historical evolution of the doctrine, in order to be able to look at the influence that this evolution has had on Imamism's basic teachings. Such an outline will help us to understand better the historical fate of Imamism, on the one hand, and to evaluate the relationship that the faithful believer is supposed to maintain with the imam during the Occultation, on the other. [693] Let us look first at the case of Imamite jurisprudence (*fiqh*), since it is the discipine that touches daily religious life most closely. It is jurisprudence that codifies and regulates the most concrete aspects of dogma, and it appears to have been the discipline that was most immediately touched by the problems posed by the Occultation. Imamite *fiqh* came into existence as a discipline of its own, so to speak, during the Imamates of Muḥammad al-Bâqir and especially Jaʿfar al-Ṣâdiq, even though its systematic methodology was not worked out until later.[694] For a long time the principles of jurisprudence (*uṣûl al-fiqh*) included only the Qur'an and the hadith, the latter comprising the traditions of the Prophet and those of the imams, those of the imams being able to abrogate those of the Prophet. As we have seen, the imams are extremely critical of both reasoning by analogy (*qiyâs*) and the use of personal opinion (*ra'y*) in religious matters.[695] We have also seen that in the early "esoteric nonrational" tradition, *ʿaql* not only had the meaning of a dialectic faculty of discernment, but it also referred to a cosmic force, like the Imam of Creation, actualized in individuals in the form of a faculty of metaphysical apperception and considered as the individual imam of each faithful believer.[696] Even among the first great "rationalist" theologians like al-Mufîd (d. 413/1022) and his disciple al-Murtaḍä (d. 436/1044), the Qur'an and the hadith are recognized as being the only bases of law. *Ijtihâd* (the "personal interpretation" of the doctor/theologian), of great importance in later Imamism, was rejected as being a disguised form of the "reasoning by analogy" that was criticized by the imams.[696bis] The "consensus" (*ijmâʿ*) of the Doctors of the Law, as it is described by these two authors, comes in a typically Shîʿite form: the "consensus" is of no value unless it includes the will of the imams, a will that must be shown through their words. The value of the "consensus" is thus "effaced" by the validity of the hadith.[697] The same opinions of *ijtihâd* and *ijmâ'* are found in Abû Jaʿfar al-Ṭûsî (d. 460/1067), but in his case we can already see the first influences of Muʿtazilism: *ʿaql* begins to lose its early definition and approaches the reasoning faculty of the dialecticians.[698] It appears as though the somewhat later al-ʿAllâma al-Ḥillî (d. 726/1325) was the first of the great Imamite scholars to have classified *ijtihâd*, and consequently *ʿaql* (in its acceptation as dialectical reasoning) as methodological principles of jurisprudence to be used along with the Qur'an and the hadith.[699] In its early stage, then, the bases of Imamite law were practically limited to the Qur'an and the hadith.[700] As we will see, it will not be until about the tenth/sixteenth century, that the two ideas of *ijtihâd* and *ʿaql* are effectively considered to be two bases for jurisprudence, that the doctor/theologians will acquire significant political and social power.

As far as "applicable branches" (*furûʿ*) are concerned, transactions (*muʿâmalât*) in Imamite law are with very few exceptions identical to those in Sunni schools of law.[701] Problems become more thorny when we get into the field of duties regarding worship (*ʿibâdât*) and precepts (*aḥkâm*); here, even in Imamism, scholars have long debated certain points. Let us begin with duties regarding worship, divided into prayer (both individual and collective), fasting, the religious "taxes," pilgrimage, *jihâd* (in the sense of "holy war"), and ordering what is good and forbidding what is evil. From what can be gleaned from the notes of Aqâ Bozorg al-Ṭihrânî in his *al-Dharîʿa*, a colossal collection of Shîʿite works, fierce debates were waged on the practice of two of these, collective prayer and holy war. In essence, what characterizes these two is their need for a "leader" or a "guide" to be practiced appropriately. We know that in Imamism this "leader" can only be the imam himself, or someone designated by him. According to the early corpus of the imams, the collective prayer of the two feasts of the Sacrifice at the end of the month of Ramaḍân are specifically declared as impossible to perform in the absence of the imam or his delegate.[702] On the other hand, since the leaders of the Imamite collective prayer on Fridays were named by the imams, once the imam is absent, it appeared as though the Friday prayer could no longer be practiced, or that it was at least "suspended" (*mutawaqqif al-ijrâ'*) until the

Return of the Mahdî and his designating new leaders for prayer. This situation prevailed throughout the pre-Safavid period, since at the beginning of the Safavid dynasty (circa 927/1520 to 1009/1600) nearly a hundred books or treatises were written to justify the legal status of Friday prayer.[703] The composition of these books was linked to the religious politics of the Safavids, specifically to attempts at setting up another Islamic "pole" in the face of the Ottoman Empire, on the one hand, and the "ideologization" of Imamism, on the other. We shall return to this.

We find ourselves facing the same phenomenon when it comes to the holy war. With the arrival of the Safavids, a number of polemical works were composed to prove the legal or illegal status of *jihâd* in the absence of the imam.[704] A solution was finally reached through compromise, and the doctor-theologians distinguished between two different holy wars: the offensive *jihâd*, declared to be "suspended" during the period of Occultation, and the defensive, legal *jihâd*, which may be obligatory in the case of an attack from outside. The polemics and the juridical-theological debates in the Safavid and post-Safavid periods show that the question was still moot until relatively recently.

Among the *aḥkâm*, religious jurisdiction (*ḥukûma/qaḍâ'*) and legal punishments (*ḥudûd*) were subject to this debate. The need for justice based on the Law and religious science of the judge being beyond question, the question remains as to whether the judge should be a religious person, in the sense of a religious "professional," or not. The problem is raised by later sources, once again starting in the time of the Safavids and the constitution of a class of Imamite religious professionals. Actually, among the early Imamites, the theologian-judges (*ḥukkâm/quḍât al-sharʿ*) were named directly by the imams; some of the imams' remarks regarding the difficulty of just jurisdiction[705] appear to have led Imamite doctors to wonder whether, in the absence of the imam, a religious judge, all the more likely to make judgment errors since he is not designated by the infallible person of the imam, could exercise such a responsibility without compromising both the Law and religion. The number of works written from the Safavid period on against this argumentation encourages us to think that it was effectively used by Imamites in earlier times.[706] Imamite law divides legal punishments into two categories:[707] there are first of all those punishments instituted by the Qurʾan and whose application is designated by the expression "God's right" (*ḥaqq Allâh*); next, there are the punishments applied to errors not foreseen by the Sacred Text and whose commission is called "man's right" (*ḥaqq al-nâs*). Since the imam is the only person with the ability to apply Qurʾanic precepts to individual cases appropriately, the practice of "God's right" can be carried out only by Him, or by the person specifically designated by Him. "Man's right," on the other hand, can be carried out by an individual whose virtue and religious knowledge are recognized by everyone. The final part of al-Murtadä's treatise,

Risâlat al-ghayba, summarizes and illustrates quite well this somewhat discomforting and ambiguous situation that we are examining.[708] The somewhat stilted language of the text is from A. Sachedina's translation:

> The doctrine of the *ḥudûd* [legal punishment] during the *ghayba* is clear. It is like this that if [the *ḥadd*] was to be implemented on a person, if the Imâm appears and if that person is still alive and if it is proved on him by imputation and confession of having been committed by him, the Imâm will impose the legal punishment on him. But if the punishment was not implemented because of his having died, the sin is on those who have frightened the Imam and forced him to go into *ghayba*. The *Sharîʿah* does not get abrogated in the execution of the *ḥudûd*, because abrogation is at that time when there is a possibility of implementing the punishment and when obstacles preventing its enforcement have been removed. But under the condition we have mentioned, it does not get abrogated. . . . "[709]

This short excerpt seems to sum up the early Imamite concept as concerns the social application of jurisprudence: as long as the imam remains in hiding, it is impossible for the Law to function correctly on the collective level. There is no one but the hidden imam who, once he comes back, can carry out all the precepts applicable to the collective religious life. The Imamites could not have been ignorant of the inevitable implications of a complete Occultation: without the designation of the imam, no chosen delegate could be named; without the delegate, there could be no "leader" or "guide" for collective prayer, which, therefore, becomes "suspended." Nothing in the early corpus of the imams suggests a remedy for such a situation. The last letter of the twelfth imam will cut to the quick: not only will there not be a "representative," but no one but an imposter will claim to be one. In the face of this information, we might wonder—and here we return to our original question—if the complete Occultation did not bring about the end of the collective dimension of the Imamite doctrine, and if this doctrine did not become, from that point on, a completely interiorized, individualized, initiatory kind of "religion."

In addition to the information examined previously, there are also comments by the imams about the Occultation that appear to corroborate our idea here. The fourth imam, ʿAlî Zayn al-ʿAbidîn, after saying that the Imamate belongs to al-Ḥusayn's descendents and that the Mahdî will have two Occultations, states: " . . . As far as the [second] Occultation is concerned, its duration will be prolonged until the majority of those who profess this doctrine go back on their belief; at that time the only one who will remain steadfast will be he whose certainty [*yaqîn*] is strong [or "strengthened"] and whose knowledge [*maʿrifa*] is healthy [or "restored"], he who finds in himself no difficulty accepting what we [the imams] proclaim, he who salutes us "people of the house" [of the Prophet]."[710] The conditions required to be a true faithful believer during the period of the major Occultation are thus love (*walâya*) for the imams, absolute "certainty" about the truth of their teachings, and knowledge, which, in the technical terminology of the imams means knowledge of the initiatory secrets of the doctrine. These conditions point only to an interior and individual religious spirituality. Two of Ja'far's traditions appear to suggest that such a believer remains in contact with the hidden imam, even during the period of the major Occultation: "The Qâ'im will have two Occultations, a short one and another of long duration. During the first of these, only certain chosen Shî'ites will know where he is hidden, and during the second [Occultation], only the chosen ones among the intimate Friends in his Religion will know this place."[711] Again, Ja'far says: "The Lord of this Cause [that is, the Mahdî] will have two Occultations; one will be so long that some of [the Imamites] will say that he is dead, others that he has been killed, and still others that he has disappeared [definitively]. Only a few of his faithful will remain attached to his Cause, and none of his friends or anyone else will know where he is, except for the intimate Friend who rules over his Cause."[712] Let us not forget this other saying, constantly repeated by the imams: "Our Cause is difficult; the only ones able to bear it are a prophet sent by God, an angel of Proximity, and a faithful believer whose heart has been tested by God for faith."[713] We discern in the expression "test of the heart" an allusion to initiation into the spiritual "technique" of vision with the heart, through which the initiated discover the Light of the Imam in their hearts and thus attain esoteric Knowledge and miraculous powers. Is this tantamount to saying that "vision with the heart," with the "certainty" and "knowledge" that accompany such vision, is what makes the faithful believer become an intimate Friend of the imam? Is it what allows the faithful believer to know the "location" of his Master? This is at any rate what Imamite mystics have always claimed.[714] Only a small minority will know "the location of the hidden imam," or, in other words, only a small minority will be in contact with him. But this same handful of believers will be able to hide their privilege from the eyes of the world, so that the conditions set up by the hidden imam in his last letter may be respected. These believers are those that later sources called "men of the Invisible" (*rijâl al-ghayb*), and about whom it is said that their existence is indispensible to humanity, since they are the ones that will continue to transmit the Divine Science secretly until the Return of the hidden imam.[715]

But things evolved quickly from the beginning of the major Occultation. The Imamite Community's situation was becoming untenable. Living in a socially and ideologically hostile environment, deprived of the physical presence of its charismatic leader, in possession of a body of beliefs that appeared "heretical" and "irrational" at a time when "orthodoxy" and "rationalism" had firm footing, Imamism felt forced to adopt a solution of compromise in order to survive as a religious community. Everything seems to have begun with the slide of the meaning of the word *'aql* that, from the time of shaykh al-Mufîd, was beginning to refer to the faculty of logical reasoning. From that time on, the traditions judged to be too "irrational" were quietly left unmentioned, or were even considered suspect.[716] The door was thus open for the principle of *ijtihâd* ("the personal interpretation of the doctor-theologian regarding religious matters"), giving the doctor-theologian tremendous social and political power. The process nevertheless took a number of centuries to crystallize.[716bis] As we have seen, respect for the rules instituted by the imams began to get in the way of the application of the doctrine in collective matters. The great turning point was the rise of the Safavids in Iran. The evolution of Imamite law and the chronological placement of sources coincide directly with this political and cultural change that transformed Imamite doctrine into a state religion beginning in the tenth/sixteenth century. Before the Safavids, the problem of a government drawing its legitimacy from its adherence to a doctrine does not even seem to have been an issue among the Imamites. Imamite or pro-Imamite powers like the Buyids (334/945 to 447/1055) and the Ilkhânids (from the sixth/twelfth to the eighth/fourteenth centuries) appear never to have been forced to justify their legitimacy by their profession of faith. It is undeniable that this attitude had its political reasons, but we might also think that it was founded on the fundamental Imamite belief according to which any power before the Return of the hidden imam is by its very nature a usurper, or on some of the imams' traditions where they vehemently impugn the very idea of government.[717] Things changed radically when the Safavids took power in 907/1501. Shâh Ismâ'îl, the founder of the dynasty, publicly called himself the precursor and the "representative" of the hidden imam, and his followers looked upon him as a reincarnation of the imams. In order to create another political and religious pole in the face of the Ottoman sultan-caliphs, he ferociously imposed his ideas and ultimately declared Imamism to be the state religion of Iran. Drawing its legitimacy from its doctrinal adherence, the Safavid power needed a religious "system." Besides local doctor-theologians, religious authorities were invited from Syria, Bahrain, and Arabian Iraq to put into place a veritable "ideological" armature, in order to support the Safavid idea of Imamism. A whole religious structure, to avoid the term "official Church," controlled by the state was put into place. Simultaneously, the religious system gave birth to a body of independent Doctors of the Law vis-à-vis the powers that be.[718] The disappearance of the charisma of the sovereigns, the failure of the religious politics of the state, and serious economic crises created a condition of wavering and uncertainty, the beneficiaries of which were the independent Doctors.[719] With the exception of a few cases of desperate resistence on the part of sovereigns, it can be said that from the time of Shah Ṭahmâsb I's reign (931/1524 to 984/1576), power effectively fell into the hands of the Doctors of the Law.[720] The School of *uṣulî* ("rationalist") theologians, who carried on the thought of al-Mufîd or al-ʿAllâma al-Ḥillî, was restructured at this time, and it supplanted (although not without violence) the old *akhbârî* ("traditionalist") School; thus the idea of *ijtihâd*, supported by the theologian's personal dialectical reasoning, officially and effectively became one of the methodological bases of Imamite law.[721] *Ijtihâd* brought significant political and religious power to the jurist-theologian who used it (the *mujtahid*). The mass of faithful, incapable of reaching the level of *ijtihâd*, was relegated to relying on "imitation" (*taqlîd*), that is, to following the *mujtahid* and his instructions scrupulously. The *mujtahid* was promoted to the rank of "general representative of the hidden imam" (*nâʾib-e ʿâmm-e imâm*), and the four "representatives" of the period of the minor Occultation were henceforth named "the particular representatives of the imam" (*nâʾib-e khâṣṣ*).[722] The *fiqh*, which tends to be *uṣûlî*, easily became the dominant discipline of Islamic studies, and eclipsed the other sciences almost totally. The search for an interiorized individual religion, spiritual effort through the strength of *walâya*, "Knowledge," and "Certitude" in the hope of establishing "contact" with the hidden imam were practiced by marginalized, often persecuted groups. Political ambition and power, defined by the imams as being destroyers of the "true Religion," were from then on presented as guarantees of its just application. The religious "system" worked out by the Safavids succeeded in putting into place a "process of substitution": the jurist-theologian took the place of the imam;[723] principles of jurisprudence replaced the teachings of the imams; *walâya*, love/submission/fidelity—that all initiates owe to their initiating Master—was transformed into *taqlîd*, servile imitation of the all-powerful jurist; love for the imams was transformed into a morbid, dolorous cult whose violent group demonstrations were approved and perhaps even encouraged by clerical authority; an official, institutionalized clergy replaced the "invisible companions" of the Awaited imam. This process took place in a specific direction: its aim was to drag Imamism into the political arena, apply it on the collective level and crystallize it as an ideology.[724]

Notes

NOTES TO CHAPTER 1

1. "As far as practical solutions are concerned (in the juridical domain), the Twelvers have basically the same options as do the Sunni schools; from this point of view, divergences from Sunni thought are not called into question any more than they are among Sunnis themselves," Y. Linant de Bellefonds, "Le droit imâmite," in *Le shi'ism imâmite*, p. 185. In the appendix we shall return at greater length to this juridical tradition and its evolution.

2. For an overview of the discussions and points of disagreement among specialists, both Western and Muslim, regarding the early meaning of *'aql*, which essentially refers to the meanings that can be gleaned from the Qur'an and the hadith before the influence of Greek thought, see *L'Etrange et le Merveilleux dans l'Islam médiéval*, M. Arkoun, J. Le Goff, T. Fahd, and M. Rodinson, Paris, 1978, pp. 12, 27f., 32, 37f., 52, 56, 216.

3. See, e.g., T. Izutsu, *Ethico-religious concepts in the Qur'an*, Montreal, 1966, pp. 30f. and 69f., where the author revises and develops previous studies on the subject, particularly those of Goldziher.

4. Ch. Pellat, "Ḥilm," in *EI2*, vol. 3, p. 403; it is impossible to translate the term in one word.

5. The word *ḥilm*, undoubtedly too charged with tribal and thus profane resonance, is used infrequently in the Qur'an, where, in any case, it has either a religious connotation (it is used but two times to refer to humans, once for Abraham (9:114) and once for his son (11:75), or even a sacred connotation (*ḥalîm* becomes one of God's attributes, the thirty-third Name in the classic list of Divine Names; on this latter subject, see D. Gimaret, *Les Noms divins en Islam*, Paris, 1988, pp. 420–22). On the replacement of the idea of *ḥilm* by the idea of *'aql* in early times, see, e.g., al-Jâḥiẓ, *Kitmân al-sirr*, Ed. Kraus and Ḥâjirî, pp. 40f. (which is not surprising for a Mu'tazilite), or even al-Ghazzâlî, *Iḥyâ'*, throughout Book XXV.

6. Quite often in the speeches of the imams one encounters expressions like "*'aql* is the axis of our religion" (*al-'aql quṭb dîninâ*), "*'aql* is the axis around which the truth turns (*al-'aql huwa l-quṭb alladhî 'alayhi madâr al-ḥaqq*), "*'aql* is what one leans upon in our teaching" (*al-'aql huwa mâ yuḥtajj bihi fî amrinâ*) etc., see, e.g., al-Kulaynî, *Uṣul min al-kâfî*, vol. 1, p. 10; Ibn Bâbûye, *'Ilal al-sharâ'i'*, vol. 1, pp. 88, 107f.; Ibn Bâbûye, *Amâlî*, p. 418.

7. *Al-Kâfî fî 'ilm al-dîn/al-Uṣul min al-kâfî*, several editions; we are using the one

from Tehran, Eslâmiyye, with Persian translation and notes by Sayyid Jawâd Muṣṭafawî, n.d., 4 vol., "Kitâb al-'aql wa l-jahl," vol. 1, pp. 10–34. See e.g., also al-Barqî, *Kitâb al-maḥâsin*, vol. 1, pp. 191–98.

8. *'Aql* was the first of the "spiritual entities" (*al-rûḥâniyyûn*) to be created, and as shall be seen later (Part II), these entities are the first of God's creations. For *'aql* as an angelic being (*malak*), see also Ibn Bâbûye, *'Ilal al-sharâ'i'*, vol. 1, p. 98; for *'aql* as the first of God's creations in Sunni traditions, see I. Goldziher, "Neuplatonische und gnostiche Elemente im Hadit," in *ZA*, 1908, pp. 317f.

9. *"Inna Allâha 'azza wa jall khalaqa l-'aql wa huwa awwalu khalq min al-rûḥâniyyin 'an yamîn 'arshihi min nûrihi fa-qâla lahu adbir fa-adbara thumma qâla lahu aqbil fa-aqbala faqâla Allâhu tabârak wa ta'âlä khalaqtuka khalqan 'aẓîman wa karramtuka 'alä jamî' khalqî,"* al-Kulaynî, *Uṣûl*, vol. 1, pp. 23–24, and also the beginning of this tradition in a hadith from the fifth imam, Muhammad al-Bâqir, *Uṣûl*, vol. 1, pp. 10–11. For other references to this tradition, see Shahrastânî, *Livre des religions et des sectes*, trans. and notes by D. Gimaret and G. Monnot, Louvain, 1986, p. 226, note 30 (Gimaret's note).

10. *"Thumma khalaqa l-jahl min al-baḥr al-ujâj ẓulmâniyyan fa-qâla lahu adbir fa-adbara thumma qâla lahu aqbil fa-lam yuqbil fa-qâla lahu 'stakbarta fa-la'anahu,"* al-Kulaynî, *Uṣûl*, vol. 1, p. 24.

11. *"Ja'ala li l-'aql khamsatan wa sab'în jundan fa-lammâ ra'a l-jahl mâ akrama Allâhu bihi l-'aql wa mâ a'ṭâhu aḍmara lahu l-'adâwa fa-qâla l-jahl yâ rabbi hâdhâ khalqun mithlî khalaqtahu wa karramtahu wa qawwaytahu wa anâ ḍidduhu wa lâ quwwa lî bihi fa-a'ṭinî min al-jund mithla mâ a'ṭaytahu fa-qâla na'am fa-in 'aṣayta ba'da dhâlik akhrajtuka wa jundaka min raḥmatî qâla raḍîtu fa-a'ṭâhu khamsatan wa sab'în jundan,"* al-Kulaynî, *Uṣûl*, vol. 1, p. 24.

12. Al-Kulaynî, *Uṣûl*, vol. 1, pp. 24–26. Good (*al-khayr*) is the minister of *'aql*; its oposite, Evil (*al-sharr*) is the minister of Ignorance. The enumeration of the 75 qualities and defects follows, side by side: faith (*îmân*) and its adversary infidelity (*kufr*). . . .Clemency (*raḥma*), with anger (*ghaḍab*) . . . asceticism (*zuhd*) with desire (*raghba*) . . . wisdom (*ḥikma*) with passion (*hawâ'*), etc. We might point out that *ḥilm* and its opposite *safah* are also present.

13. Although Ibn al-Muqaffa' (d. circa 140/757), the author of one of the very first treatises on logic in the Greek style, was a contemporary of the fifth and sixth imams, we are nevertheless far, in this cosmogonic presentation, from the kind of Greek thought where no substance, no disposition even, is opposed to the intellect and where ignorance is simply the absence of any form in the intellect; but certain similarities between Imamite and Greek ideas can be perceived in their ethics and soteriology. On the other hand, the similarity of certain ideas with (late?) Mazdean dualism is remarkable: a dualism not at the level of God, but at that of creation: *'aql* has an opposite on the same ontological level, namely *jahl* (cosmic Ignorance); the struggle that opposes the Armies of *'aql* and those of *jahl* is an irresistible reminder of the perpetual combat between such entities as innate Wisdom (*âsn xrad*, read *âshn khrad*) and Ignorance (*dusâkâsîh*, read *dushâkâsih*), corresponding, respectively, with Vohuman and Akoman (see *Le Troisième Livre de Dênkart*, trans J. de Menasce, Paris, 1973, s. v.) or the Iranian myth about the Primordial War as it is told by al-Shahrastânî (*Livre des religions et des sectes*, p. 639 and the notes by G. Monnot). In the course of the present

study, there is only time to allude quickly to similarities, sometimes flagrant, to other doctrines. It is hoped that these points can be dealt with in more detail in our work (in preparation) on the prehistory of Shî'ism.

14. *"Al-'aql ḥibâ' min Allâh wa l-adab kulfa fa-man takallafa l-adab qadara 'alayhi wa man takallafa l-'aql lam yazdad bi-dhâlik illâ jahlan,"* al-Kulaynî, *Uṣûl*, vol. 1, p. 27.

15. Al-Kulaynî, *Uṣûl*, vol. 1, p. 30. The disciple in question is Isḥâq b. 'Ammâr (Abû Hâshim al-Kûfî al-Ṣayrafî), who knew the teachings of the sixth and seventh imams. For more information about him see, for example, al-Ṭûsî, *Rijâl*, Najaf, 1380/1961, p. 149, num. 135 and p. 342, num. 3; Ardabîlî, *Jâmi' al-ruwât*, Qumm, 1331 solar/1953, vol. 1, pp. 82–87.

16. "*. . . Dhâka man 'ujinat nuṭfatuhu bi-'aqlih . . . fa-dhâka lladhî rukkiba 'aqluhu fîhi fî baṭn ummih . . . fa-dhâka lladhî rukkiba 'aqluhu fîhi ba'da mâ kabura. . . .*"

17. For our translation of *'ilm* as "initiatory Knowledge" (French: *science initiatique*), "science," "wisdom" (*science-sagesse*), or sacred Knowledge (*science sacrée*) see below; throughout the present work particular attention is paid to detecting these important technical terms and their translation.

18. Al-Kulaynî, *Uṣûl*,, vol. 1, p. 34.

19. Cf. the expression "recognition of sacred knowledge is made through *'aql*" (*ma'rifat al-'ilm bi'-'aql*) (al-Kulaynî, *Uṣûl*, vol. 1, p. 20, words of the seventh imam, Mûsä al-Kâẓim; Ibn Bâbûye, *'Ilal al-sharâ'i'*, vol. 1, pp. 100–1, Ja'far's words; Ibn Bâbûye, *Ma'ânî al-akhbâr*, 78, words of the eighth imam, 'Alî al-Riḍâ). It is emphasized that "this knowledge cannot be received but by the divine sage"—one of the appellations of the imams (*lâ 'ilm illâ min 'alim rabbânî*) (cf., for example, al-Kulaynî, *Uṣûl*, vol. 1, p. 20). The interdependence and the complementarity of *'aql* and *'ilm* are stated emphatically: " *'Aql* [goes] with *'ilm* (*al-'aql ma'a al-'ilm*)," or vice versa (al-Kulaynî, *Uṣûl*, vol. 1, p. 16); *'ilm* constitutes the sixth Army of *'aql* and is opposed by *jahl*, the same adversary as that of *'aql* (al-Kulaynî, *Uṣûl*, vol. 1, p. 24).

20. About him, see W. Madelung's article in *EI2*, vol. 3, pp. 513–15.

21. Al-Kulaynî, *Uṣûl*, vol. 1, pp. 14–23.

22. See also al-Kulaynî, *al-Rawḍa min al-kâfî*, vol. 1, p. 274 and vol. 2, p. 50; Ibn Bâbûye, *'Ilal al-sharâ'i'*, vol. 1, pp. 98 and 107–108; Ibn Bâbûye, *al-Muqni' wa al-hidâya*, p. 68. The idea according to which the heart is the seat of psychic or spiritual powers is common not only to Muslims (especially before the progressive influence of Greek medicine) and the Semites, but also to a great number of ancient peoples (cf. on this subject A. Guillaumont, "Le sens du nom du coeur dans l'Antiquité," in the issue of the *Études Carmélitaines* dedicated to the "heart," 1953, and in *Dictionnaire de spiritualité ascétique et mystique*, the article on "coeur" by A. Cabassut and A. Hamon, vol. II, 1953, pp. 1023–51). But this idea takes on a particular importance in the Imamology of early Imamism because it appears to constitute the speculative basis of a spiritual "technique," perhaps the most important of the early doctrine: that is, the practice of " vision with (or through) the heart" (*al-ru'ya bi'l-qalb*). (See Part II-3).

23. Al-Kulaynî, *Uṣûl*, vol. 1, p. 19.

24. Cf., for example, the words of the tenth imam, 'Alî al-Naqî, where he elevates *'aql*, in its function of proof, to the same level as the miracles of the prophets (the mag-

ical powers of Moses, Jesus' powers to heal, the power of Muhammad's words) (al-Kulaynî, *Uṣûl*, vol. 1, p. 28); or those of the sixth imam: "The proof between God and his servants is the prophets and the imams, and the proof between the servants and God is *ʿaql* (al-Kulaynî, *Uṣûl*, vol. 1, p. 29); it must be added finally that the very term *ḥujja* is one of the titles of the imams (plural: *ḥujaj*).

25. *"Iʿjâb al-marʾ binafsihi dalîl ʿalä ḍaʿf ʿaqlih"* (al-Kulaynî, *Uṣûl*, vol. 1, p. 32).

26. Al-Kulaynî, *Uṣûl*, vol. 1, p. 11. The author is tempted to choose to read "*ḥayât*" (Life, in the sense of an existence in relation to God) rather than "*ḥayâʾ* (modesty), since it is not easy to understand the reason for placing modesty on equal footing with *ʿaql* and religion; such an interpretation appears to be confirmed in another tradition attributed to ʿAlî : " . . . I cannot pardon the absence of two things [in people]: *ʿaql* and religion; for without religion there is no safety (*amn*), and without safety life is nothing but anguish (*makhâfa*); and without *ʿaql* there is no point to Life (*ḥayât*). He who has no *ʿaql* can only be compared to the dead (*lâ yuqâs illâ bi l-amwât*)" (al-Kulaynî, *Uṣûl*, vol. 1, pp. 31–32).

27. *"Man kâna ʿâqilan kâna lahu dînun wa man kâna lahu dîn dakhala l-janna,"* Al-Kulaynî, *Uṣûl*, vol. 1, p. 12. Cf. also the expression "no religion for him who is deprived of humanity, and no humanity for him who is deprived of *ʿaql*" (*lâ dîn li-man lâ muruwwa lahu wa lâ muruwwa li-man lâ ʿaql lahu*) (Al-Kulaynî, *Uṣûl*, vol. 1, p. 22, also Ibn Bâbûye, *Maʿânî al-akhbar*, 22).

28. Al-Kulaynî, *Uṣûl*, vol. 1, p. 13.

29. Muʿâwiya b. Abî Sufyân, the first Umayyad caliph (from 40 to 60/661–680), is one of the individuals most abhorred by Shiʿites (primarily because of his battle against ʿAlî at Ṣiffîn, and the eviction and, according to the Shiʿites, poisoning of Ḥasan b. ʿAlî); his personality and his politics are still discussed even in Sunni circles (cf. H. Lammens, *Études sur le règne du calife omeyyade Moʾawiya Ier*, Beirut, 1908, pp. 191–97 and 209–13; and the article in *EI1* by L. Della Vida, vol. 3, p. 1054). Jaʿ-far's aim appears to have been to focus on a Sunni point of view that made Muʿâwiya a champion of religious piety (cf. H. Lammens, *Études sur le règne . . .*, p. 213), a point of view that was defended particularly vigorously in Ḥanbalite circles (cf. Ibn Rajab, *Kitâb al-dhayl ʿalä ṭabaqât al-ḥanâbila*, Cairo, 1953, vol. 1, p. 78; regarding Qâḍî Abû al-Ḥusayn, d. 526/1131 and vol. 1, p. 355; regarding ʿAbd al-Mughîth al-Ḥarbî, d. 583/1187).

30. *"Mâ l-ʿaql ? qâla mâ ʿubida bihi l-raḥmân wa ʾktusiba bihi l-jinân qultu fa-lladhî kâna fî Muʿâwiya ? fa-qâla tilka l-nakrâʾ tilka l-shayṭana wa hiya shabîha bi l-ʿaql wa laysat bi l-ʿaql,"* al-Kulaynî, *Uṣul*, vol. 1, p. 11.

31. Jaʿfar reports Muhammad as saying, "When you hear talk about someone's religious qualities (*ḥusn ḥâl*), consider the quality of his *ʿaql* (*ḥusn ʿaqlihi*), for he will be rewarded according to his *ʿaql*" (*Uṣul*, vol. 1, p. 13). (Regarding the translation of *ḥusn ḥâl* by "religious quality," see the other tradition of the Prophet reported by Jaʿfar (al-Kulaynî, *Uṣul*, vol. 1, p. 31): "When you see someone who says a lot of prayers and fasts several times [a year], do not admire him; first consider his *ʿaql*.")

32. Al-Kulaynî, *Uṣul*, vol. 1, p. 10, and Ibn Bâbûye, *Amâlî*, 418.

33. Al-Kulaynî, *Uṣul*, vol. 1, p. 12.

34. *"Idhâ qâma qâʾimunâ waḍaʿa Allâh yaduhu ʿalä ruʾûsi l-ʿibâd fa-jamaʿa*

bihâ 'uqûlahum wa kamalat bihi aḥlâmuhum," Al-Kulaynî, *Uṣul,* vol. 1, p. 29; Ibn Bâbûye, *Kamâl al-dîn,* 675 (a slightly different "reading": "*. . . fa-jama'a bihâ 'uqûlahum wa kamalat bihâ aḥlâmuhum*"). Here again, *ḥilm* is an intelligence applied to the worldly domain, as distinguished from *'aql,* intelligence, intuition or knowledge applied to the sacred domain.

35. " *Inna awwal al-umûr wa mabda'ahâ wa quwwatahâ wa 'imâratahâ allatî lâ yuntafa' bi-shay'in illâ bihi l-'aql alladhî ja'alahu Allâh zînatan li-khalqih wa nûran lahum fa-bi l-'aql 'arafa l-'ibâd khâliqahum wa annahum makhlûqûn wa annahu l-mudabbir lahum wa annahum al-mudabbarûn wa annahu l-bâqî wa humu l-fânûn wa 'stadallû bi-'uqûlihum 'alä mâ ra'aw min khalqih min samâ'ih wa arḍih wa shamsih wa qamarih wa laylih wa nahârih . . . wa 'arafû bihi l-ḥasan min al-qabîḥ wa anna l-ẓulma fî l-jahl wa anna l-nûr fî l-'ilm,"* al-Kulaynî, *Uṣul,* vol. 1, pp. 33–34.

36. The articles entitled "'Aql" in *L'Encyclopédie de l'Islam* (*EI2*, vol. 1, pp. 352–53, by T.J. De Boer and F. Rahman) and *Encyclopedia Iranica* (vol. 1, p. 194–98) by F. Rahman and W. Chittick) do not take this semantic evolution into account. N. Pourjavady outlined such a study in "Taḥlîlî az mafâhîm-e *'aql* va jonûn dar *'uqalâ' al-majânîn,*" *Ma'âref,* 4, 2 (1366 sun/1987), pp. 7–38 (in Persian). For the different philosophical and theological acceptations of the word *'aql* and the fact that it has been adopted to translate several technical terms in Greek belonging to different philosophical contexts (*noûs, logos, dianoia . . .*), see al-Fârâbî, *Risâla fî l-'aql,* ed, M. Bouyges, Beirut, 1938; (it is interesting to note that this author also uses the example of Mu'âwiya, cf. notes 29 and 30); regarding problems faced by Latin translators in dealing with the term, see J. Jolivet, "Intellect et intelligence. Note sur la tradition arabo-latine des XIIe et XIIIe siècles" in *Mélanges offerts à H. Corbin,* Tehran, 1977, pp. 681–702.

37. See Ḥasan b. Md Abû al-Qâsim al-Nîsâbûrî's quite interesting work *Kitâb 'uqalâ' al-majânîn,* ed. Wajîh b. Fâris, second ed., Damascus, 1405/1985, especially the author's introduction. The study of the evolution of the idea of *'aql* in the mystics also provides an interesting field for research; while in the first centuries of Islam ascetics and mystics were looked upon as the true "sages" (*'uqalâ'*) of the Community, from the third century on, certain categories of these same groups were perceived as being the "mad" (*majânîn*) (*Kitâb 'uqalâ' al-majânîn*; see especially the notes and anecdotes dedicated to such mystics as Uways al-Qaranî, Sa'dûn, Abû Naṣr al-Juhanî, and Sumnûn al-Muḥibb); it also appears that, starting at about this time, the mystics themselves began to describe themselves as such, since *'aql* in its new acceptation not only had no reason to exist in mystical life, but was perceived as being a hindrance to spiritual progress; expressions like "the mad sages" or "the intelligent idiots" (*aṣḥâb 'uqûl bilâ 'uqûl*), "the fools of the Truth (*majânîn al-ḥaqq*), and so on, were all created by mystics after the beginning of the third/ninth century (cf. Pourjavady, "Taḥlîlî az mafâhîm-e *'aql* va jonûn dar *'uqalâ' al-majânîn,"Ma'âref,* 4,2 (1366 sun/1987), pp. 26–35).

38. Cf. for example, al-Mufîd, *Awâ'il al-maqâlât fî l-madhâhib al-mukhtârât,* ed. 'A. Sh. Wâ'iẓ, second ed. Tabrîz, 1371/1951, pp. 11–12 (with a French translation by D. Sourdel in *L'Imâmisme vu par le cheikh al-Mufîd,* Paris, 1974, p. 45 [257]); also, al-Mufîd, *al-Fuṣûl al-mukhtâra min al-'uyûn wa l-maḥâsin,* third ed., Najaf, 1962, pp. 78–79.

39. *Awâ'il al-maqâlât*, 12 (for the complementarity of *ʿaql* and *samʿ*); see also his *Kitâb Sharḥ ʿaqâ'id al-Ṣadûq aw taṣḥîḥ al-iʿtiqâd*, ed. ʿA. Wajdî, second ed., Tabriz, 1371/1951, pp. 46–47 (for the parallel relationship between *ʿaql* and the imam).

40. See M. J. McDermott, *The Theology of al-Shaikh al Mufîd*, Beirut, 1978, chapters II, XII, and XVII.

41. See his "al-Uṣûl al-iʿtiqâdiyya" in *Nasfâ'is al-makhṭṭât*, ed. Al Yâsîn, Baghdad, 1954, p. 79.

42. *Jumal al-ʿilm wa l-ʿamal*, Najaf, 1967, p. 36 ff.

43. In the technical terminology of Imamism, *al-mu'min* (the faithful believer) refers to the "true Shîʿite" (one initiated into the esoteric secrets of the religion; this topic will be dealt with at greater length), he who believes firmly in the completeness of the message of the imams. As such, he is to be distinguished from the *muslim*, who is just a Sunni Muslim or the Muslim who does not know the complete Imamite doctrine and believes only partially in it. In response to the question, What is the difference between Islam and faith (*îmân*)? Jaʿfar said: "Islam consists of the following exterior aspects to which people adhere (*al-islâm huwa l-ẓâhir alladhî ʿalayhi l-nâs*): the two testimonies about the unicity of God and the mission of the Prophet Muhammad, prayer, alms, the pilgrimage to Mecca, and fasting during the month of Ramadan. In addition to all that, faith is knowledge of our teachings (*maʿrifa amrinâ*); he who professes and practices the former without knowing the latter has gone astray, even if he is a Muslim (*kâna musliman wa kâna ḍâllan*)" (al-Kulaynî, *Uṣûl*, "kitâb al-îmân wa l-kufr," vol. 3, p. 39). He further says: "Islam is the profession of divine unicity and acceptance of the mission of our Prophet; it is through Islam that the blood price is paid, and the conditions of marriage and inheritance are reglemented; it is [a group of] exoteric laws (*ẓâhir*) that the majority of people obey (*jamâʿat al-nâs*, one of the names given by the imams to Sunni Muslims, called also *akthar al-nâs*, as opposed to the "minority" *aqall al-nâs*, the name given to the Shiʿites). However, faith is a guidance (*hudä*) that is shown to the heart; exoterically, faith is associated with Islam, while esoterically Islam is not associated with faith (*inna l-îmân yushârik al-islâm fî l-ẓâhir wa l-islâm lâ yushârik al-îmân fî l-bâṭin*); faith is thus superior (*arfaʿ*) to Islam (al-Kulaynî, *Uṣûl*, "kitâb al-îmân wa l-kufr," vol. 3, pp. 41–42; for the identification established between faith in the imam and religion (*al-dîn*), see al-Nuʿmânî, *Kitâb al-ghayba*, pp. 131 and 188, and Ibn Bâbûye, *Amâlî*, p. 639f.). As far as our present purpose is concerned, see the expression "*al-ʿaql dalîl al-mu'min*"(e. g. al-Kulaynî, *Uṣûl*, vol. 1, p. 29), which can thus be translated: "hiero-intelligence is the guide of the initiated Imamite."

44. See especially his *Sharḥ ʿaqâ'id al-Ṣadûq*, patricularly pp. 26f., 46f., and 66f.

45. See, for example, his *Amâlî*, Cairo, 1954, p. 81, and especially his *Kitâb al-shâfî fî l-imâma*, lith. ed. Tehran, 1301/1884, the entire introductory section, and pp. 98f.

46. Without being particularly centered on the idea of *ʿaql*, the latter two parts of McDermott's work, dedicated to a comparative study of the thought of Ibn Bâbûye, al-Mufîd, and al-Murtaḍâ, give an idea of the rationalist evolution of early Imamism (*The Theology of Shaikh al-Mufîd*, chapters 12 to 17).

47. These names appear to have arisen quite late; at the time of the earliest polemics, the names were of course given by adversaries. The "traditionalists" were called *ḥashwiyya*, *muqallida*, *ahl al-ḥadîth*, *aṣḥâb al-khabar* . . . (cf. al-Mufîd, *Awâ'il*

al-maqâlât, pp. 80-81, 86 ff., 92, 101, 118; al-Mufîd, *Sharḥ ʿaqâʾid al-Ṣaduq*, 186, 222; al-Mufîd, *al-Radd ʿalä aṣḥâb al-ʿadad*, in ʿAlî al-ʿÂmilî, *al-Durr al-manthûr*, p. 124; al-Ṭûsî, *ʿUddat al-uṣûl*, p. 248; al-Ṭûsî, *Kitâb al-ghayba*, p. 3) and "the rationalists": *muʿtazila* or *kalâmiyya* (cf., for example, Shahrastânî, *Milal*, pp. 169 and 178). The expressions *akhbârî* and *uṣûlî* appear to have been first used in the sixth/twelfth century by ʿAbd al-Jalîl al-Qazwînî (cf. his *Kitâb al-naqḍ*, pp. 3, 236, 272, 282, 285, 529, 568 . . .) and al-Shahrastânî (*Milal*). See also on this subject J. Calmard, "Le chiisme imamite en Iran à l'époque seldjoukide d'après le Kitâb al-naqḍ"; Scarcia Amoretti, "L'Imamismo in Iran nell'epoca selgiuchide: a proposita del problema delle "communita"; E. Kohlberg, "Akhbâriyya" in *Encyclopedia Iranica*; J. R. Cole, "Shiʿi clerics in Iraq and Iran: the Akhbari-Usuli conflict reconsidered."

48. That is, from the time of Muhammad Amîn Astarâbâdî (d. 1030/1624), who is considered to be the elaborator of the *akhbârî* system, and who was instrumental in the constitution of the *uṣûlî* system. See E. G. Browne, *A Literary History of Persia*, vol. 4, s.v.; G. Scarcia, "Intorno alle controversie tra Akhbârî e Usûlî presso gli Imâmiti di Persia," *RSO*, XXXIII, 1958 (for other bibliographical references, see the latter article, pp. 218 ff.).

49. Regarding the expression "proto-Shiʿite," see W. M. Watt, *The Formative Period of Islamic Thought*, s. v. On these first traces, cf. H. Modarressi Tabâtabâʾi, *An Introduction to Shîʿi Law*, chapter 4; H. Modarressi Tabâtabâʾi,, "Rationalism and Traditionalism in Shîʿi Jurisprudence: A Preliminary Survey," *SI*, vol. 59, 1984 (taken almost word-for-word from the first part of the preceding work); M. Momen, *An Introduction to Shiʿi Islam*, Chapter 12; E. Kohlberg, "Shîʿi Ḥadîth," pp. 299 ff.; W. Madelung, "Imâmism and muʿtazilite theology"; W. Madelung, the article on "al-Kulaynî" in *EI2*, vol. 5, p. 364; W. B. Hallaq, "On the Origins of the Controversy About the Existence of Mujtahids and the Gate of Ijtihâd," *SI*, vol. 63, 1986, and especially Andrew Joseph Newman's excellent doctoral thesis, *The Development and Political Significance of the Rationalist . . . and Traditionalist . . . School in Imami Shiʿi History* . . . (especially the first part).

50. Regarding the date of the death of the latter, see W. Madelung's article "Hishâm b. al-Ḥakam," *EI2*, and especially J. Van Ess, "Ibn Kullâb und die Miḥna," in *Oriens*, 18–19, 1967, 115. On these individuals, the fragments of their doctrines, and the titles of their writings, see al-Ashʿarî, *Maqâlât al-islâmiyyin*, s.v.; al-Baghdâdî, *al-Farq*, s.v.; al-Shahrastânî, *Milâl*, s. v.; Ibn al-Nadîm, *Kitâb al-Fihrist*, ed. Tajaddod, s.v.; al-Ṭûsî, *Fihrist kutub al-shîʿa*, pp. 143, 323, and 355f.; Muhammad ʿAlî Mudarris, *Rayḥânat al-adab*, s.v.; al-Ardabîlî, *Jâmiʿ al-ruwât*, s. v.

51. Cf. W. Madelung, "The Shiite and Khârijite Contribution to Pre-Ashʿarite *kalâm*"; J. Van Ess, *Une lecture à rebours* . . . s.v., and also under "chiites" and "chiites anthropomorphistes."

52. Husayn M. Jafri, *Origins and early development of Shiʿa Islam*, p. 305f; and especially Modarressi Tabâtabâʾi, *An Introduction* . . . , p. 24f.

53. For refutations of the theological theses of the disciples of the imams, see, e.g., al-Kulaynî, *al-Rawḍa*, 228; Ibn Bâbûye, *Kitâb al-tawḥîd*, p. 100 ff; Ibn Bâbûye, *Amâlî*, pp. 277, 342, 546, 552; al-Kashshî, *Rijâl* (abridged by sl-shaykh al-Ṭûsî, *Ikhtiyâr maʿrifat al-rijâl*, Mashhad, 1348 solar/1969, pp. 279–80; Asad Allâh al-Tustarî al-Kâẓimî (d. 1234/1818–19), *Kashf al-qinâʿ*, pp. 71–84.

54. Cf. al-Kashshî, *Rijâl*, p. 280; the titles of some the treatises that these theologians composed against one another have come to us via biographical and bio-bibliographical sources, for example, two of Hishâm b. al-Ḥakam's writings, *Kitâb al-radd ʿalä Hishâm al-Jawâlîqî* (*Fihrist*, p. 224), and *Kitâb ʿalä Shayṭân al-Ṭâq* (*Fihrist*, p. 224 and al-Najâshî, *Rijâl*, Tehran, 1337 solar/1959, p. 338; *Risâla fî maʿânä Hishâm* (i.e., b. al-Ḥakam) *wa Yûnus* (i.e., Yûnus b. ʿAbd al-Raḥmân, disciple of the seventh and eighth imams)" by ʿAlî b. Ibrâhîm b. Hâshim al-Qummî (*Rijâl* al-Najâshî, p. 197); "*Risâla fî l-radd ʿalä ʿAlî b. Ibrahîm b. Hâshim fî maʿnä Hishâm wa Yûnus*," by Saʿd b. ʿAbdAllâh al-Ashʿarî (*Rijâl* al-Najâshî, p. 134).

55. See, e.g., al-Ṭûsî, *Fihrist*, 132 (the note dedicated to Abû Jaʿfar al-Sakkâk, disciple of Hishâm b. al-Ḥakam) or the case of Abû Jaʿfar Muhammad b. Qibba (fourth/tenth century) and his theses against "impeccability" (*ʿiṣma*) and the inspired Science of the imams in his *Kitâb al-inṣâf fî l-imâma*" (Ibn al-Nadîm, *Fihrist*, p. 225); Ibn Qibba's theses were admired and reported by al-Murtaḍä (*al-Shâfî*, p. 100f.), and subsequently by other representatives of the rationalist current (for example, al-Ṭûsî, *Fihrist*, p. 133f.; see also Ibn Shahrâshub, d. 588/1192, *Maʿâlim al-ʿulamâʾ*, p. 85f.; al-ʿAllâma al-Ḥillî [d. 726/1325], *Khulâṣat al-aqwâl*, p. 143; al-Kâẓimî, *Kashf al-qinâʿ*, pp. 200 and 305).

56. Cf. al-Ashʿarî, *Maqâlât al-islâmiyyin*, pp. 37f, 60f., 331, 344, 369, 493f.; ʿAbd al-Jabbâr, *al-Mughnî*, vol. 5, p. 20; O. Pretzl, "Die frühislamische Atomenlehre," *Der Islam*, XIX, 1931, pp. 117–30, especially p. 129.

57. Cf. *Maqalât al-islâmiyyin*, pp. 44f., 272, 280, 494 (on the doctrine of Jahm b. Ṣafwân (d. 128/745), pp. 181, 346, 518, 589)); R. M. Frank, "The Neo-Platonism of Gahm ibn Safwân," *Muséon*, vol. 78, 1965, pp. 395f.; J. Van Ess, "Ḍirâr b. ʿAmr und die 'Cahmîya'," pp. 258f.

58. Regarding the "tactical" utility of *kalâm* in polemics, see, e.g., al-Kulaynî, *Uṣûl*, vol. 1, p. 95f.; Ibn Bâbûye, *Kitâb al-tawḥîd*, chapters 63 and 64; Ibn Bâbûye, *ʿUyûn akhbâr al-Riḍâ*, vol. 1, pp. 141, 173, 189; vol. 2, pp. 440, 653f; regarding the safeguarding of the unity of the imamites, see, e.g., al-Kashshî, *Rijâl*, p. 489 (the request made of traditionalists in the city of Qumm to stop hostilities and polemics against the Imamite *mutakallimûn*, for the purpose of avoiding division) and 498–99 (an attempt at appeasing too angry Imamite theologians).

59. The words of Jaʿfar in al-Kulaynî, *Uṣûl*, vol. 1, "kitâb faḍl al-ʿilm," p. 72: *Inna aṣḥâb al-maqâʾîs ṭalabû l-ʿilm bi l-maqâʾîs fa-lam tazidhumu l-maqâʾîs min al-ḥaqq illâ buʿdan wa inna dîn Allâh lâ yuṣâb bi l-maqâʾîs*."

60. Al-Kulaynî, *Uṣûl*, vol. 1, p. 73-74 (in other traditions from this chapter of the *Kitâb faḍl al-ʿilm*," *qiyâs* and *raʾy* are said to be "blameworthy innovations," *bidʿa*); see also Ibn Bâbûye, *Amâlî*, 6; al-Nuʿmânî, *Kitâb al-ghayba*, 77 (against *qiyâs*, *raʾy*, *ijtihâd*); on Samâʿa b. Mihrân, see e.g. al-Barqî, *Rijâl*, s. v.; al-Najâshî, *Rijâl*, s.v.; al-Ardabîlî, *Jâmiʿ al-ruwât*, s. v. (read "Sâʿima" as Samâʿa).

61. Al-Kulaynî, *Uṣûl*, vol. 1, p. 76; for the traditions that condemn recourse to *raʾy*, see also al-Ṣaffâr al-Qummî (d. 290/902-3), *Baṣâʾir al-darajât*, pp. 301 and 518; al-Nuʿmânî, *Kitâb al-ghayba*, pp. 77 and 79.

62. Ibn Bâbûye, *Amâlî*, pp. 552–53 (the words of Jaʿfar).

63. Ibn Bâbûye, *Kitâb al-tawḥid*, pp. 454 and 457 (the words of the fifth and sixth imams, respectively). Against *kalâm* in general and theological polemics (*jidâl*, *mirâʾ*,

khuṣûma), cf. chapter 67; or Ibn Bâbûye *Amâlî*, p. 417; or Ibn Bâbûye, *Kamâl al-dîn*, p. 324.

64. Ibn Bâbûye, *Kitâb al-tawḥid*, p. 458 (the words are Ja'far's). For the Imamite idea of *taslîm* (submission to the imams and scrupulous application of their directives, presented as being the ideal healthy attitude to be adopted when faced with questions about sacred ideas, as well as being the "antidote" to the temptation to enter into theological discussions), see al-Ṣaffar, *Baṣâ'ir*, p. 520, "fî l-taslîm lî-âl Muḥammad"; al-Kulaynî, *Uṣûl*, vol. 2, p. 234, "bâb al-taslîm wa faḍl al-musallimîn"; al-Nu'mânî, *Kitâb al-ghayba*, p. 79; Ibn Bâbûye, *Kitâb al-tawḥid*, p. 458f.; Ibn Bâbûye, *Kamâl al-dîn*, p. 324 (the words of the fourth imam, 'Alî b. al-Ḥusayn al-Sajjâd: "God's religion can be acquired only by submission; he who is submissive to us [the imams] is saved (*fa-man sallama lanâ salima*) . . . while he who has recourse to reasoning by analogy and to his own personal opinion is lost (*wa man kâna ya'mal bi l-qiyâs wa l-ra'y halaka*)."

65. None of those defending the idea according to which the imams supported *kalâm* and the Imamite *mutakallimûn* and professed a "rational" doctrine while relying on dialectical argumentation and reasoning has quoted any of the statements that we have just cited. More seriously still, their references are to relatively late texts (beginning with the work of al-Mufîd), all belonging to the "rationalist" current, or in the rare case where a reader is referred to older texts belonging naturally to the "traditionalist" current references become quite imprecise if not patently erroneous; see H. Modarressi Tabâtabâ'i, *An Introduction to Shî'î Law*, p. 24f. "The period of the presence of the imams"; references to al-Kulaynî or Ibn Bâbûye (p. 26, notes 1, 4, 6; p. 28, notes 13 and 14) do not at all reinforce the ideas of the author, except in extrapolations or interpretations out of context; on p. 28 the author attempts to posit that the imams practiced and approved of the use of *ra'y* and *qiyâs* and refers (p. 28 note 3), besides later sources, to only one early work, Ṣaffâr al-Qummî's *Baṣâ'ir al-darajât*, p. 301, where there is a whole chapter on the position of the imams *against* the use of *ra'y* and *qiyâs* (ch. 15 of section 6): "*Bâb fî l-a'imma inna 'indahum jamî' mâ fî l-Kitâb wa l-Sunna wa lâ yaqûlûn bi ra'yihim wa lam yurakhkhiṣû dhâlika shî'atahum.*" We have used this passage of the *Baṣâ'ir* to support our own remarks (note 61). Modarressi Tabâtabâ'i suggests no explanation for the predominance of the "traditionalist" current up to the second half of the fourth/tenth century, to which he himself furtively alludes on page 40 of his work.

66. See, e.g., J. A. Newman, *The Development and Political Significance of the Rationalist . . . and Traditionalist . . . School in Imami Shi'i History* , especially the conclusion of the first part. On the "Intermediary School" and its representatives, see Muḥaqqiq al-Ḥillî (d. 676/1277), al-*Mu'tabar*, p. 7; al-Kâẓimî, *Kashf al-qinâ'*, p. 139; 'Abbâs Eqbâl, *Khânedân-e Nawbakhtî*, p. 6f; Modarressi Tabâtabâ'i, *An Introduction to Shî'î Law*, p. 39.

67. All these data will be returned to at length in parts II and III of our study. The general index at the end of the book will assist the reader who is pressed to find them. At present, because of the needs of a comparative outline, the themes will only be mentioned.

68. Additonal details about these first compilations and their authors will be presented in the third part of this introduction, when the principle sources for the present study are introduced.

69. *Baṣâ'ir,* section II, chapters 6 to 21; section I, chapters 9 and 10; section IX, chapter 11; section 8, chapter 8.

70. *Uṣûl,* vol. 2, pp. 2–20, and vol. 2, pp. 25–34.

71. Cf., e.g., *Kitâb al-tawḥid,* p. 319; *'Uyûn akhbâr al-Riḍâ,* vol. 1, p. 262; *'Ilal al-sharâ'i',* vol. 1, pp. 5, 23, 34, 65-66, 116, 118, 122, 144, 183 . . . , vol. 2, chapter 1; *Amâlî,* pp. 75, 132, 182, 236, 347, 461, 593, 612 . . . ; *Kamâl al-dîn,* pp. 254, 275, 319, 335, 669. . . .

72. Al-Mufîd, *al-Ikhtiṣâṣ,* pp. 43, 154; al-Murtaḍä, *al-Shâfî,* pp. 32, 115.

73. *Baṣâ'ir,* all of section 3; section 4, chapters 7, 9; section 5, chapters 3f.; section 9, chapters 7–10; section 7, chapters 3 and 8. Al-Kulaynî deals with the first four series, using a lesser number of traditions: *Uṣûl,* vol. 1, pp. 321–30, 376–81, 388–91, 393; vol. 2, p. 20; and allusion to the sixth series is made in his *Rawḍa,* vol. 1, p. 182. Ibn Bâbûye reproduces only partially the three first series and vague allusions to the fourth: *'Ilal al-sharâ'i',* vol. 1, chapters 103, 108; *Amâlî,* p. 596; *Kamâl al-dîn,* pp. 223, 263. Al-Mufîd reports only traditions from series 3 and 4, being content for the rest with maintaining that the imams have the benefit of favors from God, that they can receive divine inspiration, and that they are capable of working wonders, cf. *al-Ikhtiṣâṣ,* pp. 65, 102f, 181; also, *Awâ'il al-maqâlât,* chapter 38; Al-Murtaḍä does likewise, *al-Shâfî,* pp. 87–88.

74. *Baṣâ'ir,* fourth section, chapters 4, 9, and those that follow; section 6, chapters 3–9; section 8, chapters 12 and those that follow; section 9, chapter 1. With the exception of the fourth and sixth series, al-Kulaynî writes about all of the powers, although as usual he fails to report all the traditions transmitted by his master, al-Ṣaffâr al-Qummî, cf. *Uṣûl,* vol. 1, pp. 334–42, 276; *al-Rawḍa,* vol. 1, p. 283; vol. 2, pp. 9, 67, 230. Ibn Bâbûye does likewise, *'Uyûn akhbâr al-Riḍâ,* vol. 1, p. 96; vol. 2, p. 227; *'Ilal al-sharâ'i',* vol. 1, chapter 139; *Amâlî,* pp. 63, 71–72, 112, 148, 289, 467; *Ma'ânî al-akhbâr,* pp. 67, 107; *Kamâl al-dîn,* pp. 327, 377, 537, 673–74. Al-Mufîd and al-Murtaḍä report only certain elements of series one and three (in the framework of general theory, professed equally by the majority of Sunni Muslims, of the possibility of saints working miracles—*karâmât* and rarely *mu'jizât;* cf. al-Mufîd, *al-Irshâd,* the *manâqib* and the *mu'jizât* of each imam; al-Mufîd, *al-Ikhtiṣâṣ,* pp. 54, 92, 171; al-Murtaḍä, *al-Shâfî,* pp. 90, 105; al-Murtaḍä, *Jumal al-'ilm wa l-'amal,* pp. 17, 35. Al-Murtaḍä vehemently criticizes the "traditionalist" traditionists for having reported certain hadith concerning supernatural powers of the imams that are preposterous from a reasonable point of view, like "the power to walk upon clouds," "travel in diverse regions of the heavens and the earth" or magical practices; cf. *al-Shâfî,* pp. 91, 100f., 124.

75. *Baṣâ'ir,* section 3, chapter 11; section 4, chapters 6–7; *Uṣûl,* vol. 1, pp. 325, 332; vol. 4, pp. 435f.; *al-Rawḍa,* vol. 1, pp. 3, 75, 83, 181, 265–66, 286; vol. 2, pp. 2–3, 60, 113–14, 231, 247f.

76. Ibn Bâbûye, e.g., *Ma'ânî al-akhbâr,* pp. 86f; *Risâlat al-i'tiqâdât,* English trans. by A. A. A. Fyzee, *A Shi'ite Creed,* pp. 84–85.

77. An entire section of the present work will be dedicated to "the Qur'an of the Imams." This question is of paramount importance for a proper understanding of several early ideas in Imamism, for example, the sources of the imams' *'ilm,* Imamite ideas on the destiny of the Muslim Community, and the famous idea of *sabb al-ṣaḥâba,* the return of the hidden imam.

78. Al-Nu'mânî, *Kitâb al-ghayba*, pp. 330f., 336–39, 378–79, 443–54, 473f.; see also al-Kulaynî, *Uṣûl*, vol. 2, pp. 117–20, 449f., 486; and al-Kulaynî, *Rawḍa*, vol. 2, pp. 145f.

79. Ibn Bâbûye, *Kamâl al-dîn*, pp. 229, 372, 384, 407, 417, 424, 434, 654, 671f.; see also Ibn Bâbûye, *Amâlî*, pp. 176f., 228, 284, and 288.

80. Al-Ṭûsî, *Kitâb al-ghayba*, p. 148f. The author's emphasis is on the "rational" proof of the phenomenon of the Occultation; it is thus normal for him to not have dealt with the "nonrational" elements reported. Before him, al-Mufîd and al-Murtaḍä did likewise; cf. al-Mufîd, *al-Fuṣûl al-'ashara fî l-ghayba*, Najaf, 1951, and *Khams rasâ'il fî ithbât al-Ḥujja*, Najaf, 1951 (the first *risâla* entitled "al-Fuṣûl al-'ashara" is another edition of the preceding work). By al-Murtaḍä, cf. "Mas'ala wajîza fî l-ghayba," in *Nafâ'is al-makhṭûṭât*, Baghdad, 1954, vol. 4.

81. The coming to power of the Buyids (334/945–447/1055) in no way altered what we are speaking of here; they were not able, nor in all probability did they want to neutralize either the effects of the Occultation or those of the almost general "rationalization," despite some resistance especially among cultivated Ḥanbalite minds. Moreover, political opportunity was pushing them to deal tactfully with the caliphs and the Sunni majority in Iraq as well as in Iran, where the Imamite community constituted only a small minority. It is nevertheless certain that "rationalist" Imamism took advantage of the moderate Shî'ism of the Buyids to consolidate its position and increase its social, economic, and religious influence (the introduction in Baghdad of the Shî'ite feasts of 'Âshûrâ and Ghadîr Khumm, official honors at 'Alid tombs especially in Iraq, moderate Shî'ism having become an "in" doctrine and attracting, subject to *tashayyu' ḥasan*, a number of intellectuals); see Cl. Cahen's article in *EI2*, vol. 1, pp. 390–97; H. Busse, *Die Buyiden und das Chalifat*, Beirut, 1969; F. Gabrieli, "Imâmisme et littérature sous les Bûyudes," in *Le Shî'isme imâmite*, pp. 105–13; 'A. A. Faqîhî, *Âl-e Bûye*, 3rd ed., Tehran, 1366 solar/1987.

82. The word "irrational" is deliberately eschewed because of its overly negative implications in the West. "Nonrational," which in this case could be substituted by "suprarational," is not meant to suggest anything formless, stupid, or gratuitously illogical, but simply that which is not necessarily subject to the control of reason, that which remains opposed to rationalization. We will attempt to isolate further and appropriately identify those elements by means of "guidemarks" associated with esoteric doctrines in order to minimize the possibility of errors in our discussion, and to lend to the discussion the universally valid character of a scientific inquiry. We are not referring here to rationalizing the nonrational, which would properly be impossible, but rather to taking hold of it and identifying its elements, and thus to contrast the solidity of a spiritual doctrine with the fantasies of the "irrational." These distinctions are all the more important since spiritual "suprarationalism" is most often seen as the opposite of both the extravagances of religious "irrationalism" and the petrification of dogmatic "rationalism."

83. On these collections of traditions, see, e.g., Aḥmad b. Muḥammad al-Barqî (d. 274 or 280/887 or 893), *al-Rijâl*, ed. Muḥaddith Urmawî, Tehran, 1342 solar/1963; al-Kashshî, *Ikhtiyâr ma'rifat al-rijâl*; Ibn al-Nadîm, *al-Fihrist*, section 5, chapter 2, pp. 223–27 and chapter 5, pp. 244-47; section 6, chapter 5, pp. 275–79; al-Ṭûsî, *Fihrist kutub al-shî'a*; F. Sezgin, *GAS*, vol. 1, pp. 525–52.

84. Al-Ṭûsî, *ʿUddat al-uṣûl*, pp. 25–63; H. Modarressi Tabâtabâ'i, *An Introduction to Shî'i Law*, pp. 44f.

85. See. M. Shafâ'î, "ʿUddat al-uṣûl-e shaykh Ṭûsî va naqsh-e ân dar madâr-e târîkh-e ʿelm-e oṣûl" in *Yâdnâme-ye shaykh al-ṭâ'ifa Abû Jaʿfar Md. b. Ḥasan-e Ṭûsî*, Mashhad, University of Mashhad, 1348 solar/1970, pp. 167–83; A. J. Newman, *The development and political significance . . .*, part II.

86. In the impressive corpus of Imamite literature from its origins to the present day (Shaykh Âqâ Bozorg Tehrânî's bibliographical encyclopedia, *al-Dharîʿa ilä taṣânîf al-shîʿa*, includes 25 volumes in-octavo, each of some 400 pages) there is an astonishing paucity of works dedicated to esoteric, mystical, occult, or otherwise "suprarational" traditions of the earliest compilations. Most often, these are the works of mystics or Imamite philosophers with a tendency toward sufism, all of which are either marginal or marginalized (e.g., the work of Sayyid Ḥaydar Amolî, seventh/fourteenth century, the *Mashâriq al-anwâr* of Rajab al-Ḥâfiẓ al-Bursî, eighth–ninth/fourteenth–fifteenth century; or the philosophical commentaries of al-Kulaynî's *Kâfî* by Muhammad Bâqir Mîr Dâmâd, d. 1040/1630, *al-Rawâshiḥ al-samâwiyya fî sharḥ al-aḥâdith al-imâmiyya*; or, by Mullâ Ṣadrâ al-Shîrâzî, d. 1050/1640, *Sharḥ uṣûl al-Kâfî*) or certain *akhbârîs* (e.g., the work of Muḥammad Amîn Astarâbâdî, d. 1030/1624) or authors belonging to the mystical Imamite brotherhoods of the last two centuries (the *shaykhiyya*, *dhahabiyya*, the *niʿmatullâhiyya*, the *oveysî* . . .). On the other hand, thousands of works have been dedicated to the corpus of juridical traditions of these compilations. It must be noted that the Imamite "Four Books" (*al-kutub al-arbaʿa*, that is, Kulaynî's *Kitâb al-kâfî*, Ibn Bâbûye's *Kitâb man lâ yaḥḍuruhu l-faqîh*, and *Tahdhîb al-aḥkâm* and the *Kitâb al-istibṣâr*, both by Ṭûsî), that are often hastily compared to the Sunni "Six Books," appear to have been recognized as such only rather recently; the first author who presented them as authoritative works par excellence in the matter of Imamite hadith seems to be al-Muḥaqqiq al-Ḥillî, d. 676/1277 (cf. especially his *al-Muʿtabar*, pp. 7–8, and his *Nukat al-nihâya in al-Jawâmiʿ al-fiqhiyya*, Tehran, 1276/1859, p. 373). The "Four Books" serve as an authority essentially in the matter of *fiqh*. Finally, let it be added that the criteriological science of Imamite hadith (*ʿilm dirâyat al-ḥadîth*, the Shîʿite equivalent of the Sunni *ʿilm al-jarḥ wa l-taʿdîl*) in its definitive form is a still later development, dating from the tenth/sixteenth century (beginning with the work of al-shahîd al-thânî Zayn al-Dîn b. ʿAlî al-ʿÂmilî, d. 966/1559, especially his *al-Dirâya*; cf. Modarressi Tabâtabâʿi, *An Introduction to Shîʿi Law*, pp. 5–6). Discussion on this science has nevertheless remained open to the present time (cf., e.g., the criticism of the Imamite "rationalists" *ʿilm al-dirâya* by Sarkâr Âqâ Ebrâhîmî, the shaykhî master assassinated in 1979, in *Fehrest-e kotob-e . . . mashâyekh . . . va kholâṣe-ye aḥvâl-e îshân*, Kermân, 1957, pp. 237–53). On this subject see K. Modîr Shânehtchî, "Kotob-e arbaʿe-ye ḥadîth-e shîʿe," in *Nâme-ye Âstân-e Qods*, num. 38–39, 1350 solar/1971, Mashhad; A. Arioli, "Introduzione allo studio del *ʿilm al-rijâl* imâmita : le fonti," in *Cahiers d'Onomastique Arabe*, 1979, pp. 51–89; E. Kohlberg, "Shîʿî Hadith," in *Arabic Literature to the End of the Umayyad Period*, Cambridge, 1983, pp. 299–307.

87. On him, see. e.g., al-Najâshî, *Rijâl*, s.v.; al-Ṭûsî, *Fihrist kutub al-shîʿa*, pp. 143–44; Baghdâdî Ismâʿîl Pâshâ, *Hidyat al-ʿârifîn*, Istanbul, 1951–55; vol. 2, p. 24; Md ʿAlî Mudarris, *Rayḥânat al-adab*, vol. 3, p. 453; ʿUmar Riḍâ Kaḥḥâla, *Muʿjam al-*

mu'allifîn, vol. 9, p. 208; Âqâ Bozorg Tehrânî, *al-Dharî'a*, vol. 3, pp. 124–25, num. 416. See my article 'Al-Ṣaffâr al-Qummî (d. 290/902–3) et son *Kitâb Baṣâ'ir al-darajât*," *Journal Asiatique*, vol. 280, num. 3–4, 1992, pp. 221–50.

88. A few collections of juridical traditions, all apparently lost, have also been attributed to him: *Kitâb al-ashriba, Kitâb al-janâ'iz, Kitâb al-wuḍû', Kitâb al-ṣalât*, and so on (cf. Mudarris, *Rayḥânat al-adab*).

89. This is the title of the majority of the manuscripts presented by Brockelmann, *GAL*, SI, p. 319, and Sezgin, *GAS*, vol. 1, p. 538, num. 29; this work is not to be confused with the *Baṣâ'ir al-darajât* by the Imamite Sa'd b. 'Abd Allâh al-Ash'arî (d. 299 or 301/910 or 912), the author of the famous *Kitâb al-maqâlât wa l-firaq* (ed. M. J. Mashkûr, Tehran, 1963); cf. Tehrânî, *al-Dharî'a ilä taṣânîf al-shî'a*, num. 415; Sezgin, *GAS*, vol. 1, p. 538, num. 30.

90. Edited by Mîrzâ Muḥsin Kûtchehbâghî, Tabrîz, n.d. (the editor's introduction is dated 1380/1960). No reference information is given for the manuscripts used, but it is evident that the editor had access to the lithographed edition of 1285/1868, done in Iran and with the assistance of the "readings" of the *Biḥâr al-anwâr* of Md. Bâqir al-Majlisî (d. 1111/1699). The work has on its first page the title *Kitâb Baṣâ'ir al-darajât al-kubrä fî faḍâ'il âl Muḥammad.*

91. On this subject, see the article "al-Kulaynî" by W. Madelung in *EI2*, vol. 5, p. 364, and also al-Sam'ânî, *al-Ansâb*, facsimile edition and introduction by D. S. Margoliouth, Leiden-London, 1912, 486a; al-Kantûrî, *Kashf al-ḥujub*, pp. 418-19; al-Sayyid al-'Âmilî, *A'yân al-shî'a*, Damascus, 1935-61, juz' 47, pp. 152–53; Ḥusayn 'AbdAllâh Maḥfûẓ, *Sîrat Md b. Ya'qûb al-Kulaynî,* in Kaḥḥâla, *Mu'jam al-mu'allifîn*, vol. 12, p. 116.

92. Several editions have been done in Iran or in Iraq; we will use that of Sayyid Jawâd Muṣṭafawî, with Persian translation and annotations, Tehran, n.d., 4 vols. (the fourth volume is translated by Sayyid Hâshim Rasûlî Maḥallâtî and is dated 1386/1966).

93. Edition with Persian translation and notes by Rasûlî Maḥallâtî, 2 books in one volume in octavo, Tehran, 1389/1969.

94. See al-Najâshî, *Rijâl*, s.v.; al-Kantûrî, *Kashf al-ḥujub*, p. 452; Khwânsârî, *Rawḍât al-jannât*, p. 555; 'Abbas al-Qummî, *Hidyat al-aḥbâb*, p. 46; Kaḥḥâla, *Mu'jam al-mu'allifîn*, vol. 8, p. 195; Brockelmann, *GAL*, SI, p. 321, 9a; Sezgin, *GAS*, vol. 1, p. 543, num. 38.

95. Cf. Tehrânî, *al-Dharî'a ilä taṣânîf al-shî'a*, vol. 4, p. 318; P. Nwyia, *Exégèse coranique et langage mystique*, p. 159 (the author gives, although with no reference, the date 328/940 as the date of Nu'mânî's death; Nu'mânî had read the complete version of his *Kitâb al-ghayba* to Md. b. 'Alî Abû l-Ḥusayn al-Shajâ'î al-Kâtib in 342/953; cf. *Kitâb al-ghayba*, p. 18).

96. Al-Nu'mânî, *Kitâb al-ghayba*, ed. 'A. A. Ghaffârî, Tehran, 1397/1977. We are also using the edition and the Persian translation by M. J. Ghaffârî, Tehran, 1985.

97. See A. A. A. Fyzee's article "Ibn Bâbawayh" in *EI2*, vol. 3, pp. 749–50; add to the bibliography Tehrânî, *al-Dharî'a ilä taṣânîf al-shî'a*, vol. 2, p. 226; Kaḥḥâla, *Mu'jam al-mu'allifîn*, vol. 11, p. 3; Zirikli, Khayr al-dîn, *al-A'lâm*, Cairo, 1954-59, vol. 7, p. 159; Brockelmann, *GAL*, S I, p. 321; Sezgin, *GAS*, vol. 1, p. 544, num. 44.

98. For Ibn Bâbûye's bibliography, see S. Nafîsî's introduction to the edition of

the *Muṣâdaqat al-ikhwân*, Tehran, n.d., pp. 1–18; A. A. A. Fyzee, *A Shiʿite Creed*, p. 12f.

99. The Najaf Edition, 1385/1966, 2 books in one volume in octavo, with introduction by M. Ṣ. Baḥr al-ʿulûm.

100. *Kamâl al-dîn wa tamâm al-niʿma*, ed. ʿA. A. Ghaffârî, Qumm, 1405/1985; the majority of manuscripts have the title *Ikmâl al-dîn wa itmâm al-niʿma* (the author had undoubtedly read the Qurʾanic verse "*. . . al-yawm akmaltu lakum dînakum wa atmamtu ʿalaykum niʿmatî . . .*" Qurʾan 5:3); on this subject, see D. Gimaret, *Kitâb Bilawhar wa Bûdhasaf*, French trans., Paris-Geneva, 1971, pp. 27f.

101. Ed. Sayyid Hâshim al-Ḥusaynî al-Tehrânî, Tehran, 1398/1978; see also H. Corbin, "Le Livre du Tawhîd de Shaykh Sadûq et son commentaire par Qâzî Saʿîd Qummi," in *Annuaire EPHE* (sciences religieuses), volumes 73 and 74, pp. 102–9 and 106–14.

102. Tehran ed., with Persian trans. and notes by M. B. Kamareyî, 1404/1984 (containing 92 *majlis*).

103. Ed. Sayyid Mahdî Ḥusaynî Lâjevardî, Tehran, 1378/1958, 2 books in one volume in octavo.

104. *Ṣifât al-shîʿa wa Faḍâʾil al-shîʿa*, Tehran ed., with Persian trans. and introduction (in Persian) by Ḥ. Fashâhî, 1342 solar/1964.

105. *Maʿânî al-akhbâr*, ed. ʿA. A. Ghaffârî, Tehran, 1379/1959; *Kitâb al-khiṣâl*, text and Persian trans. by M. B. Kamareyî, Tehran, 1361 solar/1982; *al-Muqniʿ wa al-Hidâya*, ed. Md. Wâʿiẓ Khurâsânî, Tehran, 1377/1957; *Kitâb man lâ yaḥḍuruhu l-faqîh*, ed. Ḥ. al-Mûsawî al-Kharsân, Tehran, 5th ed., 1390/1970; "Risâlat al-iʿtiqâdât," in ʿAllâma al-Ḥillî, *al-Bâb al-ḥâdî ʿashar*, Tehran, 1370/1950.

106. Al-Barqî, *Kitâb al-maḥâsin*, ed. J. al-Muḥaddith al-Urmawî, Tehran, 1370/1950.

107. There are numerous editions of this work; we are using the one by Sayyid ʿA. N. Fayḍ al-islâm, *al-Ṣaḥîfa al-kâmila al-sajjâdiyya*, with Persian translation and notes, n.l., 1375/1955; cf. now the English translation by William Chittick: *The Psalms of Islam*, London, 1988.

108. *Tafsîr Jaʿfar al-Ṣâdiq*, ed. P. Nwyia, in *Mélanges de l'Université Saint Joseph*, volume 43, 1968, fasc. 4, pp. 188–230 (redone by ʿA. Zayʿûr, *al-Tafsîr al-ṣufî li l-Qurʾan ʿinda l-Ṣâdiq*, Beirut, 1979); this is a recension by the mystic al-Sulamî (d. 412/1021) in his *Ḥaqâʾiq al-tafsîr* that, in comparison with the text quoted by al-Nuʿmanî (mss. Bankipore 1460 and Istanbul, Nafiz Pasa 65, one part of which is edited with the title *al-Muḥkam wa l-mutashâbih* under al-Murtadä's name, lith. ed., Iran, n.d.) was purged of any reference to Shîʿism and any allusion to *ahl al-bayt*. See also Massignon, *Essai*, pp. 201–6; P. Nwyia, *Exégèse coranique*, pp. 156f.

109. Al-ʿAskarî, *Tafsîr*, Qumm, 1407/1987. Despite its early date of composition (it is cited numerous times by Ibn Bâbûye in several of his works), it is not certain that this *tafsîr* is the work of the eleventh imam; a "traditionalist" author with the breadth of knowledge of Muḥsin al-Fayḍ al-Kâshânî (d. 1019/1680) actually calls it "the *Tafsîr* attributed to al-ʿAskarî" (cf. his *Tafsîr al-Ṣâfî*, n.l. [Iran] 1266/1849, p. 19; al-Kâskanî, *al-Nawâdir fî jamʿ al-aḥâdîth*, Tehran, 1960, p. 3); see also al-Tihrânî's points of view, *al-Dharîʿa*, vol. 4, pp. 285–93.

110. Furât, *Tafsîr*, ed. Muḥammad al-Kâẓim Tehran, 1410/1990.

111. Al-Qummî, *Tafsîr*, Najaf, 1386-87/1966–68.

112. Al-ʿAyyâshî, *Tafsîr*, Qumm, 1380–1960; in a recent article, M. Bar-Asher claims to have completed a doctoral thesis in Hebrew under the direction of Professor Kohlberg at the Hebrew University of Jerusalem entitled *Etudes sur l'exégèse imâmite ancienne du Coran (III-IV/IX-X^e^* siècles) (cf. "Deux traditions hétérodoxes dans les anciens commentaires Imamites du Coran," *Arabica*, vol. 37, 1990, p. 291); the publication and translation of this work are eagerly awaited).

113. *Kâmil al-ziyârât*, lith. ed., Iran, n.d.

114. *Kifâyat al-athar*, lith. et., Tehran, 1305/1888.

115. *Muqtaḍab al-athar* Tehran, 1346/1927.

116. We are using the Tehran edition, 1392/1972, with Persian translation and notes by ʿA. N. Fayḍ al-islâm, 6 books in one volume in octavo, 1340 pages. The authenticity of the *Nahj al-balâgha* was in doubt by figures as early as Ibn Taymiyya (d. 728/1328; see his *Kitâb minhâj al-sunnat al-nabawiyya*, vol. 4, pp. 157–59, or H. Laoust, *Essai sur les doctrines . . . d'Ibn Taimîya*, p. 108). Regarding doubt about the authenticity of ʿAlî's famous letter to Mâlik al-Ashtar al-Nakhaʿî, governor of Egypt (*Nahj al-balâgha*, pp. 988f.), see W. al-Qâḍî, "An early Fâṭimid political document," in *SI*, vol. 48, 1978, pp. 71–108; on the general state of the question, see the remarkable study by L. Veccia Vaglieri, "Sul *Nahg al-balâghah* e sul suo compilatore ash-Sharîf ar-Raḍî," in *AIUON*, special num. 8, 1958, pp. 1–46. On the importance of the *Nahj al-balâgha* for the development of Shîʿite thought, see H. Corbin, *Histoire de la philosophie islamique*, first part, Paris, 1964, pp. 57–59; it should be mentioned that ʿAlî's conversation with his disciple Kumayl b. Ziyâd about the Truth (known especially through Shîʿite mystical sources by the name "*mâ l-ḥaqîqa ?*") to which Corbin refers on p. 58 is not in the *Nahj al-balâgha*.

117. *Ithbât al-waṣiyya*, Najaf, al-Maktabat al-Murtaḍawiyya, al-Maṭbaʿat al-Ḥaydariyya, n.d. Regarding the Imamites' claim to al-Masʿûdî, see, e.g., al-Najâshî, *Rijâl*, p. 178; al-ʿAllâma al-Ḥillî, *Khulâṣat al-aqwâl*, p. 56; Khwânârî, *Rawḍât al-jannât*, pp. 379-80; al-Mâmaqânî, *Tanqîḥ al-maqâl*, s. v. (under "ʿAlî b. al-Ḥusayn b. ʿAlî al-Masʿûdî"); Tehrânî, *al-Dharîʿa*, vol. 1, p. 110, num. 536. Among the Sunnites, Ibn Taymiyya (*Kitâb minhâj al-sunnat al-nabawiyya*, vol. 2, pp. 129–31) and Ibn Ḥajar al-ʿAsqalânî (*Lisân al-mîzân*, vol. 4, pp. 224–25, the first part of the note has been left out) accuse him of Shîʿism; others have considered him a Muʿtazilite (e.g., al-Dhahabî, *Mîzân al-iʿtidâl*, s. v.; al-Subkî, *al-Ṭabaqât al-shâfiʿiyya*, vol. 2, p. 307). On this subject, see especially C. Pellat's article "Masʿûdî et l'imâmisme," in *Le Shîʿisme imâmite*, pp. 69–90; as Pellat well states, the *Ithbât al-waṣiyya* is "a text the authenticity of which, if it were proven, would make Masʿûdî the first "historian" of the imams" (p. 77), although it is here a question of what H. Corbin calls "hierohistory" (*ibid.*, p. 90). Counter to Pellat's tendency to opt for authenticity in attributing the book to al-Masʿûdî, see the skeptical and sometimes quite pertinent remarks by T. Khalidi in *Islamic historiography: the histories of Masʿûdî*, Albany, 1975, pp. 138, note 2 and 163–64.

118. These are what the Imamites now call the "four books" of the "three Muhammads" (Md. b. Yaʿqûb al-Kulaynî, Md b. ʿAlî Ibn Bâbûye, and Md b. Ḥasan al-Ṭûsî); numerous editions of the works have been published in Iran or Iraq.

119. See, e.g., Syed Ameer Ali, *Mohammedan Law*, Calcutta, 1928, vol. 2, pp. 398f.; H. Löschner, *Die dogmatischen Grundlagen des shiʿitischen Rechts*, Erlangen-

Nürnberg, 1971; G. Lecomte, "Aspects de la littérature du ḥadîth chez les Imâmites" in *Le Shî'isme imâmite*, pp. 91–101; Y. Linant de Bellefonds, "Le droit imâmite," in *Le Shî'isme imâmite*, pp. 183–99; E. Kohlberg, "Shî'i Hadith"; T. Rauscher, *Sharî'a: islamischer Familienrecht der Sunna und Shî'a*, Frankfurt, 1987.

120. Official recognition of *ijmâ'* (the consensus of the religious authorities) and *'aql* (in the sense of logical reasoning) as two other "principles of jurisprudence" (*uṣûl al-fiqh*) is a later addition and is used only by the "rationalists"; the first source to include them seems to have been *al-Sarâ'ir al-ḥâwî li taḥrîr al-fatâwî* (Tehran, 1270/1853, p. 3) by Ibn Idrîs al-'Ijlî al-Ḥillî (d. 598/1202); see H. Modarressi Tabâtabâ'i, *An Introduction to Shî'i Law*, chapter 1, pp. 3f.

121. *"Mâ min shay' illâ wa fîhi kitâbun aw sunnatun,"* al-Kulaynî, *Uṣûl*, vol. 1, p. 77.

122. *"Kullu shay' mardûd ilä l-Kitâb wa l-Sunna wa kullu ḥadîth lâ yuwâfiqu Kitâb Allâh fahuwa zukhruf,"* al-Kulaynî, *Uṣûl*, vol. 1, p. 89.

123. The imam is the "initiated and initiating Sage" par excellence; in Part III we shall deal in detail with the Knowledge of the imam.

124. " . . . *Inna fîhi 'ilm mâ maḍä wa 'ilm mâ ya'tî ilä yawm al-qiyâma wa ḥukma mâ baynakum wa bayân mâ aṣbaḥtum fîhi takhtalifûn fa-law sa'altumûnî 'anhu la'allamtukum,"* al-Kulaynî, *Uṣûl*, vol. 1, pp. 78–79, num. 7 *in fine*.

125. *"Qad walandanî rasûl Allâh wa anâ a'lamu Kitâb Allâh wa fîhi bad' al-khalq wa mâ huwa kâ'in ilä yawm al-qiyâma wa fîhi khabar al-samâ' wa khabar al-arḍ wa khabar al-janna wa khabar al-nâr wa khabar mâ kâna wa khabar mâ huwa kâ'in a'lamu dhâlika kamâ anẓuru ilä kaffî inna Allâha yaqûl fîhi tibyân kulli shay'."* al-Kulaynî, *Uṣûl*, vol. 1, p. 79.

126. *"Ḥadîthî ḥadîthu abî wa ḥadîthu abî ḥadîthu jaddî . . . wa ḥadîthu rasûl Allâh qawl Allâh,"* al-Kulaynî, *Uṣûl*, vol. 1, p. 68. For the commentaries see Mullâ Ṣadrâ, *Sharḥ Uṣûl al-Kâfî*, p. 41; Mullâ Khalîl al-Qazwînî, *al-Shâfî fî sharḥ al-Kâfî*, p. 76; Md Bâqir al-Majlisî, *Mir'ât al-'uqûl*, p. 112.

127. Al-Kulaynî, *Uṣûl*, vol. 1, pp. 65-66; see also al-Nu'mânî, *Kitâb al-ghayba*, p. 127 ("Our creation is one, our Science is one, our worth is one, we are all one . . . ": "*Khalqunâ wâḥid wa 'ilmunâ wâḥid wa faḍlunâ waḥid wa kullunâ waḥid* . . . ") and p. 183 ("To deny one of the living imams is tantamount to denying all those who preceded him": "*Man ankara wâḥidan min al-aḥyâ' faqad ankara l-amwât*"); Ibn Bâbûye, *Kamâl al-dîn*, pp. 14–15 (the same tradition, and also: "He who denies our last one denies also our first one": "*Al-munkir li-âkhirinâ ka l-munkir li-awwalinâ*"). Having here taken a phenomenological approach, we shall also consider the teaching of the imams as a whole to which each of them supposedly brings elements and information that complete what was brought by his predecessors. It would likewise be interesting to undertake a study to see whether the teachings of each of them contained elements specific to that particular imam.

128. On the progressive importance and elaboration of the methodology of *isnâd*, see J. Horovitz, "Alter und Ursprung des Isnâd," *Der Islam*, vol. 8, 1918, pp. 39–47; J. Robson, "Ibn Isḥâq's use of the *isnâd*," *The John Rylands Library*, vol. 38, 1955–56, pp. 449–65; J. Robson, "al-djarḥ wa al-ta'dîl," *EI2*, vol. 2, pp. 473–74; W. M. Watt, "The Materials Used by Ibn Isḥâq," *Historians of the Middle East*, London, 1962, pp. 23–34, especially pp. 27f.

129. Cf. J. Robson, "Ḥadîth," *EI2*, vol. 3, pp. 24f.; Ṣubḥî al-Ṣâliḥ, *'Ulûm al-ḥadith wa muṣṭalaḥahu*, Damascus, 1379/1959.

130. The only exception to this rule appears to be the case of the famous Companion Jâbir b. 'AbdAllâh al-Anṣârî, faithful to the cause of the imams, from whom the Imamis report traditions without passing through an imam as intermediary; cf. E. Kohlberg, "An unusual Shî'i *isnâd*," *IOS*, vol. 5, 1975, pp. 142–49.

131. See al-Kulaynî, *Uṣûl*, vol. I, pp. 65-66, num. 4, and p. 67, num. 12. On *ijâza*, vol. 1, p. 66, num. 6, and p. 68, num. 15.

132. On the qualities of the transmitter, see al-Kulaynî, *Uṣûl*, vol. 1, p. 86, num. 10 and p. 89, num. 8; also, Ṣaffâr, *Baṣâ'ir*, section 10, chapter 22, p. 537. Let it be added that at the time, the term *fiqh* did not yet have, at least when the imams used it, the restricted sense of "canon law"; in the early texts it meant all knowledge of a religious nature, and thus was part of *'ilm*, the holy initiatory Science (cf., e.g., its use throughout the "kitâb faḍl al-'ilm" of al-Kulaynî's *Uṣûl*).

133. Al-Kulaynî, *Uṣûl*, vol. 1, p. 80, num. 1, and *Nahj al-balâgha*, pp. 665–67.

134. Ṣaffâr, *Baṣâ'ir*, section 10, chapter 22, pp. 537–38; al-Kulaynî, *Uṣûl*, vol. 1, p. 62, num. 6.

135. Al-Kulaynî, *Uṣûl*, vol. 1, pp. 86-88. The disciple in question was 'Umar b. Ḥanẓala al-'Ijlî al-Bakrî Abû Ṣakhra al-Kûfî, disciple of the fifth and sixth imams; on him, see al-Ṭûsî, *Rijâl*, p. 131, num. 64 and p. 251, num 451; al-Ardabîlî, *Jâmi' al-ruwât*, vol. 1, p. 633.

136. Al-Kulaynî, *Uṣûl*, vol. I, p. 65, num. 2; five of Ja'far's disciples were called Muhammad b. Muslim; the best known is Md b. Muslim b. Rabâḥ al-Thaqafî Abû Ja'-far al-A'war, who, according to Ṭûsî (*Rijâl*, p. 300, num. 317), was nearly seventy in 150/767; see also al-Ardabîlî, *Jâmi' al-ruwât*, vol. 2, p. 193.

137. Al-Kulaynî, *Uṣûl*,, vol. 1, p. 65, num. 63. Dâwûd b. Rarqad Abû Yazîd al-Asadî al-Kûfî was the disciple of the sixth and seventh imams; on him, see al-Najâshî, *Rijâl*, s.v.; al-Ṭûsî, *Rijâl*, p. 189, num. 4, and p. 349, num. 2; al-Ṭûsî, *Fihrist kutub al-shî'a*, p. 97; al-Ardabîlî, *Jâmi' al-ruwât*, vol. 1, p. 305.

138. On the idea of abrogation, see, e.g., al-Kulaynî, *Uṣûl*, "kitâb faḍl al-'ilm," bâb ikhtilâf al-ḥadîth, vol. 1, pp. 80f.

139. *"Man 'arafa annâ lâ naqûlu illâ ḥaqqan fa-l-yaktafî bi-mâ ya'lamu minnâ fa'in sami'a minnâ khilâf mâ ya'lamu anna dhâlika difâ'un minnâ 'anhu,"* al-Kulaynî, *Uṣûl*, vol. 1, p. 85, num. 6. According to al-Nawbakhtî, from the earliest times of the imams, their adversaries claimed that ideas like *taqiyya* or *badâ'* (changing divine decisions) were nothing more than reasons for hiding the errors and contradictions in Imami doctrine (cf. al-Nawbakhtî, *Firaq al-shî'a*, French trans. and notes by M. J. Mashkour, *Les Sectes shiites*, 2d ed., Tehran, 1980, pp. 79–80.

140. "Write down [Tradition], for you will only remember it in this way"; "Through writing the heart finds confidence (*al-qalb yattakil 'alä l-kitâba*)"; "vocalize our words aloud, for we [the imams] are eloquent people (*qawm fuṣaḥâ'*)," al-Kulaynî, *Uṣûl*, vol. 1, pp. 66–67.

141. For "original" as one of the early meanings of *aṣl*, pl. *uṣûl* (just as is the case for "copy" as one of the meanings of *far'*, pl. *furû'*) see R. G. Khoury, "L'importance d'Ibn Lahî'a et de son papyrus conservé à Heidelberg dans la tradition musulmane du deuxième siècle de l'Hégire," *Arabica*, vol. 22, num. 1, 1975, p. 8; M. M. A'ẓamî,

Studies in Early Hadith Literature, 2nd ed., Indianapolis, 1978, p. 29; on the "400 books" see E. Kohlberg's excellent article "al-Uṣûl al-arbaʿumiʾa," *JSAI*, 10, 1987, pp. 128-166 (we fail to find the author's argument for not translating *aṣl* by *original copy* convincing; *ibid.*, pp. 128-29). See also the following note.

142. See also Tihrânî, *al-Dharîʿa*, vol. 2, pp. 125–67 (on the classical bibliography of this subject, see pp. 129-34); K. Modîr Shânetchî, "kotob-e arbaʿe-ye ḥadîth-e shîʿe," *Nâme-ye Âstân-e Qods*, num. 1, new series, vol. 38, pp. 165–92. Kohlberg presents three manuscripts of fragments still extant from the "400 books" (*ibid.*, pp. 150f.); we shall on occasion use that of the University of Tehran (num. 962) although this text presents no particular interest for the subject before us.

143. The number of traditions coming from the fifth and sixth imams and reported by early compilations is far superior to the number of those from the ten other imams, the Prophet, and Fatima combined. Using the example of the "four books," al-Kulaynî's contains 16,100 traditions, Ibn Bâbûye's contains 9044, and al-Ṭûsî's two works, *Takdhîb al-aḥkâm* and *Istibṣâr*, contain 13,590 and 5511, respectively. Of these roughly 38,000 traditions, nearly 8000 come from al-Bâqir and Jaʿfar; cf. Modîr Shânetchî, *Kotob-e arbaʿe . . .* " p. 171; *Y. Richard,* Le shîʿisme en Iran, p. 30. It must be remembered that Twelver Shiʿism is also called Jaʿfarite Shiʿism (*al-shîʿa al-jaʿfariyya, al-madhhab al-jaʿfarî*).

144. On these well-known events and their related bibliography, we refer the reader to F. M. Pareja *et al.*, *Islamologie*, s. v., and to H. Laoust, *Les Schismes dans l'Islam*, s. v. To the bibliographical sources of these two works, let us add one early source with historical import of the first order: the anonymous *Akhbâr al-dawlat al-ʿabbâsiyya*, ed. ʿA. ʿA. al-Dûrî, Beirut, 1971; the title chosen by the editor seems erroneous; classical sources call it *Kitâb ʿAbbâsî*, *Kitâb al-ʿAbbâs*, or even *Akhbâr al-ʿAbbâs* (see, e.g., Ḥasan b. Md al-Qummî, *Taʾrîkh Qumm*, pp. 236–37). An abridged version dating from probably the eleventh/seventeenth century was edited by P. Griaznevich in Moscow in 1960 with the title *Nabdha min kitâb al-taʾrîkh al-majhûl min al-qarn al-ḥâdî ʿashar*. See also M. Sharon, "The ʿAbbasid Daʿwa reexamined on the basis of a new source," XXI–XLI.

145. Al-Kulaynî, *Uṣûl*, vol. 1, p. 67, num. 11; Jaʿfar's partner in conversation is none other than his famous disciple al-Mufaḍḍal b. ʿUmar al-Juʿfî al-Kûfî, who was also the disciple of the seventh imam; on him, see Najâshî, *Rijâl*, s. v.; Kashshî, *Rijâl*, p. 383; Ṭûsî, *Rijâl*, p. 314, num. 554 and p. 360, num. 23; ʿAllâma al-Ḥillî, *Khulâṣa*, p. 182.

146. Al-Kulaynî, *Uṣûl*, vol. 1, p. 66, num. 10.

147. Ibn Kathîr, *al-Bidâya wa l-nihâya*, vol. 11, pp. 309-12; Ibn Athîr, *al-Kâmil fî l-taʾrîkh*, sub anno 381f; Yâqût al-Ḥamawî, *Muʿjam al-buldân*, s. v. "bayn al-sûrayn."

148. Ibn Kathîr, *al-Bidâya wa l-nihâya*, vol. 11, pp. 333–36 and 347–48, vol. 12., pp. 3, 19, 53f.; see also H. Laoust, *Les Schismes dans l'Islam*, pp. 182-83 and *La Profession de foi d'Ibn Baṭṭa*, notes 221 and 222.

149. Modarressi Tabâtabâʾî, *An Introduction to Shîʿi Law*, p. 6f.; the totality of the "four books," with the exception of part of the *Uṣûl* of *al-Kâfî*, is concerned with canon law (cf. note 86).

150. This is why the adjective "theosophic" is more fitting to qualify this phase of Imamite doctrine; first of all, it differentiates between dialectical theology (*kalâm*) and

philosophy inspired by the Greeks (*falsafa*), both of which are later developments. Also taken into account are the etymological sense of the term (Greek *theosophia*, "the knowledge of God") and its modern meaning in Western languages, with magical and occult connotations. The remainder of this study will justify these reflections.

NOTES TO CHAPTER 2

151. In contrast to the semantic complexity of the term *walâya* in the administrative, social, and religious language of the beginnings of Islam and later in the technical terminology of sufism, *walâya*, in the context of early Shî'ism, has a quite simple translation with two interdependent and complementary meanings: applied to the imams of different prophets, it refers to their ontological status or their sacred initiatory mission; several nuances of the root *wly* are found in this meaning: the *walî*-imam is the "friend" and the closest "helper" of God and His prophet; he immediately "follows" the latter in his mission; he is the "chief," the "master" of believers par excellence. In this acceptation, *walî* is a synonym of *waṣî* (the inheritor, the heir [of the Sacred Cause of the prophets]) or the *mawlä* (applied to the imam, this term means the master, the guide, the protector, the *patronus*). Applied to the faithful of the imams, *walâya* denotes the unfailing love, faith, and submission that the initiated owe to their holy initiating guide; in this acceptation, the term becomes the equivalent of *tawallî* (being the faithful friend or the obedient protegé of someone); "true Shî'ites" are called the *mutawallî* of the imams. Throughout our study, we will see evidence of this double meaning of *walâya* in the early texts.

152. Doctrinal information concerning the person of Fâṭima is rare in Imamism's early texts. A mystical doctrine of sorts has developed around her, either in Ismâ'îli circles, or in the works of later Imamite authors. For the first of these, see especially L. Massignon's studies "Der Gnostische Kult der Fâṭima im Shiitischen Islam," "La Mubâhala de Médine et l'hyperdulie de Fâṭima," "La notion du voeu et la dévotion musulmane à Fâṭima," in *Opera minora*, vol. 1, pp. 514–22, 550–72, 573–91 respectively; H. Corbin, *Corps spirituel et Terre céleste*, pp. 82–99. For the second case, see Mme T. Sabri's thesis, based exclusively on later Imamite sources and in particular on the *Biḥâr al-anwâr: L'hagiographie de Fâṭima d'après le Biḥâr al-Anwâr de Md Baqîr Majlisî (d. 1111/1699)*, Paris III, June 1969. Let us point out finally the near inexistence of an early Imamite bibliography of Fâṭima in H. Lammens's work *Fâṭima et les filles de Mahomet*, Rome, 1912, and in the quite well documented article by L. Veccia Vaglieri in *EI2*, vol. 2, pp. 861–70. In the course of the present work we will have occasion to see some early information regarding Fâṭima.

153. There is no need to delve deeply into this basic information here, as it is found in almost all studies dedicated to Imamism; the best presentation, despite its being only vaguely historical in parts, is that of Henry Corbin; see, e.g., *En Islam iranien*, vol. 1, all of Book One, "Aspects du shî'isme duodécimain" and *Histoire de la philosophie islamique*, first part, II, A, 3 and 4, pp. 69–85.

154. The numbers cited most frequently are 2000, 7000, and 14,000 years before the creation (*al-khalq*) of Adam or before the world (*al-dunyâ*); for 2000 years, see, e.g., Ibn Bâbûye, *'Ilal*, ch. 116, p. 134; ch. 139, p. 174/Ibn Bâbûye, *Amalî*, "majlis" 18, p. 75; al-Nu'mânî, *Kitâb al-ghayba*, p. 131; Ibn Shahrâshûb al-Mâzandarânî (d. 588/1192), *Manâqib*, vol. 1, p. 183. For 7000 years, see, e.g., Ibn Bâbûye, *'Ilâl*, ch.

156, pp. 208f. For 14000 years, see, e.g., Ibn Bâbûye, *Kamâl al-dîn*, pp. 275 and 335–36; Ibn al-Biṭrîq al-Ḥillî (d. 600/1203), *Kitâb al-ʿumda*, p. 75 (referring to Aḥmad b. Ḥanbal: "*Kuntu anâ wa ʿAlî nûran bayna yadayiʾ llâh ʿazza wa jalla qabla an yakhluqa Âdam bi arbaʿa ʿashara alfa ʿâmin,*"; this tradition does not appear in the *Musnad*).

155. A Qurʾanic expression (Qurʾan 3:7; 13:39; and 43:4). See Ibn Bâbûye, *ʿIlâl*, chapter 70, pp. 79f. Among Sunni sources, see al-Suyûṭî, *al-Khaṣâʾiṣ al-kubrä*, vol. 1, p. 10 (referring to Aḥmad b. Ḥanbal: "*Innî ʿinda ʿllâh fî ummî l-kitâb la-khâtamu l-nabiyyîn wa inna Âdam la-munjadil fî ṭînatihi*"; cf. *Musnad*, vol. 4, pp. 127–28 where only *ʿinda* is read *ʿabd*.

156. "*Inna Muḥammadan wa ʿAliyyan kânâ nûran bayna yadayy Allâh qabla khalq al-khalq bi-alfay ʿâm . . . dhâlika l-nûr . . . lahu aṣlan qad tashʿʿaba minhu shuʿâʿ lâmiʿ . . . hâdhâ nûrun min nûrî aṣluhu nubuwwa wa farʿuhu imâma ammâ l-nubuwwa fa li Muḥammad ʿabdî wa rasûlî wa ammâ l-imâma fa li ʿAlî ḥujjatî wa waliyyî wa law lâ humâ lamâ khalaqtu khalqî . . . qâla ʿAlî anâ min Muḥammad/Aḥmad ka l-ḍawʾ min al-ḍawʾ . . . ,*" a tradition attributed to Jaʿfar, Ibn Bâbûye, *ʿIlâl*, ch 139, p. 174; for the traditions of the other imams, see *ibid.*, ch 111, pp. 131f.

157. "*Khuliqtu anâ wa ʿAlî min nûr wâḥid qabla an tukhlaqa l-dunyâ,*" Ibn Bâbûye, *Amâlî*, "*majlis*" 41, num. 10, p. 236; Ibn al-Biṭrîq, *al-ʿUmda*, pp. 44–45; Ibn al-Biṭrîq, *Khaṣâʾiṣ waḥy al-mubîn*, pp. 37–38 and 109–110. On the light of ʿAlî, often called "the shimmering light" (*nûr shaʿshaʿânî*), see Ibn Bâbûye, *ʿIlâl*, ch. 120, p. 144 and vol. 2, ch. 1, p. 313; Ibn Bâbûye, *Amâlî*, "*majlis*" 55, pp. 347–48, num. 6.

158. Ibn Bâbûye, *ʿIlâl*, ch. 116, pp. 134–35.

159. Ibn Bâbûye, *Kamâl al-dîn*, vol. 1, ch. 23, p. 252, num. 2; Ibn Bâbûye, *ʿUyûn*, vol. 1, ch. 6, num. 27, p. 58; al-Nuʿmânî, *Kitâb al-ghayba*, p. 137; al-Khazzâz al-Râzî, *Kifâyat al-athar*, pp. 152–53; Ibn ʿAyyâsh al-Jawharî, *Muqtaḍab al-athar*, p. 23; al-Ṭûsî, *Kitâb al-ghayba*, p. 95. We shall not here return to the concept of *nûr muḥammadî* dealt with by other Sunnites; on this subject, see, e.g., I. Goldziher, "Neuplatonische und Gnostische Elemente in Hadît," pp. 324f.; T. Andrae, *Die Person Muhammeds*, pp. 313f.; F. Rosenthal, *Knowledge Triumphant*, p. 157 f.; L. Massignon, "Nûr Mûḥammadî," *EI1*; U. Rubin, "Pre-existence and Light, Aspects of the Concept of Nûr Muḥammad," *IOS*; for the traditions concerning Muḥammad as the first creation and his light in non-sufi works, see, e.g., Ibn Hishâm, *al-Sîrat al-nabawwiyya*, vol. 1, pp. 164-66; Ibn Saʿd, *Ṭabaqât*, vol. 1, pp. 1–60; al-Ṭabarî, *Taʾrîkh*, vol. 2, p. 243f.; al-Bayhaqî, *Dalâʾil al-nubuwwa*, vol. 1, pp. 64–86. The concept found its widest developments in the mystics (e.g., Ibn Sabʿin describes more than 33 modalities of Muḥammadan light; see *Rasâʾil Ibn Sabʿîn*, ed. ʿA. R. Badawî, "Risâla fî anwâr al-nabî," Egypt, n.d., pp. 201–11) and for a bibliography we refer the reader to the Western studies cited previously. For the Sunni reactions to Shîʿite traditions about the primordial lights of the Prophet and the imams, see T. Andrae, *Die Person Muhammeds*, pp. 319f.; U. Rubin, "Pre-Existence and Light, Aspects of the Concept of Nûr Muḥammad," *IOS*, pp. 113–14.

160. See, e.g., Ibn Bâbûye, *ʿIlal*, chapter 116, pp. 135f.; Ibn Bâbûye, *Kamâl al-dîn*, chapter 31, p. 319; Ibn Bâbûye, *Khiṣâl*, vol. 2, pp. 307–10; al-Khazzâz al-Râzî, *Kifâyat al-athar*, pp. 110–11 and 169–70.

161. Ibn Bâbûye, *'Ilal*, chapter 116, p. 135; Ibn al-Biṭrîq, *al-'Umda*, p. 120; Ibn al-Biṭrîq, *Khaṣâ'iṣ*, p. 145; al-Ḥurr al-'Amilî (d. 1104/1692), *al-Jawâhir al-saniyya*, pp. 233, 278, 304–5, 307.

162. See the fragments from al-Nu'mânî 's recension of Ja'far's *Tafsîr*, which appeared under al-Murtaḍä's name, under the title *al-Muḥkam wa l-mutashâbih*, lith. Iran, n.d., p. 72; this passage does not appear in either of the two editions of the *Tafsîr* edited by P. Nwyia and 'A. Zay'ûr; it is true that these editions were edited using the recension of the mystic al-Sulamî in his *Ḥaqâ'iq al-tafsîr*, where the author expurgated any typically Shî'ite allusion from the original text of the *Tafsîr*. The only manuscript of the *Ḥaqâ'iq* where this passage curiously appears is that of Yeni Cami 43 (cf. P. Nwyia, *Exégèse coranique*, p. 159, note 3). See also note 108. It must be added that the Imamite interpretation of the *âyat al-nûr* (Qur'an 24:35) sees in the different modalitites and instruments of light cited in this verse allusions to the lights of the different individuals that make up the Fourteen Impeccables; see, e.g., al-Kulaynî, *Uṣûl*, "Kitâb al-ḥujja," bâb inna l-a'imma . . . nûr Allâh," vol. 1, p. 278, num. 5; Ibn al-Biṭrîq, *al-'Umda*, pp. 186, 219–20; Ibn Shahrâshûb, *Manâqib*, vol. 1, p. 240f.; al-Majlisî, *Biḥâr al-anwâr*, vol. 23, pp. 304f.

163. " . . . *Al-'arsh laysa huwa Allâh wa l-'arsh ism 'ilm wa qudra wa 'arsh fîhi kullu shay'*," al-Kulaynî, *Uṣûl*, "Kitâb al-tawḥid," bâb al-'arsh wa l-kursî, vol. 1, p. 177, num. 2; see also vol. 1, p. 179, num. 6, Ja'far's words where the Throne is associated with Knowledge.

164. *"Al-'arsh dîn al-ḥaqq,"* Ibn 'Ayyâsh al-Jawharî, *Muqtaḍab al-athar*, p. 75.

165. " . . . *Li'annahumâ bâbân min akbar abwâb al-ghuyûb wa humâ jamî'ân ghaybân wa humâ fî l-ghayb maqrûnân li'anna l-kursî huwa l-bâb [huwa l-ta'wîl] al-ẓâhir min al-ghayb alladhî minhu maṭla' al-bad' wa minhu l-ashyâ' kulluhâ wa l-'arsh huwa l-bâb al-bâṭin alladhî yûjad fîhi 'ilm al-kayf wa l-kawn wa l-qadr wa l-ḥadd wa l-'ayn wa l-mashî'a wa ṣifat al-irâda wa 'ilm al-alfâẓ wa l-ḥarakât wa l-tark wa 'ilm al-'awd wa l-bad' . . . ,*" Ibn Bâbûye, *Kitâb al-tawḥid*, chapter 50 (bâb al-'arsh wa ṣifâtih), pp. 321–22, num. 1; the text is difficult: why this irregular enumeration? Does the *al-mashî'a wa ṣifat al-irâda* group always depend on *'ilm*? Is this not rather a case of the Divine Will being placed on the same plane as Knowledge? Does *al-tark* (lit. "abandonment," "desertion," "tranquility") really mean "immobility" in this case? (The Persian translator of the work, Md 'Alî b. Md Ḥasan Ardakânî, reproduces the word as such: *Asrâr-e towḥîd*, Tehran, n.d., p. 369).

166. *"Ḥamalat al-'arsh," Uṣûl,* "Kitâb al-tawḥîd," bâb al-'arsh wa l-kursî, vol. 1, p. 179, num. 6.

167. *"Ḥamala dînî wa 'ilmî," Uṣûl,* "Kitâb al-tawḥîd," bâb al-'arsh wa l-kursî, vol. 1, p. 179, num. 7.

168. Ibn Bâbûye, *'Ilal*, ch. 18, p. 23; also ch. 156, p. 208; see also, e.g., al-Majlisî, *Biḥâr*, vol. 11, pp. 150f. and 192f. (citing al-Ḥasan al-'Askarî's *Tafsîr*); in Sunni literature, the expression *ashbâḥ nûr*, or simply *ashbâḥ*, probably borrowed from the Shî'ites, refers in general to the form of the angels, described as being "luminous subtle bodies" (*ajsâm laṭîfa nûrâniyya*); cf. al-Zurqânî, *Sharḥ 'alä al-mawâhib*, vol. 1, pp. 9f.

169. Ibn Bâbûye, *'Ilal*, ch. 130, p. 162; Ibn Bâbûye, *Kamâl al-dîn*, vol. 2, ch. 33, pp. 335–36 num. 7.

170. Al-Nu'mânî, *Kitâb al-ghayba*, p. 328; Ibn 'Ayyâsh, *Muqtaḍab*, p. 95; al-

Majlisî, *Biḥâr*, vol. 15, p. 25 (citing al-Kulaynî); sometimes these shadows of light are described as being green, cf. *ibid.*, vol. 15, pp. 23 and 24. "We [the imams] were near our Lord, and other than us there was no one; we were enveloped in green shadows": "*kunnâ ʿinda rabbinâ laysa ʿindahu ghayrunâ fî ẓillatin khaḍrâ . . .*"; "the first of God's creations was Muḥammad and us members of the family (*ahl al-bayt*), out of the Light of His Majesty (*min nûr ʿaẓamatihi*); then He made the same number of green shadows (*fa awqafanâ aẓilla khaḍrâʿ*) placed before Him; and at that time the sky and the earth, the day and the night, the sun and the moon had not yet come into being."

171. *"Fa l-imâm . . . ẓillan qabla khalqihi nasamatan ʿan yamîn ʿarshihi . . . ,"* al-Nuʿmânî, *Kitâb al-ghayba*, p. 328; al-Khazzâz al-Râzî, *Kifâyat al-athar*, p. 112.

172. See, e.g., al-Nuʿmânî, *Kitâb al-ghayba*, pp. 274 and 309; Ibn Bâbûye, *Amâlî*, "majlis" 89, p. 612, num. 9.

173. " *ʿAn al-Ḥusayn b. ʿAlî ʿan al-nabiyy . . . qâla akhbaranî Jabraʾîl . . . yâ rabb hadhâ l-ism al-maktûb fî surâdiq al-ʿarsh ʾarinî aʿazza khalqika ʿalayka (sic) qâla fa-ʾarâhu ʾllâhu ʿazza wa jall ithnay ʿashara ashbâḥan abdânan . . . hâdhâ nûr ʿAlî . . . ,"* al-Khazzâz, *Kifâya*, pp. 169–70. It is noteworthy that here the lights of the imams are contained in the name of Muḥammad, and constitute the reality of this name.

174. See, e.g., al-Khazzâz, *Kifâya*, pp. 1110–11; Ibn Bâbûye, *Khiṣâl*, vol. 1, p. 156; according to the Imamite tradition, the Prophet had a number of ascensions, the most frequently tendered number being 120; see al-Majlisî, *Biḥâr*, vol. 18, pp. 387f. (citing especially al-Ṣaffâr al-Qummî and Ibn Bâbûye).

175. *"Muʿallaqa"* (lit. "suspended") or *"bayn al-samâʾ wa l-arḍ"* (lit. "between the heaven and the earth," but thus must be understood in the sense of "floating," since neither the heaven nor the earth was yet created).

176. *" . . . Ithnay ʿashara ashbâḥan min nûr bayn al-samâʾ wa l-arḍ . . . yuwaḥḥidûna ʾllâh ʿazza wa jall wa yumajjidûnahu,"* prophetic hadith, see al-Khazzâz, *Kifâya*, p. 170; Ibn ʿAyyâsh, *Muqtaḍab*, p. 123.

177. A tradition that dates back to the fourth imam, ʿAlî b. al-Ḥusayn: *"Innaʾl-lâha tabârak wa taʿâlä khalaqa Muḥammadan wa ʿAliyyan wa l-aʾimmat al-aḥad ʿashar min nûr ʿaẓamatih arwâḥan fî ḍiyâʾ nûrih yaʿbudûnahu qabla khalqi l-khalq yusabbiḥûnaʾllâh ʿazza wa jall yuqaddisûnahu . . . ,"* Ibn Bâbûye, *Kamâl al-dîn*, chapter 31, num. 1, pp. 318–19; on this subject see also Ibn Bâbûye, *ʿIlal*, ch. 19, p. 23; ch. 97, p. 118, and pp. 208–9; Ibn Bâbûye, *ʿUyûn*, vol. 1, ch. 25, pp. 262f.; al-Khazzâz, *Kifâya*, p. 171; Ibn ʿAyyâsh, *Muqtaḍab*, p. 125; al-Majlisî, *Biḥâr*, vol. 15, p. 26.

178. See, e.g., al-Ṣaffâr, *Baṣâʾir*, pp. 67 and 69; al-Nuʿmânî, *Kitâb al-ghayba*, p. 137; Ibn ʿAyyâsh, *Muqtaḍab*, p. 58; Jaʿfar b. Md al-Qummî, *Kâmil al-ziyârât*, pp. 26–27; in Imamite tradition, the *jinn*, although classified as being among the *rûḥâniyyûn*, are nevertheless generally considered to be obedient to the imams, and thus beneficent. In this point of view, they are opposed to the *nasnâs* (or *nisnâs*), a kind of maleficent supernatural monsters that live on earth and are compared to the faithful of the adversaries of the imams. Regarding the belief in *jinn* among Muslim Doctors in general, interesting information may be found in Shihâb al-Dîn b. Ḥajar (d. 973/1565), *al-Fatâwä al-ḥadîthiyya*, Cairo, 1325/1907, pp. 166f.; for the early literature on this subject, see Ibn al-Nadîm, *al-Fihrist*, ed. Flügel, p. 308.

179. See, e.g., al-Ṣaffâr, *Baṣâʾir*, pp. 70, 74–75; Ibn Bâbûye, *ʿIlal*, ch. 101, p.

122; Ibn ʿAyyâsh, *Muqtaḍab*, p. 41; al-Majlisî, *Biḥâr*, vol. 51, pp. 149f.; for the list of *ûlû l-ʿazm* prophets (cf. Qur'an 46:35) and the reasons why Adam cannot be counted among them, see e.g., Ibn Bâbûye, *ʿIlal*, all of chapter 101.

180. See, e.g., al-Ṣaffâr, *Baṣâ'ir*, pp. 79–80; al-Kulaynî, *Uṣûl*, "kitâb al-imân wa l-kufr," vol. 3, pp. 12f.; Ibn Bâbûye, *Faḍâ'il al-shîʿa*, pp. 11–12. On the opposition of *mu'min/muslim*, see note 43; on the plane of manifestation perceptible by the senses during the time of the historical imams of Islam, these two terms referred, respectively, to "the true Shîʿites," those initiated by the imams, and the mass of Muslims, meaning the Sunnites or those who were only nominally Shîʿites: those who had not been initiated into the esoteric side of Islam.

181. On the idea of *mîthâq* and its later developments, especially in mystical literature, see L. Massignon, "Le Jour du Covenant," in *Oriens*, vol. 15, 1962; L. Massignon, *La passion de Hallâj*, s.v. "*mîthâq*"; L. Gardet, "Les Noms et les Statuts," *SI*, vol. 5, 1956; L. Gardet, "Fins dernières selon la théologie musulmane," *Revue Thomiste*, vol. 2, 1957.

182. In reply to the question "How then did they [the pure beings] respond if they were only particles?" (*Kayfa ajâbû wa hum dharr*), Abû ʿAbdAllâh Jaʿfar al-Ṣâdiq said: "In the world of the Pact, [God] instilled in them that which they needed to answer his questions" (*Jaʿala fihim mâ idhâ sa'alahum ajâbû yaʿnî fî l-mithâq*); al-Kulaynî, *Uṣûl*, "kitâb al-îmân wa l-kufr," vol. 3, p. 19. Although the statement of the sixth imam remains vague, the commentators did not hesitate to see in it an allusion to conscience (*shuʿûr*), to the faculty of perception-comprehension (*idrâk*), or the faculty of emitting sounds (*nuṭq*) (cf. al-Majlisî, *Mir'at al-ʿuqûl*, vol. 2, pp. 12-13, citing particularly al-Mufîd and al-Murtaḍä). The disciple who asked Jaʿfar the question was Abû Baṣîr; the sixth imam had three disciples with this *kunya*: Layth b. al-Bukhturî al-Murâdî, ʿAbd-Allâh b. Md al-Asadî al-Kûfî, and Yaḥyä b. Abi l-Qâsim al-Asadî al-Makfûf (cf. Mudarris, *Rayḥânat al-adab*, vol. 7, pp. 34–37); the first appears to have been the closest of the three since he was known as being one of the "apostles" (*ḥawârî*) of the sixth imam (al-Kashshî, *Rijâl*, pp. 7 and 113).

183. This is why, in Imamite tradition, the plural *mawâthîq* is often used; see, e.g., al-Ṣaffâr, *Baṣâ'ir*, pp. 70-71 and 80–81; al-Kulaynî, *Uṣûl*, vol. 3, pp. 12–13; al-Nuʿmânî, *Kitâb al-ghayba*, p. 274; Ibn Bâbûye, *ʿIlal*, vol. 1, ch. 97, p. 117 and ch. 104, p. 124; vol. 2, chapter 1, pp. 312f.; al-Ḥurr al-ʿÂmilî, *al-Jawâhir al-saniyya*, p. 215; al-Majlisî, *Biḥâr*, vol. 26, pp. 279–80.

184. Al-Ṣaffîr, *Baṣâ'ir*, section 2, chapter 7, num 2; see also al-Kulaynî, *Uṣûl*, "kitâb al-îmân wa l-kufr," vol. 3, p. 12, num. 1451; al-Majlisî, *Biḥâr*, vol. 26, p. 279, num. 22. As it is reported in what follows in this tradition, Adam, who is also a prophet, remains indecisive and lacks the resolve to take the oaths of *walâya*; he thus does not deserve to be counted among the *ûlû al-ʿazm*; the Qur'anic verse "We had already made a Pact with Adam, but he forgot it; We have found no firm resolve in him" (*Wa laqad ʿahidnâ ilä Âdam min qablu fa-nasiya wa lam najid lahu ʿazman*, Qur'an 20:115) is understood in this sense. In other traditions, we are told only later, after being materially created, he recognizes the sacred supremecy of the Impeccables, repents and takes the fourfold oath of fidelity and is redeemed (see, e.g., al-Majlisî, *Biḥar*, vol. 21, pp. 311–12, citing al-Kulaynî and Ibn Bâbûye). For the oaths of other shadows of pure beings (the angels, the "spirituals," or the believers), even though the

four oaths do not appear all in one tradition, see the references in note 183, as well as Ibn 'Ayyâsh, *Muqtaḍab al-athar*, p. 59; Ja'far b. Md al-Qummî, *Kâmil al-ziyârât*, p. 26.

185. *"Kunnâ arwâḥ nûr fa-nu'allimu l-aẓilla asrâr 'ilm al-tawḥîd wa l-taḥmîd,"* Ibn 'Ayyâsh, *Muqtaḍab al-athar*, p. 63.

186. *"Kunnâ ashbâḥ nûr nadûru ḥawla 'arsh al-Raḥmân fa-nu'allimu l-malâ'ika al-tasbîḥ wa l-tahlîl wa l-taḥmîd,"* Ibn Bâbûye, *'Ilal*, chapter 18, p. 23.

187. With slight variations, Ibn Bâbûye reports this tradition a number of times, in several of his works:*'Ilal*, ch. 7, pp. 5f.; *Kamâl al-dîn*, ch. 23, pp. 254–55, num. 4; *'Uyûn*, vol. 1, ch. 25, pp. 262f., num. 22. Our translation is from the version of the *'Ilâl* that appears to be the most complete. The author most probably took the tradition from one of his no longer extant reference books: the *Kitâb tafḍîl al-anbiyâ' wa l-a'imma 'alä l-malâ'ika* (cf. *'Ilâl*, pp. 20–27 and 211f.), a work by Md b. Baḥr al-Ruhnî (from Ruhn, not far from Kirmân, in Iran), the Imamite author of at least three known works; apparently, all three have been lost, but fragments have survived thanks to later authors. They are the just mentioned, *al-furûq bayna l-abâṭîl wa l-ḥuqûq* (cf. Ibn Bâbûye, *'Ilal*, pp. 211–20) and finally *al-ḥujja fî ibṭâ' al-qâ'im* (cf. *Kamâl al-dîn*, vol. 2, pp. 352–57 and 417–23, and al-Ṭûsî, *Kitâb al-ghayba*, pp. 104–8 and 124–28). (We are greatly indebted to Professor Etan Kohlberg, who, since the original French publication of this work, has pointed out a fourth title of al-Ruhnî's, *Muqaddimât 'ilm al-qur'ân*, cited by Ibn Ṭâwûs in his Sa'd al-su'ûd, Najaf, 1369/1950, pp. 227–28 and 279–81.) Al-Ruhnî lived from the middle of the third century A.H. to the beginning of the fourth; he is considered as an "extremist" (*ghâlî*) by some authors of Imami *Ṭabaqât*; we shall return to this point in the last part of the book. On Ruhnî, see e.g., al-Kashshî, *Ikhtiyâr ma'rifat al-rijâl*, p. 147; al-Najâshî, *Rijâl*, pp. 189, 219, 271; al-Ṭûsî, *al-Fihrist*, ed. Najaf, 1356/1937, p. 132; Ibn Dâwûd al-Ḥillî, *Rijâl*, Najaf, 1972, pp. 270 and 277.

188. The noun *ḥawl* has two principal meanings in early Arabic. The first is force, and the second is change, upheaval, transformation. Although in the holy words *lâ ḥawl wa lâ quwwa illâ bi'llâh* only the first of these meanings can be applied, in the words of the Prophet *lâ ḥawl lanâ wa lâ quwwa illâ bi'llâh* (where just the word *lanâ* is inserted into the sacred phrase), the ambiguity appears to have been kept on purpose, and applying the second meaning to the phrase, we have "We are not subject to change and we have our Power only through God"; we find this latter in the versions of *'Ilal al-sharâ'i'* (p. 6) and *'Uyûn akhbâr al-Riḍâ* (vol. 1, p. 263), but in *Kamâl al-dîn* (p. 255), the word *lanâ* is taken out of the Prophet's words, and one finds the sacred phrase as such.

189. Let us note that in what is taught during this Primoridal Initiation we find four phrases common to all Muslims, as well as four phrases from the mystics' *dhikr*: *lâ ilâha illâ llâh, Allâhu akbar, lâ ḥawl wa lâ quwwa illâ bi'llâh*, and *al-ḥamdu li'llâh*; in the very first phase of initiation, although the phrase taught is not specified, it might be supposed that it is *subḥâna'llâh* (we began to praise God . . . " *fa-sabbaḥnâ*), another phrase of *dhikr*. According to the mystics, these phrases are extremely powerful and contain multiple spiritual, even magical, secrets. Cf. also the words of Ja'far: " . . . We taught the secrets of the Science of Unification and Glorification to the shadows" (note 185).

190. We have already seen that dark Ignorance (*al-jahl*) was created from the "briny ocean" (*al-baḥr al-ujâj*), while Hiero-Intelligence (*al-'aql*), in the same way as the Impeccables, was that which was first created by God, proceeding from the divine light and taken from the right side of the Throne (cf. Part I-1).

191. Al-Ṣaffâr, *Baṣâ'ir*, section 2, chapter 7, pp. 70 and 71, nums 2 and 6.; cf. also the same tradition with slight variations in al-Kulaynî, *Uṣûl*, "kitâb al-îmân wa l-kufr," chapter 1, num. 1449, vol. 3, p. 10, num. 2. In tradition number 1448 from this same work, it is said that "the People of the Right" are the people of obedience (*ṭâ'a*) and Paradise, while "the People of the Left" are those of disobedience (*ma'ṣiya*) and Hell; on the *aṣḥâb al-yamîn* and the *aṣḥâb al-shimâl*, see also Ibn 'Ayyâsh al-Jawharî, *Muqtaḍab al-athar*, pp. 9–10. The two expressions are from the Qur'an (56: 27 and 41).

192. See al-Kulaynî, *Uṣûl*, bâb fiṭrat al-khalq 'alä l-tawḥîd, vol. 3, pp. 19–21; there are five traditions here, four of which date to Ja'far, and the other to al-Bâqir. The five commentate on the following verses: Qur'an 7:172 (cited above); 30:30 " . . . according to the original nature that God gave to men . . . " (. . . *fiṭrat Allâh allatî faṭara l-nâs 'alayhâ*); 31:25 "And if you ask them who created the heavens and the earth, they answer: God . . . " (*wa la'in sa'altahum man khalaqa l-samâwât wa l-arḍ la-yaqûlunna Allâh . . . ,*" as well as in commentary on the Prophetic tradition: "Any newborn child has the original nature" (*kullu mawlûd yûlad 'alä l-fiṭra*). The aim of these elements seems evident: first, to give an ontological and archetypal dimension to the opposition *mu'min/muslim*, and then to denounce the implicit infidelity of the "Sunnite"/exoteric Muslims who fail to recognize *walâya*. The choice of the terms *islâm* and *muslim* to denote submission to the exoteric part of religion to the exclusion of the esoteric is evidently not gratuitous.

193. There are both traditions that allude to, and traditions that deal directly with this gift of pre-existential "seeing" of the Impeccables (called *ru'ya*, vision, or *'ilm al-ṭîna*, the knowledge of clay, by the texts). "The Day of Alliance with the Particles, God received the oaths of our faithful regarding the recognition of our mission as imams, recognition of his own lordship, and recognition of the prophetic mission of Muḥammad. Then he showed Adam's descendents to Muḥammad while they were still in the clay, in the form of shadows; then he created them from the clay with which he had created Adam, and the Messenger of God knew them and he made them known to 'Alî, and we [the other imams] also knew them (words of Abû Ja'far Md al-Bâqir, "*inna'llâha akhadha mîthâq shî'atinâ bi l-walâya lanâ wa hum dharr yawma akhdh al-mîthâq 'alä al-dharr wa l-iqrâr lahu bi l-rubûbiyya wa li-Muḥammad bi l-nubuwwa wa 'araḍa' llâh 'alä Muḥammad banî Âdam fî l-ṭîn wa hum aẓilla wa-khalaqahum min al-ṭînat allati khalaqa minhâ Âdam wa 'arafahum rasûl Allâh wa 'arrafahum 'Alîyyan wa naḥnu na'rifuhum*"), al-Ṣaffar, *Baṣâ'ir*, p. 89. "The iman knows the characteristics and the names of his faithful as well as those of his enemies, because he knows the clay from which they were created" (the words of Ja'far, "*inna l-imâm ya'rifu shî'atahu wa a'dâhu bi-wujûhihim wa asmâ'ihim bi 'ilm al-ṭînat allati khuliqû minhâ*") Ibn 'Ayyâsh, *Muqtaḍab*, p. 41; also, Baṣâ'ir, p. 390; see also in this latter source, section 2, chapters 14–16 (*bâb fî rasûl Allâh annahu 'arafa mâ ra'a fî l-aẓilla wa l-dharr; bâb fî amîr al-mu'minîn annahu 'arafa mâ ra'a fî l-mîthâq; bâb fî l-a'imma annahum ya'rifûna mâ ra'aû fî l-mîthâq*), pp. 83–90; for allusions to this subject, see, e.g., Ibn Bâbûye, *'Ilal*,

ch. 139, p. 173; Ibn Bâbûye, *ʿUyûn*, vol. 2, p. 227; Ibn Bâbûye, *Faḍâʾil al-shîʿa*, p. 31, num. 27.

194. See, e.g., al-Ṣaffâr, *Baṣâʾir*, section 1, ch. 9 and 10, pp. 14–25; al-Kulaynî, *Uṣûl*, "kitâb al-ḥujja," bâb khalq abdân a l-aʾimma wa arwâḥihim wa qulûbihim, vol. 2, pp. 232–34, and "kitâb al-imân wa l-kufr," bâb ṭinat al-muʾmin wa l-kâfir, vol. 3, pp. 2–16. These traditions are not always clear, and in the work of al-Kulaynî, in particular, the confusion between the entities created on the one hand and the provenance of the Clay from which they were formed on the other, destroys the balance and the correspondence of the system. Al-Ṣaffâr al-Qummî appears to be more methodical than his disciple in this regard; one of the traditions he reports seems to constitute a kind of systhesis of details on the subject, namely *Baṣâʾir al-darajât*, section 1, ch. 9, p. 14, num. 2: The fifth imam said, "God created [the bodies of] Muḥammad and his family [i.e., Fâṭima and the imams] from the Clay of *ʿIlliyyin*, and he created their spirits and their hearts from a Clay located above the *ʿIlliyyin*. He created [the bodies] of our faithful as well as [those] of the prophets from a Clay found beneath the *ʿIlliyyin*, while he created their spirits and their hearts from the Clay of the *ʿIlliyyin* itself. This is why the hearts of our faithful come from the bodies of the family of Muḥammad. Likewise, God created the enemy of the family of the Prophet [his spirit, his heart, and his body] as well as the spirits and the hearts of his partisans, from the Clay of the *Sijjîn*, and [the bodies of] the latter from a clay located below the *Sijjîn*; this is what explains how the hearts of the partisans come from the bodies of the others [i.e., their leaders, the enemies of the imams], and why all hearts long for their bodies." Further explanation for this last phrase, "All hearts long for their body," will be forthcoming when we enter into a study of the spiritual "technique" of "vision with the heart" (Part II-3). On this subject, see also Ibn Bâbûye, *ʿIlal*,, cha. 96, p. 117, num. 12–15. We see here a kind of dualism. The Qurʾan speaks of a number of creatures made of different substances (the angels of light, the *jinn* of fire, and human beings of clay), but in no case are creatures made of two different substances. This is of course not a principial dualism, but it does constitute a dualism of nature. The pre-existential "worlds" are reminiscent of Iranian speculations about the creation in the *mênôg* state; the cosmic battle from the origin of creation has shades of the Iranian myth of the Primordial War (cf. note 13). Nonetheless, this radical dualism is sometimes nuanced by rare traditions; see, e.g., *Baṣâʾir*, section 1, ch. 9, pp. 15–17, numbers 5, 7, 8, 10 (the "mixture of Clays").

195. *Kallâ inna kitâb al-abrâr la-fî ʿilliyyin/wa mâ adrâka mâ ʿilliyyûn/kitâbun marqûm/yashhaduhu l-muqarrabûn.*

196. *Kallâ inna kitâb al fujjâr la-fî sijjîn/wa mâ adrâka mâ sijjîn/kitâbun marqûm.*

197. According to a tradition attributed to al-Bâqir, *ʿIlliyyin* and *Sijjîn* denote, respectively, the "seventh heaven" and the "seventh earth" (al-Qummî, *Tafsîr*, *sub* Qurʾan 83:7–9, 18–21); in a tradition that the same author attributes to Jaʿfar, "the impious" of the Qurʾanic verse are identified as Abû Bakr and ʿUmar, just as "the pure" are identified as the Fourteen Impeccables (*ibid.*). In Jaʿfar al-Ṣâdiq's *Tafsîr* there are interesting details about "the pure" (*abrâr*) and "the impious" (*fujjâr*) that the Qurʾanic text directly relates to *ʿIlliyyin* and *Sijjîn*, respectively. Commentating on Qurʾan 82:12–13: "Yes, the pure [will be plunged] into felicity and the impious into a furnace" (*inna l-abrâra la-fî naʿîm wa inna l-fujjâra la-fî jaḥîm*), Jaʿfar says, "Felicity is knowl-

edge and contemplation (*al-na'îm al-ma'rifa wa l-mushâhada*) and the furnace is ignorance and obscurity"(*al-jaḥîm al-jahl wa l-ḥijâb*, lit. "being hidden behind a veil"); another "reading": the furnace is those [carnal] souls for whom the fires of Hell have been lit," *al-jaḥîm al-nufûs fa-inna lahâ nayrân tattaqid* (ed. by P. Nwyia, p. 228 [50]). Although in al-Sulamî's recension the technical terms used take on a connotation of orthodox "mysticism," it must be pointed out that in an early Imamite context, these terms are charged with doctrinal meanings; "knowledge" is divine knowledge, of course, but this is not possible except through knowledge of the Imam, who by his ontological status and because of his cosmic role is that aspect of God that can be known; "contemplation" is vision of the luminous entity of the Imam in the subtle center of the heart, thus constituting the vision of the "Face of God" (cf. Part II-3); the terms "ignorance" and "obscurity" are likewise to be understood in this context. For the different interpretations of *'Illiyîn* in the Imamite tradition, see al-Majlisî, *Biḥâr*, vol. 3, p. 65; for a general view, see R. Paret in *EI2*, s.v.

198. In Imamism, the idea of "Book" (*kitâb*) is of particular doctrinal importance; the "Book" is the container, the vehicle of essential knowledge, of the science of realities in a general as well as a particular sense; a certain correspondence can be detected between the "Superior Books" (*umm al-kitâb, 'Illiyin*) that contain "information" of a divine order and "the speaking book" that the imam is, the vehicle for all the sacred sciences (cf. the expression *kitâb nâṭiq/Qur'ân nâṭiq*, referring to the imam; see, e.g., the "index" of the *Biḥâr*, entitled *Safînat al-Biḥâr*, by 'Abbâs al-Qummî, ed. 1355/1936, s.v.); this correspondence might similarly be considered as being between Sijjîn's "Inferior Book" and the Enemies of the Imams, the Guides of Darkness (*a'immat al-ẓalâm*).

199. Al-Kulaynî, *Uṣûl*, "kitâb al-ḥujja," bâb khalq abdân al-a'imma . . . , num. 2, vol. 2, pp. 232–33; for the replacement of *'Illiyyin* by *'arsh*, see also al-Ṣaffâr, *Baṣâ'ir*, section 1, chapter 9, num. 12, p. 17. It would be interesting to point out that in Sunni tradition, Mecca (and sometimes Medina) constitutes the terrestrial counterpart to the celestial Abode with the Clay from which the Prophet was created; cf. e.g., al-Zurqânî, *Sharḥ*, vol. 1, p. 43; al-Ḥalabî, *al-Sîrat al-ḥalabiyya*, vol. 1, p. 147; for other sources, see M. J. Kister, "You shall only set out for Three Mosques," *Muséon*, vol. 82, 1969, p. 187, note 63. The mention of Medina is undoubtedly due to the belief that the Clay of each individual comes from the place where he will be buried (*turbatu 'l-shakhṣ madfanuhu*), see, e.g., al-Zurqânî, *Sharḥ*, vol. 1, pp. 42–43. On this subject, see also H. Corbin, *Temple et contemplation*, s.v. Ka'ba and Mekke.

200. Cf. Part II-3 (excursus).

201. This most probably refers to Adam in the present cycle of humanity; actually, the belief in cyclical creations and successive humanities exists in early Imamism, although no specific details or developments are furnished on the subject by the imams; the tradition upon which this belief is based is found in a commentary by al-Bâqir on Qur'an 50:15: "Are We [God is speaking] then fatigued from the first creation, such that they are indoubt about a new creation?" (*'A fa-'ayînâ bi l-khalq al-awwal bal hum fî labsin min khalqin jadîd*); al-Bâqir: "When these creatures and this world are annihilated by God (*Inna llâha 'azza wa jall idhâ afnä hâdhâ l-khalq wa hâdhâ l-'âlam*) and the people of Paradise and Hell inhabit the Abodes that they deserve, God will create a new world different from this one, with other creatures, not divided into male and

female (*min ghayr fuḥûla wa lâ unâth*), who will worship Him and will bear witness to His Unicity; and He will create a new earth to support them, and to give them refuge He will create a new sky. Do you think that this is the only world God created? That he did not create other races of humanity than you (*basharan ghayrakum*) ? Certainly not, for He has created thousands upon thousands of worlds with thousands upon thousands of Adams, and you dwell upon only the last of these worlds, in the midst of the last of these Adamic humanities (*laqad khalaqa Allâh alfa alf 'âlamin wa alfa alf Âdama anta fî âkhir tilka l-'awâlim wa ulâ'ika al-âdamiyyîn*). Cf. Ibn Bâbûye, *Kitâb al-tawhîd*, ch. 38, p. 277, num. 2; the speaker for the fifth imam is here Abû 'AbdAllâh Jâbir b. Yazîd al-Ju'fî (d. 128/745 or 132/749), the famous disciple of the fifth and sixth imams, and to whom we owe the transmission of a great number of traditions of a theosophical nature; on him, see, e.g., al-Kashshî, *Rijâl*, p. 126; al-Najâshî, *Rijâl*, s.v.; al-Ṭûsî, *Rijâl*. p. 111, num. 6, and p. 163, num. 30; al-Ardabîlî, *Jâmi' al-ruwât*, vol. 1, p. 144; The doctrinal developments of the theme of successive creations are especially due to Ismâ'îli authors; on this subject, see especially H. Corbin, *Temps cyclique et gnose ismaélienne*, Paris, Berg International, 1982.

202. Cf. also Qur'an 7:11f.; 15:26f.; 17:61f.; 18:50; 38:74f. Iblîs (Satan, from the Greek *diabolos*?) is considered in Imamite traditions as the archetypal personification of the "guides of darkness," the "enemies of the imams and of the Shî'ites" (the *nawâṣib* in general); he is the first to have failed to recognize the light of prophecy [the Imamate]; from this perspective, he may be identified with *jahl*, the universal counterpower of Ignorance and Darkness.

203. The hadith of "the superiority of the Prophet and the Proofs over the angels," Ibn Bâbûye, *'Ilal*, p. 6, Ibn Bâbûye, *Kamâl al-dîn*, p. 255 (cf. also note 187): "... *Thumma inna llâha tabârak wa ta'âlä khalaqa Âdam fa-awda'anâ ṣulbahu wa amara l-malâ'ika bi l-sujûd lahu ta'ẓîman lanâ wa ikrâman wa kâna sujûduhum li'llâh 'azza wa jall 'ubûdiyyatan wa li-Âdam ikrâman wa ṭâ'atan li-kawninâ fî ṣulbih....*"

204. Ibn Bâbûye, *'Ilal*, vol. 1, ch. 156, p. 209; the phrase about "the loins of the fathers and the wombs of the mothers" being free from any impiety or infidelity refers to the religious status of the genealogical ancestors of the Prophet, a problem dealt with at length in the literature of the *sîra* and the hadith; from the Imami point of view, all the ancestors of the Prophet, and consequently of the imams, were "Muslims" in the sense of being "monotheists," and practiced the religion of Abraham, that of the *ḥanîf*; this fact implies, among other things, that their children were not illegal, and thus the allusion to "adultery due to infidelity" (cf., e.g., Ibn Bâbûye, *Amâlî*, majlis 89, p. 614, num. 11; Ibn Shahrâshûb, *Manâqib âl Abî Ṭâlib*, vol. 1, pp. 37f. and 132f.; al-Majlisî, *Biḥâr*, vol. 11, pp. 10f., and vol. 15, pp. 117–27 and 172f.: "*Ittafaqati'l-imâmiyya 'alä anna wâlidayi'l-rasûl wa kulla ajdâdih ilä Âdam kânû muslimîn bal kânû min al-ṣiddîqîn wa l-ḥunafâ'*"). A great number of Sunni authors are of the same opinion, emphasizing especially the monotheism of 'Abd al-Muṭṭalib and his two sons, 'AbdAllâh and Abû Ṭâlib (see, e.g., Ibn Sa'd, *Ṭabaqât*, vol. 1, pp. 1, 2, 5, 31: the Prophet: *Innamâ kharajtu min nikâḥ wa lam akhruj min sifâḥ min ladun Âdam lam yuṣibnî min sifâḥ ahl al-jâhiliyya shay'un*; al-Bayhaqî, *Dalâ'il al-nubuwwa*, vol. 1, pp. 131f.; al-Suyûṭî, *al-Khaṣâ'iṣ al-kubrä*, vol. 1, pp. 93–96; Ibn al-Jawzî, *al-Wafâ bî aḥwâl al-Muṣṭafä*, vol. 1, pp. 35f. and 77–78; al-Qasṭallânî, *Irshâd al-sârî*, vol. 6, pp. 31f.; al-Ḥalabî, *al-Ṣîrat al-ḥalabiyya*, vol. 1, pp. 42f.; al-Zurqânî, *Sharḥ*, vol. 1, pp. 66f., 174f.). It seems to have been espe-

cially the Hâshimite tradition, pro-Shî'ite but especially pro-'Abbâsid, that glorified the religious excellence of the Prophet's ancestors in general, and that of 'Abd al-Muṭṭalib in particular, in its propaganda against the Umayyads; let it be remembered that 'Abd al-Muṭṭalib is the common ancestor of 'AbdAllâh, Abû Ṭâlib, and al-'Abbâs; as ancestor, he is presented as a monotheist, as pious and emanating the light of prophecy that he carried within him; Umayya, the ancestor of the Umayyads, is presented as his exact opposite (cf., e.g., Ibn Hishâm—the Hâshimite sympathies of his teacher, Ibn Isḥâq, are well known—*al-Sîrat al-nabawiyya,* vol. 1, p. 180; al-Balâdhurî, *Ansâb al-ashrâf,* vol. 4b, p. 18—the words of 'AbdAllâh b. Abbâs against the Umayyad caliph Yazîd b. Mu'âwiya and reported by 'Awâna b. al-Ḥakam (d. 147/764; on him and his pro-Abbasid sympathies, see *GAS*, vol. 1, p. 307, and especially A. A. Dûrî, *Nash'at al-'ilm al-ta'rîkh*, pp. 36f.; for the opposition of 'Abd al-Muṭṭalib and Umayya, see also Abû al-Faraj al-Iṣfahânî, *Kitâb al-aghânî*, vol. 1, pp. 8-9). Fakhr al-Dîn al-Râzî, while deductively demonstrating the truth of this detail concerning "genealogical purity," implicitly recognizes its Shî'ite origin (al-Râzî, *al-Tafsîr al-kabîr*, vol. 24, pp. 173–74); actually, a certain number of Sunni scholars, beginning with the famous Muslim, reacted rather quickly to the assertion according to which the immediate ascendents of the Prophet were "Muslims." Muslim relates the hadith where the Prophet states to a convert: "My father and yours are now in hell" (Muslim, *Ṣaḥîḥ*, vol. 1,. pp. 132–33; see also al-Zurqânî, *Sharḥ*, vol. 1, p. 79, where he refers to Muslim, adding that by his father the Prophet actually meant Abû Ṭâlib, who had raised him: *Wa arâda bi-abîhi annahu Abû Ṭâlib wa li-annahu rabbâhu wa al-'arab tussamî l-murabbî aban*; see also al-Ḥalabî, *al-Ṣîrat al-ḥalabiyya*, vol. 1, p. 29; al-Ṭabarî, *Jâmi' al-bayân*, vol. 11, pp. 30–31). For other Sunni sources, see C. Gilliot, "Muqâtil . . . ," *JA*, pp. 68–70.

205. On this subject and the sources, both Shî'ite and Sunni, see Uri Rubin, "Pre-Existence and Light, Aspects of the Concept of Nûr Muḥammad," *IOS*, vol. 5, 1975, pp. 62–119; for the light of 'Abd al-Muṭṭalib, pp. 94-96; for that of 'AbdAllâh and Âmina, pp. 84–89; for that of Abû Ṭâlib, pp. 75–76.

206. Ibn Bâbûye, *'Ilal*, ch. 116, pp. 134–35; see also Ibn Bâbûye, *Kamâl al-dîn*, vol. 1, ch. 24, p. 275, num. 25. For the presence of the light of *nubuwwa/walâya* in Adam, see also Ibn 'Ayyâsh, *Muqtaḍab*, p. 82; al-Majlisî, *Biḥâr*, vol. 21, pp. 311–12; in Abraham, see Ibn 'Ayyâsh, *Muqtaḍab*, p. 83; al-Majlisî, *Biḥâr*, vol. 21, p. 315; in Moses, see Ibn 'Ayyâsh, *Muqtaḍab*, p. 41; and al-Majlisî, *Biḥâr*, vol. 51, p. 149. The idea of Muḥammad's prophetic ascendence is also admitted in the Sunni tradition, but despite the opinion of Goldziher, who sees a neo-Platonic kind of spiritual transmission ("Neuplatonische und Gnostische Elemente im Hadît," p. 340), it appears to be more a case for Sunni authors of a physical transmission via seminal fluid; cf. Ibn Sa'd, *Ṭabaqât*, vol. 1, pp. 1, 5 (. . . *Wa min nabiyyin ilä nabiyyin wa min nabiyyin ilä nabiyyin ḥattä akhrajaka nabiyyan*), also Ibn Kathîr, *Tafsîr*, Beirut, 1966, vol. 5, p. 215 (. . . *Ya'nî taqallubahu min ṣulbi nabiyyin ilä ṣulbi nabiyyin ḥattä akhrajahu nabiyyan*); al-Suyûṭî, *al-Khaṣâ'iṣ*, vol. 1, p. 94 (*Mâ zâla l-nabiyyu yataqallabu fî aṣlâb al-anbiyâ' ḥattä waladathu ummuhu*); cf. also al-Zurqânî, *Sharḥ*, vol. 1, p. 67 and al-Ḥalabî, *al-Ṣîrat al-ḥalabiyya*, vol. 1, p. 29. For some authors it was the "seal" marked on the body of the Prophet by the prophetic light that made him the "Seal of the prophets"; on this subject and on theological discussions on this theme, which ended up being an Islamic article of faith, see H. Birkland, *The Legend of Opening of*

Muḥammad's Breast, Oslo, 1955; Y, Friedmann, "Finality of Prophethood in Sunni Islam," *JSAI*, vol. 7, 1986, pp. 177–215.

207. This double genealogy is reminiscent of the double "natural" and "royal" ascendence of Jesus (in Luke 3:23–38 and Matthew 1: 1–17, respectively); as will be seen, there is considerable overlap in the ancestors who appear on the two lists.

208. *Ithbât al-waṣiyya li l-imâm ʿAlî b. Abî Ṭâlib ʿalayhi l-salâm*, attributed to al-Masʿûdî, Najaf, al-Maṭbaʿat al-Ḥaydariyya, n.d.; on this work and the problems of its attribution, see Ch. Pellat, "Masʿûdî et l'imâmisme," in *Le Shîʿisme imâmite*, pp. 69–90, and note 117.

209. Cf., e.g., Ibn ʿAyyâsh, *Muqtaḍab*, pp. 51–52; *Ithbât al-waṣiyya*, pp. 75–90; compare with al-Masʿûdî, *Murûj al-dhahab*, ed. Barbier de Meynard, vol. 1, pp. 80–83, and vol. 4, p. 115.

210. Cf., e.g., Ibn Bâbûye, *Kamâl al-dîn*, vol. 1, ch. 22, pp. 211–13, num. 1, ch. 58, num. 4 and 5, and vol. 2, ch. 58, p. 644; Ibn Bâbûye, *Kitâb al-faqîh*, vol. 4, ch. 72, pp. 129–30; this spiritual filiation takes up nearly 70 pages of the *Ithbât al-waṣiyya* (pp. 8–74), where the list is more than twice as long (75 names instead of 35); the author attempts to place the prophets and their heirs "historically" by giving the names of contemporary kings; Biblical kings are listed, also kings from Persia and from Greece; compare with the *Murûj al-dhahab*, vol. 1, pp. 72–73. See also the excellent article by E. Kohlberg, "Some Shîʿi Views on the Antediluvian World," *SI*, vol. 52, 1980, pp. 41–66.

211. *"Anâ sayyid al-anbiyâ' wa waṣiyyî sayyid al-waṣiyyin wa awṣiyâ'uhu sâda l-awṣiyâ' . . . al-ʿulamâ' warathat al-anbiyâ' . . . ʿulamâ' ummatî ka-anbiyâ' Banî Isrâ'îl,"* cf., e.g., al-Ṣaffâr, *Baṣâ'ir*, section 1, chapter 2; Ibn Bâbûye, *Kamâl al-dîn*, pp. 211-12. For comparisons between the Impeccables and the prophets and saints of the Bible, see, e.g., Ibn Bâbûye, *Kamâl al-dîn*, pp. 25–26 (ʿAlî has the qualities of the earlier prophets); Ibn Shahrâshûb, *Manâqib*, vol. 3, p. 46 (the relationship between the Prophet and ʿAlî is compared to that of Moses and Joshua; al-Shahrastânî takes the origin of this idea back to the mysterious partisan of ʿAlî, ʿAbdAllâh b. Saba', cf. *Milal*, ed. Kaylânî, vol. 1, p. 174; E. G. Hodgson, "Abd Allâh b. Saba," *EI2*), vol. 2, p. 219 (ʿAlî and Aaron), vol. 3, p. 166 (al-Ḥasan and al-Ḥusayn and the two sons of Aaron, Shabar and Shubayr), vol. 2, p. 164 (ʿAlî and Shem), vol. 1, p. 258 (the twelve imams and the twelve chiefs, *naqîb*, of the Tribes of Israel); *Ithbât al-waṣiyya*, p. 259 (the twelve imams and the twelve apostles of Jesus); al-Khawârizmî, *al-Manâqib*, Najaf, 1965, p. 85 (al-Ḥasan and Abraham, al-Ḥusayn and Moses, ʿAlî b. al-Ḥusayn and Aaron); according to certain traditions, the imams are considered prophets, even by their adversaries (al-Kulaynî, *Rawḍa*, vol. 1, p. 173, the words of the Umayyad Hishâm b. ʿAbd al-Malik; Ibn Bâbûye, *Amâlî*, majlis 47, p. 278, num. 4, the words of the Khawârij). On this theme, see also A. J. Wensinck, "Muḥammad und die Propheten," in *Acta Orientalia*, vol. 2, 1924; R. Selheim, "Prophet, Chalif und Geschichte," in *Oriens*, XVIII-XIX, 1965–66; M. J. Kister, "Ḥaddithû ʿan Banî Isrâ'îl," *IOS*, vol. 2, 1972.

212. The "Sacred Legacy" is composed of a certain number of material objects, also: the Sacred Books of the earlier prophets, the Secret Books (Jafr, Jâmiʿa . . .), and certain objects with supernatural powers that belonged to the prophets (Adam's cloak, the Arc of the Covenant from Moses, Muḥammad's weapon . . .). Here again, we find

the two ideas of Knowledge and Power that characterized the pre-existence of the Imams and that will continue to characterize their existence (cf. Part III). We shall return to this at length in the third part of this study. "The written investiture" (*al-naṣṣ*) is merely the evidence of the transmission of the "Legacy" destined to prove to the faithful the authenticity of the heir (on the *naṣṣ* of the imams, see, e.g., al-Kulaynî, *Uṣûl*, "Kitâb al-ḥujja," vol. 2, pp. 40–120; al-Mufîd, *al-Irshâd*, the section dedicated to the *naṣṣ* of each imam within the chapter about him). According to a tradition attributed to Ja'far al-Ṣâdiq, *al-waṣiyya* is also the name of a Sealed Book (*kitâb makhtûm*) that descended from heaven for the Prophet; this book contained twelve sealed letters containing the mission reserved for each imam (al-Nu'manî, *Kitâb al-ghayba*, pp. 82–83).

213. On this subject, see Rainer Freitag, *Seelenwanderung in der islamischen Häresie*, Berlin, 1985, s.v.; Guy Monnot, "La transmigration et l'immortalité," in *Islam et religions*, Paris, 1986, ch. 12, pp. 279–95.

214. " . . . *Fa-stawda'ahum fî afḍal mustawda'in wa aqarrahum fî khayr mustaqarr tanâsakhat-hum karâ'im al-aṣlâb ilä muṭahharât al-arḥâm* . . . ," *Nahj al-balâgha*, p. 279, num. 93; the seeds of belief in certain forms of reincarnation are found in the early writings of the imams; the word *maskh* in the sense of a debasing reincarnation in an animal form is seen a number of times (cf., e.g., al-Ṣaffâr, *Baṣâ'ir*, section 7, ch. 16, ch. 16, pp. 353–54; al-Kulaynî, *Rawḍa*, vol. 1, p. 285; vol. 2, p. 37; Ibn Bâbûye, *'Uyûn*, vol. 1, ch. 17, p. 271; al-Nu'mânî, *Kitâb al-ghayba*, p. 387). This theme is more amply developed in the literature of Baṭinite Shî'ites and especially in the Jâbirian writings, where we see the appearance, perhaps for the first time, of a whole series of terms to refer to different kinds of reincarnations: *naskh* (reincarnation in another human form), *maskh* (reincarnation in an animal form), *faskh* (in a vegetable form), *raskh* (in a mineral form) (cf. *The Arabic Work of Jâbir b. Ḥayyân*, ed. E. J. Holmyard, Paris, 1928, "Kitâb al-bayân," p. 11; *Mukhtâr rasâ'il Jâbir b. Ḥayyân*, ed. P. Kraus, Paris-Le Claire, 1935, "Kitâb al-ishtimâl," pp. 549–50; *Zeitschrift für Geschichte des arabischen-islamischen Wissenschaften*, Arabic texts ed. M. 'A. Abû Ridâ, vol. 1, 1984, "Kitâb al-ma'rifa," p. 57; Shahrastânî, *Livre des religions*, trad. Gimaret-Monnot, p. 512).

215. *"Mâ bayna Ḥawwâ'a in nusibta ilä/Âminata 'tamma nabtuka l-hadabû Qarnan fa-qarnan tanâsukhuka laka/'l-fiḍḍatu minhâ bayḍâ'a wa l-dhahabû,"* Kumayt, *Ḥâshimiyyât*, Qumm, n.d., p. 69.

216. I. Goldziher, *Muslim Studies*, ed. S. M. Stern, London, 1971, vol. 1, pp. 45f. and 135f.; Goldziher, *Vorlesungen über den Islam*, Heidelberg, 1910, pp. 217f.; M. E. S. Hodgson, "How Did Early Shî'â Become Sectarian?," *JAOS*, vol. 75, 1955, pp. 1–13; W. M. Watt, "Shî'ism Under the Umayyads," *JRAS*, 1960, pp. 158-72; U. Rubin, "Prophets and Progenitors in the Early Shî'a Tradition," *JSAI*, vol. 1, 1979, pp. 41-64; M. Sharon, "The Development of the Debate Around the Legitimacy of Authority in Early Islam," *JSAI*, vol. 5, 1984, pp. 121–42, especially pp. 139–41; M. Momen, *An Introduction to Shî'i Islam*, chapter 2.

217. "Theology" here is not to be interpreted in the sense of *kalâm* (dialectical speculative theology), which, as we saw in our introduction, was severely criticized by the imams; "theology" here is the word *tawḥîd*, or the expression *'ilm al-tawḥîd*, literally, "the science of divine unicity." In the early corpus of the imams, theological data

attempt to show the sterility, if not the impossibility, of a purely speculative approach to God, at the same time emphasizing, as is seen in the present section of this work, the necessity of direct knowledge of God through experience, where the role of the imam remains absolutely decisive. H. Corbin calls this theology "apophatic Shîʿite theology" (cf. the following note), stating that the expression is a translation of the word *tanzîh*, literally, "transcendence." It must be added that this term, widely used by Ismâʿîlî theologians and philosophers, is rarely found in this sense in the Imamite tradition that, in this context, as has been said, prefers the word *tawḥîd* (cf., e.g., al-Kulaynî, *Uṣûl*, "Kitâb al-tawḥîd"; Ibn Bâbûye, *Kitâb al-tawḥîd*; Ibn Bâbûye, *ʿUyûn*, bâb al-tawḥîd, etc.). As has been seen, things changed beginning with the school of shaykh al-Mufîd and the influence of Muʿtazilite rational theology.

218. See, e.g., A. A. A. Fyzee, *Shiʿite Creed*, introduction; Hassan al-Amin, *Islamic Shiʿite Encyclopaedia*, s.v.; L. Arnold, "Le Credo du Shîʿisme duodécimain"; M. Ḥ. Tabâṭabâʾî, *Shîʿe dar Eslâm*, especially chapter 3 (English translation by S. H. Nasr, *Shiʿite Islam*, London, 1975); P. Antes, *Zur Theologie der Schîʿa*, Freibourg, 1971; H. Corbin, *En Islam iranien*, s.v. "tawḥîd," "tanzîh"; H. Corbin, "Le Livre du Tawḥîd de Shaykh Ṣadûq . . . "; H. Corbin, *Le Paradoxe du monothéisme*, especially part 3; W. Madelung, "The Shiʿite and Khârijite Contribution to Pre-Ashʿarite Kalâm," in *Religious Schools*, part 8.

219. Al-Kulaynî, *Uṣûl*, Kitâb al-tawḥîd, bâb iṭlâq al-qawl bi-annahu shayʾ, vol. 1, p. 109, num. 2; Ibn Bâbûye, *Kitâb al-tawḥîd*, ch. 7, p. 104, num 1.

220. *"Huwa shayʾun bi-khilâf al-ashyâʾ irjiʿ bi-qawlî "shayʾun ilä ithbât maʿnan wa annahu shayʾun bi-ḥaqîqat al-shayʾiyya ghayr annahu lâ jism wa lâ ṣûra,"* Ibn Bâbûye, *Kitâb al-tawḥîd, ibid.*, num 2.

221. *"ʾA tuwahhima shayʾan? fa-qâla naʿam ghayr maʿqûl wa lâ maḥdûd fa-mâ waqaʿa wahmuka ʿalayhi min shayʾ fa-huwa khilâfuhu lâ yushbihuhu shayʾ wa lâ tudrikuhu l-awhâm wa huwa khilâf mâ yuʿqal wa khilâf mâ yutaṣawwar fî l-awhâm innamâ yutawahhamu shayʾun ghayr maʿqûl wa lâ maḥdûd,"* Ibn Bâbûye, *Kitâb al-tawḥîd, ibid.*, num 6; al-Kulaynî, *Uṣûl, ibid.*, num. 1. On ʿAbd al-Raḥmân b. Abî Najrân al-Tamîmî al-Kûfî, disciple of the eighth and ninth imams, see, e.g., al-Najâshî, *Rijâl*, s.v.; al-Ṭûsî, *Rijâl*, p. 380, num. 9 and p. 403, num. 7; al-Ṭûsî, *Fihrist*, p. 135, num. 476; al-Mâmaqânî, *Tanqiḥ al-maqâl*, s.v.; al-Ardabîlî, *Jâmiʿ al-ruwât*, vol. 1, p. 444. On applying the word "thing" to God in the Muslim *kalâm* and discussions about it, see D. Gimaret, *Les Noms divins en Islam*, pp. 142–50.

222. Cf., e.g., al-Kulaynî, *Uṣûl*, vol. 1, pp. 140f. (bâb al-nahy ʿaniʾl-jism wa l-ṣûra); Ibn Bâbûye, *Kitâb al-tawḥîd*, pp. 97f. (bâb annahu ʿazza wa jall laysa bi-jism wa lâ ṣûra).

223. Cf., e.g., al-Kulaynî, *Uṣûl*, vol. 1, pp. 169f. (bâb al-ḥaraka wa l-intiqâl); Ibn Bâbûye, *Kitâb al-tawḥîd*, ch. 28, pp. 173f. (bâb nafy al-makân wa l-zamân wa l-sukûn wa l-ḥaraka wa l-nuzûl wa l-ṣuʿûd ʿaniʾllâh ʿazza wa jall) and pp. 31f.; ch. 2 (bâb al-tawḥîd wa nafy al-tashbîh); Ibn Bâbûye, *ʿUyûn*, vol. 1, ch. 11, pp. 114f. (mâ jâʾa ʿani-l-Riḍâ ʿalayhi l-salâm fî l-tawḥîd).

224. On the attributes of Essence and Act, see, e.g., al-Kulaynî, *Uṣûl*, vol. 1, bâb ṣifât al-dhât, pp. 143–47, bâb ṣifât al-dhât, and bâb ṣifât al-fiʿl, pp. 148–51, bâb ṣifât al-fiʿl; Ibn Bâbûye, *Kitâb al-tawḥîd*, bâb ii (bâb ṣifât al-dhât wa ṣifât al-afʿâl), pp. 139f. (bâb ṣifât al-dhât al-dhât wa ṣifât al-afʿâl).

225. We are here dealing with the ontological Imam, of course, the perfect, cosmic divine Man of whom the historical imam is the manifestation on the sensible plane; see, e.g., al-Ṣaffâr, *Baṣâ'ir*, section 2, pp. 61–66 (the last pages of which are commentaries on the word *wajh* in the Qur'an); al-Kulaynî, *Uṣûl*, "kitâb al-tawḥîd," bâb al-nawâdir, vol. 1, p. 196; "kitâb al-ḥujja," bâb jâmi' fî faḍl al-imâm wa ṣifâtihi,vol.1, p. 283; Ibn Bâbûye, *Kitâb al-tawḥîd*, ch. 12, pp. 149f. (bâb tafsîr: kullu shay'in hâlik illâ wajhahu "everything is perishable except his Face [i.e., the Imam]" (Qur'an 28:88), ch. 22, bâb ma'nä janb Allâh 'azza wa jall, pp. 164f., ch. 24, bâb ma'nâ l-'ayn wa l-udhu wa l-lisân, pp. 167f.; Ibn Bâbûye, *'Uyûn*, vol. 1, ch 11, pp. 114f., and especially pp. 115–16 and 149-153, khuṭbat al-Riḍâ fî l-tawḥîd (khuṭbat al-Riḍâ fi l-tawḥîd); Ibn Bâbûye, *Kamâl al-dîn*, vol. 1, ch. 22, p. 231.

226. Cf., e.g., al-Ṣaffâr, *Baṣâ'ir,* section 2, ch. 3, pp. 16–17; Ibn Bâbûye, *Amâlî*, majlis 9, p. 35, num. 9; majlis 10, pp. 38–39, num. 6; al-Majlisî, *Biḥâr*, vol. 22, pp. 212–13, vol. 34, pp. 109–10.

227. Ibn Bâbûye, *'Ilal*, ch. 9, 'illa khalq al-khalq, p. 9, num. 1 (the tradition is reported by Ja'far: al-Ḥusayn: *inna'llâha jalla dhikruhu mâ khalaqa l-'ibâd illâ li-ya'rifûhu fa-idhâ 'arafûhu 'abadûhu fa-idhâ 'abadûhu' staghnaû bi-'ibâdatihi 'an 'ibâda man siwâh, fa-qâla lahu rajul famâ ma'rifat Allâh? qâla ma'rifa ahl kulli zamân imâmahum alladhî yajibu 'alayhim ṭâ'atuhu*).

228. *"Man 'arafanâ faqad arafa Allâh . . . wa man ankaranâ faqad ankara Allâh,"* cf., e.g., al-Ṣaffâr, *Baṣâ'ir,* section 1, ch. 3, p. 6; Ibn Bâbûye, *Kamâl al-dîn*, ch. 24, p. 261, num. 7; *Nahj al-balâgha*, p. 470.

229. *"Binâ 'urifa Allâh wa binâ 'ubida Allâh,"* see Ibn Bâbûye, *Kitâb al-tawḥîd*, ch. 12, p. 152, num. 9 *in fine.*

230. "Law lâ Allâh mâ 'urifnâ wa law lâ naḥnu mâ 'urifa Allâh," see Ibn Bâbûye, *Kitâb al-tawḥîd*, ch. 41, p. 290, num. 10.

231. Ja'far: " . . . *wa ja'alanâ 'aynahu fî 'ibâdihi wa lisânahu l-nâṭiq fî khalqih wa yadahu l-mabsûṭa 'alä 'ibâdihi bi l-ra'fa wa l-raḥma wa wajhahu'lladhî yu'tä minhu wa bâbahu alladhî yadullu 'alayhi wa khazâ'inahu fî samâ'ihi wa arḍih . . . bi 'ibâdatinâ 'ubida Allâh law lâ naḥnu mâ 'ubida Allâh,"* see Ibn Bâbûye, *Kitâb al-tawḥîd*, ch. 12, pp. 151–52, num. 8.

232. For general information on the question in mystical or Sunni theological literature in the classical age, see J. Van Ess, *Die Gedankenwelt des Ḥârit al-Muḥâsibî*, pp. 213–15 and 218f.; J. Van Ess, "Ibn Kullâb und die Miḥna,"; L. Gardet, *Dieu et la destinée de l'homme*, pp. 338–45; G. Vajda, "Pour le dossier de naẓar"; L. Ibrahim, "The Problem of the Vision of God in the Theology of az-Zamakhsharî and al-Bayḍâwî"; N. Pourjavady, "Ru'yat-e mâh dar âṣmân"; for Hanbalism, see H. Laoust, *La Profession de foi d'Ibn Baṭṭa*, s.v. "ru'ya" and "vision de Dieu"; for Mu'tazilism, see 'Abd al-Jabbâr, *al-Mughnî*, vol. 4, pp. 32–240; Ibn Mattûye, *al-Majmû'*, pp. 208–11; Mânakdîm Aḥmad b. Aḥmad, *Sharḥ*, pp. 233–77; for critiques of Mu'tazilite theses, see, e.g., al-Bâqillânî, *Kitâb al-tamhîd*, pp. 266–79; al-Baghdâdî, *Uṣûl al-dîn*, pp. 98f.; Ibn Ḥazm, *al-Fiṣal*, vol. 3, pp. 2f.; for Ash'arite theses, see D. Gimaret, *La Doctrine d'al-Ash'arî*, s.v. vision (*ru'ya*) and especially the second part, chapter 10.

233. Ibn Bâbûye, *Kitâb al-tawḥîd*, ch. 8, mâ jâ'a fi'l-ru'ya, p. 107, num. 1.

234. Al-Kulaynî, *Uṣûl*, Kitâb al-tawḥîd (bâb fî ibṭâl al-ru'ya), ch. 9, vol. 1, p. 128, num. 2; Ibn Bâbûye, *Kitâb al-tawḥîd*, pp. 110–11, num. 9. On the complex idea of *zan-*

daqa (and of the *zindîq*, pl. *zanâdiqa*, which has been here translated as "heretics" for the sake of simplicity), see Melhem Chokr's doctoral thesis *Zandaqa et Zindîqs en Islam jusqu'à la fin du II/VIIIe siècle,* Paris III, 1987–88, a thesis that masterfully completes the classical studies of G. Vadja on this subject.

235. It is here the tenth imam, ʿAlî b. Muḥammad al-Hâdî, who in reality is Abû' l-Ḥasan V, but since this *kunya* is rarely used in the case of the first and fourth imams (Abû' l-Ḥasan I and II), Imamites conventionally call the seventh imam Abû'l-Ḥasan I (although he is in reality the third), the eighth imam Abû' l-Ḥasan III (actually the fifth); moreover, Aḥmad b. Isḥâq al-Râzî was a disciple of the tenth imam (on him see, e.g., al-Ṭûsî, *Rijâl*, p. 410, num. 14; al-Ardabîlî, *Jâmiʿ al-ruwât*, vol. 1, p. 41). It would be of use here to add some practical information; in the corpus of the imams, these latter names are almost never cited, except with one of their surnames (*laqab*) or under one of their many *kunya*. Sometimes one *kunya* is used by several imams, and in this case one can identify them only by the person with whom they are speaking. Given that the compilations of traditions or the biographical notices do not always furnish this information, we take the liberty of presenting here the list of imams with their respective surnames and *kunya*:

1. ʿAlî b. Abî Ṭâlib (40/661), Amîr al-muʾminîn, al-Shahîd, al-Murtaḍä, Abû l-Ḥasan (I), Abû Turâb.
2. al-Ḥasan b. ʿAlî (49/669), al-Mujtabä, Abû Muḥammad (I).
3. al-Ḥusayn b. ʿAlî (61/680), Sayyid al-shuhadâʾ, Abû ʿAbdAllâh (I).
4. ʿAlî b. al-Ḥusayn (92 or 95/711 or 714), al-Sajjâd, Zayn al-ʿÂbidîn, Abû l-Ḥasan (II), Abû Muḥammad (II).
5. Muḥammad b. ʿAlî (circa 115/733–34), al-Bâqir, Abû Jaʿfar (I).
6. Jaʿfar b. Muḥammad (148/765), al-Ṣâdiq, Abû ʿAbdAllâh (II).
7. Mûsä b. Jaʿfar (183/799), al-Kâẓim, ʿAbd Ṣâlih, Abû l-Ḥasan (in reality III but usually I), Abû Ibrâhîm.
8. ʿAlî b. Mûsä (203/818), al-Riḍâ, Abû l-Ḥasan (in reality IV but usually II).
9. Muḥammad b. ʿAlî (220/835), al-Taqî, al-Jawâd, Abû Jaʿfar (II).
10. ʿAlî b. Muḥammad (254/868), al-Naqî, al-Hâdî, Abû l-Ḥasan (in reality V, but usually III), Abû l-Ḥasan al-ʿAskarî,.
11. al-Ḥasan b. ʿAlî (260/874), al-ʿAskarî, Abû Muḥammad (III).
12. Muḥammad b. al-Ḥasan (the hidden imam), al-Qâʾim, al-Mahdî, Ḥujjat Allâh, Baqiyyat Allâh, Ṣâḥib al-zamân, Abû l-Qâsim.

236. *"Lâ yajûz al-ruʾya mâ lam yakun bayna l-râʾî wa l-marʾî hawâʾun yanfuduhu l-baṣar fa-idhâ ʾnqaṭaʿa l-hawâʾ wa ʿudima l-ḍiyâʾ bayna l-râʾî wa l-marʾî lam taṣiḥḥa l-ruʾya wa kâna fî dhâlik al-ishtibâh liʾanna l-râʾî matä sâwä l-marʾî fî l-sabab al-mawjib baynahumâ fî l-ruʾya wajaba l-ishtibâh wa kâna dhâlik al-tashbîh,"* al-Kulaynî, *Uṣûl*, vol. 1, p. 130, num. 4; Ibn Bâbûye, *Kitâb al-tawḥîd*, p. 107, num. 7. Notice the insufficiency and the tentative manner of expression that is evident at this archaic stage of abstract reflection in Islam; in this regard, the words of the famous Hishâm b. al-Ḥakam, one of the sixth imam's partisans, are significant; he clumsily

attempts to harmonize the Aristotelian theory of perception, undoubtedly learned through translations of elementary summaries, with the Imamite context of the impossibility of ocular vision of God: "Things can be apprehended in two manners only: through the senses or through the heart. Perception via the senses takes place through three modalities [lit. "senses," *ma'ânin*]: interpenetration (*mudâkhala*), contact (*mumâssa*), [and perception] without either interpenetration or contact. Perception by interpenetration includes auditory, olfactory, or gustative perception [lit. "sounds, smells, and tastes," *al-aṣwât wa l-mashâmm wa l-ṭu'ûm*]. Perception via contact includes knowledge of (geometric) figures like the square [lit. "quadrature," *al-tarbî'*] or the triangle [lit. "triangulation," *al-tathlîth*], as well as that which is polished or rough [lit. "the soft and the rude," *al-layyin wa al-khashin*], or hot and cold. Perception through neither of the above includes sight, since it perceives things without either contact or interpenetration, and without things being in its own domain (*ḥayyiz*), but in domains beyond it. Vision requires [lit. "possesses," *lahu*] a milieu [lit. "a way," *sabîl*] and a means (*sabab*); its milieu is air and its means is light . . . [there follows a more or less analogous argument to that developed in the hadith of the tenth imam, but even more complex and less clear than the previous reasoning, to prove the impossibility of a vision of God]," cf. al-Kulaynî, *Uṣûl*, vol. 1, pp. 138–39, num. 12. The distance separating purely religious, rich terminology, and groping language that wishes to be logical can be seen.

237. " . . . *Katabtu ilä Abî Md as'aluhu kayfa ya'budu l-'abd rabbahu wa huwa lâ yarâh fa-waqqa'a yâ Abû Yûsuf jalla sayyidî wa mawlâya wa l-mun'im 'alayya wa 'alä âbâ'î an yurä . . . wa sa'altuhu hal ra'a rasûl Allâh rabbahu fa-waqqa'a inna'l-lâha tabârak wa ta'âlä arâ rasûlahu bi-qalbih min nûr 'aẓamatih mâ aḥabba,*" al-Kulaynî, *Uṣûl*, vol. 1, pp. 127–28, num. 1; Ibn Bâbûye, *Kitâb al-tawḥîd*, p. 107, num. 2; on Abû Yûsuf Ya'qûb b. Isḥâq al-Barqî, disciple of the tenth and eleventh imams, see, e.g., al-Ṭûsî, *Rijâl*, p. 426, num. 6 and p. 437, num. 3; al-Ardabîlî, *Jâmi' al-ruwât*, p. 345.

238. " . . . "*Yâ Abâ Ja'far ayyu shay'in ta'budu qâla Allâh ta'âlä qâla ra'aytahu qâla bal lam tarahu l-'uyûn bi-mushâhadat al-abṣâr wa lâkin ra'athu l-qulûb bi-ḥaqâ'iq al-îmân lâ yu'rafu bi l-qiyâs wa lâ yudraku bi l-ḥawâss wa lâ yushbihu bi l-nâs mawṣûf bi l-âyât ma'rûf bi l-'alâmât* . . . " al-Kulaynî, *Uṣûl, ibid.*, num. 5; Ibn Bâbûye, *Kitâb al-tawḥîd, ibid.*, num. 5.

239. Al-Kulaynî, *Uṣûl, ibid.*, num. 6; Ibn Bâbûye, *Kitâb al-tawḥîd, ibid.*, num. 6.

240. Cf. G. Vajda, "Le problème de la vision de Dieu (*ru'ya*) d'après quelques auteurs shî'ites duodécimains," in *Le Shî'isme imâmite*, pp. 31–53; N. Poorjavady, "Ru'yat-e mâh dar âsmân," in *Nashr-e Dânesh* (in Persian), 10th year, num. 2, 1990, especially pp. 12–15; the two authors only allude to the question of vision with the heart without dedicating a bit of their work to it.

241. There are reasons to believe that this fragmentation of details was voluntary; in the remainder of this chapter we will have occasion to see that the spiritual practice of vision with the heart appears as one of the most jealously guarded secrets in early Imamism. In the case of such secrets, both the imams and Shî'ite authors, especially the mystics and the esotericists, used a written "technique" of transmission called "dispersion of information" (*tabdîd al-'ilm*); we shall return to this subject.

242. In his *En Islam iranien*, H. Corbin dedicates a few pages to the question of

vision with the heart (vol. 1, pp. 226–35), but his analysis is essentially founded on a few traditions, reported by al-Kulaynî, and interpreted by the relatively late philosopher Mullâ Ṣadrâ (d. 1050/1640–41); despite two undeveloped allusions (p. 232 and p. 234, note 213), the approach thus remains exclusively philosophical, which is already an extrapolation as far as speech of the imams is concerned; the most significant traditions have not been reproduced and the practical, initiatory, even magical aspects that, to our thinking, constitute the essence of the question have remained neglected. On the other hand, see Corbin's admirable lines on this subject in Ibn 'Arabi in his *L'imagination créatrice . . .*, Part 2, pp. 7–8.

243. *"Thalâth min al-'abîd ilä rabbihim maḥâll al-tajallî wa l-waṣla wa l-ma'rifa falâ 'ayn tarâhu wa lâ qalb yaṣilu ilayhi wa lâ 'aql ya'rifuhu . . . ,"* Ja'far al-Ṣâdiq, *Tafsîr*, ed. P. Nwyia, pp. 196–97; ed. Zay'ûr, p. 141. It is here a question of God's Essence in its unfathomable abstruseness, since God, in His manifest aspect, can be known by *'aql*, the organ of the Sacred, through knowledge of the Imam; He can be reached by vision with the heart.

244. *"Dhâka idhâ lam yakun baynahu wa bayn Allâh aḥad dhâka idhâ tajallä 'llâh lahu,"* Ibn Bâbûye, *Kitâb al-tawḥîd*, p. 115, num. 15.

245. On the "eye of the heart" (*'ayn* or *'aynâ al-qalb*) see, e.g., al-Kulaynî, *Rawḍa*, vol. 2, p. 15; Ibn Bâbûye, *Kitâb al-tawḥîd*, ch. 60, pp. 366–67, num. 4.

246. Cf., e.g., al-Kulaynî, *Rawḍa*, vol. 1, p. 274 and vol. 2, p. 15; *Nahj al-balâgha*, p. 582; Ja'far, *Tafsîr*, ed. Nwyia, p. 203 (commentary on Qur'an 14:1), ed. Zay'ûr, p. 156.

247. *"Mathal al-'aql fî l-qalb ka-mathal al-sirâj fî wasaṭ al-bayt,"* a prophetic hadith reported by the first imam, Ibn Bâbûye, *'Ilal*, vol. 1, ch. 86, ch. 86, p. 98, num. 1.

248. Cf., e.g., al-Kulaynî, *Rawḍa*, vol. 1, p. 195; al-Nu'mânî, *Kitâb al-ghayba*, p. 217; Ibn Bâbûye, *'Ilal*, vol. 1, ch. 96, pp. 107-8, nums. 3 and 6; *Nahj al-balâgha*, 1223; Ja'far, *Tafsîr*, ed. Nwyia, p. 221 (commentary on Qur'an 46:13), ed. Zay'ûr, p. 197, and commentary on Qur'an 108:1 (ed. Nwyia, p. 230).

249. The words of al-Bâqir: *"la-nûr al-imâm fî qulûb al-mu'minîn anwar min al-shams al-muḍî'a bi l-nahâr,"* al-Kulaynî, *Uṣûl*,, vol. 1, "kitâb al-hujja," bâb inna l-a'imma nûr Allâh 'azza wa jall, p. 276, num. 1 and p. 278, num. 4; see also the identification of the Imam with light in the famous sermon of al-Riḍâ in the mosque in Marw. For example, the Imam is there referred to as "the luminous sun" (*al-shams al-muḍî'a*), "the shining full moon" (*al-badr al-munîr*), "the brilliant lamp" (*al-sirâj al-zâhir*), "the shining light" (*al-nûr al-sâṭi'*); cf., e.g., al-Ṣaffâr, *Baṣâ'ir*, section 7, chapter 18; al-Nu'mânî, *Kitâb al-ghayba*, pp. 315f.; Ibn Bâbûye, *Amâlî*, pp. 674f.; Ibn Bâbûye, *Kamâl al-dîn*, pp. 675f.

250. The words of Ja'far: *"inna manzilat al-qalb min al-jasad bi-manzalat al-imâm min al-nâs al-wâjib al-ṭâ'a 'alayhim,"* Ibn Bâbûye, *'Ilal*, vol. 1, ch. 96, p. 109, num. 8.

251. Cf. e.g., al-Kulaynî's chapter of the "kitâb al-ḥujja" entitled "the imams are the Light of God" (note 249); let us remark that in the Qur'an, the only "thing," the only "substantive" with which God is identified is light: "God is the Light of the heavens and the earth"), Qur'an 24:35.

252. " . . . *Al-'arsh khalaqahu Allâh ta'âlä min anwâr arba'a nûr aḥmar minhu 'ḥmarrat al-ḥumra wa nûr akhḍar minhu 'khḍarrat al-khuḍra wa nûr aṣfar minhu*

'ṣfarrat al-ṣufra wa nûr abyaḍ minhu 'byaṢṢa al-bayâd wa huwa l-'ilm alladhî ḥammalahu Allâh al-ḥamala wa dhâlika nûrun min 'aẓamatihi fa-bi 'aẓamatihi wa nûrihi abṣara qulûb al-mu'minîn . . . ," al-Kulaynî, *Uṣûl*, "kitâb al-tawḥîd," bâb al-'arsh wa l-kursî, vol. 1, p. 175, num. 1.

253. "*Al-shams juz' min sab'în juz'an min nûr al-kursî juz' min sab'în juz'an min nûr al-ḥijâb wa l-ḥijâb juz' min sab'în juz'an min nûr al-sitr fa'in kânû ṣadiqîn falyamla'û a'yunahum min al-shams laysa dûnahâ saḥâb,"* al-Kulaynî, *Uṣûl*, vol. 1, bâb fî ibṭâl al-ru'ya, pp. 131–32, num. 7; Ibn Bâbûye, *Kitâb al-tawḥîd*, ch. 8, p. 108, num. 3.

254. *"Dhâka Muḥammad kâna idhâ naẓara ilä rabbihi bi-qalbihi ja'alahu fî nûrin mithl nûr al-ḥujub ḥattä yastabîna lahu mâ fî l-ḥujub inna nûr Allâh minhu'khḍarra mâ'khḍarra wa minhu'ḥmarra mâ'ḥmarra wa minhu'byaḍḍa mâ'byaḍḍa wa minhu ghayr dhâlik,"* Ibn Bâbûye, *Kitâb al-tawḥîd*, p. 114, num. 13.

255. See L. Massignon, *Essai* and *Passion de Hallâj*, s.v. "qalb"; E. Dermenghem, "Techniques d'extase en Islam"; L. Gardet, "La mention du nom divin (*dhikr*) en mystique musulmane"; in the article "qalb" from *EI1* (vol. 4, pp. 507–10, by L. Gardet and J. C. Vadet), there is no mention of vision with the heart. Among the classics of sufism, see, e.g., Abû l-Ḥasan al-Nûrî, *Maqâmât al-qulûb* in "Textes mystiques inédits d'Abû l-Ḥasan al-Nûrî" in *MUSJ*, vol. 44, fasc. 9; al-Qushayrî, *al-Risâlat al-qushayriyya*, pp. 47f.; al-Hujwîrî, *Kashf* al-maḥjûb, pp. 246f.; al-Sulamî, *Risâ la al-malâmatiyya* in E. E. 'Afîfî, *al-Malâmatiyya wa l-ṣûfiyya*, pp. 100 and 104; al-Ḥakîm al-Tirmidhî, *al-Farq bayna l-ṣadr wa l-qalb . . .*

256. Ed. F. Meier, *Die Rawâ'iḥ al-jamâl wa fawâtiḥ al-jalâl des Najm ad-dîn al-Kubrâ*, Akademie der Wissenschaften und der Literatur, Veröffentlichungen der Orientalischen Komission, Wiesbaden, 1957.

257. Najm al-Dîn al-Râzî, *Mirṣâd al-'ibâd* (in Persian), ed. Shams al-'Urafâ', chapters 18 and 19, pp. 165–73; ed. M. A. Riyâḥî, chapters 17 and 18 of ch. 3, pp. 299–315 (*dar bayân-e mushâhadât-e anwâr wa marâtib-e ân; dar bayân-e mukâshafât wa anwâ'-e ân*).

258. 'Alâ' al-Dawla al-Simnânî, *al-'Urwa li ahl al-khalwa wa l-jalwa*, ed. of the Arabic text and an early Persian translation by N. Mâyel Herawî, s.v., *laṭâ'if rûḥânî* and *laṭîfa*.

259. On this question see the excellent book by H. Corbin, *L'Homme de lumière dans le soufisme iranien*, Paris, 1971 (English translation, *The Man of Light in Iranian Sufism*, Boulder & London, 1978). Corbin here studies, among others, the teachings of Najm al-Dîn al-Kubrä (chapter 4), Najm al-Dîn al-Râzî (chapter 5), and 'Alä al-Dawla al-Simnânî (chapter 6). He refers to the latter's *Tafsîr*, which has not been edited and which we have unfortunately not been able to consult, but exactly the same theses are found therein as in *al-'Urwa*, to which we have referred (N. M. Herawî is presently preparing a critical edition of al-Simnânî's *Tafsîr*).

260. Al-shaykh Muḥammad Amîn al-Kurdî al-Shâfi'î al-Naqshbandî, *tanwîr al-qulûb*, with a biographical sketch by his successor (*khalîfa*), al-shaykh Salâma al'Azzâmî, sixth ed., Cairo, 1348/1929, pp. 548–58.

261. We are indebted to Professor Guy Monnot, a specialist in Qur'anic commentaries, for pointing out that the relationship of the *'arsh* and the *kursî* with the *qalb* and the *sirr* is also found in the commentators, particularly al-Ṭabarî and al-Nîsâbûrî.

262. Md Taqî b. Md Kâẓim Muẓaffar 'Alî Shâh Kirmânî, *Kibrît-e aḥmar* (+ Baḥr

al-asrâr), ed. J. Nûrbakhsh, p. 5: "*Maḥall-e zuhûr-e nûr-e khodâ wa â'îne-ye tajaliyyât-e ḥudûr-e mawlä ḥaqîqat-e qalb ast ke ân laṭîfa îst rabbânî wa mujarradîst rûḥânî wa ḥaqîqat-e qalb-e rûḥânî râ ṣûratîst jismânî ke ʿibârat az muḏgha-ye ṣinawbariyya-ye wâqiʿa dar aysar-e tajwîf-e ṣadr ast wa har tajallî-ye maʿnawî ke dar qalb-e maʿnawî wâqiʿ mîshawad dar în qâlab-e ṣinawbarî ke be manzila-ye rowzane-ye ân laṭîfa-ye rabbânî wa be mathâba-ye khalîfa-ye ân mujarrad-e rûḥânîst ṣûratî muṭâbiq-e ân maʿnä wa mithâlî muwâfiq-e ân tajallî jilwagar mîgardad wa har gâh ân tajallî az tajalliyyât-e jâmiʿa bâshad lâ maḥâla ṣûrat-e mutmaththila ṣûratî jâmiʿ kh(w) âhad bûd . . . ṣûrat-e insânîst.*" In the continuation of the treatise, the author rather abstrusely and in densely worded language points out both phrases to be used in *dhikr* and the signs that should be visualized, especially at the level of the heart. The editor, a present-day master of a branch of the brotherhood, without going as far as to reveal technical secrets, has nevertheless judged it necessary to clarify a number of sentences with explanatory notes.

263. Mullâ ʿAlî b. Mullâ Sulṭân Md Gunâbâdî Nûr ʿAlî Shâh Thânî, *Ṣâliḥiyya* (written in Persian in the name of his son and successor, Ṣâliḥ ʿAlî Shâh, d. 1386/1966), second ed., Tehran, 1387/1346 solar/1967.

264. "*Zuhûr-e nûr dar del nûr-e Imâm ast wa nûr-e Imâm dar del-e mu'min anwar az shams . . . balke ṭaraf-e nisbat nabâshand . . . nûr-e Imâm zuhûr-e nûr-e ḥaqq ast wa nûr-e shams zulmat wa ghubâr ast . . . "Maʿrifatî bi l-nûrâniyya maʿrifat Allâh wa maʿrifat Allâh maʿrifatî bi l-nûrâniyya man ʿarafanî bi l-nûrâniyya kâna muʿminan imtaḥana 'llâhu qalbahu li l-îmâm . . . ,*" Ṣâliḥiyya, "ḥaqîqa," 86, pp. 159–60. The final sentence on the subject of the "believer whose heart has been tested by God for faith" is an important, consecrated expression to which we shall return.

265. "*Del râ do rû' st rû-ye zâhir-e ân ke ḥayât ast jân bakhsh-e quwä wa tan ast wa în wajhe qâʿida-ye nûr ast wa rû-ye bâtin-e ân ke bâtin-e qalb ast wa zuhûr-e û be ṣadr ast majmaʿ wa maḥall-e zuhûr-e asmâ' wa ṣifât-e ilâhî' st liḥâdhâ ʿarsh gûyand . . . liḥâdhâ ʿAlî ʿarsh ast ke be rûy-e bâṭin Allâh ast ke majmaʿ-e asrâr ast,*" Ṣâliḥiyya, "ḥaqîqa," 587, p. 330.

266. Ṣâliḥiyya, pp. 149–50, 156, 328f., respectively.

267. On the "invocations of the heart" (*dhikr qalbî*) of this branch of the Niʿmatullâhiyya, see also Mullâ Sulṭân Md Gunâbâdî Sulṭân ʿAlî Shâh (d. 1327/1909), *Walâyat Nâmeh* (in Persian), second ed., Tehran, 1385/1344 solar/1965, especially bâb 9, chapters 2 to 5, pp. 171–89.

268. Jamâl al-Dîn shaykh Md Qâdir Bâqiri Namînî, *Dîn wa del* ("religion and the heart," in Persian), Tehran, 1356 solar/1977 (numerous references to the works of the masters of the Order, e.g., Jalâl al-Dîn ʿAlî Mîr Abû l-Faḍl (d. 1323/1905), Mîr Quṭb al-Dîn Muḥammad (d. 1962) or Shâh Maqṣûd Ṣâdiq ʿAnqâ' (d. 1986).

269. See, e.g., Ḥasan b. Ḥamza b. Md Palâsî Shîrâzî, *Tadhkira-ye shaykh Md b. Ṣâdiq al-Kujujî* (translated in Persian in 811/1404 by Najm al-Dîn Ṭârumî), Shiraz, n.d., pp. 14, 18, 25, 38, 68 and passim; Ḥaḍrat Râz Shîrâzî (Mîrzâ Abû l-Qâsim Âqâ Mîrzâ Bâbâ, one of the great masters of the Order, d. 1286/1869), *Kitâb mirṣâd al-ʿibâd*, Tabrîz, n.d., pp. 4, 10, 11, 17, 21, and passim; anonymous, *Qaṣâ'id wa madâ'iḥ dar sha'n-e mawlâ-ye muttaqîyân Ḥaḍrat-e Shâh-e walâyat ʿAlî ʿalayhi l-salâm*, Tabrîz, n.d., poems num. 10 and 11; anonymous, *Yek qismat az târîkh-e ḥayât wa karâmât-e sayyid Quṭb al-Dîn Md Shîrâzî*, Tabrîz, 1309/1891, pp. 7-8, 37. All these sources are in Persian.

270. This dialogue constitutes the last text in a Dhahabi collection of eleven texts, Tehran, 1367/1947, pp. 112–50 (the title of the text is *Risâla-ye ḥall-e ishkâl-e dawâz-dah su'âl-e jenâb-e Râ'iḍ al-Dîn Zanjânî quddisa sirruh az pîr-e waḥîd-e 'ârif-e kâmil-e khod ḥaḍrat-e Mîrzâ Abû l-Qâsim ma'ruf be Âqâ Mîrzâ Bâbâ-ye Râz-e Shîrâzî qud-disa sirruh*).

271. *Risâla-ye ḥall-e ishkâl* . . . pp. 125-26; see also p. 150 (an allusion to the fact that the light of faith in the heart is a ray of Light from the Imam). For Khâksâr sufi spiritual practices based on the vision of the Light of the Imam in the heart, see Sayyid Aḥmad Dehkordî (d. 1339/1920), *Burhân nâme-ye ḥaqîqat*, Tehran, n.d., pp. 81f. ("Description of the septuple Mountains of the heart and the rising of the Real Sun"). For general information and bibliography on Imamite mystical orders, see R. Gram-lich, *Die schiitischen Dewischorden Persiens*, Wiesbaden, 3 vol., 1981 (3rd edition).

272. These same elements are found in other esoteric and mystical traditions, like certain Hindu traditions and the orthodox Hesychast monks. The earliest accounts come from the Vedas: "This Light residing in the hearts of all, omniscient and all-pene-trating, this Spirit that is the Divine Instructor; it is this Spirit that, with its strength, makes the wise person into a Seer" (*Rg Veda*, VII, 88, 4). "Searching in their hearts, the sages discover the source and the cause of existence in the depths of the nonexistent" (*ibid.*, X, 129, 4). Further clarification comes in the *Brâhmanas* and the *Upanishads*: "The Self is like a grain of rice, as small as a fragment of golden millet; form residing in the cave of the heart, shining like a smokeless fire, the Self bigger than the sky" (*Shatapata Br.*, 10, 6, 2 and 4). "Such a sage assumes the very form of the light that he perceives with his interior vision, his glance, guided by the Supreme Master [Shiva], perceives the shining Sun of Intelligence hidden in the cave of the heart" (*Advaya Târaka Up.*, 12–13). All the relevant Yoga literature contains information on "the sub-tle center" (*chakra*) of the heart, some of which is more detailed than the rest; we limit ourselves here to a few lines from the yogic *Upanishads*: "At the center of the chalice of the lotus of the heart is found the mystic syllable AUM, immobil, brilliant as a never-extinguished lamp . . . it is no more than the Lord, the size of a thumb, and the form of the hidden Lord is revealed like a flame in the heart" (*Dhyânabindu Up.*, 19–22). "In the region of the heart, there is a lotus in the center of which there is a circle the size of an atom wherein is found the individual soul, which is light. . . . When thought rests in the very center of the lotus, it attains Knowledge (*ibid.*, 93). On the other hand, the method of prayer and meditation of the Hesychast monks can be summed up as follows: sitting in the darkness, lower your head, fix your gaze on the center of your body, attempt to discover the location of the "true heart," persevering in this exercise day and night, always accompanying it with the prayer "Lord Jesus Christ, Son of God, have pity on me" said with the slowest rhythm of breath possible; "thus will you find 'the location of the heart' and in it all kinds of knowledge and marvels, the crown of which is the discovery of the Light of Christ." The subtle center of the heart is found, according to the Greek Fathers, a little above the left nipple (cf. e.g., I. Hausherr, "La méthode d'oraison Hésychaste"; A. Bloom, "Contemplation et ascèse, contribution orthodoxe"; A. Bloom, "L'Hésychasme, yoga chrétien?"; *Petite philo-calie de la prière du coeur*.

273. The imams knew "concentration of the heart"; they often use expressions like "the concentrated [= "concentered"] heart" (*al-qalb al-mujtama'*) (Ibn Bâbûye,

Amâlî, "majlis" 1, num. 6, p. 4; Ibn ʿAyyâsh, *Muqtaḍab*, p. 55) or "the protection of the heart against associative thoughts" (*ḥifẓ al-qalb min al-khawâṭir*; Jaʿfar, *Tafsîr*, ed. Nwyia, p. 195, a commentary on Qurʾan 6:79, and also p. 229, commentary on Qurʾan 104:6–7).

274. On the sacred phrases and virtues of their repetition, see, e.g., al-Kulaynî, *Uṣûl*, "kitâb al-îmân wa l-kurf," bâb al-inṣâf wa l-ʿadl, vol. 3, p. 216, num. 9, and especially "kitâb al-duʿâʾ," ch. 23-29 (on the *dhikr*, the Remembrance of God) and ch. 31-51 (on the sacred phrases), vol. 4, pp. 245–65 and 267–90; on illumination of the heart by prayer, cf. the words of the third imam in al-Nuʿmânî, *Kitâb al-ghayba*, p. 92. The Imamite mystics claim to have received their *dhikr* from the imams via an uninterrupted chain of spiritual masters.

275. For heresiological sources, see, e.g., al-Ashʿarî, *Maqâlât al-islâmiyyin*; al-Baghdâdî, *Farq*; al-Shahrastânî, *Milal*, s.v., or under "Hishâmayn." For Imamite sources and the refutations of the imams, see, e.g., al-Kulaynî, *Uṣûl*, vol. 1, "kitâb al-tawḥîd," bâb al-nahy ʿani l-jism wa l-ṣûra, p. 140, num. 1; Ibn Bâbûye, *Kitâb al-tawḥîd*, ch. 6, pp. 97f., nums. 1, 2, 4, 6, 7 etc., and ch. 8, pp. 113–14, num. 13 (the anthropomorphist remarks are here attributed to two other companions, also, al-Maythamî and "Muʾmin" al-Ṭâq); Ibn Bâbûye, *Amâlî*, "majlis" 47, p. 277, nums. 1 and 2. The teachings of these companions (Hishâm b. Sâlim was part of the entourage of the fifth, sixth, and seventh imams, Hishâm b. al-Ḥakam was in the entourage of the latter two) are too little known; they are considered either as anthropomorphists or as anti-anthropomorphists; they are at times presented as intimate disciples of the imams, and at other times as opposed to them, if not condemned by the imams because of their beliefs; it is for this reason that we hesitate to use the word "disciple." See, e.g., W. Madelung, "Hishâm b. al-Ḥakam," *EI2*; W. Madelung, "The Shiite and Kharijite Contribution," especially pp. 129-30, note 10; Shahrastânî, *Livre des religions*, pp. 531–38 (especially D. Gimaret's notes on pp. 531–32 and 535), and also in the present work, s.v.

276. Cf. Part I-2, especially Ibn Bâbûye, *Kitâb al-tawḥîd*, ch. 67 (bâb al-nahy ʿani l-kalâm), pp. 454–61.

277. When speaking about the Light that is seen at the level of the heart, the imams are speaking either of God or of the Imam; they sometimes even keep this ambiguity about themselves, as plenary manifestations of the ontological Imam. For example, in Jaʿfar's remarks resembling the "paradoxes"(*shaṭaḥât*) of the sufis: Abû Baṣîr (cf. note 182):

> "Tell me if, on the Day of Ressurection, the believers will be able to see God."
>
> Jaʿfar: "Yes, but they have already seen Him well before the coming of that day."
>
> "When?"
>
> "When He asked them 'Am I not your Lord?' and they replied, 'Verily'" (Qurʾan 7: 172).

Abû Baṣîr reports that then his master remained silent for a long time, then said:

> "The believers see Him already in this world before the Day of Resurrection, *do you not see Him right now*?
>
> "Could I have your authority to report these words?"

"No, because a negator, not knowing the deep meaning of these words, would use them to accuse us of assimilationism and infidelity. Vision with the heart differs from vision with the eyes, and God transcends the descriptions of the assimilationists and the heretics" (Ibn Bâbûye, *Kitâb al-tawḥîd*, ch. 8, num. 20, p. 117).

In another tradition attributed to Ja'far al-Ṣâdiq an identity is established between the Lord and the Imam; commenting on Qur'an 39:69 ("And the earth will be illumined by the light of its Lord" —*wa ashraqat al-arḍ bi-nûri rabbihâ*), the sixth imam said: "The Lord of the earth is the Imam of the earth," and to the question "What will happen to it when the Imam appears?" he replies: "Then men will no longer need the sun, for the light of the Imam will suffice them" (al-Qummî, *Tafsîr*, under Qur'an 39:69). Remarks of the same tenor are reported in Jâbir's corpus, a corpus whose early date of composition and affiliation with Shî'ism there can no longer be any doubt about: "Then I [it is Jâbir b. Ḥayyân who is speaking] prostrated myself before him [imam Ja'far]. He said "If your prostration were addressed to me, you would be among the happy ones. Your ancestors already were prostrate before me [an allusion to the "voyage" of the divine light of the Imam through the ages of humanity]. But in being prostrate before me, o Jâbir, you actually are prostrate before yourself [an allusion to the presence of the interior Imam in each initiated believer]. By God, you are well above [such prostrations]!" "But I prostrated myself again." He then said, "O Jâbir, you have no need of all that." "You are right, my lord," I replied. He said: "We know what you mean and you know what I mean. So obtain that which you desire." (*Mukhtâr rasâ'il Jâbir b. Ḥayyân*, "kitâb ikhrâj ilä l-quwwa mî fî l-fi'l," pp. 79-80; French trans. P. Lory, *Dix traités d'alchimie*, p. 296, note 160. For the vision of light of the Imam with the heart in Jâbir's works, see P. Lory, *Alchimie et mystique*, pp. 38, 61, 104, 157.

278. Once again we are assisted by indices from an Indian text: "Through concentration on the center of the heart, the yogi gains limitless knowledge, knows the past, the present, and the future; he possessed clairvoyance and "clairaudience"; he can see the gods and goddesses, and he masters the supernatural beings that move in space. He who, each day, fixes his interior gaze on the hidden Flame of the Heart, obtains the power of moving through the air and that of showing up anywhere in the world at will" (*Shiva Samhitâ*, V, 86-88). It is interesting to note that the prodigious faculties that the Shivaist text lists for the ascetic who concentrates on the "Flame of the Heart" are exactly those that are attributed to the imams, and sometimes to some of their initiates, especially the "representatives" of the hidden imam: for knowledge of the past, present, and future, see, e.g., al-Kulaynî, *Uṣûl*, vol. 1, "kitâb al-ḥujja," bâb jihât 'ulûm al-a'imma, pp. 393f.; for clairvoyance and clairaudience, see al-Ṣaffâr, *Baṣâ'ir*, section 9, ch. 1, 7, and 12; for the control exercises on supernatural or nonhuman beings, see *Baṣâ'ir*, section 7, ch. 14–16 and section 10, ch. 16–18; on "magic displacement" and "striding over clouds," see *Baṣâ'ir*, section 8, ch. 12–15; on the supernatural powers of the hidden imam's representatives, see, e.g., Ibn Bâbûye, *Kamâl al-dîn*, chapter 45, especially pp. 482f. All of these points will be returned to at length.

279. Ja'far: "*Amrûna* [*amr*: "affair," "cause," "order"; it is our sense that "doctrine" contains all these meanings to a certain extent] *sirr fî sirr wa sirr mustasirr wa sirr lâ yufîdu illâ sirr wa sirr muqanna' bi-sirr,*" *Baṣâ'ir*, section 1, ch. 12, p. 28, num. 1.

280. Al-Bâqir: "*Inna amranâ hâdhâ mastûr muqanna' bi l-mîthâq* (it could also

be translated: "Our doctrine is hidden, veiled since the time of the preexistential World of the Pact") *man hatakahu adhallahu 'llâh,*" *Baṣâ'ir, ibid.*, num. 2.

281. Jaʿfar: *Inna amranâ huwa l-ḥaqq wa ḥaqq al-ḥaqq wa huwa l-ẓâhir wa l-bâṭin wa bâṭin al-bâṭin wa huwa l-sirr wa sirr al-sirr wa sirr mustasirr wa sirr muqannaʿ bi l-sirr,*" *Baṣâ'ir, ibid.*, num. 4, p. 28.

282. It is perhaps in this sense that the recursive words of the imams, repeated like a leitmotive throughout the ensemble of their works, should be understood: "We are the Treasure (*khazâna*) and the Treasurers (*khuzzân/khazana*) of God's secret and our initiated [*shîʿatunâ*, lit. "our Shîʿites," "our "partisans"; this translation will be justified in part III-2] are our treasures and our treasurers," cf. e.g., *Baṣâ'ir*, section 2, ch. 3; al-Kulaynî, *Uṣûl*, "kitâb al-ḥujja," ch. 13–14; al-Kulaynî, *Rawḍa*, vol. 1, p. 101; Ibn Bâbûye, *ʿUyûn*, vol. 1, ch. 19-20; Ibn Bâbûye, *Maʿânî al-akhbâr*, p. 132; Ibn Bâbûye, *Ṣifât al-shîʿa*, pp. 60f.; Ibn ʿAyyâsh, *Muqtaḍab*, p. 89.

283. The traditions of several imams: "*Ḥadîthunâ* (var.: *amrunâ*) *ṣaʿb mustaṣʿab lâ haḥtamiluhu (var.: lâ yuʿminu bihi) illâ nabî mursal aw malak muqarrab aw mu'min imtaḥana'llâhu qalbahu li l-îmân,*" cf. e.g., al-Ṣaffâr, *Baṣâ'ir*, section 1, ch. 11, pp. 20–28; Furât, *Tafsîr*, p. 55; we find here the three categories of "pure beings" initiated by the luminous entities of the Impeccables in the pre-existential World of the Pact, which corroborates the idea according to which on one hand the teaching of the imams and on the other the practice of vision with the heart are the reactualization of the primordial Initiation. Certain traditions add another element, having the capacity to add faith to the teaching of the imams: "a fortified city" (*madîna ḥaṣîna*), which according to the imams is "a concentrated heart" (*al-qalb al-mujtamaʿ*), cf. *Baṣâ'ir*, section 1, ch. 11, p. 21, num. 3; Ibn Bâbûye, *Amâlî*, "majlis" 1, p. 4, num. 6; Ibn Bâbûye, *Maʿânî al-akhbâr*, p. 189. The believer with a proven heart, one who has managed to pass the initiatory test of vision with the heart, is thus the true faithful of the imams, "the true Shîʿite."

284. Cf. al-Ṣaffâr, *Baṣâ'ir*, section 9, chapter 12, pp. 440–42, num. 4; al-Kulaynî, *Uṣûl*, vol. 2, "kitâb al-ḥujja," bâb mawâlîd al-a'imma, pp. 225–28, num. 1.

285. According to traditions attributed to the fifth and sixth imams, the prophets and the imams are endowed with five spirits: 1) the holy spirit (*rûḥ al-quds*) who obtains Knowledge for them and because of whom they can carry the repository of prophecy; 2) the spirit of faith (*rûḥ al-îmân*), through which they have faith, fear of the Lord and justice; 3) the spirit of strength (*rûḥ al-quwwa*), through which they can expend effort in obedience to God; 4) the spirit of longing (*rûḥ al-shahwa*), through which they desire to serve God and satisfy their natural needs; and 5) the spirit of movement (*rûḥ al-madraj*), or the spirit of life (*rûḥ al-ḥayât*), which allows them to move. Cf. al-Ṣaffâr, *Baṣâ'ir*, section 9, ch. 14, pp. 445–50; al-Kulaynî, *Uṣûl*, vol. 2, "kitâb al-ḥujja," bâb fîhi dhikr al-arwâḥ allatî fî l-a'imma, pp. 15–17.

286. The imam is identified with the Word (*kalima*) of God. In the Qur'an, the only man identified with the Word, with the Logos, is Jesus Christ, the son of Mary (cf. Qur'an 3:39 and 45; 4:171). In the domain that we are in the midst of presenting, there is a parallel to be found between Christ and the imams, on the one hand, and between Fâṭima and Mary, on the other; on this subject see Mahmoud M. Ayoub, "Towards an Islamic Christology: An Image of Jesus in Early Shîʿi Muslim Literature," *MW*, 66, 1976, pp. 163–88; Henry Corbin, *En Islam Iranien*, s.v. "christiansime et shîʿisme" and "christologie"; the studies are cited in note 152.

287. The mention of the "Supreme Horizon" (*al-ufuq al-a'lä*) is not gratuitious; the expression is used once in the Qur'an: "By the star when it disappears/Your Companion (the Prophet Muḥammad) has not gone astray, nor does he err/He does not speak under the command of his own impulse/It is only a Revelation which has been inspired to him/The Powerful, the Almighty made it known to him/The Powerful was held in majesty/When he found himself on the Supreme Horizon/Then he approached and remained suspended/He was at a distance of two bowshots or less/And he revealed to his servant what he revealed" (Qur'an 53:1–10); although it is difficult to differentiate between the names represented by "he" in the last four verses [God, the angel Gabriel, or the Prophet himself], the Imamite commentary, in accord with the majority of Sunni commentaries, has identified him who "found himself at the Supreme Horizon" as the angel Gabriel (cf. al-Ḥasan al-'Askarî, *Tafsîr*, p. 298; 'Alî b. Ibrâhîm al-Qummî, *Tafsîr*, under Qur'an 53:1–10; Furât, *Tafsîr*, under Qur'an 53:1–10). Thus the imam would be, from the moment of his birth, summoned by the angel of Revelation, the angel of the prophets, who transmits the divine message to him. It is the superiority of the imams over the prophets that is thus implicitly emphasized, and therefore that of esotericism over exotericism.

288. Cf. note 182.

289. Certain elements irresistibly recall the legend of the conception of Zoroaster, as it is described by al-Shahrastânî: ". . . Then [God] put the spirit of Zoroaster in a tree that He had grow at the summit of *'Illiyûn*. . . . He then mixed the spirit of Zoroaster with some cowmilk. Zoroaster's father drank it, and it became sperm, and then an embryo in his mother's womb . . . ," *Livre des religions*, p. 643 (trans. G. Monnot: see the translator's notes; compare with *Dênkart*, VII, 2, 1f., and M. Molé, *La Légende de Zoroastre selon les textes pehlevis*, Paris, 1967, pp. 15f.).

290. Al-Kulaynî, *Uṣûl*, "kitâb al-ḥujja," bâb mawâlîd al-a'imma, vol. 2, pp. 228f., num. 2f.

291. Al-Kulaynî, *Uṣûl*, *ibid.*, num. 5.

292. The parallel established with the Qur'anic account of the conception of Jesus and the visit of the angel to Mary is evident (cf. Qur'an 19:15f.).

293. Ibn Bâbûye, *'Ilal*, ch. 147, p. 183, num. 1. According to some traditions, the seed of the imam comes from a celestial dew upon a piece of fruit or a blade of grass that his father absorbed; cf., e.g. *Baṣâ'ir*, section 9, ch. 7, pp. 431–34.

294. Ibn Bâbûye, *'Ilal*, *ibid.*, num. 2; it should be emphasized that according to the Imamite idea, the numerous celestial ascensions of the Prophet, just as much as the "supernatural translocations" or "striding upon clouds" of the imams (see later discussion), take place corporally; on the question of the *mi'raj*, the literature about it, and the polemics between holders of the "spiritual" thesis and those of the "corporeal" thesis, see the erudite introduction by N. Mâyel Herawî to his edition of *Mi'raj Nâme-ye Abû 'Alî Sînâ be enḏemâm-e taḥrîr-e ân az Shams al-Dîn Ibrâhîm Abarqûhî* (in Persian), Tehran, 1365 solar/1987, pp. 11–67.

295. There are numerous variations of the traditions concerning these characteristics; we report here only those details that are encountered most frequently in most of the traditions; cf. al-Ṣaffâr, *Baṣâ'ir*, section 9, chapters 11–12; al-Kulaynî, *Uṣûl*, "kitâb al-ḥujja," bâb mawâlîd al-a'imma, numbers 4, 5, 6, 8.

296. This is the definition given by the Prophet, for the word *al-batûl*, the sur-

name shared with Mary, the mother of Jesus, and Fâṭima (cf. Ibn Bâbûye, *ʿIlal*, ch. 144, p. 181); the word usually has the meaning of "pious virgin," but in our context it could be translated as "immaculate" (although in the Christian tradition relative to Mary, the term has more the meaning of "without sin," or "not soiled by sin").

297. We have counted 46 in the early sources (al-Ṣaffâr, *Baṣâ'ir*, section 9, chapters 7–12, pp. 431–43; al-Kulaynî, *Uṣûl, ibid.*, vol. 2, "kitâb al-ḥujja," bâb mawâlîd al-a'imma, pp. 225f, and especially 229–31; al-Kulaynî, *al-Rawḍa*, vol. 1, pp. 182–83; for more recent sources, see al-Ṭurayḥî, *Majma' al-baḥrayn*, s.v. "ʿamûd," "nûr"). Of the 46 traditions, 35 are attributed to Jaʿfar, 8 to al-Bâqir, and 3 to al-Riḍâ. What once again confirms the determining role of these first two individuals, and particularly that of Jaʿfar, in the systematic elaboration of Imamite doctrine (also called Jaʿfarite doctrine), is the fact that Jaʿfar is considered by Muslim esotericists as the "father" of Muslim occult sciences. On discussions regarding Jaʿfar's founding role in Islamic occultism, see J. Ruska, *Arabischer Alchemisten*, Heidelberg, 1924; P. Kraus, *Jâbir b. Ḥayyân*; and the responses of: F. Sezgin, *GAS*, vol. 4, especially pp. 191f.; T. Fahd, "Gaʿfar aṣ-Ṣâdiq et la tradition scientifique arabe," in *Le Shîʿisme imâmite*; T. Fahd, *La Divination arabe*, s.v. Gaʿfar aṣ-Ṣâdiq; P. Lory, *Alchimie et Mystique en terre d'Islam*, pp. 44f.

298. *"ʿAmûd al-nûr, ʿamûd min nûr,"* cf., e.g., al-Ṣaffâr, *Baṣâ'ir*, pp. 431–33, 435–36, 442.

299. *Manâr min nûr,"* al-Ṣaffâr, *Baṣâ'ir*, pp. 432, 435; al-Kulaynî, *Uṣûl*, vol. 2, p. 231, num. 6.

300. *"Miṣbâḥ min nûr,* al-Ṣaffâr, *Baṣâ'ir*, pp. 432, 433.

301. *"Nûr mithl sabîkat al-dhahab,"* al-Kulaynî, *Uṣûl*, vol. 2, p. 230, num. 5.

302. Al-Ṣaffâr, *Baṣâ'ir*, pp. 439, 440, 442.

303. Al-Ṣaffâr, *Baṣâ'ir*, p. 440: *"Jaʿala Allâh baynahu wa bayna l-imâm ʿamûdan min nûr . . . idhâ arâda ʿilma shay'in naẓara fî dhâlika l-nûr fa-ʿarafahu."*

304. Al-Ṣaffâr, *Baṣâ'ir*, p. 432; see also the following hadith: " . . . A minaret of light with which [the imam] sees the actions of the servants (. . . *manâran min nûr yanẓuru bihi ilä aʿmâl al-ʿibâd*)" or on page 431: " . . . For him is established a column made of light, [stretching] between the heavens and the earth, and by which he sees the actions of people and knows their intentions (. . . *Nuṣiba lahu ʿamûdan min nûr min al-samâ' ilä l-arḍ yarä bihi aʿmâl al-nâs wa yaʿrifu niyyâtihim*)."

305. Al-Ṣaffâr, *Baṣâ'ir*, pp. 434, 437; sometimes the word *bilâd* (lit. country, region), here translated as "place," is replaced by the word *qarya* (village) (e.g., on pages 437–38).

306. To clarify certain elements of early Imamite teaching, what we have called "nonrational esoteric Imamism," we have often been led to consult occult or magical literature, not only in the confines of the Muslim world where texts are for the most part inaccessible or too hermetic and little studied, but also in other esoteric and occult traditions that are more completely studied and richer in resources. Regarding the Column of Light, an analogous phenomenon can be discerned in the occultists of India or Tibet, as well as in the medieval West. In Hindu cosmology, *Âkâsha* (often translated as "ether") is the fifth element and the Mother of the four others; it is a sacred cosmic material of extreme subtlety; it is thus invisible to the physical eye, but it fills all of space, penetrating everything. For Indian occultists, *Âkâsha* has, among other properties, that of

recording in itself everything that happens in the universe, from events of a cosmic scale to the slightest movements of thought; this is why it is also called *Chitâkâsha* (*Âkâsha*—universal mind). The occultist yogi can obtain the ability to visualize *Âkâsha* with his spiritual eye, with the eye of his heart, or with the eye of Shiva located between his eye-brows. At the moment of vision, *Âkâsha*, the universal mind, is perceived as a "divine" Light reflecting in the individual mind of the yogi, who thus "sees" all, or sees the object of his personal quest within the totality of everything else (H. Carrington, *Hindu magic*, London, 1909, ch. 11; Prakasam Pillai, *Hindu Occultism*, 1967, p. 180f.). It is claimed that the esotericist magicians of the Himalayan countries have been able to focus the famous crystal ball, apparently of Tibetan origin, utilizing the same cosmological information; a crystal ball made according to the strict rules and precedures required can concentrate the rays of light reflected by *Âkâsha* into those of the eye of Shiva; this is the way that the yogi-magician can see, e.g., "what is happening in the minds of men" or "what is happening in the farthest places of the earth and the cosmos" (F. Johnston, *Himalayan Tantric Magic*, Bombay, 1949, pp. 131–35). Among the occultists of the western Middle Ages, exactly the same characteristics are found for what is called "astral light," "golden light," or "quintessential light" (from "quint-essence," the Fifth Element), where the magician contemplates the mysteries of the world and draws from it his magical powers (e.g., *Grimoire de Salomon*, Paris, 1930, p. 61). As was underscored in the section on "vision with the heart," is is not our attempt here to draw direct parallels, but rather to use these references from other traditions in our context, showing a strong presence of esoteric elements in the practices of early Imamism, an initiatory doctrine where an occult presence—of religious as well as "mythical" expression—runs in filigree and occupies a much more important place than purely speculative theological-philosophical discourse. Although we do not believe that a symbolic meaning can be given to the Imamite Column of Light, it seems worthwhile to remember that in the Judeo-Christian tradition the luminous column (of fire during the night, a cloud during the day) symbolizes the active presence of God, guiding the Chosen People (cf. Exodus 13:21–22). Finally, let it be borne in mind that the Imamite Column of Light, which to our thinking is of a magical nature, appears to have no relationship to its mystical-philosophical Ismâ'îli homonym (cf. Corbin, *Trilogie ismaélienne*, s.v.).

NOTES TO CHAPTER 3

307. See, e.g., Ibn Kathîr, *al-Bidâya wa l-nihâya*, vol. 7, pp. 225f.; 'Abd al-Qâhir al-Baghdâdî, *al-Farq bayna l-firaq*, pp. 58f.; Ibn Taymiyya, *Kitâb Minhâj al-sunnat al-nabawiyya*, vol. 2, pp. 182f.; al-Mufîd, *Irshâd*, pp. 6f.; L. Veccia Vaglieri, *EI2*, vol. 1, p. 392; I. Poonawala and E. Kohlberg, in *Encyclopedia Iranica*, vol. 1, fasc. 8; H. Laoust, "Le rôle de 'Alî dans la *sîra* shî'ite," *REI*, vol. 30, 1962; J. Eliash, *'Alî b. Abî Ṭâlib in Ithnâ 'asharî—shî'î belief*, doctoral thesis, University of London, June, 1966; Md Ibrâhîm al-Muwaḥḥid, *'Alî fî l-aḥâdîth al-nabawiyya*, Beirut, 1404/1984, especially the introduction.

308. See, e.g., al-Mufîd, *Irshâd*, pp. 167f., Ibn Shahrâshûb, *Manâqib*, pp. 112f.; al-Dhahabî, *Kitâb duwal al-islâm*, vol. 1, pp. 21f.

309. On this episode, see, e.g., Ibn Kathîr, *al-Bidâya wa l-nihâya*, vol. 8, pp. 50–52; H. Lammens, *Etudes sur le règne du calife Omeyyade Mu'âwiya I* (complement with the corresponding articles from *Encyclopédie de l'Islam*).

310. For the reasons behind these pro-Shîʿite politics, the conflicts between the two brothers al-Ma'mûn and al-Amîn, and the early sources, see F. Gabrieli, *Al-Ma'mûn e gli Alidi*, especially pp. 40f.; F. Gabrieli, "Amîn" in *EI2*, vol. 1, pp. 449–5; D. Sourdel, "La politique religieuse du calife abbasside al-Ma'mûn," *REI*, vol. 30, 1962; D. Sourdel, "Barâmika," in *EI2*, vol. 1, p. 1064; H. Laoust, *Les Schismes dans l'Islam*, pp. 98f.; W. Madelung, "New documents concerning al-Ma'mûn, al-Faḍl b. Sahl, and ʿAlî al-Riḍâ," *Studia Arabica et Islamica, Festschrift for Iḥsân ʿAbbas*, ed. W. al-Qâḍî, Beirut, 1981, pp. 333-46.

311. Cf. the long and famous sermon by al-Riḍâ in the Great Mosque of Marw, shortly after his arrival in the city; the imam (in the Shîʿite sense of the word, of course), his rank and mission are described as being beyond political considerations; the imam's cause is beyond the imperfect understanding of those who do not possess the necessary criteria to be able to choose one; subjecting the rank of the imam to election by human choice lowers the rank to that of an ordinary earthly sovereign, while in reality the imam was chosen by God since before the time of creation and announced by the prophets in the holy books in order to bring the Light of Truth to his faithful. The imam is the proof of God on earth; whether or not he is elected by humanity in no way changes his divine selection; for the text of this sermon and the slight variations the early texts give of it, see al-Nuʿmânî, *Kitâb al-ghayba*, pp. 315–26; Ibn Bâbûye, *Amâlî*, "majlîs" 97, pp. 674–80; Ibn Bâbûye *ʿUyûn*, ch. 20, pp. 216–22, num. 1; Ibn Bâbûye, *Kamâl al-dîn*, vol. 2, ch 58, pp. 675–81, num. 31.

312. See, e.g., Ibn Saʿd, *Ṭabaqât*, vol. 5, pp. 156–64; Ibn Kathîr, *al-Bidâya*, vol. 9, pp. 103f.; Ibn Taymiyya, *Minhâj*, vol. 2, pp. 125f.; al-Mufîd, *Irshâd*, pp. 234–41; see also W. Chittick's introduction to his translation of the work of the fourth imam, *al-Ṣaḥîfa al-Sajjâdiyya, The Psalms of Islam*, London, Muhammadi Trust, 1988.

313. See, e.g., al-Mufîd, *Irshâd*, pp. 241f.; Ibn Kathîr, *al-Bidâya*, vol. 9, pp. 309f.; Ibn Taymiyya, *Minhâj*, vol. 3, pp. 114–15. Zayd was the son of the fourth iman. The eponym of the "five-imam Shîʿites," he is known especially for his revolt against the Umayyads in Kufa near the end of the caliphate of Hishâm in 122/740. His armed insurrection was quickly repressed by the forces of Yûsuf al-Thaqafî, the governor of Iraq; Zayd and a few hundred of his partisans met their deaths on that occasion (see R. Strothmann, "Zayd b. ʿAlî," *EI1*, vol. 4, p. 1260). One of Zayd's sons, Yaḥyâ, managed to escape the massacre and take over the Zaydi revolt, this time from Khurâsân, under the caliphate of Walîd II. He managed to raise a part of eastern Iran against the Umayyad power for nearly three years; he was assassinated at Jûzjân, not far from Herat, in 125/743 (see C. Von Arendonk, "Yaḥyâ b. Zayd," *EI1*, vol. 4, pp. 1214–15).

314. See, e.g., al-Mufîd, *Irshâd*, pp. 249f.; Ibn Kathîr, *al-Bidâya*, vol. 10, pp. 105f.; see also the studies cited in note 297 *in fine*, and *EI2*, vol. 2, pp. 384–85.

315. Cf., e.g., *Târîkh-e shîʿe wa firqa-ha-ye islâmî*, the Persian translation of *Kitâb al-Farq bayna l-firaq* by ʿAbd al-Qâtir al-Baghdâdî, by Md Jawâd Mashkûr, Tehran, 1339 solar/1960, p. 80, and note; Ibn Ṭaqṭaqä, *Târîkh-e Fakhrî*, p. 208; al-Yaʿqûbî, *Ta'rîkh*, pp. 103–4.

316. The Zaydi revolt of the Ḥasanids Md b. ʿAbdAllâh, called al-Nafs al-Zakiyya, and his brother Ibrâhîm, was the largest armed Shîʿite insurrection of the reign of the second Abbasid caliph, al-Manṣûr (137–59/754–75). Open hostility began shortly after the assassination of Abû Muslim in 138/755; for seven years the two

brothers stirred up insurrection in a number of centers of the caliphate, especially in Iraq, the Ḥijâz, and Khurâsân, while always avoiding a test of strength. In 145/762, the revolt became open and armed, almost at the same time, with Muḥammad in Medina and Ibrâhîm in Baṣra. Within a few months the revolt was violently repressed by the forces of the governor of Kûfa, 'Isâ b. Mûsä, and the two brothers were killed (cf., e.g., Ibn Kathîr, *Bidâya*, vol. 10, pp. 93f.; C. Von Arendonk, *Les Débuts de l'imâmat zaydite du Yémen*, pp. 44f.; C. Von Arendonk, "al-Nafs al-Zakiyya," *EI1*, vol. 3, p. 710). It must be noted that one of the reasons given by the imams for their passive and negative attitude, or what might today be called their "apolitical stance," especially as regards their refusal to support the Zaydi revolts is the following: the imams have revealed books, called the Books (*kutub*) of 'Alî and Fâtima, in their possession. These books contain the names of all the sovereigns as well as the names of their fathers up until the end of time; the names of the Zaydi insurgents do not appear in the books, and thus they will never attain power. The imams thus know beforehand that these revolts are doomed to fail (cf. al-Ṣaffâr, *Baṣâ'ir*, section 4, bâb fî l-a'imma 'indahum al-kutub allatî fîhâ asmâ' al-mulûk, pp. 168–70; in the next part of this study we will return to the sacred and secret Books of the imams in greater detail). In general, according to the imams, any Shî'ite revolt before the Return of the hidden imam will be crushed violently. In the words of Ja'far: "None of those of us from the house of the Prophet has ever rebelled or will ever rebel against oppression to defend a just cause without the great calamity ripping out his roots; and this will be the case until the time of the coming of our Resurrector. Any rebellion by any of us will be only one more cause for suffering both for us (the imams) and for our faithful" (*Mâ kharaja wa lâ yakhruj minnâ ahl al-bayt ilä qiyâm qâ'iminâ aḥadun li-yadfa'a ẓulman aw yan'asha ḥaqqan illâ'ṣṭalamathu l-baliyya wa kâna qiyâmuhu ziyâdatan fî makrûhinâ wa shî'atinâ*"; "fî bayân isnâd al-Ṣaḥîfa," first part of *al-Ṣaḥîfat al-Sajjâdiyya* by the fourth imam, 'Alî Zayn al-'Âbidîn, p. 22, num. 62). See also al-Kulaynî, *al-Rawḍa*, vol. 2, p. 121; al-Nu'mânî, *Kitâb al-ghayba*, pp. 244, 248, 283, 286, 291 (traditions of al-Bâqir and Ja'far). Again, according to Ja'far, he and his fathers (i.e., the imams in the Twelver line) call people to life, although his uncle Zayd and the Zaydis—for whom armed revolt against an oppressor is an article of faith—call them to death ('Alî Zayn al-'Âbidîn, *op. cit*, p. 18, num. 47). We will soon see how al-Ḥusayn's battle at Karbalâ is explained not as a revolt with political implications but as a predestined act with mystical implications.

317. See, e.g., al-Mufîd, *Irshâd*, pp. 263f.; Ibn Taymiyya, *Minhâj*, vol. 2, pp. 114f.; Abû l-Faraj al-Iṣfahânî, *Maqâtil al-ṭâlibiyyin*, pp. 172–76.

318. See, e.g., al-Mufîd, *Irshâd*, pp. 288f.; Ibn Taymiyya, *Minhâj*, vol. 2, pp. 127–28; Abû l-Faraj al-Iṣfahânî, *Maqâtil al-ṭâlibiyyin*, pp. 182–85.

319. See, e.g., al-Mufîd, *Irshâd*, pp. 229f.; Ibn Taymiyya, *Minhâj*, vol. 2, pp. 129f.; the imam 'Alî b. Muḥammad is the eponym of the Alawite Shî'ites. On al-Mutawakkil and his successors' anti-Shî'ite politics of repression (the demolition in 236/850 of al-Ḥusayn's mausoleum, persecutions, imprisonments, torture), see Ibn Kathîr, *al-Bidâya*, vol. 10, pp. 311f.; al-Ṭabarî, *Ta'rîkh*, vol. 7, pp. 265f.; D. Sourdel, "La politique religieuse des successeurs d'al-Mutawakkil," *SI*, vol. 31, 1973.

320. See, e.g., al-Mufîd, *Irshâd*, pp. 311 f.; Ibn Taymiyya, *Minhâj*, vol. 2, pp. 134f.; also, al-Nawbakhtî, *Firaq al-shî'a*, pp. 75–77.

321. See what is perhaps the earliest source on this event, Abû Mikhnaf Lûṭ b. Yaḥyä al-Azdî al-Ghâmidî al-Kûfî (d. circa 158/774), *Maqtal al-Ḥusayn aw Waq'at al-Ṭaff*, ed. M. H. Yûsufî Gharawî, Qumm, 1367 solar/1988; see also. e.g., al-Mufîd, *Irshâd*, pp. 179–224; for discussions by Sunnites and Shî'ites, see Ibn Taymiyya, *Minhâj*, vol. 2, pp. 225, 237–56; cf. Ibn Kathîr's historiographical Sunni account, *al-Bidâya*, vol. 8, pp. 172f.; for other sources, see L. Vecchia Vaglieri's remarkable article "al-Ḥusayn b. 'Alî," *EI2*; for information about the period, see H. Lammens, *Le caliphat de Yazîd I* (this study is to be complemented with the corresponding articles from the *Encyclopédie de l'Islam*).

322. *"Anzala'llâhu ta'âlä al-naṣr 'alä l-Ḥusayn ḥattä kâna bayna l-samâ' wa al-arḍ thumma khuyyira al-naṣr aw liqâ' Allâh fa-akhtâra liqâ' Allâh ta'âlä,"* al-Kulaynî, *Uṣûl*, "kitâb al-ḥujja," bâb anna l-a'imma ya'lamûn matä yamûtûn, num. 672, vol. 1, p. 387.

323. Ibn Bâbûye, *'Uyûn*, ch. 17, num. 1, pp. 209–10.

324. E.g., Ibn Bâbûye, *'Ilal*, chap. 156, pp. 205–10; chap. 178, p. 243; Ibn Bâbûye, *Amâlî*, pp. 126, 131, 136, 140, 144, 164, 579; Ibn Bâbûye, *'Uyûn*, ch. 31, vol. 2, p. 26, num. 6. We have evidence of a similar view of things among the Bâtinites in the *Kitâb al-haft al-sharîf*, a collection of esoteric dialogues between the imâm Ja'far and his disciple Mufaḍḍal al-Ju'fî. Ja'far claims that al-Ḥusayn was pre-existentially destined to be sacrificed for God; after having been Ishmael (Abraham's son; in the Islamic tradition it was he and not Isaac who was to be sacrificed by his father) and Jesus, he reached the goal and the perfection of his destiny in Karbalâ, in the same way that the assassins of the imam were pre-existentially destined to perdition (*Kitâb al-haft al-sharîf*, ed. M. Ghâlib, chap. 39, "fî ma'rifa qatl al-Ḥusayn fî l-bâṭin," pp. 92–95, and chap. 40, "fî ma'rifa qatl al-Ḥusayn 'alä l-bâṭin fî zamân banî Umayya," pp. 96–102; ed. A. Tamer under the title *Kitâb al-haft wa l-aẓilla*, pp. 97–107. On this book, see H. Halm's erudite study, *Das "Buch der Schatten,"* in *Der Islam*, vol. 55, 1978); for a mystical version of the drama of Karbalâ, see also M. Ayoub, *Redemptive Suffering in Islam: A Study of the Devotional Aspects of* 'âshûrâ *in Twelver Shî'ism*, The Hague, 1978; for a nonpolitical vision of the battle of Karbalâ, see also H. M. Jafri, *Origins and Early Development of Shî'a Islam*, s.v., and especially pp. 200-4. For a general study, see J. Calmard, *Le Culte de l'imâm Ḥusayn: Etude sur la commémoration du drame de Karbalâ dans l'Iran pré-ṣafavide*, doctoral thesis, Paris, 1975.

325. *" . . . Qâtil wa'qtul wa tuqtal wa'khruj bi-qawmin li l-shahâda lâ shahâda lahum illâ ma'aka,"* al-Nu'mânî, *Kitâb al-ghayba*, ch. 3, pp. 82-83, nums. 3 and 4; also, Ibn Bâbûye, *Kamâl al-dîn*, ch 58, vol. 2, pp. 669–70, num. 15.

326. See *ALSERAT: Papers from the Imam Husayn Conference, London, 6th-9th July 1984*, Muhammadi Trust, London, 1986, *al-Serat*, vol. XII (especially the second part dedicated to historical and doctrinal perspectives).

327. Cf. the recurrent expression of the imams: "Any banner raised before the rising of the Resurrector belongs to a rebel against God" (*Inna kulla râyatin turfa'u qabla qiyâm al-qâ'im fâ-ṣâḥibuhâ ṭâghût*), e.g., al-Kulaynî, *Rawḍa*, vol. 2, pp. 121f.; al-Nu'mânî, *Kitâb al-ghayba*, all of chapter 5, pp. 161–68, and chapter 14, p. 393, num. 53. The word *ṭâghût* is used eight times in the Qur'an, there referring to all kinds of rebels against Allâh's Order (idols, demons, or sovereigns).

328. *"Yâ ma'shar al-shî'a lâ tudhillû riqâbakum bi-tark ṭâ'a sulṭânikum fa-'in*

kâna ʿâdilan fa'sʾalûʾllâh taʿâlä baqâʾahu wa ʾin kâna jâʾiran fa'sʾalûʾllâh taʿâlä iṣlâḥahu fa-inna ṣalâḥakum fî ṣalâḥ sulṭânikum wa anna l-sulṭân al-ʿâdil bi-manzilat al-wâlid al-raḥîm fa-aḥibbû lahu mâ tuḥibbûn li-anfusikum wa krahû lahu mâ takrahûn li-anfusikum," cf. Ibn Bâbûye, *Amâlî*, pp. 161–62; cited also by J. Homâʾî in the introduction to his edition of al-Ghazzâlî's *Naṣîḥat al-mulûk* (Tehran, 1351 solar/1972, new edition p. xii), an introduction containing interesting remarks on the political passivity of early Imamism.

329. Al-Kulaynî, *Uṣûl*, "Kitâb al-îmân wa l-kufr," bâb ṭalab al-riʾâsa, vol. 3, pp. 405–7; six of the traditions come from Jaʿfar, one from al-Bâqir, and one from al-Riḍâ (the latter being called by the *kunya* Abû l-Ḥasan—tradition num. 1—and is identifiable thanks to his disciple Muʿammar b. Khallâd [b. Abî Khallâd al-Baghdâdî]; on him, see al-Najâshî, *Rijâl*, s.v.; al-Ardabîlî, *Jâmiʿ al-ruwât*, vol. 2, p. 252). The word *riʾâsa* refers to both political and religious power of command; a *raʾîs* can be a political chief, a "leader," or a theologian who is the "head" of a school (cf. al-Ṭurayḥî, *Majmaʿ al-baḥrayn*, s.v. On "leadership" (*riʾâsa*) in general, see al-Majlisî, *Biḥâr*, vol. XV/3, pp. 102–4; on "those who pretend to be leaders" (*mutaraʾisûn*) see al-Kashshî, *Rijâl*, pp. 148, 152, 207).

330. *"Man ṭalaba l-riʾâsa halaka," "Man arâda l-riʾâsa halaka,"* al-Kulaynî, *Uṣûl*, *ibid.*, nums. 2, 7.

331. *"Iyyâkum wa hâʾulâʾ al-ruʾasâʾ alladhîna yataraʾasûn fa-waʾllâhi mâ khafaqat al-niʿâl khalfa rajulin illâ halaka wa ahlaka,"* al-Kulaynî, *Uṣûl*, *ibid.*, num. 3.

332. *"Malʿûn man taraʾʾasa malʿûn man hamma bihâ malʿûn man ḥaddatha bihâ nafsahu,"* al-Kulaynî, *Uṣûl*, *ibid.*, num. 4.

333. *"Iyyâka wa l-riʾâsa wa iyyâka an taṭaʾa aʿqâb al-rijâl,"* al-Kulaynî, *Uṣûl*, *ibid.*, num. 5.

334. "W*ayḥaka yâ Abâ l-rabîʿ lâ taṭlubanna l-riʾâsa wa lâ takun dhiʾban wa lâ taʾkul binâ l-nâs fa-yufqiruka Allâh wa lâ taqul fînâ mâ lâ naqûl fî anfusinâ fa-innaka mawqûf wa masʾûl lâ maḥâla fa-ʾin kunta ṣâdiqan ṣaddaqnâka wa ʾin kunta kâdhiban kadhdhabnâka,"* al-Kulaynî, *Uṣûl*, *ibid.*, num. 6. The fifth imam is speaking with Abû l-Rabîʿ al-Ḥasan b. Maḥbûb al-Shâmî, whom al-Ṭûsî fails to name among the imam's disciples; on him, see al-Najâshî, *Rijâl*, s.v.; al-ʿAllâma al-Ḥillî, *Khulâṣa*, s.v.; al-Ardabîlî, *Jâmiʿ al-ruwât*, vol. 2, p. 385.

335. It has been suggested, albeit unconvincingly, that the secret political activities of the imams were quite structured, their organization being referred to as *al-tanẓîm al-sirrî* (Javad ʿAlî, "Die beiden ersten Safire des Zwölften Imams," pp. 197f.); we have never encountered this expression anywhere in the early texts, and it appears to have a frankly modern resonance (lit. "secret organization"). Jassim M. Hussain uses the expression with no indication of references (*The Occultation of the Twelfth Imam*, p. 79); he thinks it can be replaced with the more classical term *wikâla* (lit. "intendancy," "procuration"), which nevertheless means nothing political, properly speaking: "The main purpose of the *wikâla* was to collect the *khums*, the *zakât* and other kinds of alms for the Imam from his followers" (p. 79); this does not keep the author from ascribing a political and subversive meaning to the word throughout his work. W. Madelung uses a single tradition attributed to Jaʿfar (it comes from the *Furûʿ min al-kâfî*) to corroborate his theses on the political stance of the imams: "If the Umayyads had not found someone who would write for them, collect the land tax for them, fight on their behalf, and witness their communal prayer, they would not have deprived us of

our right" ("A treatise of the Sharîf al-Murtaḍâ on the legality of working for the government," p. 19); the remarks may be considered as much a statement of fact as an invitation to disobey power. In the same sense, see also J. Wellhausen, *Die religiös-politischen Oppositionsparteien im alten Islam*, s.v.; G. Scarcia, "A proposito del problema della sovranita presso gli imâmiti"; J. Eliash, "The Ithnâ 'asharî Shî'î Juristic Theory of Political and Legal Authority"; Roy P. Mottahedeh, *Loyalty and Leadership in an Early Islamic Society*; M. Sharon, "The Development of the Debate Around the Legitimacy of Authority in Early Islam." It is interesting to note that the specifically political theses of Imamism do not begin to develop until the time of al-Mufîd and the domination of the "theological-juridical-rational" current. Regarding the different theses on the "apoliticalism" of early Imamism, see our article "Le shî'ism doctrinal et le fait politique"; N. Calder, *The Structure of Authority in Imâmî Shî'î Jurisprudence*; N. Calder, "Accommodation and Revolution in Imâmi Shî'i Jurisprudence: Khumaynî and Classical Tradition." For an overview of the subject see E. Kohlberg, "Some Imâmî Shî'î Interpretations of Umayyad History," *Belief and Law . . .*, part 12.

336. Cf. my article "Le shî'isme doctrinal et le fait politique," pp. 85f.

337. Cf. D. Amaldi, "Osservazioni sulle catene di trasmissione in alcuni testi di rijâl imamiti," *Cahiers d'Onomastique Arabe*, 1979; M. Robson, "Hadith," *EI2*; J. Matînî, "'Ilm wa 'ulamâ' dar zabân-e Qur'ân wa aḥâdîth," *Iran-Nameh*, vol. 2, num. 3, 1363 solar/1984; C. H. A. Juynboll, *Muslim Tradition*, s.v. (see also the summary of this work by R. G. Khoury, "Pour une nouvelle compréhension de la transmission des textes dans les trois premiers siècles islamiques," *Arabica*, vol. 34, num. 2, July 1987). The only exception is the article by E. Kohlberg, "Imam and Community in the Pre-Ghayba Period," in *Authority and Political Culture in Shî'ism*, New York, 1988, where the author outlines some quite interesting developments in strictly Imamite *'ilm*; see also, by the same author, "The Term Muḥaddath in Twelver Shî'ism," *Studia Orientalia memoriae D. H. Baneth dedicata*, Jerusalem, 1979, pp. 39–47.

338. *"Ṭalab al-'ilm farîḍa 'alä kulli muslim inna 'llâha yuḥibbu bughât al-'ilm,"* *Baṣâ'ir*, section 1, ch. 1, p. 3, num. 1.

339. It is our belief that the remainder of this chapter will justify this translation of the term *'ilm*. With this "anticipated" translation in the body of our text, we hope to avoid too frequent use of Arabic terms from the same family as *'ilm*.

340. *"Anâ madînat al-'ilm [al-ḥikma] wa 'Alî bâbuhâ"*; cf. e.g., Furât, *Tafsîr*, pp. 63–64; Ibn Bâbûye, *Amâlî*, pp. 268–69, 345, 388, 561; Ibn Bâbûye, *Kamâl al-dîn*, ch. 22, p. 241, num. 65; Ibn Bâbûye, *Kitâb al-tawḥîd*, ch. 43, p. 307, num. 1. It must be repeated that here again, according to the doctrine of the imams, aside from the historical individuals, Muḥammad represents lawgiving prophecy (*nubuwwa*), the exoteric part of the religion, while 'Alî represents the Imamate (*walâya*), the esoteric teaching.

341. *"Abä Allâh an yujriya l-ashyâ' illâ bi l-asbâb fa-ja'ala li-kulli sabab sharḥan wa ja'ala li-kulli sharḥ miftâḥan wa ja'ala li-kulli miftâḥ 'ilman wa ja'ala li-kulli 'ilm bâban nâṭiqan man 'arafahu 'arafa Allâh wa man ankarahu ankara Allâh dhâlika rasûl Allâh wa naḥnu,"* *Baṣâ'ir*, section 1, ch. 3, p. 6, num. 2.

342. *Baṣâ'ir*, section 1, ch. 6, pp. 9–10.

343. *Baṣâ'ir*, section 2, ch. 19, pp. 103–6.

344. *Baṣâ'ir*, section 4, ch. 10–11, pp. 202–7.

345. *Baṣâ'ir*, section 7, ch. 5–7, pp. 319–26 and section 8, ch. 1, pp. 368–74; see

also al-Kulaynî, *Uṣûl*, "kitâb al-ḥujja," bâb anna l-a'imma muḥaddathûn mufahhamûn, vol. 2, pp. 13–15; al-Nu'mânî, *Kitâb al-ghayba*, pp. 95, 126; Ibn Bâbûye, *'Ilal*, vol. 1, ch. 146, pp. 182–83.

346. *Baṣâ'ir*, section 8, ch. 1, pp. 368–74; al-Kulaynî, *op. cit.*, vol. 2, p. 14, num. 4 (a tradition from Ja'far: "*Al muḥaddath* hears the sound [or "the voice"] and does not see "the person" . . . *yasma'u l-ṣawt wa lâ yarä l-shakhṣ*"). On difficulties posed by the term *shakhṣ* in early Arabic, see G. Monnot, *Islam et religions*, s.v. and for the bibliography referring thereto, see p. 256, note 41; see also D. Gimaret, *Les Noms divins en Islam*, p. 158.

347. Al-Kulaynî, *op. cit.*, bâb anna l-a'imma tadkhulu l- malâ'ika buyûtahum wa taṭa'u busuṭahum wa ta'tîhim bi l-khabar ("the angels come into the intimacy of the imams—lit, "tread upon their carpets"—and bring them information"), vol. 2, pp. 240f.

348. Cf. *Baṣâ'ir*, section 7, ch. 5, p. 320, num. 4; ch. 6, pp. 321–22, num. 3; p. 324, num. 13; al-Kulaynî, *Uṣûl*, "kitâb al ḥujja," bâb anna l-a'imma muḥaddathûn mufahhamûn, vol. 2, pp. 14-15, num. 5.

349. Cf. e.g., al-Kulaynî, *Rawḍa,* vol. 1, pp. 173, 176 (the Umayyad caliph Hishâm b. 'Abd al-Malik recognizes that the inhabitants of Kûfa consider the imam al-Bâqir to be a prophet); al-Nu'mânî, *Kitâb al-ghayba*, p. 145 (according to the author, the imams have the same religious importance that the Prophet had); Ibn Bâbûye, *Amalî*, "majlis" 47, p. 278, num. 4 (one of the Khawârij is said to have recognized the "prophetic mission," *risâla*, of Ja'far).

350. *Baṣâ'ir*, section 8, ch. 1, pp. 368–74; al-Kulaynî, *Uṣûl,* "kitâb al-ḥujja," bâb al-farq bayna l-rasûl wa l-nabî wa l-muḥaddath, vol. 1, pp. 248-50.

350 bis. On this problem as a whole, see E. Kohlberg's monograph, "The Term 'Muḥaddath' in Twelver Shî'ism," *St. Or. memoriae . . . Baneth dedicata . . .* Jerusalem, 1979.

351. Al-Kulaynî, *Uṣûl*, bâb anna l-a'imma tadkhulu l-malâ'ika buyûtahum . . . , vol. 2, pp. 240–41, num. 1 ("*Wa yaẓharûna [i.e., al-malâ'ika] lakum? fa masaḥa yadahu 'alä ba'ḍi ṣibyânihi fa-qâla hum alṭaf bi-ṣibyâninâ minnâ bihim*"). The disciple in question was Misma' b. 'Abd al-Malik Kirdîn Abû Sayyâr al-Kûfî al-Baṣrî, who also knew the teaching of al-Bâqir; on him, see al-Najâshî, *Rijâl*, s.v.; al-Ṭûsî, *Rijâl*, p. 136, num. 23, and p. 321, num. 657; al-Ardabîlî, *Jâmi' al-ruwât*, vol. 2, p. 230.

352. On al-Rûḥ, see e.g., *Baṣâ'ir*, section 9, ch. 18–19, pp. 460–64; al-Kulaynî, *Uṣûl*, bâb al-rûḥ allatî yusaddidu'llâh bihâ l-a'imma, vol. 2, p. 17–20.

353. Cf. *Baṣâ'ir*, section 5, ch. 3, pp. 220–25; al-Nu'mânî, *Kitâb al-ghayba*, pp. 94–95; al-Kulaynî, *Uṣûl*, "kitâb al-ḥujja," bâb fî sha'n "innâ anzalnâhu fî laylati'l-qadr" (Qur'an 97:1) wa tafsîrihâ, vol. 1, pp. 350–72. To corroborate what they say, the imams refer to two Qur'anic passages in particular: 97:1–5 "We had it [the Qur'an] come down during the Night of the Decree/How could you conceive what the Night of the Decree is?/The Night of the Decree is better than a thousand months/The angels and al-Rûḥ come down during this Night, with the permission of their Lord, to order all things/This Night is peace up to the rising of the dawn"; and 44:2–3: "By the clear Book/That We revealed during the Blessed Night, Verily We have been the warner." According to a suggestion of the ninth imam, Muḥammad al-Jawâd, the Night of the Decree is the 23rd night of Ramaḍân (al-Kulaynî, *op. cit.*, vol. 1, p. 370, the last sentence of number 8: "When the month of Ramaḍân comes, recite each night a hundred

times the Sura of the Smoke [Sura 44], and the 23rd of the month, you will see what you have just asked me about come true").

354. A cryptic allusion to a third kind of Knowledge revealed during the Night of the Decree should also be pointed out; in the ninth imam's tradition already cited, someone asks him, "Besides what they [the imams] already know, is there a[nother] Science that is revealed to them (*famâ yuḥaddathu lahum fî layâlî al-qadr 'ilmun siwä mâ 'alimû*)? The imam replies: "This is part of what the imams have been ordered to keep hidden (*hâdhâ mimmâ umirû bi-kitmânihi).* Only God—may He be exalted and glorified—knows the explanation to what you have just asked (*wa lâ ya'lamu tafsîr mâ sa'alta 'anhu illâ'llâh 'azza wa jall*)." For an explanation of the ideas of *mujmal* and *tafâsîr*, see also Ibn Bâbûye, *'Uyûn*, vol. 1, pp. 145f.; al-Majlisî, *Biḥâr*, vol. 8, p. 205; al- Majlisî, *Mir'ât al-'uqûl*, vol. 3, p. 97; for an overview, see E. Kohlberg, "Imam and Community . . . ," pp. 28–29.

355. *"Wallâhi inna arwâḥanâ wa arwâh al-nabiyyin la-tuwâfî l-'arsh layla kull jumu'a fa-mâ turaddu fî abdâninâ illâ bi-jamm al-ghafîr min al-'ilm," Baṣâ'ir*, section 3, ch. 8, p. 132, num. 6.

356. *" . . . Fî layâlî al-jumu'a . . . yu'dhanu li-arwâḥ al-anbiyâ' al-mawtä wa arwâḥ al-awṣiyâ' al-mawtä wa rûḥ al-waṣî alladhî bayna ẓahrânaykum ya'ruju bihâ ilä l-samâ' ḥattä tuwâfiya 'arsha rabbihâ fa-taṭûfu bihi usbû'an wa tuṣalliya 'inda kulli qâ'ima min qawâ'im al-'arsh rak'atayn thumma turaddu ilä l-abdân allatî kânat fîhâ fa-yuṣbiḥu l-anbiyâ' wa l-awṣiyâ' qad muli'û surûran wa yuṣbiḥu l-waṣî alladhî bayna ẓahrânaykum wa qad zîda fî 'ilmihi mithl jamm al-ghafîr,"* al-Kulaynî, *Uṣûl*, bâb fî anna l-a'imma yazdâdûn fî laylat al-jumu'a 'ilman, vol. 1 pp. 372–73, num. 1.

357. *"Idhâ kâna laylat al-jumu'a wâfä rasûl Allâh—ṣl'm—al-'arsh wa wâfä l-a'imma wa wâfaytu ma'ahum famâ arji'u illâ bi-'ilmin mustafâd wa law lâ dhâlika la-nafida mâ 'indî,"* al-Kulaynî, *Uṣûl, ibid.*, vol. 1 pp. 373–74, num. 3; actually, it is said that the Knowledge of the imam must inexorably increase or disappear; thus, initiation must continue throughout his life (cf. *Baṣâ'ir*, section 3, ch. 8, p. 130, num. 1 and p. 131, num. 5; al-Kulaynî, *Uṣûl*, bâb law lâ anna l-a'imma yazdâdûn la-nafida mâ 'indahum, vol. 1, pp. 374–75).

358. *"Fa bihi 'arafû l-ashyâ'" / "'arafû mâ taḥta al-'arsh ilä mâ taḥta al-tharä" / "ḥaml amânat al-nubuwwa / ḥaml al-nubuwwa," Baṣâ'ir*, section 9, ch. 14, pp. 445–50 and ch. 15, pp. 451–54 (in the latter chapter's traditions, the nature of *rûḥ al-quds* remains ambiguous; in it, the imams are asked how they can make a (juridical?) decision concerning a case that they encounter for the first time. They reply that they obtain knowledge about it through "the holy spirit." Is this still referring to the first of the five spirits of the imam, or to the angelic being, assimilated into the Angel Gabriel, mentioned in the Qur'an? Are we permitted to think that the first is an interior and spiritual projection of the second? See also al-Kulaynî, *Uṣûl*, bâb fîhi dhikr al-arwâḥ allatî fî l-a'imma, vol. 2, pp. 15–17; al-Kulaynî would have already thought about making the comparison between the imams' faculty of celestial inspiration and the constitution of their spirit, since he had the chapter dealing with the five spirits (vol. 2, pp. 15–17) precede the chapter dealing with the imam *al-muḥaddath al-mufahham* (vol. 2, pp. 13–15).

359. "Marking of the heart" (*makt/qadhf/qar' [fî] al-qalb*) and "piercing of the eardrum" (*naqr/nakt fî al-udhn/al-sam'/al-asmâ'*—lit. "piercing or marking *in* the ear; it is due to the presence of the particle *fî* [in] that we have chosen to translate as

"eardrum"); the words for which action is performed are sometimes interchanged, according to the tradition. Cf. especially *Baṣâ'ir,* section 7, ch. 3, pp. 316–18; and al-Ṭurayhî, *Majma' al-baḥrayn*, s.v.

360. *Baṣâ'ir*, ch. 4, pp. 318–19; al-Kulaynî, *Rawḍa*, vol. 1, p. 182.

361. The phrase is the following: "The Sage (*'âlim=* imam) has his heart marked and his eardrum pierced." There are no other details about the nature of the phenomenon; in only one place, one of Ja'far's traditions, it is said that "the piercing of the eardrum is the matter (or the order) of the angel (*wa ammâ al-naqr fî al-asmâ' fa-amr al-malak*)," al-Kulaynî, *Uṣûl,* "kitâb al-ḥujja," bâb jihât 'ulûm al-a'imma, vol. 3, p. 394, num. 3.

362. *Baṣâ'ir,* section 7, ch. 3, nums. 5, 8, 10; al-Kulaynî, *Uṣûl*, the same num. 3 (Ja'far; "the marking of hearts is the inspiration, *wa ammâ l-nakt fî l-qulûb fa'l-ilhâm*).

363. *"Yankatu fî udhnihi fa-yasma'u ṭanînan ka-ṭanîn al-ṭast aw yuqra'u 'alä qalbihi fa-yasma'u waq'an ka-waq' al-silsila 'alä al-ṭast,"* *Baṣâ'ir*, section 7, ch. 6, p. 324, num. 13; Sunni collections of prophetic traditions report analogous experiences by the Prophet during the "descent" of Revelation (cf. A. J. Wensinck, *Concordances*, s.v. *jaras* or *ṣalṣala*).

364. The practice is called lithomancy (*al-ṭarq bi l-ḥaṣä*), and consists of 1) throwing the stones and observing how they fall, 2) throwing the stones and divining an answer based on their positions respective to one another; or else 3) dropping the pebbles from one hand into the other and studying their positions. Regarding the practice, its antecedents in other magical traditions and the bibliography pertaining to it, see T. Fahd, *La Divination arabe*, pp. 195-96, as well as the section on lithoboly (*ramy al-jimâr*), pp. 188–95.

365. *Baṣâ'ir*, section 8, ch. 7, pp. 389–90; the chapter contains seven traditions, six of which are from al-Bâqir, and one from Ja'far; the one who practices *rajm* is always 'Alî b. Abî Ṭâlib. Elsewhere, it is said that when faced with "difficult cases" the imam receives inspiration, *ilhâm* (*ibid*., section 5, ch. 9, p. 234).

366. *Baṣâ'ir*, section 6, ch. 5, pp. 274–82.

367. *"Yamût man mâta minnâ wa laysa bi-mayyit,"* *Baṣâ'ir*, section 6, ch. 5, p. 275, num. 4.

368. *Baṣâ'ir*, p. 278, num. 13; see also al-Ṭurayhî, *Majma' l-baḥrayn*, s.v.

369. *Baṣâ'ir*, p. 282, num. 19.

370. *Baṣâ'ir*, p. 276, num. 8; on Samâ'a b. Mihrân Abû Md al-Ḥaḍramî al-Kûfî, a disciple of the sixth and seventh imams and a Wâqifite (believing in the occultation and Return of the seventh imam as the Mahdî), see, e.g., al-Najâshî, *Rijâl*, s.v.; al-Ṭûsî, *Rijâl*, p. 214, num. 196 and p. 351, num. 4; 'Allâma al-Ḥillî, *Khulâṣat al-aqwâl*, s.v.; al-Ardabîlî, *Jâmi' al-ruwât*, vol. 1, pp. 384f.

371. *Baṣâ'ir*, nums. 2, 7, 9, 10, 11, 14, 17. Besides their esoteric and occult scope, the polemic motivation of this tradition is also evident; Abû Bakr, convinced after this supernatural demonstration, appears to be ready to return power to 'Alî, but he meets 'Umar who persuades him not to by saying that it was an act of magic (*siḥr*), and that the magical practices of the Banû Hâshim (or of the Banû 'Abd al-Muṭṭalib) were known to all.

372. *Baṣâ'ir*, section 6, ch. 6, pp. 282-84.

373. *"Idhâ anâ muttu fa-ghassilnî wa ḥanniṭnî wa kaffinnî thumma'q'udnî wa*

ḍa'yadaka 'alä ṣadrî wa salnî mâ shi'ta fa-wa'llâhi lâ tas'alunî 'an shay'in illâ ajabtuka," *Baṣâ'ir, ibid.*, nums. 2,3,8,9.

374. *Baṣâ'ir, ibid.*, nums. 1, 4, 5, 6, 7.

375. *"Anba'anî bimâ huwa kâ'in ilä yawm al-qiyâma," ibid.*, num. 10; here 'Alî claims to have "received" the teaching from the Prophet without having placed his hand on the Prophet's breast, but by putting his mouth to the mouth of the Prophet (this will be returned to when we introduce the subject of the imams' ways of transmitting the Initiatory Knowledge); one tradition ascribed to Ja'far and reported by al-Kulaynî supplies occult information about the post mortem condition of the Prophet; warning a group of his disciples, the sixth imam said: "I do not like one of them [my disciples] to get up on the Prophet's grave, for I warn him [lit., I cannot guarantee his safety] that he will see something there that will make him blind, or else he might see [the Prophet] in prayer or in the company of one of his wives (*Mâ uḥibbu li-aḥad minhum an ya'luwa fawqahu [fawq qabr al-nabî] wa lâ âmanahu an yarä shay'an yadhhabu minhu baṣaruhu aw yarâhu qâ'iman yuṣalliya aw yarâhu ma'a ba'ḍ azwâjihi*)" (*Uṣûl*, "kitâb al-ḥujja," bâb al-nahy'an il-ishrâf 'alä qabr al-nabî, vol. 2, p. 346, num. 1 [= 1224]).

376. *"Yaqra'ûna kutub al-anbiyâ' wa ya'rifûnahâ 'alä ikhtilâf alsinatihâ," Baṣâ'ir*, section 1, ch. 21, p. 47; section 3, ch. 9–10, pp. 132–39; section 7, ch. 13, pp. 340–41; and section 9, ch. 17, pp. 458–60; al-Kulaynî, *Uṣûl*, bâb anna l-a'imma warithû 'ilm al-nabî wa jamî' al-anbiyâ', vol. 1, pp. 324–29; bâb anna l-a'imma 'indahum jamî' al-kutub allatî nazalat min 'ind Allâh wa annahum ya'rifûnahâ 'alä ikhtilâf alsinatihâ, vol. 1, pp. 329–31; Ibn 'Ayyâsh al-Jawharî, *Muqtaḍab al-athar*, pp. 72–81. The revealed Books specifically named are those of Abraham, Solomon, David, Moses, Jesus, and of course Muḥammad. On the role of the biblical prophets and the presence of Judeo-Christian elements in Shî'ism, one can quite profitably consult W. Aichele's "Biblische Legenden der Schî'iten aus dem Prophetenbuch des Hoseinî," *MSOS*, vol. 18, 1915, pp. 27–57; G. Vajda, "Deux *Histoires des Prophètes*, selon la tradition des shî'ites duodécimains," *Revue des Etudes Juives*, 106, 1945-46, pp. 124–33; G. Vajda, "De quelques emprunts d'origine juive dans le ḥadîth shî'ite," *Studies in Judaism and Islam presented to S. D. Goitein*, ed. S. Morag *et al.*, Jerusalem, 1981, pp. 45–53; Ramzî Na'nâ'a, *al-Isrâ'îliyyât wa atharuhâ fî kutub al-tafsîr*, Damascus, 1390/1970; E. Kohlberg, "From imâmiyya to ithnâ 'ashariyya," pp. 521–34, especially pp. 526f.; U. Rubin, "Prophets and Progenitors in the Early Shî'a Tradition," pp. 41–65, especially pp. 51f., 55f., 59f., and 60, note 112. Inversely, for the presence of Shî'ite elements in esoteric Judaism, see S. Pines, "Shî'ite Terms and Conception in Judah Halevi's *Kuzari*," *JSAI*, vol. 2, 1980, pp. 165–251.

377. Cf. especially *Baṣâ'ir*, section 1, ch. 12–14, pp. 44–48; section 3, pp. 142–61; section 4, ch. 1–3, pp. 162–73; section 6, ch. 2, pp. 266-69; al-Kulaynî, *Uṣûl*, bâb fîhi dhikr al-ṣaḥîfa wa l-jafr wa l-jafr wa l-jâmi'a wa muṣḥaf Fâṭima, vol. 1, pp. 344–50; Ibn Bâbûye, *Kamâl al-dîn*, vol. 2, pp. 352f.

378. Ibn Bâbûye, *Kamâl al-dîn*, vol. 1, ch. 27, pp. 306-7; Ibn Bâbûye, *'Uyûn*, vol. 1, ch. 6, pp. 40–41, num. 1.

379. On the *ḥadîth al-lawḥ*, see al-Kulaynî, *Uṣûl*, "kitâb al-hujja," bâb mâ jâ'a fî l-ithnä 'ashar wa l-naṣṣ 'alayhim, vol. 2, pp. 470–74, num. 3 [=1383]; al-Nu'mânî, *Kitâb al-ghayba*, pp. 96–101; Ibn Bâbûye, *Kamâl al-dîn*, vol. 1, ch. 28, pp. 308–12; Ibn Bâbûye, *'Uyûn*, vol. 1, ch. 6, pp. 41–45, num. 2; *Ithbât al-waṣiyya*, pp. 143–45; Shâd-

hân b. Jibra'îl al-Qummî, *Kitâb al-faḍâ'il*, Najaf, n.d., p. 113; al-Ṭûsî, *Amâlî*, vol. 1, pp. 297–98; Ibn Shahrâshûb al-Mâzandarânî, *Manâqib*, vol. 1, pp. 296–98; Md b. Md al-Ṭabarî, *Bishârat al-Muṣṭafä*, pp. 183–84; al-Ḥurr al-'Âmilî, *al-Jawâhir al-saniyya*, pp. 201–9; al-Majlisî, *Biḥâr al-anwâr*, vol. 9, p. 221 (referring to al-'Askarî's *Tafsîr*); for modern sources, see Ḥ. Ṭârumî and 'A. Ṭâli'î, *Aḥâdîth-e qudsî pîrâmûn-e ḥaḍrat-e Mahdî*, Tehran, 1407/1987, p. 75. On Jâbir b. 'Abd Allâh al-Anṣârî, see al-Dhahabî, *Tadhkirat al-ḥuffâẓ*, vol. 1, pp. 43–44; al-Dhahabî, *Siyar a'lâm al-nubalâ'*, vol. 3, pp. 126–29; Ibn Ḥajar al-'Asqalânî, *Tahdhîb al-tahdhîb*, vol. 2, pp. 42–43; on his particular role in certain chains of transmission of Imamite traditions, see E. Kohlberg, "An Unusual Shî'î isnâd," *IOS*, 5, 1975. For an overview of *lawḥ*, see the article by A. J. Wensinck and C. E. Bosworth, *EI2*, vol. 4, p. 703.

380. Al-Nu'mânî, *Kitâb al-ghayba*, pp. 82–83, nums. 3,4; Ibn Bâbûye, *Kamâl al-dîn*, ch. 58, vol. 2, pp. 669–70, num. 15.

381. *"'Allama rasûl Allâh 'Aliyyan alfa bâb [ḥadîth, kalima] yuftaḥu min kulli bâb alfu bâbin."* Cf., e.g., *Baṣâ'ir*, section 6, ch. 18, pp. 309–12 (here the Prophet justifies the fact that he has chosen 'Alî for initiation, saying "I struggle [using the support of] the exoteric part of Revelation, and 'Alî struggles [using the support of] the esoteric interpretation of Revelation (*anâ uqâtilu 'alä l-tanzîl wa 'Alî yuqâtilu 'alä l-ta'wîl*—on *tanzîl* and *ta'wîl*, see H. Corbin, *Histoire de la philosophie islamique*, s.v.; H. Corbin, *En islam iranien*, s.v.), section 7, ch. 1, pp. 313–15; Ibn Bâbûye, *Khiṣâl*, vol. 3, pp. 326f.

382. See, e.g., the sentence "God conferred his Secret to the Angel Gabriel (*asarra'llâhu sirrahu ilä Jabra'îl*), the Angel Gabriel conferred it to the Prophet, who conferred it to 'Alî, 'Alî conferred it to al-Ḥasan, who conferred it to al-Ḥusayn, and he to his son 'Alî . . . " *Baṣâ'ir*, section 8, ch. 3, pp. 377–78.

383. *"Lâ yu'allimu'llâhu Muḥammadan 'ilman illâ wa amarahu an yu'allimahu 'Alîyyan," Baṣâ'ir*, section 6, ch. 11, pp. 292–94. (We have reported the first of five traditions concerning "the two pomegranates." It might be remarked that here initiatory Knowledge (*'ilm*), which goes hand in hand with *nubuwwa*, is used as a synonym for the Imamate/*walâya*. The account of the two fruits of the pomegranate tree might be compared with another, reported by Ibn Bâbûye in his *Amâlî* (majlis 87, p. 596, num. 3): told by Ibn 'Abbâs, it is a story about the "Five of the Cloak": the Prophet, 'Alî, Fatima, al-Ḥasan, and al-Ḥusayn. The angel Gabriel brings an apple (*tuffâḥa*) to the Prophet; he kisses the fruit and passes it to 'Alî, who kisses it and returns it to the Prophet; the three others do likewise after receiving the apple from the hand of the Prophet; then the fruit falls to the ground and splits in half; a ray of light springs forth, lighting up the sky and carrying the inscription: "In the name of God, the gracious, the merciful, here is a gift (*tuḥfa*) from God to Muḥammad *al-Muṣṭafä* (the Best), 'Alî *al-Murtaḍä* (the Chosen One), Fatima *al-Zahrâ'* (the Resplendent), al-Ḥasan and al-Ḥusayn, the two grandsons of the Prophet Messenger from God (*sibṭay rasûl Allâh*) This is a guarantee against the fires of hell, the Day of Resurrection, for those who love them (*amân li-muḥibbîhim yawm al-qiyâma min al-nâr*)."

384. Cf. e.g., *Baṣâ'ir*, section 3, ch. 1, pp. 114–16, 118–21, and section 9, ch. 22, pp. 468–70; al-Kulaynî, *Uṣûl*, "kitâb al-ḥujja," bâb anna l-a'imma warithû 'ilm al-nabî wa jamî' al-anbiyâ' wa l-awṣiyâ' alladhîna min qablihim, vol. 1, pp. 324–29; al-Kulaynî, *al-Rawḍa*, vol. 1, p. 162, and vol. 2, p. 108; Ibn Bâbûye, *Kamâl al-dîn*, ch. 22, p. 223, num. 14 and p. 224, nums. 18, 19.

385. "*Inna al-ʿilm yutawârath wa lî yamût ʿâlimun minnâ illâ yuʿallimu man baʾ-dahu mithl ʿilmihi,*" *Baṣâʾir*, section 3, ch. 2, pp. 117–18.

386. "*Umanâʾ Allâh fî l-arḍ,*" *Baṣâʾir*, section 3, ch. 3, pp. 118–20.

387. *Baṣâʾir*, section 4, ch. 11, pp. 204–7; here the imams maintain that they are designated by the Qurʾanic verse "Yes, they are manifest signs in the breasts of those to whom knowledge has been given"—*bal huwa âyâtun bayyinât fî ṣudûriʾllâdhîna ûtûʾl-ʿilm*, Qurʾan 29:49. Generally, all Qurʾanic allusions, regardless their form or expression, to "those who hold the science" are interpreted in this manner. To the famous hadith "*al-ʿulamâʾ warathatuʾl-anbiyâ*" (usually translated as "the scholars are the inheritors of the prophets," and where "the scholars" are understood as being the jurist-theologians versed in the exoteric religious sciences), the imams add: "*al-ʿulamâʾ* are the imams/or the Heirs (*al-ʿulamâʾ al-aʾimma/al-awṣiyâʾ*)" (e.g., *Baṣâʾir*, section 1, ch. 6–7, pp. 9–12); in the context of early Imamism, the hadith should be translated by "The initiated Sages are the inheritors of the prophets"; see also the case of the hadith: "*Ṭalab al-ʿilm farîḍa ʿalä kulli muslim*" ("The search for initiatory Knowledge is a canonical duty for every Muslim," cf. note 338; we wonder whether here it would not be better to read *musallim* instead of *muslim*; in Imamite technical terminology, *musallim*—lit., "those who have submitted"—is one of the names for the faithful disciples of the imams, while *muslim*, as opposed to *muʾmin*, refers to the simple Muslim faithful to exoteric religion).

388. Cf. al-Kulaynî, *al-Rawḍa*, vol. 1, p. 106 and vol. 2, p. 78; Ibn Bâbûye, *Maʿânî al-akhbâr*, pp. 86–87.

389. *Baṣâʾir*, section 6, ch. 6, pp. 282–84 (ʿAlî places his hand on the breast of the deceased Prophet in order to welcome his Knowledge); al-Kulaynî, *al-Rawḍa*, vol. 2, p. 213.

390. *Baṣâʾir*, section 7, ch. 1, p. 313, num. 1: . . . *qâla ʿAlî ḥaddathanî bi-alf ḥadîth yaftaḥu kullu ḥatîth alf bâb wa ʿariqtu wa ʿariqa rasûl Allâh fa-sâla ʿalayya ʿaraquhu wa sâla ʿalayhi ʿaraqî.*

391. *Baṣâʾir*, section 8, ch. 8, p. 390, num. 1; according to this tradition, the Prophet's saliva gave ʿAlî's eyes vision of the Pretemporal Pact (*mîthâq*) and of those who were present (and to distinguish them from who were not) when the Pact was made (cf. earlier discussion); ʿAlî was from then on able to recognize the "pure beings" who had made the Pact and took oaths of fidelity to the imams.

392. Al-Nuʿmânî, *Kitâb al-ghayba*, ch. 10, p. 204, num. 3.

393. Ibn Bâbûye, *Amâlî*, "majlis" 55, p. 341, num. 1 (*Salûnî qabla an tafqidûnî hâdhâ safaṭ al-ʿilm hâdhâ luʿâb rasûl Allâh mâ zaqqanî rasûl Allâh zaqqan zaqqan salûnî fa-inna ʿindî ʿilm al-awwalîn wa al-âkhirîn*).

394. Ibn Bâbûye, *Amâlî*, "majlis"28, p. 136, num. 5 (the Prophet places his tongue into the mouth of the newborn al-Ḥusayn, who begins to suck it—" . . . *lammâ saqaṭa l-Ḥusayn min baṭn ummih fa-dafaʿathu ilä l-nabî fa-waḍaʿa l-nabî lisânahu fî famihi wa aqbala l-Ḥusayn ʿalä lisân rasûliʾllâh yamuṣṣuhu*"); Ibn Bâbûye, *Kamâl al-dîn*, vol. 2, ch. 42, p. 425, num. 1 (here the scene takes place between the eleventh imam, al-Ḥasan al-ʿAskarî, and his newborn son, the future hidden imam: " . . . [the father] placed his hands on the child's thighs (or calves) and back, and placed the child's feet against his breast; then he slipped his tongue into the child's mouth and passed his hand over his eyes, his ears, and his joints— . . . *fa-waḍaʿa yadayhi taḥta*

alyatayhi wa ẓahrihi wa waḍa'a qadamayhi 'alä ṣadrihi thumma adlä lisânahu fî fîhi wa amarra yadahu 'alä 'aynayhi wa sam'ihi wa mafâṣilih; further on, it is said that the father slipped his tongue into the child's mouth as if nourishing him with milk or honey— . . . *adlä lisânahu fî fîhi ka'annahu yughadhdhîhi labanan aw 'asalan*"). Cf. also Ibn Bâbûye, *Ma'ânî al-akhbâr*, p. 57, num. 6.

395. Ibn Ishqâ, *Sîra*, ed. Md Ḥamîdullâh (from a manuscript from Fez and a recension transmitted by Yûnus b. Bakîr) pp. 103, 161, 257. Cf. also the miracles attributed to Jesus Christ's saliva, e.g., Mark 8:23 or John 9:6.

396. F. Johnston, *Himalayan Tantric Magic: Theory and Practice*, Bombay, 1949, pp. 201–2.

397. *Baṣâ'ir*, section 2, ch. 21, pp. 109–12; al-Kulaynî, *Uṣûl*, "kitâb al-ḥujja," bâb anna l-a'imma ya'lamûn jamî' al-'ulûm allatî kharajat ilä l-malâ'ika wa l-anbiyâ wa l-rusul, vol. 1, pp. 375–76.

398. Cf. the remarks of the third imam, al-Ḥusayn: "God created his servants so that they might know him . . . knowledge of God . . . is knowledge of the imam . . . (cf. previous discussion).

399. The details are given elsewhere, in other traditions. We had an early look at this when we discussed the sources and means of transmission of Knowledge, and it will be seen again when we deal with the imams' "prodigious powers," which are described as being the results of their Knowledge.

400. *Baṣâ'ir*, section 9, ch. 22, pp. 468–70; "the Marks of the Knowledge of prophecy" seems to refer to the contents of the Sacred Books of the earlier prophets and "the Heritage of Knowledge" to the contents of the seven Secret Books and the tablets of the imams.

401. *"Fa-ammâ l-mâḍî fa-mufassar wa ammâ l-ghâbir fa-mazbûr wa ammâ l-ḥâdith fa-qadhf fî l-qulub wa naqr fî l-asmâ',"* *Baṣâ'ir*, section 7, ch. 4, pp. 318–19; al-Kulaynî, *Uṣûl*, "kitâb al-ḥujja," bâb jihât 'ulûm al-a'imma, vol. 1, pp. 393–94; al-Kulaynî, *al-Rawḍa*, vol. 1, p. 182; the phrase is said by the sixth and seventh imams, who then add: "The present is the marking of hearts and the piercing of eardrums, and this constitutes our supreme Science, and there is no prophet after our Prophet (*al-ḥâdith . . . huwa afḍal 'ilminâ wa lâ nabî ba'd nabiyyinâ*)." This last phrase is obviously pronounced in order to prevent any ambiguity or any confusion between an inspired imam and a prophet, on the one hand, and to emphasize the article of Imamite faith by which Muḥammad is the last lawgiving prophet in this cycle of humanity, on the other. The idea of *khatm al-nubuwwa* (the sealing of the prophecy after Muḥammad) was discussed at length in the first centuries of Islam, and it ultimately became an article of faith; on these discussions and the historical antecedents of the idea, see, respectively, Y. Friedmann, "Finality of Prophethood in Sunni Islâm," *JSAI*, 7, 1986, pp. 177–215; G. Stroumsa, "*Seal of the Prophets*: The Nature of a Manichean Metaphor," *JSAI*, 7, 1986, pp. 61–74.

402. *"Khâzin 'ilm Allâh,"* *"ma'din 'ilm Allâh,"* *"'âlim al-Qur'ân,"* *"al-râsikh fî l-'ilm,"* *"wârith al-'ilm,"* etc. These phrases could be found by merely consulting, e.g., the table of contents of the "Book of the Proof" (*Kitâb al-ḥujja*) of al-Kulaynî, *Uṣûl min al-kâfî*.

403. *"Yaghdû l-nâs 'alä thalâtha ṣunûf 'âlim wa muta'allim wa ghuthâ' fa-naḥnu l-'ulamâ' wa shî'atunâ l-muta'allimûn wa sâ'ir al-nâs ghuthâ',"* *Baṣâ'ir*, sec-

tion 1, ch. 5, pp. 8–9 (Jaʿfar's traditions). This division is seen in a number of other places: "Men are of three kinds: the noble of pure descendence [lit., "the Arab"], the protected client, and the vile of impure heritage [lit, "the non-Arab," "the savage with no religion"] (*al-nâs thalâtha ʿarabî wa mawlä wa ʿilj*—which could also be translated "the lord, the client, and the barbarian"); we are the noble, our faithful are the clients, and those who do not have the same doctrine as we [*man lam yakun ʿalä mithl mâ naḥnu ʿalayhi*] are the vile" (al-Kulaynî, *al-Rawḍa*, vol. 2, p. 30, one of Musä al-Kâẓim's traditions). In similar parlance we encounter the division "descendents of Hâshim/Arabs of noble lineage [*al-ʿarab*] /Bedouin Arabs of low heritage [*al-aʿrâb*] (al-Kulaynî, *al-Rawḍa*, vol. 1, p. 244). In one of al-Ḥusayn's traditions, reported by his son, ʿAlî, it is said that humanity is formed from three groups: "men, those who are similar to men, and monsters with human appearance [*al-nâs/ashbâh al-nâs/al-nâsnâs* (or *al-nisnâs*: a fabulous and malefic being, half-man and half-beast)]." "The men" are the imams; "those who are similar to men" are the disciples of the imams: "our faithful, and they are from us (*shîʿatunâ wa hum minnâ*)"; and finally "the monsters with human appearance are the others, the "majority," and with his hand he pointed to the mass of people" [*al-sawâd al-aʿẓam wa ashâra bi-yadihi ilä jamâʿat al-nâs*]" (al-Kulaynî, *al-Rawḍa*, vol. 2, p. 54; see also Furât, *Tafsîr*, p. 64). At the beginning of one of his conversations with his intimate disciple Kumayl b. Ziyâd al-Nakhaʿî, ʿAlî states: ". . . Men are of three kinds: the Divine Sage, the initiated disciple [travelling] on the road to Deliverance, and dumb sheep following any call whatsoever and distracted by any wind; these latter are in no way illumined by the light of Knowledge, and have no firm pillar on which to lean . . . [*Al-nâs thalâtha ʿâlim rabbânî wa mutaʿallim ʿalä sabîl najât wa hamajun raʿâʿ atbâʿ kulli nâʿiq yamîlûn maʿa kulli râḥ lam yastaḍîʾû bi-nûr al-ʿilm wa lam yaljaʾû ilä ruknin wathîq*]" (Ibn Bâbûye, *Kamâl al-dîn*, ch. 26, p. 290, num. 2; *Nahj al-balâgha*, p. 1155; also, H. Corbin, *En Islam iranien*, vol. 1, p. 113). The Jâbirian corpus uses this tripartite division, cf., *Mukhtâr rasâʾil Jâbir b. Ḥayyân*, ed. P. Kraus, Paris-Cairo, 1935, *Kitâb al-baḥth*, pp. 502–3; also, P. Lory, *Alchimie et mystique en terre d'Islam*, pp. 51, 107.

404. As was seen in the second part, the Imam is ontologically superior to other creatures. There are additionally, as will be seen later, certain aspects of the imams' Knowledge and Powers that belong to them exclusively, and which cannot be transmitted to disciples.

405. *"Anna l-ʿâlim wa l-mutaʿallim fî l-ajr siwâʾ yaʾtiyân yawm al-qiyâma kafarasay rihân yazdaḥimân," Baṣâʾir*, section 1, ch. 2, p. 3, num. 1.

406. Al-Kulaynî, *Uṣûl*, "kitâb al-ʿaql wa l-jahl," vol. 1, p. 26, num. 14 *in fine*; *Ithbât al-waṣiyya*, pp. 2–3. As far as we know, no specialist has yet mentioned this essential point of Imamism, that the initiated disciple can reach "the degree" occupied by the imam; even H. Corbin does no more than mention a vague "spiritual initiation" (cf., e.g., *En Islam iranien*, s.v.) and appears to consider effective initiatory transmission as belonging to Ismâʿîli Shîʿism.

407. Cf. e.g., *Baṣâʾir*, section 1, ch. 20; section 2, ch. 13; section 6, ch. 15; section 8, ch. 6, 7; al-Kulaynî, *Uṣûl*, "kitâb faḍl al-ʿilm," bâb al-radd ilä l-kitâb wa l-sunna; vol. 1, pp. 76-80, bâb al-akhdh bi l-sunna wa shawâhid al-kitâb, vol. 1, pp. 88–90.

408. *". . . Kullu ḥadîth lâ yawâfiqu kitâb Allâh fahuwa zukhruf,"* al-Kulaynî, *Uṣûl, ibid.*, p. 89, num. 3.

409. *"Qad waladanî rasûl Allâh wa anâ a'lamu kitâb Allâh wa fîhi bad' al-khalq wa mâ huwa kâ'in ilä yawm al-qiyâma wa fîhi khabar al-samâ' wa khabar al-arḍ wa khabar al-janna wa khabar al-nâr wa khabar mâ kân wa mâ huwa kâ'in a'lamu dhâlika kamâ anẓuru ilä kaffî . . . ,"* al-Kulaynî, *Uṣûl*, vol. 1, p. 79, num. 8; cf. also *Baṣâ'ir*, section 3, ch. 5–7, pp. 124–30.

410. "Chapitre inconnu du Coran," publié et traduit pour la première fois par M. Garcin de Tassy, *JA*, vol. 13, May 1842, pp. 431–39.

411. Since the end of the eighteenth century, through numerous scientific discussions regarding the subject of the identity of the author of the *Dabestân*, two names have remained in the forefront: Muḥsin Fânî Kashmîrî, and Mobed Shâh 'Alî Ardistânî Sayyid Dhû l-fiqâr; but since the time of a study headed by Raḥîm Reḍa Zâdeh Malek that followed his edition of the complete text of the work, it now appears as though the author is Key Khosrow Esfandiyâr, apparently the son of the famous Iranian Zoroastrian priest Âdhar Keyvân, a philosopher and esoterist, who emigrated to India with his disciples toward the end of the sixteenth or the beginning of the seventeenth century (cf. Sir J. J. Modi, "A Parsee High Priest (Dastûr Azar Kaiwân 1529–1614 A.D.) with his Zoroastrian Disciples in Patna in the 16th and 17th Century A.C.," *The Journal of the K. R. Cama Oriental Institute*, vol. 20, 1932, pp. 1-85; M. Mo'în, "Âdhar Keyvân wa peyrovân-e û," *Majalle-ye Dâneshkade-ye Adabiyyât-e Dâneshgâh-e Tehrân*, num. 3, 4th year, 1336 solar/1958); the text of the sura of the two Lights: *Dabestân-e madhâhib*, ed. R. Reḍâ Zâdeh Malek, Tehran, 1362 solar/1983, vol. 1, pp. 246–47.

412. "Observations de Mirzâ Alexandre Kazem-Beg, professeur de langues orientales à l'université de Casan, sur le *Chapitre inconnu du Coran*," *JA*, vol. 14, December 1843, pp. 373–429.

413. St Clair Tisdall, "Shi'ah Additions to the Koran," *MW*, III, July 1913, num. 3, pp. 227–41.

414. Cf. Schwally-Nöldeke, *Geschichte des Qorans*, vol. 2: *Die Sammlung des Qorans*, Leipzig, 1919, pp. 94–102; R. Blachère, *Introduction au Coran*, Paris, 1958, pp. 184–86.

415. Cf. A. Jeffery, "The Qur'ânic Readings of Zaid b. 'Alî," *RSO*, vol. 16, 1936; J. Hollister, *The Shî'a of India*, London, 1955, pp. 28–29; D. Rahbar, "Relation of Shî'a Theology to the Qur'an," *MW*, vol. 51, num. 3, July 1961, pp. 92–98, vol. 52, num. 1, Jan 1962, pp. 17–21 and vol. 52, num. 2, April 1962, pp. 124–28; J. Eliash, "The Shî'ite Qur'ân. A Reconsideration of Goldziher's Interpretation," *Arabica*, vol. 16, 1969; S. Husain M. Jafri, *Origins and Early Development af Shî'a Islam*, pp. 313f.; [H. Modarressi Tabâtabâ'i, "Early Debates on the Integrity of the Qur'ân," *Studia Islamica*, vol. 77, 1993, pp. 5–39].

416. Cf. I. Goldziher, *Vorlesungen über den Islam*, Heidelberg, 1910, pp. 201–78; I. Goldziher, *Die Richtungen der islamischen Koranauslegung*, Uppsala, 1913 (reedited Leipzig, 1952), especially pp. 263–309; Pareja, Hertling, Bausani, Bois, *Islamologie*, Beirut, 1957–63, p. 820; E. Kohlberg, "Some Notes on the Imamite Attitude to the Qur'ân," *Islamic Philosophy and the Classical Tradition: Essays Presented to R. Walzer*, Jerusalem, 1972, pp. 209–24; J. A. Newman, *The Development and Political Significance . . .* , pp. 185-88. For a scholarly presentation of questions regarding this subject, see also A. Falaturi, "Die Zwölfer-Schia aus der Sicht eines Schiiten: Problem ihrer Untersuchung," *Festschrift Werner Caskel*, Leiden, 1968, pp. 62–95; M.

Ayoub, "The Speaking Qur'ân and the Silent Qur'ân: A Study of the Principles and Development of Imami Shîʿi *tafsîr,*" *Approaches to the History of the Interpretation of the Qur'ân*, ed. A. Rippin, Oxford, 1988, pp. 177–98.

417. A tradition of al-Bâqir: "*Mâ min aḥad min al-nâs yaqûlu annahu jamaʿa l-Qur'ân kullahu kamâ nazzalahu'llâh illâ kadhdhâb wa jamaʿahu wa ḥafiẓahu kamâ nazzalahuʿllâh taʿâlä illâ ʿAlî b. Abî Ṭâlib wa l-a'imma min baʿdihi,*" *Baṣâ'ir*, section 4, ch. 6, p. 193, num. 2; al-Kulaynî, *Uṣûl*, "kitâb al-ḥujja," bâb annahu lam yajmaʿ al-Qur'ân kullahu illâ l-a'imma, vol. 1, p. 332, num. 1.

418. A tradition of al-Bâqir: "*Mâ yastaṭîʿu aḥadun an yaddaʿiya annahu jamaʿa [anna ʿindahu jamîʿ] al-Qur'ân kullihi ẓâhirihi wa bâṭinihi ghayr al-awṣiyâ,*" *Baṣâ'ir*, *ibid.*, num. 1; al-Kulaynî, *Uṣûl*, *ibid.*, num. 2.

419. A tradition of Jaʿfar: "*Inna l-Qur'ân alladhî jâ'a bihi Jabra'îl ilä Muḥammad sabʿata ʿashara alfa âya,*" al-Kulaynî, *Uṣûl*, "kitâb faḍl al-Qur'ân, vol. 4, p. 446, num. 3582.

420. " . . . *Akhrajahu [al-kitâb] ʿAlî ilä al-nâs ḥîna farigha minhu wa katabahu fa-qâla lahum hâdhâ kitâbu 'llâh ʿazza wa jall kamâ anzalahu ʿalä Muḥammad wa qad jamaʿtuhu min al-lawḥayn fa-qâlû hawdhâ ʿindanâ muṣḥaf jâmiʿ fîhi l-Qur'ân lâ ḥâja lanâ fîhi faqâla amâ wa'llâhi mâ tarawnahu baʿd yawmikum hâdhâ abadan innamâ kâna ʿalayya an ukhbirakum ḥîna jamaʿtuhu li-taqra'ûhu,*" *Baṣâ'ir*, section 4, p. 193, num. 3; al-Kulaynî, *Uṣûl*, "kitâb faḍl al-Qur'ân, vol. 4, p. 443–44, num. 3577.

421. This is the beginning of the same tradition by Jaʿfar mentioned in the preceding note: "*Fa-idhâ qâma l-qâ'im qara'a kitâb Allâh ʿazza wa jalla ʿalä ḥaddihi wa akhraja l-muṣḥaf alladhî katabahu ʿAlî.*"

422. Al-Kulaynî, *Uṣûl*, bâb fî kam yuqra'u l-Qur'ân wa yukhtam, vol. 4, pp. 422–23, num. 3526; on al-Ḥusayn b. Khâlid b. Ṭahmân Abû ʿAlî al-Kûfî al-ʿÂmirî, called Ibn Abî'l-ʿAlâ, a disciple of the fifth and sixth imams, see e.g., al-Najâshî, *Rijâl*, s.v.; al-Kashshî, *Rijâl*, p. 233; al-Ardabîlî, *Jâmiʿ al-ruwât,* vol. 1, pp. 231, 239.

423. Al-Kulaynî, *Uṣûl*, bâb al-nawâdir, vol. 4, pp. 440–41, num. 3570; a premonitory vision of ʿAlî reported by al-Nuʿmânî includes the same information: Al-Aṣbagh b. Nubâta said "I heard ʿAlî say, 'I can see from here the non-Arabs [*al-ʿajam*; i.e., the Companions of the hidden imam at the time of his final return] under their tents set up in the mosque at Kûfa; they are teaching the people the Qur'an as it was revealed (*yuʿallimûn al-nâs al-Qur'ân kamâ unzila*)'; I asked, 'O Prince of Believers ! Is not [the Qur'an] now as it was when it was revealed (*a wa laysa huwa kamâ unzila*)?' 'No,' he replied, 'The names of 70 members of the Quraysh tribe have been taken out (*muḥiya minhu*), as well as the names of their fathers; the name of Abû Lahab has been left only to humiliate the Prophet, since Abû Lahab was his uncle'" [al-Nuʿmânî, *Kitâb al-ghayba*, ch 21, p. 452, num. 5]. We will return to the theme of "premonitory visions" (*malâḥim*) when we take up the subject of the special powers of the imams. On Aḥmad b. Md b. Abî Naṣr Abû ʿAlî al-Bazanṭî al-Kûfî, a disciple of the eighth and ninth imams, see al-Najâshî, *Rijâl*, s.v.; al-ʿAllâma al-Ḥillî, *Khulâṣa*, s.v.; al-Mâmaqânî, *Tanqîḥ al-maqâl*, s.v. On al-Aṣbagh b. Nubâta al-Tamîmî al-Ḥanẓalî, a confidant and disciple of the first imam, see these same sources, and al-Ardabîlî, *Jâmiʿ al-ruwât*, vol. 1, p. 106.

424. Al-Kulaynî, *Uṣûl*, bâb fî kam yuqra'u l-Qur'ân wa yukhtam, vol. 4, p. 436, num. 3558, a tradition of al-Bâqir: "*Nazala l-Qur'ânu arbaʿa arbâʿin rubʿ fînâ wa rubʿ*

fî 'aduwwinâ wa rub' sunan wa amthâl wa rub' farâ'iḍ wa aḥkâm." In num. 3556 (vol. 4, p. 435), 'Alî says that the Qur'an is divided into three parts: a third dedicated to the Impeccables and their enemies, a third to the sayings and parables, and the last third to canonical duties and precepts. In the following number (p. 436) Ja'far proposes a division of the Qur'an into four parts: that which is illicit, that which is licit, sayings and precepts, and an account of the events of the past and the future and the arbitration of differences.

425. Tradition of Ja'far; "*Wa'ttaba'û mâ tatlû al-shayâṭîn* bi walâyat al-shayâṭîn *'alä mulk Sulaymân*" al-Kulaynî, *al-Rawḍa*, vol. 2, p. 114, num. 440.

426. Tradition of 'Alî: "*Wa idhâ tawallä sa'ä fî l-arḍ li-yufsida fîhâ wa yuhlika l-ḥarth wa l-nasl* bi-ẓulmihi wa sû'sîratihi *wa'llâhu lâ yuḥibbu l-fasâd*"; al-Kulaynî, *al-Rawḍa*, vol. 2, p. 113, num. 435.

427. Tradition of Ja'far; " *Sal banî Isrâ'îla kam âtaynâhum min âyatin bayyina* fa-minhum man âmana wa minhum man jahada wa minhum man aqarra wa minhum man baddala *wa man yubaddil ni'mata'llâh min ba'di mâ jâathu fa-inna'llâha shadîd al-'iqâb*"; al-Kulaynî, *al-Rawḍa*, vol. 2, p. 114, num. 440.

428. Tadition of Mûsä; "*Lahu mâ fî l-samâwât wa mâ fî l-arḍ* wa mâ baynahumâ wa mâ taḥta l-tharä 'âlam al-ghayb wa 'âlam al-shahâda al-raḥmân al-raḥîm *man dhâ alladhî yashfa'u 'indahu illâ bi-idhnih,*" al-Kulaynî, *al-Rawḍa*, vol. 2, p. 113, num. 437.

429. Tradition of Ja'far; "*Wa kuntum 'alä shafâ ḥufratin min al-nâr fa-anqad-hakum minhâ* bi-Muḥammad," al-Kulaynî, *al-Rawḍa*, vol. 1, p. 265, num. 208

430. Tradition of 'Alî; "*Ulâ'ika lladhîna ya'lamu'llâh mâ fî qulûbihim fa-a'riḍ 'anhum* fa-qad sabaqat 'alayhim kalimat al-shaqâ' wa sabaqa lahum al-'adhâb [here *wa 'iẓhum* is missing] *wa qul lahum fî anfusihim qawlan balîghan,*" al-Kulaynî, *al-Rawḍa*, vol. 1, p. 266, num. 211.

431. Tradition of Ja'far; "*Thumma lâ yajidû fî anfusihim ḥarajan mimmâ qaḍayta* min amr al-walî *wa yusallimû* li'llâh al-ṭâ'a *taslîman/wa law annâ katabnâ 'alayhim ani'qtulû anfusakum* wa sallamû l-imâm taslîman *awi'khrujû min diyârikum* lahu *mâ fa'alûhu illâ qalîl minhum wa law anna* ahl al-khilâf [instead of: *annahum*] *fa'alû mâ yû'aẓûn bihi lakâna khayran lahum wa ashadda tathbîtan,*" al-Kulaynî, *al-Rawḍa*, vol. 1, p. 265–66, num. 210.

432. Tradition of al-Riḍâ; "*Fa-anzala'llâh sakînatahu 'alä* rasûlihi [instead of: 'alayhi] *wa ayyadahu bi-junûdin lam tarawhâ,*" al-Kulaynî, *al-Rawḍa*, vol. 2, p. 231, num. 571; the beginning of the verse recounts the episode of the Cave where the Prophet and Abû Bakr were hidden; the passage we have cited is marked, in the official Vulgate, by a certain ambiguity as to the identity of upon whom it was that the Sakîna descended and who was sustained by the invisible Armies: was it the Prophet, or Abû Bakr? According to the imams, the original Qur'an had no such ambiguity. On the Qur'anic Sakîna, which comes from the Hebrew *shekina* (in Jewish tradition: the immanence of God, his presence in a place, or God himself; in the Christian tradition it refers to the Glory of the Lord, the divine presence) cf. D. Masson, *Le Coran*, vol. 1, Notes, Qur'an 2: 248–1. For the meaning of *sakîna* among the imams, see, e.g., Ibn Bâbûye, *Ma'ânî al-akhbâr*, pp. 284–85.

433. Tradition of Ja'far; "*Laqad jâ'a*nâ *[jâ'akum] rasûlun min anfusi*nâ *[anfusikum] 'azîzun 'alayhi mâ 'anit*nâ *(['anittum] ḥarîṣun 'alay*nâ *['alaykum] bi l-*

mu'minîn ra'ûfun raḥîm," al-Kulaynî, *al-Rawḍa*, vol. 2, p. 231, num. 570.

434. Tradition of Ja'far; *"Wa laqad 'ahidnâ ilä Adama min qablu* kalimâtin fî Muḥammad wa 'Alî wa Fâṭima wa al-Ḥasan wa al-Ḥusayn wa l-a'imma min dhurriyyatihim *fa-nasiya,"* al-Kulaynî, *Uṣûl*, "kitâb al-ḥujja," bâb fîhi nukat wa nutaf min al-tanzîl fî l-walâya, vol. 2, p. 283, num. 23.

435. Tradition of 'Alî; *"Wa mâ arsalnâ min qablika min rasûl wa lâ nabî* wa lâ muḥaddath *illâ idhâ tamannä alqä al-shayṭân fî umniyyatihi," Baṣâ'ir*, section 7, ch. 5, p. 319, num. 3, p. 321, num. 8; 'Alî b. Ibrâhîm al-Qummî, *Tafsîr*, vol. 2, p. 89; Ibn Bâbûye, *'Ilal*, p. 183; this version of the verse is old, since it appeares in 'Abd Allâh b. 'Abbâs's copy (d. 68/686. Cf. A. Jeffery, "Materials for the History of the Text of the Qur'ân," p. 202) and the famous traditionist Qatâda (d. 117–18/735–36) is said to have followed Ibn 'Abbâs's reading (Cf. al-Majlisî, *Biḥâr*, vol. 7, p. 292). For the opinion of this version by the Sunnites, see also Ibn Shahrâshûb, *Manâqib*, vol. 3, p. 115 (citing al-Ghazzâlî's *Iḥyâ'*) or al-Qasṭallânî, *Irshâd al-sârî*, vol. 6, p. 103.

436. Tradition of Ja'far; *"Wa man yuṭi'i 'llâh wa rasûlahu* fî walâyati 'Alî wa walâyati l-a'imma min ba'dihi *faqad fâza fawzan 'aẓîman,"* al-Kulaynî, *Uṣûl*, *ibid.*, vol. 2, p. 279, num. 8.

437. Tradition of al-Riḍâ; *"Shara'a lakum* yâ âl-Muḥammad *min al-dîn mâ waṣṣä bihi Nûḥan wa'lladhî awḥaynâ ilayka* yâ Muḥammad *wa mâ waṣṣaynâ bihi Ibrâhîma wa Mûsä wa 'Îsä an aqîmû dîn* âl-Muḥammad [instead of: *al-dîn*] *wa lâ tatafarraqû fîhi wa kûnû 'alä jamâ'atin kabura 'alä al-mushrikîn* man ashraka bi-walâyati 'Alî *mâ tad'ûhum ilayhi* min walâyati 'Alî *inna'llâha* yâ Muḥammad *yahdî ilayhi man yunîb* man yujîbuka ilä walâyati 'Alî [instead of: *yajtabî ilayhi man yashâ' wa yahdî ilayhi man yunîb*]," al-Kulaynî, *al-Rawḍa*, vol. 2, p. 163, num. 502; cf. also al-Kulaynî, *Uṣûl*, "kitâb al-hujja," bâb anna l-a'imma warithû 'ilm al-nabî wa jamî' al-anbiyâ' . . . , vol. 1, pp. 324–29, num. 1, and bâb fîhi nukat . . . , vol. 2, p. 285, num. 32 (with variations); St Clair Tisdall, "Shi'ah Additions to the Koran," p. 239 (with variations).

438. Tradition of 'Alî; *"Sa'ala sâ'ilun bi-'adhâbin wâqi'/li l-kâfirîn* bi-walâyati 'Alî *laysa lahu dâfi'/min Allâhi dhî l-ma'ârij,"* al-Kulaynî, *al-Rawḍa*, vol. 1, p. 83, num. 18. In his "kitâb al-ḥujja," al-Kulaynî groups together in a single chapter a number of traditions in which the Qur'anic citations of the imams, containing numerous references to 'Alî, the Impeccables, and their *walâya*, present more or less marked differences with the text of the official Vulgate; some of these have already been cited, and in the interest of brevity we will here only point out the references: al-Kulaynî, *Uṣûl*, kitâb al-ḥujja, bâb fîhi nukat wa nutaf min al-tanzîl fî l-walâya, vol. 2, pp. 276–318, e.g. num. 1106 (number in the work) (= 27, number in the chapter), 1110 (= 31), 1124–27 (= 45–48), 1130 (= 51), 1137–39 (= 58-60), 1143 (= 64), 1169 (= 90), 1170 (= 91). See also the early Imamite Qur'anic commentaries, such as al-'Askarî's *Tafsîr* (ed. Lucknow), p. 33; 'Alî b. Ibrâhîm al-Qummî's *Tafsîr* (upon which the essential part of Goldziher's study of the subject is based), pp. 5–11; the *Tafsîr* by Furât b. Ibrâhîm (in *Biḥâr al-anwâr*, vol. 19/1, p. 15); or the *Tafsîr* by al-'Ayyâshî (*Biḥâr al-anwâr*, vol. 19/1, pp. 15 and 30); for other Imamite sources, see E. Kohlberg, "Some Notes on the Imâmite Attitude to the Qur'an," pp. 211–14. For other references to the imams' Qur'an, see Meir M. Bar-Asher, "Variant Readings and Additions of the Imâmî-Shi'a to the Quran," *Israel Oriental Studies*, vol. 13, 1993, pp. 39–74.

439. See, e.g., al-Kulaynî, *Uṣûl*, *ibid.*, vol. 1, p. 139, num. 69; vol. 2, pp. 2–3,

num. 247, 248, 249; vol. 2, p. 60, num. 349; al-Nu'mânî, *Kitâb al-ghayba*, ch. 14, pp. 391–92, num. 49.

440. On the famous hadith of the Two Precious Objects, particularly cherished by the Shî'ites, see, e.g., *Baṣâ'ir*, section 8, ch. 17, pp. 412–14; Ibn Bâbûye, *'Uyûn*, ch. 6, vol. 1, pp. 57-58, nums. 25, 26; Ibn Bâbûye, *Amâlî*, pp. 240, 415, 533f.; Ibn Bâbûye, *Kamâl al-dîn*, ch. 22, pp. 234f., nums. 44f.; in Sunni compilations, cf. Muslim, *Ṣaḥîḥ*, vol. 2, pp. 325–26; al-Tirmidhî, *Sunan*, vol. 2, p. 308; Ibn Ḥanbal, *Musnad*, vol. 3, pp. 3, 17, 26, 59; vol. 4, pp. 366-67; vol. 5, pp. 151–52.

441. Ibn Bâbûye, *Amâlî*, "majlis" 47, p. 280, num. 9.

442. Al-Kulaynî, *al-Rawḍa*, vol. 2, pp. 246-47, num. 586; the text is taken up by al-Sharîf al-Raḍî in his compilation of *Nahj al-balâgha* (pp. 447–48), but he omits the last sentence, that which says the most; we shall return to this.

443. Al-Kulaynî, *al-Rawḍa*, vol. 1, pp. 75-79 (a letter of al-Bâqir to Sa'd al-Khayyir, who must be Sa'd b. Ṭurayf al-Ḥanẓalî; cf. al-Ardabîlî, *Jâmi' al-ruwât*, vol. 1, pp. 354–55), vol. 1, pp. 3–20 (a letter from Ja'far to his disciples—*aṣḥâbihi*), vol. 1, pp. 179–84 (a letter from Mûsä to 'Alî b. Suwayd al-Tammâr al-Sâ'î, a disciple of the seventh and eighth imams; cf. al-Kashshî, *Rijâl*, p. 283, al-Najâshî, *Rijâl*, s.v.; al-Ṭûsî, *Rijâl*, p. 354, num. 16; al-'Allâma al-Ḥillî, *Khulâṣa*, s.v.; al-Ardabîlî, *Jâmi' al-ruwât*, vol. 1, p. 585.

444. "*. . . Kullu umma qad rafa'a' llâhu 'anhum 'ilm al-kitâb ḥîna nabadhûhu wa wallâhum 'aduwwahum . . . aqâmû ḥurûfahu wa ḥarrafû ḥudûdahu . . . ghayyarû 'urä al-dîn . . . fa 'rif ashbâh al-aḥbâr wa l-ruhbân alladhîna sârû bi-kitmân al-kitâb wa taḥrîfihi . . . a'rif ashbâhahum min hâdhihi l-umma alladhîna aqâmû ḥurûf al-kitâb wa ḥarrafûhu,*" *al-Rawḍa*, vol. 1, pp. 76–77.

445. "*. . . Lâ taltamis dîna man laysa min al-shî'a . . . fa'innahum al-khâ'inûn khânû'llâh wa rasûlahu wa khânû amânâtihimâ . . . u'tuminû 'alä kitâbi 'llâh fa-ḥarrafûhu wa baddalûhu . . . wa dullû 'alä wulât al-amr minhum fa'nṣarafû 'anhum . . .*," al-Kulaynî, *al-Rawḍa*, vol. 1, p. 181.

446. Al-Ash'arî, *Maqâlât al-islâmiyyin*, ed. H. Ritter, p. 47, and the editor's note.

447. Ibn Ḥazm, *Fiṣal*, vol. 4, p. 182.

448. Al-Isfarâ'inî Ṭâhir b. Md, *al-Tabṣîr fî l-dîn*, p. 43.

449. See, e.g., *Baṣâ'ir*, section 4, ch. 6 (against the first three caliphs); al-Kulaynî, *al-Rawḍa*, besides the references given in notes 444 and 445, vol. 1, p. 18 (against 'Umar), vol. 1, pp. 273–74 (against Abû Bakr and 'Umar), vol. 1, p. 285 (against 'Uthmân), vol. 2, p. 18 (against Abû Bakr and 'Umar), vol. 2, p. 25 (against the Banû Umayya), vol. 2, p. 55 (against Abû Bakr and 'Umar), vol. 2, p. 172 (against Abû Bakr and 'Umar), vol. 2, p. 186 (against 'Umar), vol. 2, p. 245 (against 'Uthmân); *Kitâb 'Abbâd al-'Uṣfurî in Uṣûl arba'umi'a*, ms. University of Tehran, no.. 962 (especially against 'Umar); al-Nu'mânî, *al-Muḥkam wa l-mutashâbih* (pieces of Ja'far's *Tafsîr*, a compilation published under al-Sharîf al-Murtaḍä's name), p. 12 (against the Companions); al-imâm al-'Askarî, *Tafsîr*, pp. 19–24 (against the Companions).

450. Cf. I. Goldziher, "Spottnamen der ersten Chalifen bei den Schî'iten," *ZDMG*, vol. 15, 1901; S. Dedering, "Ein Kommentar der Tradition über die 73 Sekten," *MO*, vol. 25, 1931, especially pp. 40f.; M. G. S. Hodgson, "How Did the Early Shî'a Become Sectarian?," *JAOS*, vol. 75, 1955, p. 6f.; A. Falaturi, "Die Zwölfer-Schia aus der Sicht eines Schiiten," pp. 78f.; and E. Kohlberg's excellent article, "Some Imâmî Shî'î views on the Ṣaḥâba," *JSAI*, vol. 5, 1984, pp. 146–76 (well documented,

but the erudite author makes no connection between the fact of "insulting the Companions" and questioning the imams' Qur'an; he makes no mention of al-Kulaynî's *Rawḍa*, where the majority of the traditions concerning this problem are found).

451. *"Inna l-islâm bada'a gharîban wa saya'ûdu gharîban fa-ṭûbä li l-ghurabâ',"* cf. e.g., al-Nu'mânî, *Kitâb al-ghayba*, ch. 22, pp. 455–57; al-Najâshî, *Rijâl*, p. 32; Ibn Bâbûye, *Kamâl al-dîn*, author's introduction, vol. 1, p. 66; *gharîb*, pl. *ghurabâ'*, lit. "foreign, strange, expatriated, unheard, little known." Corbin gives the phrase a gnostic slant by his use of the gnostic term *Allogène*, cf. *En Islam iranien*, s.v. "Etranger."

452. On this idea in general and the bibliography relating to it, see U. Rubin, "Barâ'a: a study of some Qur'anic passages," *JSAI*, vol. 5, p. 1985, pp. 13–32.

453. See previous discussion, especially parts II-1 and III-2; on the pairs of opposing Guides (*a'imma*) see, e.g., *Baṣâ'ir*, section 1, ch. 15–16, pp. 32f.; al-Kulaynî, *al-Rawḍa*, vol. 2, pp. 52f.; Ibn Bâbûye, *Amâlî*, pp. 345, 412.

454. All of these themes run through the compilations of Imamite traditions; on the Imamite idea of *barâ'a*, see E. Kohlberg, "Some Imâmi-Shî'î Views on the *ṣaḥâba*," *JSAI*, vol. 5, 1984; E. Kohlberg, "Barâ'a in Shî'î Doctrine," *JSAI*, vol. 7, 1986, pp. 139–75; E. Kohlberg, "Non-Imâmî Shî'i Muslims in Imâmî *fiqh*," *JSAI*, vol. 6, 1985, pp. 99–106.

455. See the references in note 443.

456. *"Kuffa 'an hâdhihi l-qirâ'a iqra' kamâ yaqra'u l-nâs* ["the people," in Imamite terminology, *al-nâs* is one of the words to refer to non-Shî'ite Muslims, the "Sunnis"] *ḥattä yaqûmu l-qâ'im fa-idhâ qâma l-qâ'im qara'a kitâb Allâh 'azza wa jalla 'alä ḥaddihi wa akhraja l-muṣḥaf alladhî katabahu 'Alî,"* al-Kulaynî, *Uṣûl*, "kitâb faḍl al-Qur'ân," bâb al-nawâdir, vol. 4, pp. 443–44, num. 23 (= 3577).

457. *"Sufyân b. al-Samṭ qâla sa'altu Abâ 'Abdi'llâh 'an tanzîl al-Qur'ân qâla'qra'û kamâ 'ullimtum,"* al-Kulaynî, *op. cit.*, num. 15 (= 3569); on Sufyân b. al-Samṭ al-Bajalî al-Kûfî, see al-Ṭûsî, *Rijâl*, p. 213, num. 164; al-Ardabîlî, *Jâmi' al-ruwât*, vol. 1, pp. 336–37. In another tradition that goes back to Ja'far, the Imamites were invited to follow the reading of the Qur'an of Ubayy b. Ka'b (cf. al-Kulaynî, *Uṣûl*, vol. 4, pp. 445–46, num. 27 (= 3581); on Ubayy, the question of differences in reading the Qur'an after 'Uthmân's imposition of Zayd b. Thâbit's recension and the bibliography that relates to it, see, e.g., R. Blachère, *Le Coran*, Paris, 1947, vol. 1, pp. 34, 39, 54, 58, 75, 92; F. M. Pareja *et al.*, *Islamologie*, pp. 604f.

458. I. Goldziher confuses 'Alî's recension of the Qur'an with one of the secret books of the imams,which he erroneously calls *Muṣḥaf Fâṭima* (*Die Richtungen* . . . , pp. 277–78).

459. Ibn Bâbûye, *Risâlat al-i'tiqâdât*, English translation by A. A. A. Fyzee, *A Shi'ite Creed*, p. 85.

460. Ibn Bâbûye, *Risâlat al-i'tiqâdât*, English translation by A. A. A. Fyzee, *A Shi'ite Creed*, pp. 86–87.

461. Al-Nu'mânî, *al-Muḥkam wa l-mutashâbih*, p. 12; al-Nu'mânî, *Kitâb al-ghayba*, p. 99. On this "turn" in the Imamite position, see also E. Kohlberg, "Some notes . . . ," pp. 212f.

462. E.g., al-shaykh al-Mufîd (413/1022), *Awâ'il al-maqâlât*, pp. 54–56 (French trans. by D. Sourdel, *L'Imâmisme vu par le cheikh al-Mufîd*, pp. 73–75); Faḍl b. al-Ḥasan al-Ṭabarsî (548/1154), *Majma' al-bayân*, vol. 1, pp. 15, 30; al-Majlisî (1110/1699), *Biḥâr al-anwâr*, vol. 19, pp. 19-20. We have seen how al-sharîf al-Raḍî

(406/1016), a "rationalist" and disciple of al-Mufîd, had censured the most telling of ʿAlî's sentences regarding the falsification of the original Qurʾan (note 442).

463. Cf. E. Kohlberg, "Some notes . . . ," pp. 214f. (on page 218, note 99, the author cites the traditionalist Md Taqî al-Nûrî (d. 1320/1905), who accuses Ibn Bâbûye of denying for the first time the traditions of the imams regarding the falsification of the integral Qur'an by the Sunnites).

464. It suffices to see just how difficult the editor-translators of the works of al-Kulaynî and al-Nuʿmânî, all of whom are religious scholars, find it to hide their embarrassment when dealing with the traditions we are discussing here. In some cases they use an arbitrary system of punctuation to attempt to prove that the "extra" Qurʾanic passages are actually the imams' commentaries. In other cases, there are equally arbitrary, and endless, discussions in notes regarding the quality of the chains of transmission of these traditions.

465. See notes 410, 412, 413. For historical and stylistic criticism, see also M. Râmyâr, *Târîkh-e Qur'ân*, pp. 167–74.

466. Th. Nöldeke, F. Schwally, *Geschichte des Qorans, vol. 2: Die Sammlung des Qorans* (Schwally), pp. 100–12 (which also outlines the theses according to which several suras were obviously abbreviated, e.g., sura *al-nûr* (sura 24) contained 100 verses instead of the 64 it presently has, sura *al-ḥijr* (sura 15) had 190 verses instead of 99, and sura *al-aḥzâb* (sura 33), which today has 73 verses, originally was the same length as sura *al-baqara*, with 286 verses).

467. R. Blachère, *Introduction au Coran*, pp. 185–86.

468. Ibn Shahrâshûb, *Mathlâib al-nawâṣib*, ms Nâṣiriyya Library, Lucknow, fol. 43a (we are indebted to M. Shûshtariyân of Tehran for allowing us to consult his photocopy of the manuscript; the pagination is by M. Shûshtariyân); Mîrzâ Ḥusayn al-Nûrî al-Ṭabarsî (d. 1320/1905) also cites this passage from Ibn Shahrâshûb in his *Faṣl al-khiṭâb fî taḥrîf al-kitâb* (lith. ed. Tehran, n.d., pp. 156–57).

469. Al-Ṭihrânî Âqâ Bozorg, *al-Dharîʿa*, vol. 3, p. 311, num. 1151, pp. 394–95, num. 1415–17, vol. 4, p. 454, num. 2022 (1 and 2); for other sources, see E. Kohlberg, "Some Notes . . . ," p. 213.

470. Manuscript collection donated by Sayyid Md Mishkât to the University of Tehran, ms. num. 842 (*Dharîʿa*, vol. 4, p. 454, num. 2022–2). The manuscript belonged to the erudite Mîrzâ Ḥusayn al-Nûrî al-Ṭabarsî and has in the margins the name, the signature, and the notes of the owner, who had certainly used it in composing his *Faṣl al-khiṭâb*. In the *Faṣl* . . . , the erudite "traditionalist," undoubtedly fearful of being considered "anathema," avoids taking a clear position on the subject of the "Qur'ân of the imams." He presents the information without ever really stating the clear conclusion, yet even this did not spare him from the vitriol of jurists who accused him of casting doubt on the integrity of the official Vulgate (e.g., al-shaykh Maḥmûd al-Muʿarrab al-Ṭihrânî, *Kashf al-irtiyâb fî ʿadam taḥrîf al-kitâb*, Tehran, 1302/1864). Âqâ Bozorg, the author of *al-Dharîʿa*, was a disciple of al-Nûrî al-Ṭabarsî. He goes to the defense of his teacher in *al-Naqd al-laṭîf fî nafy al-taḥrîf ʿan al-Qurʾân al-sharîf*, by attempting to prove that his teacher never intended to have anyone doubt the integrity of the Vulgate, and that his only error lay in having chosen a bad title for his work (cf. *al-Dharîʿa*, vol. 24, p. 278, num. 1433).

471. The text that follows, sura of the *walâya* (Divine Friendship), is from the manuscript found by St Clair Tisdall, and translated into English by him (cf. note 413); the text, in a facsimile reproduction, is divided into seven verses, and is entitled *sûra*

al-walâyat (with a long *tâ'*); it was most probably copied by a Persian, as there are Persian translations (even though they are not always faithful) between the lines:

Sûratu'ul Walâyat: Seven Verses.

In the Name of God, the Merciful, the Gracious.

(1) O ye who have believed, believe in the Prophet and in the Governor [*Al Waliyy.*], both of whom We have raised up (sent): they shall guide you to a right way. (2) A Prophet and a Governor are one of the two of them from another, and I am the Knower, the Well-Informed. (3) Verily those who faithfully perform God's covenant, to them belong the Gardens of Delight. (4) And those who, when Our verses are recited to them, have accounted Our verses lies, (5) Verily to them belongeth in hell a great place, when it is proclaimed to them on the day of the Resurrection, 'Where are the wrong-doers, those who account the Messengers liars?' (6) He created them not, the Messengers, except in the truth; and God was not about to manifest them until an appointed time near at hand. (7) And laud thou in the praise of thy Lord, and ʿAlî is [one] of the witnesses.

(*Bismi'llâh al-raḥmân al-raḥîm/yâ ayyuhâ'lladhîna âmanû âminû bi l-nabî wa bi l-walî alladhîna baʿathnâhumâ yahdiyânikum ilâ ṣirâṭin mustaqîm/nabiyyun wa waliyyun baʿḍuhumâ min baʿḍin wa anâ l-ʿalîm al-khabîr/inna'lladhîna yûfûna bi-ʿahdi'llâhi lahum jannat* (with a long *tâ'*) *al-naʿîm/wa'lladhîna idhâ tuliyat ʿalayhim âyâtunâ kânû bi-âyâtinâ mukadhdhibîn/inna lahum fî jahannama maqâman ʿaẓîman idhâ nûdiya lahum yawm al-qiyâma ayna al-ẓâlimûn al-mukadhdhibûn li l-mursalîn/mâ khalaqahum al-mursalîn* [sic, an unlikely construction] *illâ bi l-ḥaqq wa mâ kâna'llâhu li-yuẓhirahum ilä ajalin qarîb/wa sabbiḥ bi-ḥamdi rabbika wa ʿAliyyun min al-shâhidîn*).

472. Later, the miracles performed by the sufis will appear to be less surprising; why? According to what historical, social, or religious procedure was *"occult dynamism,"* that is the performance of acts of a magical nature, almost universally admitted by Muslims? This is an exciting field of study that leads to the sources of occultism in Islam; for further direction in research in this area, in a number of different branches of Islam (theologians, philosophers, scholars, jurists, mystics, milieu of *adab*, etc.), see T. Fahd, "Le Monde du sorcier en Islam," or his *La Divination arabe; La Magie arabe traditionnelle* (collective work), Paris, 1976; *L'Etrange et le merveilleux dans l'Islam médiéval,* colloquium organized by the Association pour l'Avancement des Etudes Islamiques, under the direction of M. Arkoun, J. Le Goff, T. Fahd, and M. Rodinson, Paris, 1978; A. Kovalenko, *Les Concepts de magie et de sciences occultes en Islam*, doctoral thesis, Strassburg, 1979; and especially R. Gramlich, *Die Wunder der Freunde Gottes . . .* (see also the superb summary of this work by Fritz Meier, "Bemerkungen zu einem grossen Buch," *Der Islam*, vol. 65, 1988, num. 2, pp. 282–300). Despite these remarkable studies, the certain role of early Shîʿism in the development of Muslim occultism is still insufficiently explored.

473. *Baṣâ'ir*, section 4, ch. 12, pp. 208–11. Let it be noted that in the following chapter (pp. 212–16), an identity is established between the Supreme Name of God and the Science of the Book (*ʿilm al-kitâb*); cf. Qur'an 27:40, and the classical exegesis on the subject. Elsewhere, an identity is established between the Supreme Name and the sacred books taken as a whole (*Baṣâ'ir*, section 9, ch. 22, p. 469, num. 4) . . . On the

number of letters in the Supreme Name and its magical power, see also al-Kulaynî, *Uṣûl*, "kitâb al-ḥujja," bâb mâ uʿṭiya l-aʾimma min ism Allâh, vol. 1, pp. 334–35.

474. This last hidden letter is reminiscent of the primordial "Name" of God, forever hidden, that Jaʿfar refers to in mysterious, almost cosmogonic and arithmosophic terms:

> [In the beginning] God created a Name with non-sonorous letters, with an unpronounced vowel, an entity without a body; [a Name] indescribable, of a colorless color, unlimited, veiled, though not covered with a veil, from all the senses and from all imagination. God made a perfect word out of it; a word composed of four parts, none of which existed before the others; from these four parts, He showed three Names, in order to respond to a need felt by the creatures, keeping one of them veiled: the Hidden, Secret Name. Of the [three] Names shown, the exoteric name is Allâh, the Exalted, the Most High. Then He gave each of these three Names four Pillars, a total of twelve Pillars in all, and created thirty Names for each Pillar (there follows a list of some 36 Divine Names) . . . These Names added to the Most Beautiful Names make a total of 360 Names, all coming from the [first] three Names that are the Pillars and the Veils of the Single Secret Name, hidden by these three Names. . . . "

al-Kulaynî, *Uṣûl*, "kitâb al-ḥujja," bâb ḥudûth al-asmâʾ, vol. 1, pp. 151–52, num. 1; Ibn Bâbûye, *Kitâb al-tawḥîd*, ch. 29, pp. 190–91, num. 3.

475. On Juwayria b. Mus-hir al-ʿAbdî al-Kûfî, see al-Ṭûsî, *Rijâl*, p. 37, num. 4; al-Ardabîlî, *Jâmiʿ al-ruwât*, vol. 1, pp. 169–70.

476. *Baṣâʾir*, section 5, ch. 2, pp. 217–19; see also Ibn Bâbûye, *Amâlî*, "majlis" 71, pp. 467–68, num. 10 (ʿAlî states that the Supreme Name is in Syriac).

477. On ʿUmar b. Ḥanẓala, see note 135.

478. *Baṣâʾir*, section 4, ch. 12, nâdir min al-bâb, p. 210, num. 1. However, a hasty statement by Jaʿfar according to which Salmân al-Fârisî had learned the Supreme Name (al-Kashshî, *Rijâl*, p. 7; al-Mufîd, *al-Ikhtiṣâs*, p. 11) suggests that the terrifying Name was taught to initiates who had been especially tested. Is this perhaps why the imam then said that if Abû Dharr [al-Ghifârî] had received Salmân's Science he would fall into infidelity (cf. al-Mufîd, *al-Ikhtiṣâs*, p. 12; al-Majlisî, *Biḥâr*, vol. 6, p. 783)?; according to the tradition, Salmân and Abû Dharr were both close disciples of ʿAlî. The former is in a sense the prototype of an esoteric spirituality, and the latter of an ascetic spirituality. On other thaumaturgic powers of the Supreme Name, see also al-Kulaynî, *al-Rawḍa*, vol. 1, p. 283 (the power of raising the dead; according to al-Ashʿarî, al-Mughîra b. Saʿîd al-ʿIjlî (d. 119/737), an "extremist" Shîʿite who was for a time a disciple of the fifth imam, claimed to be able to bring the dead back to life with the knowledge of the Supreme Name that he had; according to him, God had created the world by pronouncing this Name; al-Ashʿarî, *Maqâlât*, ed. Ritter, pp. 7 and 9; on him, see W. F. Tucker, "Rebels and Gnostics: al-Mughîra b. Saʿîd and the mughîriyya," *Arabica*, vol. 22, 1975, pp. 33–47), and vol. 2, p. 67 (the ability to stop earthquakes). On the idea in general, with references to the Imamite traditions, see D. Gimaret, *Les Noms divins en Islam*, all of chapter 5, pp. 85–94.

479. *Baṣâʾir*, section 4, ch. 4, pp. 174-90; al-Kulaynî, *Uṣûl*, "kitâb al-ḥujja," bâb mâ ʿinda l-aʾimma min âyât al-anbiyâʾ, vol. 1, pp. 335–36, num. 4.

480. *Baṣâʾir, ibid.*; al-Kulaynî, *Uṣûl, ibid.*, Ibn ʿAyyâsh, *Muqtaḍab*, pp. 56–57.

481. Al-Kulaynî, *op. cit.*, vol. 1, p. 336, num. 5; Ibn Bâbûye, *Kamâl al-dîn*, vol. 2, ch. 58, p. 674, num. 28.

482. *Baṣâʾir, ibid.*; al-Kulaynî, *op. cit.*, nums. 1, 2.

483. *Baṣâʾir, ibid.*; al-Kulaynî, *Uṣûl*, "kitâb al-ḥujja," bâb mâ ʿinda l-aʾimma min silâḥ rasûl Allâh wa matâʿihi, vol. 1, pp. 337–43; Ibn Bâbûye, *Amâlî*, "majlis" 17, pp. 71–72, num. 2, and "majlis" 48, p. 289, num. 10. These objects are part of the prophetic Heritage, and constitute one part of the Sacred Legacy *(al-waṣiyya)* of the imams; cf. previous discussion; U. Rubin, "Prophets and Progenitors in the Early Shîʿa Tradition," pp. 46–48. The Shîʿite alchemist Aydamur b. ʿAbdAllâh al-Jaldakî (d. 750 or 761/1349 or 1360) identifies these objects listed by the imams, most notably "Moses' Staff," with so many secret symbols of the "Sublime Keys of the alchemists" (cf. H. Corbin, *Alchimie comme art hiératique,* "Le Livre des Sept Statues d'Apollonios de Tyane commenté par Jaldakî," pp. 63–143, and especially pp. 80–82).

484. *Baṣâʾir*, section 3, ch. 5–7, pp. 124–30. The imams have the ability to use both divination and prediction; the traditions that relate "visions of the future" are technically called *al-malâḥim*; cf. e.g., al-Kulaynî, *Rawḍa*, vol. 2, pp. 9, 230; Ibn Bâbûye, *Amâlî*, pp. 63, 118, 134, 140; Ibn Bâbûye, *Nahj al-balâgha*, pp. 146, 170, 296, 299, 301, etc.

485. *Baṣâʾir*, section 6, ch. 2, pp. 266–69.

486. *Baṣâʾir, ibid.*; the expression comes from the Qurʾan, where it is used only one time, when speaking about King David: 38:20: "And We have reinforced his kingdom, We have given him wisdom and the *faṣl al-khiṭâb*"; it is translated by "the art of pronouncing judgments—*l'art de prononcer des jugements*" (Masson), "the art of arbitration—*l'art d'arbitrer*" (Blachère), "eloquence—*l'éloquence*" (Kasimirski); the Qur'an gives no explanation of the term. The literal meaning is the strength or force of words or speech. Although the imams provide no further details either, it nevertheless appears as though the expression means "the art of arbitration," since in certain traditions it is accompanied by the terms *waṣâyâ* and *qaḍâyâ* ("decrees" and "judgments," cf. *Baṣâʾir, ibid.*, nums. 7 and 15), but it can also be thought of as "the effective Word," a well-known thaumaturgic practice in occult traditions.

487. *Baṣâʾir*, section 5, ch. 10–12, pp. 234–53.

488. *Baṣâʾir*, section 5, ch. 16–17, pp. 259–61; see also, e.g., Ibn Bâbûye, *ʿIlal*, vol. 1, ch. 139, pp. 173–74; Ibn Bâbûye, *ʿUyûn*, vol. 2, ch. 53, p. 227; Ibn Bâbûye, *Kamâl al-dîn*, vol. 1, ch. 32, p. 327, num. 7; vol. 2, ch. 36, p. 377, num. 1; vol. 2, ch. 38, p. 384, num. 1; *Nahj al-balâgha*, p. 55; for mind reading the usual expression is "and he (i.e., the imam) told me first—*fa-qâla lî mubtadiʾan,"* that is, that the disciple did not need to ask his question, since the imam "read" his mind.

489. *Baṣâʾir*, section 7, ch. 11–13, pp. 333–41; see also, e.g., Ibn Bâbûye, *ʿUyûn*, vol. 2, p. 227.

490. *Baṣâʾir*, section 7, ch. 14–16, pp. 341–54; the "metamorphosized" are most often reincarnations of the "enemies of the imams"; cf. also al-Kulaynî, *al-Rawḍa*, vol. 1, p. 285, and vol. 2, p. 37 (the metamorphosis of ʿUthman and the Umayyads); al-Nuʿmânî, *Kitâb al-ghayba*, p. 387 (the adversaries of the imams); Ibn Bâbûye, *ʿUyûn*, vol. 1, ch. 27, p. 271; cf. also note 214; on the idea of reincarnation and transmigration in Islam, and the related bibliography on this subject, cf. G. Monnot, "La transmigration et l'immortalité," *Islam et religions*, pp. 279–95.

491. *Baṣâ'ir*, section 2, ch. 18, pp. 95–103; al-Kulaynî, *Uṣûl*, "kitâb al-ḥujja," bâb anna l-jinn ya'tîhim fa-yas'alûnahum 'an ma'âlim dînihim, vol. 2, pp. 242–46.

492. *Baṣâ'ir*, section 5, ch. 13, pp. 253–57, and section 10, pp. 501–4.

493. As has been pointed out, this point deals primarily with visits from prophets and saints and from the Prophet Muḥammad in particular; the imams can also see and make visible their deceased enemies; cf. the case of the Umayyad caliph Mu'âwiya, who was seen by the fifth and sixth imams and their disciples wandering around in the form of a thirsty man in chains, *Baṣâ'ir*, section 6, ch. 7, pp. 284–86.

493bis. *Baṣâ'ir*, section 10, ch. 15, pp. 494–95.

494. *Baṣâ'ir*, section 6, ch. 3–4, pp. 269–74.

495. *Baṣâ'ir*, *ibid*., pp. 270–71, num 4–6. On Abû Baṣîr, cf. note 182 (note that one of the three disciples of Ja'far with this *kunya* was blind, *al-makfûf*.; cf. *ibid*., p. 272: the imam momentarily restored his sight, but he took it away again so that his miraculous power would not be known).

496. *Baṣâ'ir*, section 8, ch. 12, pp. 397–401.

497. On ornithomancy and divinatory knowledge of the earth (*qiyâfat al-athar*) among the Arabs, see T. Fahd, *La Divination arabe*, pp. 403f and 432f. The use of the words *'ilm* and *'ulamâ'* in this context confirms once again the translations we have proposed throughout this study: *'ilm*/Initiatory Knowledge, *'âlim*, pl. *'ulamâ'*/initiated Sage (in the early Imamite context, of course).

498. The opposition of night/day in the respective remarks of the Yemenite and the sixth imam do not appear anodine; are we to understand that the magic practiced by the Yemenites is presented as "black magic," while that practiced by the imams is "white magic"?

499. *Baṣâ'ir*, *ibid*., p. 401, num. 14 and 15.

500. *Baṣâ'ir*, section 8, ch. 13, pp. 402–7.

501. *Baṣâ'ir*, section 8, ch. 15, p. 409. Ibn Qûlûye al-Qummî, *Kâmil al-ziyârât*, pp. 71–72.

502. 'Alî al-Riḍâ: "We [the imams] are equal in Knowledge and in courage, but in [supernatural] gifts it depends upon what commandments we have received [*Naḥnu fî l-'ilm wa l-shajâ'a sawâ' wa fî l-'aṭâyâ 'alä qadri mâ nu'maru bihi*]"; *Baṣâ'ir*, section 10, ch. 8, p. 480, num. 3. Ja'far: "Some imams have more [thaumaturgic] Knowledge than others [*al-a'imma ba'ḍuhum a'lam min ba'd*]"; *Baṣâ'ir*, section 10, ch. 8, p. 479, num. 2. For another view of this last tradition, see E. Kohlberg, "Imam and Community . . . ," p. 30.

503. Dhû l-qarnayn (Qur'ân 18:83-98) was especially known among the Semites as a symbol of Power, both on the temporal plane and on the spiritual plane; his legend is identified with that of Alexander the Macedonian, preserved in the Syriac version of pseudo-Callisthenes and Jacques de Sarouj (cf. A. W. Budge, *The History of Alexander the Great, being the Syrian Version of the Pseudo-Calisthenes*, Cambridge, 1889; M.S. Southgate, "Alexander in the works of Persian and Arab Historians of the Islamic area" in *Iskandarnamah, a Persian Medieval Alexander Romance*, English trans. by M. S. Southgate, New York, 1978; Ch. H. de Fouchécour, *Moralia*, part 4.1.0, pp. 69–73); the themes of the trip to the West and the East, to the Fountain of Life located in the center of the Darkness, of marvelous accounts and magical practices, all themes common to accounts of initiatory travels are present in the work.

504. Ideas also professed by the "extremists" Sabâ'iyya and Bayâniyya; cf. Shahrastânî, *Livre des religions*, p. 510, and note 18 (by D. Gimaret) from the same page.

505. *Baṣâ'ir*, section 9, ch. 1, pp. 419–23.

506. *Baṣâ'ir*, p. 421, num. 10. Cf. also all of Part II-3, on "vision with the heart."

507. *Baṣâ'ir*, p. 422; the disciple who asks the question is Khâlid b. Nujayḥ al-Kûfî, who also knew the teachings of the seventh imam, Mûsä al-Kâẓim; on him, see al-Najâshî, *Rijâl*, s.v.; al-Ṭûsî, *Rijâl*, p. 186, num. 7 and p. 349, num. 1; al-Tafrishî, *Naqd al-rijâl*, s.v.; al-Astarâbâdî, "Ṣâḥib rijâl," *Manhaj al-maqâl* (or *Rijâl kabîr*),s.v.; al-Ardabîlî, *Jâmi' al-ruwât*, vol. 1, p. 293.

508. The tradition remains equivocal, and appears to have a double purpose. The first is to prove that the Prophet had recourse to a certain kind of magic (theurgic magic, from the Imamite point of view) since he approves of Abû Bakr's words. The second is implicitly to accuse Abû Bakr of a lack of respect toward the Prophet, since the idea of *siḥr* (in the sense of goetic magic) was nevertheless condemned by the Qur'ân.

509. Ibn Bâbûye, *Kamâl al-dîn*, ch. 49, ḥadîth Ḥubâbat al-wâlibiyya, vol. 2, pp. 536–37.

510. Al-Nu'mânî, *Kitâb al-ghayba*, ch. 4, pp. 129–31, num. 18; it is said that the imam then picked one of the dates of the miraculously produced tree, that he cut it in two, and took from it a fine white scale upon which were inscribed two lines: the first was: "There is no god but God, and Muhammad is the Prophet of God [*lâ ilâha illâ Allâh/Muḥammad rasûl Allâh*; note that in Arabic, each of these two phrases contains twelve letters]; and the second is "With God and in God's Book, the day of the creation of the heavens and the earth, the months are twelve, of which four are sacred [*Inna 'id-dat al-shuhûr 'inda'llâh ithnâ 'ashara shahran fî kitâbi'llâh yawma khalq al-samâwât wa l-arḍ minhâ arba'a ḥurum*] [*sic*]; here is the Solid Religion: The Prince of Believers 'Alî b. Abî Ṭâlib, al-Ḥasan b. 'Alî, al-Ḥusayn b. 'Alî [enumeration of the twelve imams] [*al-dîn al-qayyim amîr al-mu'minîn 'Alî . . .*]" [*sic*]. Finally, Ja'far states that these inscriptions were written on the scale 2000 years before the creation of Adam.

511. Ibn Bâbûye, *Amâlî*, "majlis" 29, pp. 148–49, num. 19; Ibn Bâbûye, *'Uyûn*, vol. 1, ch. 8, pp. 95–96, num. 1.

512. Mu'allä b. Khunays Abû 'AbdAllâh al-Madanî al-Kûfî, a "client" (*mawlä*) and disciple of the sixth imam; for a while, he followed the "extremist" al-Mughîra b. Sa'^d (see note 478); cf. al-Najâshî, *Rijâl*, s.v.; al-Ṭûsî, *Rijâl*, p. 310, num. 497; al-Mâmaqânî, *Tanqîḥ al-maqâl*, s.v.

513. Al-Kulaynî, *al-Rawḍa*, vol. 2, p. 166.

514. *"Inna aṣl al-ḥisâb ḥaqq walâkin lâ ya'lamu dhâlika illâ man 'alima mawâlid al-khalq kullahum,"* al-Kulaynî, *al-Rawḍa*, vol. 2, pp. 196–97.

515. Al-Kulaynî, *al-Rawḍa*, vol. 2, p. 167.

516. 'Abd al-Raḥmân b. Siyâba al-Kûfî al-Bajalî al-Bazzâz, "client" and disciple of the sixth imam; cf. al-Ṭûsî, *Rijâl*, p. 230, num. 120; al-Ardabîlî, *Jâmi' al-ruwât*, vol. 1, p. 451.

517. As is the case for all ancient or traditional astrology, Imamite astrology combines "scientific" and "mythic" elements.

518. Al-Kulaynî, *al-Rawḍa*, vol. 1, pp. 279–80. On the favorable attitude of early

Imamism toward astrology, see Ibn Ṭâwûs, *Faraj al-mahmûm fî ta'rîkh 'ulama' al-nujûm*, Najaf, 1368/1949.

519. Cf. Qur'ân 6:97: "It is He who, on your behalf, has set the stars so that you can, with their help, guide yourselves through the darkness of land and sea, We set signs for those who know."

520. *"Ayyuhâ l-nâs iyyâkum wa ta'allum al—nujûm illâ mâ yuhtadä bihi fî barr aw baḥr fa-innahâ tad'û ilä l-kahâna wa l-munajjim ka l-kâhin wa l-kâhin ka l-sâḥir wa l-sâḥir ka l-kâfir wa l-kâfir fî l-nâr sîrû 'alä ismi'llâh," Nahj al-balâgha*, p. 177 (let us remember once again that this work, compiled by al-sharîf al-Raḍî, belongs to the "rational-theological-juridical" tradition).

521. *"Lâ ṭayr illâ ṭayruka lâ ḍayr illâ ḍayruka lâ khayr illâ khayruka wa lâ ilâh ghayruka,"* Ibn Bâbûye, *Amâlî*, "majlis" 64, p. 416, num. 16 *in fine*. Al-sharîf al-Raḍî, who reports the tradition, censures the last phrase where a "sacred divination" is witnessed by the imam; cf. *Nahj al-balâgha*, p. 177.

522. The essential role of the imams' teaching in outlining the Muslim occult sciences, although insufficiently explored, is nevertheless undeniable. Almost all of the treatises of *Jafr* (the Islamic "kabbala") are ascribed to Ja'far al-Ṣâdiq (cf. Brockelmann, *GAL*, s.v. F. Sezgin, *GAS*, vol. 4, s.v.; on this subject, see P. Lory, "La science des lettres en terre d'Islam: le chiffre, la lettre, l'Oeuvre"); see also the studies cited in note 472; for alchemy, cf. the works and studies already cited, by P. Kraus, E. J. Holmyard, and P. Lory (cf. bibliography).

NOTES TO CHAPTER 4

523. *"Yamût man mâta minnâ wa laysa bi-mayyit," Baṣâ'ir*, section 6, ch. 5, p. 275, num. 4 (note 367).

524. *Baṣâ'ir*, section 8, ch. 13, pp. 405–6, num. 5 (note 500).

525. *Baṣâ'ir*, section 9, ch. 4–5, pp. 424–28; these traditions are presented as the spiritual interpretation (*ta'wîl*) of the Qur'ânic verse: "Act! God will see your acts, as well as his messenger and the Believers [*I'malû fa-sayarä 'llâhu 'amalakum wa rasûluhu wa l-mu'minûn*; Qur'ân 9:105]"; the "Believers" in the verse refer in fact to the imams.

526. Among monographs we cite the following: G. Van Vloten, *Recherches sur la domination arabe, le chiitisme et les croyances messianiques sous le khalifat des Omeyyades*, Amsterdam, 1894; E. Moeller, *Beiträge zur Mahdilehre des Islam*, Heidelberg, 1901; I. Friedlander, *Die Messiasidee im Islam*, Frankfurt, 1903, especially pp. 116f.; MacDonald-Madelung, "Mahdî," *EI2*; A. Abel, "Changements politiques et littérature eschatologique dans le monde musulman," *SI*, vol. 2, 1954; H. Corbin, *En Islam iranien*, all of book 7, vol. 4, pp. 301–460; A. A. Sachedina, *Islamic Messianism: The Idea of the Madhi in Twelver Shi'ism*, Albany, 1981; Jassim M. Hussain, *The Occultation of the Twelfth Imam. A Historical Background*, London, 1982; J. O. Blichfeldt, *Early Mahdism. Politics and Religion in the Formative Period of Islam*, Leiden, 1985; we will have occasion to present other studies in the course of the present chapter.

527. Only Corbin has heretofore attempted to explore the esotericism of the Occultation, although his approach remains essentially philosophical, and thus leads his information away from the early corpus of the imams. Always coherent and faithful to his own methodology, Corbin attempts to elucidate points of early Shî'ite doctrine

through the interpretations of the Ismâʼîli or Imamite philosophers, all of whom wrote at a later period. Corbin also relies on gnosticism, on Christian chivalry, or on the western mystics and philosophers. His procedure is, to use his term, "meta-historical," perhaps even meta-cultural (cf. e.g., *En Islam iranien, ibid.*; "Sur le douzième imam," *Table Ronde*, Feb. 1957, pp. 7–21; "L'imam caché et la rénovation de l'homme en théologie shîʿite," *Eranos Jahrbuch*, vol. 28, 1959, Zurich, 1960, pp. 47–108; "Au «Pays» de l'imam caché," *Eranos Jahrbuch*, vol. 32, 1963, Zurich, 1964, pp. 31–87). In the early corpus of the imams, philosophical ideas strictly speaking are found only in undeveloped form; the thought is profoundly religious, the terminology is archaic, pre-philosophical, and the conceptualization is only latent. On the other hand, a spiritual, occult, and magic esotericism is ubiquitous, in actions everywhere. In this domain, we believe that this chapter restores historical esoteric foundations to the points studied by Corbin.

528 Cf. e.g., Md al-Ṣadr, *Taʿrîkh al-ghaybat al-ṣughrä*, vol. 1, Beirut, 1972, and *Taʿrîkh al-ghaybat al-kubrä*, vol. 2, Beirut, 1975; M. Momen, *An Introduction to Shîʿî Islam*, chapter 8; H. Halm, *Die Schia*, chapter 4.

529. See, e.g., L. Massignon, *Passion*, vol. 1, pp. 344f.; W. M. Watt, "The Rafîḍites: A Preliminary Study," *Oriens*, vol. 16, 1963, pp. 119f.; E. Kohlberg, "From Imâmiyya to Ithnâʿashariyya," *BSOAS*, 39, 3, 1976, pp. 521–34.

530. A. A. Sachedina lists up to thirteen different variations among the Shîʿites; cf. his *Islamic Messianism*, pp. 42–55; see also J. M. Hussain, *The Occultation*, pp. 56–67. On these different Shîʿite sects, see al-Nawbakhtî, *Kitâb firaq al-shîʿa*, ed. H. Ritter, pp. 90f.; French translation by M. J. Mashkûr (Mashkour), *Les Sectes shiites*, pp. 109f.; Saʿd b. ʿAbd Allâh al-Qummî, *Kitâb al-maqâlât wa l-firaq*, ed. M. J. Mashkûr, pp. 102f. (On the differences between these two Imamite heresiographical sources, see W. Madelung, "Bemerkungen zur imamitischen Firaq-Literatur," *Religious Schools*, Part 15, pp. 37–52); Shahrastânî, *Livre des religions*, pp. 500f.

531. Al-Ashʿarî, *Maqâlât al-islâmiyyin*, ed. H. Ritter, pp. 17f., 30f., 64.

532. Ascribing the *Uṣûl al-niḥal* (a title coined by Van Ess; cf. the following note) to al-Nâshiʾ al-Akbar has been seriously contested, with convincing reasons, by W. Madelung, "Frühe muʿtazilitische Häresiographie: das *Kitâb al-Uṣûl* des Gaʿfar b. Harb," in *Religious Schools*, Part 6, pp. 220–36.

533. Cf. J. Van Ess, *Frühe muʾtazilische Häresiographie*, Beirut, 1971, pp. 28f.

534. ʿAbd al-Qâhir al-Baghdâdî, *al-Farq*, pp. 17 and 39; see also Shahrastânî, *Livre des religions*, p. 497, D. Gimaret's note 116 according to which al-Shahrastânî (d. 548/1153) is the first to "officialize" this name in heresiographical literature.

535. Cf. particularly I. Friedlander, "The heterodoxies of the Shiites in the Presentation of Ibn Ḥazm," *JAOS*, vol. 29, 1908, pp. 150f.; E. Kohlberg, "From Imâmiyya to Ithnâ-ʿashariyya," pp. 521–22.

536. On these authors and sources, see Part I-3. Among the first authors belonging to the "theological-juridical-rational" tradition that came later, let us cite al-shaykh al-Mufîd (d. 413/1022), *al-Irshâd* (e.g., ed. Rasûlî Maḥallâtî, Tehran, 1346 solar/1968); id., *al-Fuṣûl al-ʿashara fî l-ghayba*, Najaf, 1371/1951; al-Murtaḍä ʿAlam al-Hudä, 436/1044, a disciple of al-Mufîd), *Masʾala wajîza fî l-ghayba*, Baghdad, 1955; Md b. ʿAlî al-Karâjakî (d. 449/1057, another of al-Mufîd's disciples), *al-Burhân ʿalä Ṣiḥḥa ṭûl ʿumr Ṣâḥib al-zamân*, Tabriz, n.d. (edited with the *Kanz al-fawâʾid*, by the same author), and finally Md b. al-Ḥasan al-Ṭûsî (d. 460/1067), *Kitâb al-ghayba*,

Tabriz, 1322/1904. These sources say nothing about a number of the hidden imam's esoteric and occult characteristics; we shall use them only as backup sources, and then only when the information they provide is corroborated by sources from the early "esoteric nonrational" tradition.

537. Abû Ja'far al-Barqî, *Kitâb al-maḥâsin*, ed. J. al-Ḥusaynî al-Muḥaddith, Tehran, 1370/1950; in the first chapter of the book entitled "kitâb al-ashkâl wa l-qarâ'in," the author reports traditions concerning the different meanings of numbers; he goes from the numbers 3 to 10, reporting nothing about the number 12. It is true that the book is more like a work of *adab* than a doctrinal treatise. A few decades later, Ibn Bâbûye reported, in his *Kitâb al-Khiṣâl,* a number of traditions about the number 12, among which are traditions about the twelve imams (cf. *al-Khiṣâl*, vol. 2, pp. 264–329). On al-Barqî, see F. Sezgin, *GAS*, vol. 1, p. 538, num. 28. The case of al-Ṣaffâr is both more complex and more disturbing, for in five places in his compilation he says that there were twelve imams, and thus that the Mahdî was the twelfth (cf. *Baṣâ'ir*, section 6, ch. 5, p. 280, num. 15; section 7, ch. 1, pp. 319–20, nums. 2, 4, 5; section 8, ch. 1, p. 372, num. 16). These traditions are all nested within chapters whose titles, at least, have no relationship to these details; this is perhaps why E. Kohlberg did not notice them, since he affirms that al-Ṣaffâr said nothing about the number of imams (cf. "From Imâmiyya to Ithnâ 'ashariyya," pp. 522–23); the "tactic" of "dispersion of information" (*tabdîd al-'ilm*) seems thus to be efficient; but as the Israeli scholar points out, al-Ṣaffâr appears to have transmitted nothing about the idea of *ghayba*. Moreover, it is true that the fact of his only having reported five traditions about the subject, out of the 1881 that make up the *Baṣâ'ir,* is tantamount to an almost total silence. [See now my article, "al-Ṣaffâr al-Qummî . . . ," *JA*.]

538. Al-Najâshî, *Rijâl*, pp. 12, 19; al-Ṭûsî, *Fihrist*, p. 14; Ibn Dâwûd al-Ḥillî, *Kitâb al-rijâl* (ed. Tehran, 1964), pp. 15, 416.

539. Al-Najâshî, *Rijâl*, p. 193; al-Ṭûsî, *Fihrist*, pp. 216–17.

540. Al-Najâshî, *Rijâl*, p. 39.

541. Aqâ Buzurg al-Tihrânî, *al-Dharî'a*, vol. 16, p. 76, num. 382; on his father, see al-Kashshî, *Rijâl*, pp. 288–89.

542. *Al-Uṣûl al-arba'umi'a*, ms. University of Tehran, num. 962, fol. 10a f.

543. Aqâ Buzurg, *al-Dharî'a*, vol. 21, p. 69, num. 3995; we could have mentioned Sulaym b. Qays al-Hilâlî, a companion of the first imam who, according to al-Nu'mânî, listed the twleve imams in his *Kitâb*; and where the last of the imams is the Mahdî (cf. al-Nu'mânî, *Kitâb al-ghayba*, p. 62); but the authenticity of this *Kitâb* has been questioned by the Imamites themselves (al-'Allâma al-Ḥillî, *Khulâṣa*, p. 53). Fragments of a *Kitâb Sulaym b. Qays* were published in Najaf, n.d.

544. "Kitâb Md b. al-Muthannä," in *al-Uṣûl al-arba'umi'a*, fol. 53b (perhaps an Ismâ'îli tradition?).

545. Al-Najashî, *Rijâl*, p. 191; al-Ṭûsî, *Fihrist*, p. 226.

546. Al-Najashî, *Rijâl*, pp. 235-36; Aqâ Buzurg al-Tihrânî, *al-Dharî'a*, vol. 16, p. 78, num. 395; according to Golpâyegânî, al-Faḍl b. Shâdhân essentially used the *Mashyakha* written by al-Ḥasan b. Maḥbûb al-Sarrâd (Ṣâfî Golpâyegânî, *Muntakhab al-athar*, p. 481).

547. Aqâ Buzurg, *al-Dharî'a*, vol. 16, p. 74, num. 371.

548. Al-Ṭûsî, *Kitâb al-ghayba*, pp. 112–21; on 'Alî b. Aḥmad al-'Alawî and his

work, see al-Kashshî, *Rijâl* (ed. Mashhad), pp. 296, 468–69, 555; al-Najâshî, *Rijâl*, pp. 29, 31, 53, 86, 106, 150, 199.

549. Ibn Bâbûye, *Kamâl al-dîn*, vol. 2, pp. 352–57 and 417–23; al-Ṭûsî, *Kitâb al-ghayba*, pp. 104–8 and 124–28; two other treatises by al-Ruhnî may be found in Ibn Bâbûye's works: *Tafḍîl al-anbiyâ' wa l-a'imma ʿalä l-malâ'ika* in *ʿIlal*, vol. 1, pp. 20–27, and *al-Furûq bayna l-abâṭîl wa l-ḥuqûq*, in *ʿIlal*, pp. 211–20; al-Ruhnî was considered an "extremist Shîʿite" by his own disciple, al-Kashshî, as well as by al-Ṭûsî and Ibn Dâwûd al-Ḥillî; al-Najâshî finds this accusation to be unfounded. On al-Ruhnî, see note 187 (add to the sources already mentioned Ibn Bâbûye, *Kitâb al-faqîh*, vol. 1, pp. 61–62; al-ʿAllâma al-Ḥillî, *Khulâṣa*, p. 252).

550. Al-Kulaynî, *Uṣûl*, "kitâb al-ḥujja," bâb anna l-a'imma kulluhum qâ'imûn bi amr Allâh, vol. 2, pp. 486–87; Ibn Bâbûye, *Kamâl al-dîn*, vol. 1, ch. 23, p. 251, num. 1; Ibn Bâbûye, *ʿIlal*, vol. 1, ch. 129, p. 160, num. 1; On the two principal meanings given by the imams for *qâ'im*, that is, "Resurrector" (related to the term *al-qiyâma*, the Resurrection) and "he who rises up," "he who stands up" (related to the term *al-qiyâm*, the uprising), see, e.g., J. M. Hussain, *The Occultation*, pp. 12–19.

551. *"Man takhfä ʿalä l-nâs wilâdatuhu/man ghuyyibat ʿan al-nâs wilâdatuhu,"* al-Nuʿmânî, *Kitâb al-ghayba*, ch. 10, p. 244, num. 7; Ibn Bâbûye, *Kamâl al-dîn*, vol. 1, ch. 32, p. 325, num. 2.

552. Ibn Bâbûye, *Kamâl al-dîn*, vol. 1, pp. 424–30, nums. 1 and 2; Ibn ʿAyyâsh, *Muqtaḍab*, pp. 50–58; we shall return to this account when we deal with the miraculous birth of the hidden imam.

553. Ibn Bâbûye, *Kamâl al-dîn*, vol. 1, ch. 42, p. 435; also, al-Ṭûsî, *Kitâb al-ghayba*, pp. 148–52. Sources suggest a number of dates for the birth of the twelfth imam: 255/869, 256/870, 258/871–72, and 261/874 (in the latter case, a few months after the death of his father). The date classically considered to be correct is 15 Shaʿbân 256. His first Occultation took place upon the death of his father in 260/874; at that time he would have been four or five years old.

554. Ibn Bâbûye, *Kamâl al-dîn*, vol. 1, pp. 474f.; *Ithbât al-waṣiyya*, p. 262f.; al-Ṭabarî, *Ta'rîkh*, vol. 3, pp. 1428, 1684, 1787, 1790–92, 1891, 1907; al-Mufîd, *al-Fuṣûl al-ʿashara*, pp. 13f.; Ibn Rustam al-Ṭabarî [al-shîʿî], *Dalâ'il al-imâma*, pp. 223f.; Ibn Shahrâshûb, *Manâqib*, vol. 3, p. 553 and vol. 4, p. 421f.; al-Majlisî, *Biḥâr*, vol. 50, pp. 236–38 and 355f.

555. E.g., Ibn Bâbûye, *Kitâb al-faqîh*, vol. 4, pp. 196–98; al-Mufîd, *al-Muqniʿa fî l-fiqh*, pp. 47, 58.

556. Most Shîʿites knew nothing of the twelfth imam. According to the heresiographers there were, after the death of the eleventh imam, some eleven to fifteen different schisms among his partisans. These sects can be grouped into four great families. The first were those who believed that the Imamate had come to an end. One of these subgroups did not believe in the existence of a Mahdî, and professed that al-ʿAskarî had died without having left a descendent, thus causing the end of the Imamate. Another subsect within this group likewise believed that the eleventh imam's death had occurred without his having left a son, but professed at the same time that at the End of Time one of the imams would be brought back to accomplish the mission of the expected Mahdî; it should be noted here that the word *al-qâ'im* means not "the resurrector" but "the resurrected." A second family was the Jaʿfariyya, partisans of Jaʿfar's

Imamate, Ja'far being one of the brothers of the eleventh imam; he was later called "Ja'far the liar" by the Imamites (*al-kadhdhâb*). For the sects of the Ja'fariyya, since the eleventh imam did not have a son known by all, the Imamate should devolve upon his brother. The third was the Muḥammadiyya, consisting of partisans of another of al-'Askarî's brothers, Md b. 'Alî; he was an older brother who died before his father, but his partisans believed in his Occultation and proclaimed his Return as Mahdî. The fourth was the Wâqifa of al-Ḥasan al-'Askarî, for whom the eleventh imam was the Mahdî who went into Occultation without leaving a son (cf. al-Nawbakhtî, *Firaq al-shî'a*, pp. 90f.; al-Qummî, *al-Maqâlât wa l-firaq*, pp. 102f., al-Mas'ûdî, *Murûj*, vol. 8, pp. 50f.; al-Mufîd, *al-Fuṣûl al-mukhtâra*, pp. 258–60; al-Shahrastânî, *Milal*, trans. Gimaret and Monnot, pp. 500–3). For further details on these sects, see A. A. Sachedina, *Islamic Messianism*, pp. 42f.; Jassim M. Hussain, *The Occultation*, pp. 56f.

557. This is one of nine sects that may also qualify as Qaṭ'iyya, as they categorically professed the death of the eleventh imam (cf. the same sources in the preceding note). After the beginning of the major Occultation (around 329/941) and the loss of contact with the hidden imam, this minority began, in turn, to ask questions. It is what is called the period of "perplexity" (*al-ḥayra*); if the belief in the existence of the son of the eleventh imam as the hidden imam and the expected Mahdî has ended up being an article of faith for Imamites, it is essentially due to the tenacious efforts of authors/compilers like al-Kulaynî, al-Nu'mânî, and especially Ibn Bâbûye, who, through the great mass of traditions that concern this belief, progressively managed to convince the mass of faithful. Let us remember that the complete title of Ibn Bâbûye's voluminous "monograph" is *Kamâl (Ikmâl) al-dîn wa tamâm (itmâm) al-ni'ma fî ithbât al-ghayba wa kashf al-ḥayra* (loosly translated as "The Perfection of Religion and the Performance of Good Works Through the Demonstration of the Occultation and the Effacing of Perplexity").

558. Cf. al-Kulaynî, *Uṣûl*, "kitâb al-ḥujja," bâb fî l-nahy 'an al-ism, vol. 2, pp. 126f.; al-Nu'mânî, *Kitâb al-ghayba*, ch. 16, pp. 313f.; Ibn Bâbûye, *Kamâl al-dîn*, vol. 1, ch. 33, pp. 333f.; vol. 2, ch. 35, pp. 370; ch. 56, 648.

559. *"Ṣâḥib hâdhâ l-amr lâ yusammîhi bi'smih illâ kâfir,"* al-Kulaynî, *Uṣûl*, vol. 2, p. 126, num. 3; Ibn Bâbûye, *Kamâl al-dîn*, vol. 2, p. 648, num. 1.

560. *"Lâ yurä jismuhu wa lâ yusammä bi'smihi,"* Ibn Bâbûye, *op. cit.*, num. 2.

561. Al-Kulaynî, *op. cit.*, num. 1; Ibn Bâbûye, *op. cit.*, num. 4; on Dâwûd b. Isḥâq (or b. Qâsim) b. 'AbdAllâh Abû Hâshim al-Ja'farî, a close disciple and confidant of the eighth, ninth, tenth, and eleventh imams, and one of the rare individuals who was able to see the hidden imam before his Occultation, see al-Najâshî, *Rijâl*, s.v.; al-Ṭûsî, *Rijâl*, pp. 401, 414, 431; al-Ṭûsî, *Fihrist*, p. 93, num. 278; al-'Allâma al-Ḥillî, *Khulâṣa*, s.v.

562. *"In dalaltuhum 'alä l-ism adhâ'ûhu wa in 'arafû l-makân dallû 'alayhi,"* al-Kulaynî, *op. cit.*, num. 2.

653. E.g., al-Kulaynî, *Uṣûl*, "kitâb al-ḥujja," bâb al-ishâra wa l-naṣṣ ilä ṣâḥib al-dâr ("the Lord of the House," one of the appellations of the hidden imam), vol. 2, p. 119, num. 5; al-Kulaynî, *al-Rawḍa*, vol. 1, p. 102; vol. 2, p. 76; Ibn Bâbûye, *Kamâl al-dîn*, vol. 2., ch. 42, p. 430, num. 3; ch. 43, p. 446, num. 19; Ibn Qûlûye, *Kâmil al-ziyârât*, pp. 89–90.

564. Al-Nu'mânî, *Kitâb al-ghayba*, ch. 10, p. 217, num. 9.

565. "Damned, damned be he who pronounces my name in public" (*Mal'ûn mal'ûn man sammânî fî maḥfil al-nâs," "al-nâs,"* the public, the masses, the people, is

one of the terms used to refer to the uninitiated, the exotericists), Ibn Bâbûye, *Kamâl al-dîn*, vol. 2, ch. 45, p. 482, num. 1.

566. The first text of certain authenticity that we presently possess where the names of the twelve imams are listed is the *Tafsîr* written by ʿAlî b. Ibrâhîm al-Qummî (d. 307/919). It was composed a few years after the beginning of the minor Occultation; cf. al-Qummî, *Tafsîr*, vol. 2, pp. 44f.; Jassim M. Hussain (*The Occultation*, p. 5) also cites as books composed during the period of the minor Occultation al-Nahâwandi's (d. 268/899) *Kitâb al-ghayba*, *Al-ghayba wa l-ḥayra* by ʿAbdAllâh b. Jaʿfar al-Ḥimyarî (d. after 293/905), and *Al-imâma wa l-tabṣira min al-ḥayra*, by Ibn Bâbûye (d. 329/940, the father of our frequently cited shaykh al-Ṣadûq Ibn Bâbûye). The latter text was recently published in Qumm, 1404 A.H. The other texts appear to have been lost. Al-Kulaynî composed his works during the same period, but later than ʿAlî b. Ibrâhîm al-Qummî.

567. *Muqtaḍab*, p. 9; on the two kinds of Knowledge, the "lavished" and the "hidden," see al-Ṣaffâr, *Baṣâ'ir*, section 2, ch. 21, pp. 109–12; al-Kulaynî, *Uṣûl*, vol. 1, pp. 375–76.

568. Imamite authors essentially founded their arguments on four scriptural sources: the Qur'an, Shîʿite tradition, Sunni tradition (when it is corroborated by the preceding, of course), and finally Biblical tradition (cf. E. Kohlberg's erudite expose "From imâmiyya to ithnâ ʿashariyya," pp. 525–28). The contributing Shîʿite traditions are those of the "twelve silhouettes of pre-existential light" and the "twelve lights of the imams" seen by the Prophet during his ascensions into heaven; those of "the emerald tablet of Fâṭima" recopied by Jâbir b. ʿAbdAllâh al-Anṣârî; those of the "twelve sealed Books" of the imams or the Waṣiyya of the Prophet, "the celestial Book containing Twelve Seals"; Jaʿfar's tradition of the "date seed," the seed upon which were written the names of the twelve imams. We have already had occasion to examine all these traditions in detail; let us just add Ghadîr Khumm's tradition where the Prophet, after designating ʿAlî as his successor and stating the Imamic status of both al-Ḥasan and al-Ḥusayn, announces that the Imamate will come also to the nine descendents of al-Ḥusayn (al-Nuʿmânî, *Kitâb al-ghayba*, pp. 59f.; on Ghadîr Khumm, see L. Vecchia Vaglieri's excellent article in *EI2*; ʿA. A. al-Amînî, al-*Ghadîr fî l-kitâb wa l-sunna wa l-adab*, Tehran, 1372/1952, an exclusively Imamite but well documented version).

569. *"Yakûnu ba'dî ithnâ ʿashara khalîfa kulluhum min Quraysh,"* cf. A. J. Wensinck, *Concordances*, s.v. "thny"; cf. also Ibn Ṭâwûs, *al-Malâḥim wa l-fitan* (Najaf, 1383/1963, pp. 26 and 147), who reports the hadith citing the *Kitâb al-fitan* by Nuʿaym b. Ḥammâd (d. 228/844). Evidently, each political group subsequently tries to interpret the saying in support of its own camp. The Sunni tradition has essentially retained two lines of interpretation: one pro-Umayyad line, and another, anti-Umayyad (for the first, cf., e.g., al-Qaṣtallânî, *Irshâd al-sârî*, vol. 10, p. 273, where the author seems to identify the twelve vicars of the tradition with the four first "rightly guided" caliphs and the Umayyads Muʿâwiya, Yâzid b. Muʿâwiya, ʿAbd al-Malik and his four successors, and ʿUmar b. ʿAbd al-ʿAzîz. For the second [pro-Qurayshite ? pro-Abbasid?] line, see, e.g., al-Faḍl b. Rûzbihân al-Ashʿarî and his list: the five [*sic*] "rightly guided" caliphs [the author seems to also include in this group al-Ḥasan b. ʿAlî], ʿAbdAllâh b. Zubayr, ʿUmar b. ʿAbd al-ʿAzîz, and five Abbasid caliphs; cited by ʿAlî al-Muẓaffar, *Dalâ'il al-ṣidq*, Najaf, 1372/1953, pp. 314f.).

570. Cf. especially F. Rosenthal, "The Influence of the Biblical Tradition on

Muslim Historiography"; R. Na'nâ'a, *al-Isrâ'îliyyât wa atharuhâ fî kutub al-tafsîr*; M. J. Kister, "Ḥaddithû 'an banî isrâ'îla wa lâ ḥaraja" (in English), *IOS*, vol. 2, 1972.

571. Al-Nu'mânî, *Kitâb al-ghayba*, ch. 4, pp. 126f., ch. 6, 168f.; Ibn Bâbûye, *Amâlî*, "majlis" 51, p. 309, nums. 4,5; "majlis" 91, p. 629, num. 10; Ibn Bâbûye, *Kamâl al-dîn*, vol. 1, ch. 32, p. 326; Ibn Bâbûye, *Khiṣâl*, the chapter on the number 12, vol. 2, pp. 264f.

572. Al-Nu'mânî, *Kitâb al-ghayba*, ch. 4, pp. 126f.; Ibn Bâbûye, *Kamâl al-dîn*, ch. 24, pp. 259–60, num. 5; Ibn Bâbûye, *Khiṣâl*, vol. 2, pp. 314–24 (here, according to a series of traditions, the universe is composed of twelve Worlds and twelve Oceans).

573. T. Fahd, "Djafr," *EI2*, vol. 2, pp. 386-88; T. Fahd, "Ḥurûf," *EI2*, vol. 3, pp. 616–17. See also, e.g., al-Barqî, *Kitâb al-maḥâsin*, vol. 1, p. 270, num. 360; Ibn Bâbûye, *Ma'ânî al-akhbâr*, pp. 285–86.

574. These three phrases, in particular the first, are those most frequently used in Imamite *dhikr*. The imams ask their faithful to repeat them as often as possible, and explain at length the virtues and rewards that such repetitions will bring; cf. al-Kulaynî, *Uṣûl*, "kitâb al-du'â'," chapters 23, 24, 28, 35–44.

575. The Ismâ'îlîs use a similar procedure of calculation that makes the number 7 sacred; cf. Shahrastânî, *Livre des Religions*, p. 559, and the corresponding notes by D. Gimaret.

576. This is the counting method used "to the East" of the Muslim world; the Shî'ites, who are most probably responsible for the introduction of this "science" in Islam have always used this method of numbering (cf. *Rasâ'il ikhwan al-ṣafâ*, ed. Beirut, 1957, vol. 1, pp. 51f.; P. Kraus, *Jâbir b. Ḥayyân*, p. 224). For the numbering system that is referred to as "Western" (used in North Africa and the Maghreb), see Ibn Khaldûn, *al-Muqaddima*, ed. Quatremère, vol. 1, pp. 211f. Ibn Khaldûn seems to be the first to apply the term *sîmiyâ'*, usually reserved for "white magic," to the gematric science of letters in the Arabic alphabet (*Muqaddima*, vol. 3, pp. 137f.). On these two procedures in general, see F. Rosenthal, *The Muqaddimah*, New York, 1958, vol. 3, p. 173, note 809; T. Fahd, "Ḥurûf," *EI2*.

577. This method of arithmomantic calculation is explained by shaykh Abû l-Mu'ayyad Gujarâtî (tenth/sixteenth century) in his *al-Jawâhir al-khamsa* (India, city of publication unknown), 1301/1883, pp. 126–27 (in Persian; the volume that we were able to consult has Gujarâtî's name, although the work is traditionally attributed to Muhammad Ghawth Guwâlyârî, the famous Indian sufi of the Shaṭṭariyya order who died in 970/1562; on him, see A. M. Schimmel, *Islam in the Indian Subcontinent*, Leiden, 1980, pp. 78–79 and 123.). The author claims that the chain of transmission for the science of letters goes back to Ja'far al-Ṣâdiq and his ancestors (i.e., the preceding imams).

578. Al-Kulaynî, *Uṣûl*, "kitâb al-ḥujja," bâb mâ jâ'a fî l-ithnâ 'ashar, vol. 2, pp. 468–85; al-Nu'mânî, *Kitâb al-ghayba*, ch. 10, pp. 201–81; Ibn Bâbûye, *Kamâl al-dîn*, ch. 24–38, pp. 256–385; see also, e.g., Ibn Bâbûye, *'Ilal*, chapter 122; *Nahj al-balâgha*, pp. 295, 424–25, 458, 1158, 1180, 1222.

579. Ibn Bâbûye, *Kamâl*, ch. 42, p. 432, num. 12; *Ithbât al-waṣiyya*, p. 248; al-Mufîd, *Irshâd*, vol. 2, p. 323; al-Ṭûsî, *Kitâb al-ghayba*, pp. 151f.; al-Majlisî, *Biḥâr al-anwâr*, vol. 51, p. 28.

580. Al-Kulaynî, *Uṣûl*, vol. 2, p. 432; al-Nu'mânî, *Kitâb al-ghayba*, ch. 13, pp. 330f.; *Kamâl*, vol. 1, p. 329, num. 12.

581. *Kamâl*, ch. 41, pp. 417–23; al-Ṭûsî, *Kitâb al-ghayba*, pp. 134–39; Ibn Rustam, *Dalâʾil al-imâma*, pp. 262–64.

582. Historians have mentioned no important battle between Muslims and Byzantines during this period; al-Ṭabarî writes of a skirmish in 242/856 (*Taʾrîkh*, vol. 3, p. 1434), but it is unlikely the emperor's granddaughter would have been taken prisoner in such an encounter. Moreover, no document, either from the Muslim side or from the Byzantine side, mentions any demand made by the Byzantine emperor to the Abbasid caliph for the freeing of his granddaughter. The hagiographical aspect aside, this version appears to be attempting to give the Mahdî both royal and "Christic" roots on his maternal side. An account of analogous nature identified the wife of the third imam and the mother of the fourth with a Sassanid princess; thus, the Mahdî, with his "royal" blood, is reminiscent of the "Lights" of Mazdaism, Judaism, Christianity, and Islam, that is, the four great religions known by the Muslims of the time; furthermore, it brings together in him both spiritual and temporal authority.

583. Al-Nuʿmânî, *Kitâb al-ghayba*, p. pp. 331 f.; Ibn Qûlûye, *Kâmil al-ziyârât*, pp. 54, 78, 123–24.

584. See, e.g., al-Mufîd's account, *Irshâd*, vol. 2, p. 323f.

585. *"Fa-akhadhatnî fatra wa akhadhathâ fatra," Kamâl al-dîn*, vol. 2, ch. 42, p. 425, num. 1.

586. *"Ghuyyibat ʿannî Narjis fa-lam arahâ ka-annahu ḍuriba baynî wa baynahâ ḥijâbun," Kamâl al-dîn*, vol. 2, p. 428, num. 2.

587. *Kamâl al-dîn*, vol. 2, p. 433, num. 14.

588. *Kamâl al-dîn*, vol. 2, pp. 424–34.

589. *"Wa nurîdu an namunna ʿalä'lladhîna'stuḍʿifû fî l-arḍi wa najʿalahum aʾimmatan wa najʿalahumu'l-wârithîn/wa numakkina lahum fî l-arḍ wa nuriya Firʿawna wa Hâmâna wa junûdahum minhum mâ kânû yaḥdharûn"* [*Qurʾân* 28:5–6]; this is one of the typical Qurʾanic passages whose classical Imamite interpretation applies to the idea of the Return and the final Victory of the Mahdî over his oppressors.

590. *"Iḥmilhu wa 'ḥfaẓhu wa ruddahu ilaynâ fî kulli arbaʿîn yawman," Kamâl*, vol. 2, p. 428.

591. Cf. Qur'an 28:4f.: the mother of Moses, fearful of Pharaoh's troops who were killing newborn children in order to eliminate Moses, built a box in which to place her son and threw it in the river. But in accord with Divine Providence, Moses was rescued.

592. *"Fa-qultu wa mâ hâdhâ l-ṭayr qâla hâdhâ rûḥ al-quds al-muwakkal bi l-aʾimma yuwaffiquhum wa yusaddiduhum wa yurabbîhim bi l-ʿilm [wa yuzayyinuhum bi l-ʿilm]," Kamâl*, vol. 2, p. 329. We might reasonably assume that the other birds were also "celestial messengers." Al-Kulaynî reports a tradition in which the eleventh imam claims that his absent son is far from Sâmarrâ, in Medina (al-Kulaynî, *Uṣûl*, bâb al-ishâra wa l-naṣṣ ilä ṣâḥib al-dâr, vol. 2, p. 118, num. 2; cf. also al-Nuʿmânî, *Kitâb al-ghayba*, ch. 10, p. 270, num. 36).

593. *"Inna awlâd al-anbiyâʾ wa l-awṣiyâʾ idhâ kânû aʾimma yanshaʾûn bi-khilâf mâ yanshaʾu ghayruhum wa inna l-ṣabiyy minnâ idhâ kâna atä ʿalayhi shahrun kâna ka-man atä ʿalayhi sanatun wa inna l-ṣabiyy minnâ la-yatakallam fî baṭn ummihi wa yaqraʾu l-Qurʾân wa yaʿbudu rabbahu ʿazza wa jall," Kamâl*, vol. 2, p. 329.

594. Al-Kulaynî, *Uṣûl*, bâb fî tasmiya man ra'âhu ʿalayhi l-salâm, vol. 2, pp.

120–25; Ibn Bâbûye, *Kamâl*, ch. 43, vol. 2, pp. 434–79.

595. Aḥmad b. Isḥâq al-Ash'arî al-Qummî, the famous disciple of the ninth, tenth, and eleventh imams and one of the main traditionists of Qumm in the third/ninth century; on him, see, e.g., al-Kashshî, *Rijal*, s.v.; al-Ṭûsî, *Rijal*, p. 398, num. 13; p. 427, num. 1; al-Ṭûsî, *Fihrist*, p. 50, num. 78; al-'Allâma al-Ḥillî, *Khulâṣa*, s.v.; al-Mâmaqânî, *Tanqîḥ al-maqâl*, s.v.; al-Ardabîlî, *Jâmi' al-ruwât*, vol. 1, pp. 41–42.

596. An expression dedicated to the final Return of the Mahdî: *"Alladhî yamla'u l-arḍ qisṭan wa 'adlan kamâ muli'at jawran wa ẓulman* [ẓuluman]."

597. *"Anâ baqiyyatu'llâh fî arḍih,"* one of the appellations of the Madhî. The Qur'anic expression *baqiyyat Allâh* is generally understood in a material sense by the early commentators (e.g., Qur'an 2:248); according to them, what is being referred to is sacred relics, "objects of power" like Moses' staff, the Tablets of the Law, or even Adam's turban. Comparing this verse to verses 86 and 116 of sura 11, R. Paret considers that *baqiyya*, like *sakîna*, is to be taken in a spiritual sense; in this case, it becomes a divine, victorious "Force" (cf. R. Paret, *Der Koran . . .*, ed. 1978, vol. 2, pp. 52–53; see also A. Spitaler, "Was bedewtet *baqija* im Koran?"; Shahrastânî, *Livre des Religions*, p. 442, D. Gimaret's note 35). It might also be thought that the appellation of the twelfth imam was perceived by the initiated faithful in both the material sense and the spiritual sense of the expression: his Presence inwardly contains as much "power" as a relic, his occult influence is as beneficient as a divine "Force."

598. *"Ḥâdhâ amr min amr Allâh wa sirr min sirr Allâh wa ghayb min ghayb Allâh fakhudh mâ âtaytuka wa'ktumhu wa kun min al-shâkirîn takun ma'anâ ghadan fî 'Illiyyîn," Kamâl*, vol. 2, ch. 38, pp. 384–85, num. 1. Another eyewitness account is of particular interest because it contains a fairly detailed physical description of the twelfth imam as a child; it comes from Ya'qûb b. Manqûsh (disciple of the tenth and eleventh imams; cf. al-Ṭûsî, *Rijal*, p. 429, num. 5, and p. 437, num. 5; al-Ardabîlî, *Jamî' al-ruwât*, vol. 2, p. 349). Once again at the house of al-Ḥasan al-'Askarî, Ya'qûb was asking him about the identity of the Mahdî. From a room whose door had been hidden by a veil, there came "a small boy about five spans high (*ghulâmun khamâsiyy*) who looked about eight or ten years old, with a broad forehead (*wâḍih al-jabîn*), a fair complexion (*abyaḍ al-wajh*), the whites of whose eyes were striking (*darriy al-muqlatayn*), with firm hands (*shathin al-kaffayn*) and bowed knees (*ma'ṭûf al-rukbatayn*), who had a beauty spot on his right cheek (*fî khaddihi al-ayman khâl*) and a tuft of hair sticking up from the top of his head (*fî ra'sihi dhu'âba*)." He came to sit on his father's lap and his father introduced him as the Mahdî. Then the father said to his son: "Go back, my son, until the Determined Moment (*al-waqt al-ma'lûm*)." The child went back into the room. Ya'qûb, at the request of his master, also went into the room, but found no one there; cf. *Kamâl al-dîn*, vol. 2, p. 407. On the subject of the face of the young Mahdî, it is said that he looked like Jesus, in every respect (cf., e.g., al-Nu'mânî, *Kitâb al-ghayba*, ch. 10, p. 211, num. 4, who reports other traditions, with fewer details, on the description of the Mahdî, pp. 310f.); according to some (perhaps Wâqifite) traditions, Ja'far had said the same thing about Mûsä, cf. Shahrastânî, *Livre des Religions*, p. 494).

599. Information that might be considered as having given birth to the Twelver idea of the "double Occultation" was circulating among Shî'ite groups long before this date. Some Wâqifites of the seventh imam believed that their master had been brought

back to life and then entered into Occultation before showing himself as the Mahdî and dying after the accomplishment of his mission; this is thus a case of a double death (al-Nawbakhtî, *Firaq al-shî'a*, p. 68; Sa'd b. 'AbdAllâh al-Ash'arî, *Kitâb al-maqâlât wa l-firaq*, pp. 106–8). The famous Imamite scholar Faḍl b. al-Ḥasan al-Ṭabarsî (d. 548/1154), citing the *Kitâb al-mashyakha* by al-Ḥasan b. Maḥbûb al-Sarrâd (d. 224/838) (Aqâ Buzurg al-Tihrânî, *al-Dharî'a*, vol. 21, p. 69, num. 3995), reports a tradition of al-Bâqir where it is said that the Mahdî would have two Occultations, the first of which would be short and the second of which would be long (al-Ṭabarsî, *I'lâm al-warä*, p. 443). Works later than 260/874 contain, as might be expected, a great number of traditions regarding the imams' predictions about the two Occultations, the first of which would be shorter. (See, e.g., al-Kulaynî, *Uṣûl*, "kitâb al-ḥujja," bâb fî l-ghayba, vol. 2, pp. 132–45; al-Nu'mânî, *Kitâb al-ghayba*, ch. 10, pp. 249-78; Ibn Bâbûye, *Kamâl*, vol. 1, pp. 323f. It nevertheless appears as though there was still a lack of certainty regarding the respective durations of the two Occultations. Al-Nu'mânî reports a tradition by Ja'far where the sixth imam seems to say that the first Occultation would be longer, al-Nu'mânî, *Kitâb al-ghayba*, p. 249, num. 1; this tradition does appear to be the only one of its kind.)

600. See, e.g., Javad Ali, "Die beiden ersten Safîre des Zwölften Imâms," in *Der Islam*, vol. 25, 1939, pp. 197–227; 'Emâdzâdeh Iṣfahânî, *Zendegânî-ye ḥaḍrat-e emâm-e davâzdahom* . . . Tehran, 1335 solar/1956; H. Ma'rûf al-Ḥasanî, *Sîrat al-a'immat al-ithnâ 'ashar*, Beirut, 1397/1977; J. M. Hussain, *The Occultation* . . . , chapters 4 to 7; V. Klemm, "Die vier *sufarâ'* des Zwölften Imâm. Zur formativen Periode der Zwölferschia," in *Die Welt des Orients*, Tübingen, vol. 15, 1984, pp. 126–43; H. Halm, *Die Schia*, chapter 4.

601. Ibn Bâbûye, *Kamâl al-dîn*, vol. 2, p. 486.

602. Ibn Bâbûye, *Kamâl al-dîn*, vol. 2, pp. 501–2.

603. Ibn Bâbûye, *Kamâl al-dîn*, vol. 2, p. 504.

604. Ibn Bâbûye, *Kamâl al-dîn*, vol. 2, pp. 516–17.

605. Ibn Bâbûye, *Kamâl al-dîn*, vol. 2, pp. 504, 518.

606. Ibn Bâbûye, *Kamâl al-dîn*, vol. 2, p. 522.

607. Ibn Bâbûye, *Kamâl al-dîn*, vol. 2, pp. 518–19.

608. Ibn Bâbûye, *Kamâl al-dîn*, vol. 2, pp. 509–10, 519–20.

609. Ibn Bâbûye, *Kamâl al-dîn*, vol. 2, p. 507–9.

610. *"Bi'smi'llâh al-raḥmân al-raḥîm yâ 'Alî ibn Md al-Simarrî a'ẓama'llâhu ajra ikhwânika fîka fa-innaka mayyit mâ baynaka wa bayna sittati ayyâmin fa'jma' amraka wa lâ tûṣî ilä aḥad yaqûmu maqâmaka ba'ada wafâtika fa-qad waqa'at al-ghaybat al-thâniya/al-tâmma falâ ẓuhûra illâ ba'da idhni'llâh 'azza wa jall wa dhâlika ba'da ṭûl al-amad wa qaswat al-qulûb wa imtilâ' al-arḍ jawran wa sa-ya'tî shî'atî man yadda'î l-mushâhada alâ fa-man idda'ä l-mushâhada qabla khurûj al-sufyânî wa l-ṣayḥa fa huwa kâdhibun muftarin"* . . . *"Fa-lammâ kâna l-yawm al-sâdis 'udnâ ilayhi fa huwa yajûdu binafsih fa qîla lahu man waṣiyyuka min ba'dika fa qâla li'llâh amr huwa bâlighuhu wa maḍä raḍiya'llâhu 'anh fa-hâdhâ âkhiru kalâm sumi'a minhu,"* cf. e.g., Ibn Bâbûye, *Kamâl al-dîn*, vol. 2, ch. 45, p. 516, num. 44; al-Ṭûsî, *Kitâb al-ghayba*, p. 257.

611. This classification is based on details collected by al-Kulaynî, *Uṣûl*, "kitâb al-ḥujja," bâb nâdir fî ḥâl al-ghayba, vol. 2, pp. 127–32; bâb fî l-ghayba, vol. 2, pp.

132–45; al-Nu'mânî, *Kitâb al-ghayba*, ch. 10, pp. 249–59; Ibn Bâbûye, *Kamâl al-dîn*, vol. 2, ch. 44, pp. 479–82; Ibn Bâbûye, *'Ilal al-sharâ'i'*, vol. 1, ch. 179, pp. 243–46; Ibn 'Ayyâsh, *Muqtaḍab al-athar*, pp. 34–36; al-Ṭûsî, *Kitâb al-ghayba*, pp. 73f., 109f., 214f.

612. "It is indispensible that the Qâ'im be hidden . . . for he fears assassination [or "for he fears being made a sacrifice"] [*lâ budda li l-qâ'im min ghayba . . . yakhâfu l-qatl (yakhâfu 'alä nafsihi l-dhabḥ)*]. In other traditions, after the speaker [one of the Impeccables] declares the necessity of the Occultation, he does no more than to show his stomach (*awma'a bi-yadihi ilä baṭnih*), meaning assassination [in the same way that today the throat might be shown]; traditions going back to the Prophet and to the fifth and sixth imams, cf. e.g., al-Kulaynî, *Uṣûl*, vol. 2, p. 140, num. 18; al-Nu'mânî, *Kitâb al-ghayba*, pp. 258–59, nums. 18–21; Ibn Bâbûye, *Kamâl*, vol. 2, p. 481, nos. 7–10; Ibn Bâbûye, *'Ilal*, p. 243, num. 1.

613. "Your imam will go into hiding so that at the time of his Rising he will not be linked to anyone via oath of allegiance [lit. "so that his nape will carry allegiance to no one," *inna imâmakum yaghîb . . . li'allâ takûn li-aḥad fî 'unuqihi bay'a idhâ qâma*]. The Qâ'im will rise up and will be linked to no one by pact, engagement, or oath of allegiance [*yaqûmu l-qâim wa laysa li-aḥad fî 'unuqih 'aqd wa lâ 'ahd wa lâ bay'a*]"; traditions from the fifth, sixth, and eighth imams, cf. e.g., al-Nu'mânî, *Kitâb al-ghayba*, p. 250, nums. 3,4; Ibn Bâbûye, *Kamâl al-dîn*, vol. 2, pp. 479–80, nums. 1–5.

614. Ibn Bâbûye, *Kamâl al-dîn*, vol. 2, ch. 45, p. 485, num. 4 (letter addressed to the second "representative," Md b. 'Uthmân al-'Umarî/al-'Amrî).

615. *"Innahu lâ budda li-ṣâḥib hâdhâ l-amr min ghayba li-yarji'a 'an hâdhâ l-amr man kâna yaqûlu bihi innamâ hiya miḥnatun min Allâh imtaḥana bihâ khalqahu,"* Ibn Bâbûye, *'Ilal*, vol. 1, p. 244, num. 4.

616. *"Inna li-ṣâḥib al-amr ghayba lâ budda minhâ yartâbu fîhâ kullu mubṭil,"* Ibn Bâbûye, *'Ilal*, vol. 1, pp. 245–46, num. 8; Ibn Bâbûye, *Kamâl*, vol. 2, pp. 481–82, num. 11.

617. 'AbdAllâh b. al-Faḍl al-Hâshimî, disciple of the sixth imam; on him, see al-Ṭûsî, *Rijâl*, p. 222, num. 3; al-Tafrishî, *Naqd al-rijâl*, s.v.; al-Ardabîlî, *Jâmi' al-ruwât*, vol. 1, pp. 499–500.

618. " . . . *Wajh al-ḥikma fî ghaybatihi wajh al-ḥikma fî ghaybât man taqaddamahu min ḥujaj Allâh ta'âla dhikruhu inna wajh al-ḥikma fî dhâlik lâ yankashifu illâ ba'da ẓuhûrihi kamâ lam yankashif wajh al-ḥikma fîmâ atâhu l-Khiḍr 'alayhi l-salâm min kharq al-safîna wa qatl al-ghulâm wa iqâmat al-jidâr li-Mûsä 'alayhi l-salâm ilä waqt iftirâqihimâ yâ Ibn al-Faḍl inna hâdhâ l-amr amr min amr Allâh wa sirr min sirr Allâh wa ghayb min ghayb Allâh wa matä 'alimnâ annahu 'azza wa jall ḥakîm ṣaddaqnâ bi-anna af'âlahu kulluhâ ḥikma wa in kâna wajhuhâ ghayr munkashif*"; Ibn Bâbûye, *'Ilal*, vol. 1, p. 246; Ibn Bâbûye, *Kamâl*, vol. 2, p. 482. On the story of Moses' mysterious voyage in search of the "confluence of two oceans" and his encounter with "the sage with divine Science," who later was identified with al-Khiḍr (/al-Khaḍir), see Qur'an 18: 59–82, and A. J. Wensinck, "al-Khaḍir," *EI2*, vol. 4, pp. 935–39.

619. Al-Kulaynî, *Uṣûl*, "kitâb al-ḥujja," bâb fî tasmiya man ra'âhu 'alayhi l-salâm, vol. 2, pp. 120–26; al-Nu'mânî, *Kitâb al-ghayba*, ch. 10, pp. 201–81; Ibn Bâbûye, *Kamâl*, vol. 2, ch. 43, pp. 434–79. For those accounts from later sources, see H. Corbin, *En Islam iranien*, vol. 4, book VII, ch. 2, pp. 338–89. On the resemblance to Jesus, see, e.g., al-Nu'mânî, *Kitâb al-ghayba*, pp. 210–11. For an overview of the fig-

ure of Jesus in Muslim spirituality, see, e.g., M. M. Ayoub, "Towards an Islamic Christology . . . "; and also R. Arnaldez, *Jésus dans la pensée musulmane*, Paris, 1988.

620. *Kamâl al-dîn*, vol. 2, ch. 49–55, pp. 536–643. On the length of some of the prophets' lives, see vol. 2, ch. 46, pp. 523–25 (e.g., according to one of Jaʿfar's traditions that he claimed came from the Prophet: Adam, 930 years; Noah, 2450 years; Abraham, 175 years; Moses, 126 years; David, 100 years; Solomon, 712 years). Cf. also D. Gimaret, *Kitâb Bilawhar wa Bûdhasaf*, Paris-Geneva, 1971, pp. 30–31.

621. It is Ibn Bâbûye himself who reports excerpts from Abû Sahl Ismâʿîl b. ʿAlî al-Nawbakhtî's *Kitâb al-tanbîh fî l-imâma*; the author (d. circa 294/906) is not to be confused with al-Ḥusayn b. Rawḥ al-Nawbakhtî, the third "representative" of the hidden imam, or with al-Ḥasan b. Mûsä al-Nawbakhtî, the author of the *Firaq al-shîʿa*. On the powerful Imami family of the Banû Nawbakht, see ʿA. Eqbâl's classic *Khânedân-e Nawbakhtî*, second edition, Tehran, 1966), according to which "the Proof [i.e. the hidden imam] . . . is existent in the world as regards substance and subsistent as regards essence [*mawjûd al-ʿayn fî lʿâlam wa thâbit al-dhât*]" (*Kamâl*, author's introduction, vol. 1, p. 90); however, Ibn al-Nadîm reports or interprets al-Nawbakht's doctrine otherwise; in effect, he says that according to al-Nawbakht the twelfth imam died, leaving a secret son who succeeded him, and that the line of imams would thus continue secretly from father to son until the last of them publicly showed himself to be the *Qâʾim* (*al-Fihrist*, ed. Tajaddod, p. 225).

622. Al-Kulaynî, *Uṣûl*, vol. 2, p. 125, num. 15; the spiritual symbolism is evident: the hidden imam changes dust into gold for those who seek his aid. Notice the lack of spiritual lucidity of the two "ordinary" Imamites that the account focuses on.

623. "*. . . Yashhadu l-mawâsim yarä l-nâs wa lâ yarawnahu*"; al-Nuʿmânî, *Kitâb al-ghayba*, ch. 10, pp. 256-57, nums. 13–15; Ibn Bâbûye, *Kamâl*, vol. 2, ch. 33, p. 351, num. 49.

624. " . . . [The hidden imam]walks through their marketplaces and into their homes, and they do not recognize him [*yasîru fî aswâqihim wa yaṭaʾu busuṭahum wa hum lâ yaʿrifûnahu*]"; cf. e.g., Ibn Bâbûye, *Kamâl al-dîn*, vol. 2, ch. 33, p. 341, num. 21; ch. 43, pp. 434f.; also, al-Kulanyî, *Uṣûl*, vol. 2, pp. 125–26; al-Nuʿmânî, *Kitâb al-ghayba*, p. 257.

625. " . . . *Innahum yastaḍiʾûna bi-nûrihi wa yantafiʿûn bi-walâyatihi fî ghaybatihi ka intifâʿ al-nâs bi l-shams wa in tujalliluhâ saḥâb*"; *Kamâl*, vol. 2, ch. 43, p. 253, num. 3.

626. "*. . . Wa ammâ wajh al-intifâʾ bî fî ghaybatî fa-ka l-intifâʿ bi l-shams idhâ ghayyabathâ ʿan al-abṣâr al-saḥâb*"; Ibn Bâbûye, *Kamâl*, vol. 2, ch. 45, p. 485, num. 4.

627. "*Hâdhâ min maknûn sirr Allâh wa makhzûn ʿilmihi fa-aktumhu illâ ʿan ahlihi*"; the hidden imam is sometimes said to be made of light himself; he has no shadow (*lâ yakûn lahu ẓill*); at the time of his Return, the earth will be filled with a light (*fa-idhâ kharaja ashraqat al-arḍ bi-nûrih*); Ibn Bâbûye, *Kamâl*, vol. 2, ch. 45, p. 372, num. 5.

628. Under different titles, sometimes a number of chapters are dedicated to the subject; among the titles, e.g., are "signs of the Return" (*ʿalâmât al-rajʿa*), "signs of the manifestation" (*ʿalâmât al-ẓuhûr*), "traditions concerning the Dajjâl [the Islamic Antichrist]" (*aḥâdîth al-Dajjâl*), "what is reported concerning the calamities to occur before the manifestation of the Mahdî" (*mâ jâʾa fî l-shidda allatî takûnu qabla ẓuhûr*

al-Mahdî). On this subject, see the studies cited in note 526. For Imamite sources of the early suprarational esoteric tradition, see, e.g., al-Kulaynî, *Uṣûl*, vol. 2, pp. 132f and 190f.; al-Kulaynî, *al-Rawḍa*, vol. 1, pp. 55, 244-45, and vol. 2, pp. 141f.; al-Nu'mânî, *Kitâb al-ghayba*, chapters 12, 14, 15, 18, 21; Ibn Bâbûye, *Kamâl*, chapters 47, 57, 58; Ibn Bâbûye, *'Uyûn*, vol. 1, chap. 6.

629. Whence comes the sacred phrase "The Mahdî will rise up at the End of Time and will fill the earth with justice, just as earlier it was overflowing with oppression and injustice [or "darkness"]" (*Anna l-Mahdî yakhruju fî âkhir al-zamân fayamla'a l-arḍ 'adlan kamâ muli'at jawran wa ẓulman [or "ẓuluman"]*).

630. "*. . . Idhâ amâta l-nâs al-ṣalât wa aḍâ'û l-amâna wa 'staḥallû l-kidhb wa akalû l-ribä wa akhadhû l-rushâ wa shayyadû l-bunyân wa bâ'û l-dîn bi l-dunyâ wa'sta'malû l-sufahâ' wa shâwarû l-nisâ' wa qaṭa'û l-arḥâm wa'ttaba'û l-ahwâ' wa'stakhaffû l-dimâ' wa kâna l-ḥilm ḍu'fan wa l-ẓulm fakhran wa kânat al-umarâ' fajara wa l-wuzarâ' ẓalama wa l-'urafâ' khawana wa l-qurrâ' fasaqa wa ẓaharat shahâdat al-zûr wa'stu'lina l-fujûr wa qawl al-buhtân wa l-ithm wa l-ṭughyân wa ḥulliyat al-maṣâḥif wa zukhrifat al-masâjid wa ṭuwwilat al-manârât wa ukrimat al-ashrâr wa'zdaḥamat al-ṣufûf wa'khtalafat al-qulûb wa nuqiḍat al-'uhûd . . . wa shâraka l-nisâ' azwâjahunna fî l-tijâra ḥirṣan 'alä l-dunyâ wa 'alat aṣwât al-fussâq wa'stumi'a minhum wa kâna za'îm al-qawm ardhaluhum wa'ttuqiya l-fâjir makhâfa sharrihi wa ṣuddiqa l-kâdhib wa'tumina l-khâ'in wa'ttukhidhat al-qiyân wa l-ma'âzif . . . wa rakiba dhawât al-furûj al-surûj wa tashabbaha l-nisâ' bi l-rijâl wa l-rijâl bi l-nisâ' . . . wa âtharû 'amal al-dunyâ 'alä l-âkhira wa labisû julûd al-ḍa'n 'alä qulûb al-dhi'âb . . . ," Kamâl al-dîn*, vol. 2, ch. 47, pp. 525-28, num. 1, under the title *ḥadîth al-dajjâl*.

631. "*Lâ yakûnu dhâlika l-amr ḥattä yatfula ba'ḍukum fî wujûh ba'din wa ḥattä yal'ana ba'ḍukum ba'ḍan wa ḥattä yusammiya ba'ḍukum ba'ḍan kadhdhâbîn,*" al-Nu'mânî, *Kitâb al-ghayba*, ch. 12, p. 300, num. 10.

632. "*La-tumaḥaṣṣunna yâ shî'a âl Muḥammad tamḥîs al-kuḥl fî l-'ayn wa inna ṣâḥib al-'ayn yadrî matä yaqa'u l-kuḥl fî 'aynihi wa lâ ya'lamu matä yakhruju minhâ wa ka-dhâlika yuṣbiḥu l-rajul 'alä sharî'a min amrinâ wa yumsî wa qad kharaja minhâ wa yumsî 'alä sharî'a min amrinâ wa yuṣbiḥu wa qad kharaja minhâ*"; al-Nu'mânî, *Kitâb al-ghayba*, ch. 12, p. 301, num. 12.

633. "*Wa'llâhi la-tukassarunna takassur al-zujâj wa inna l-zujâj la-yu'âdu fa-ya 'ûdu kamâ kâna wa'llâhi la-tukassarunna takassur al-fakhkhâr fa-inna l-fakhkhâr la-yatakassaru falâ ya'ûd kamâ kân wa wa'llâhi la-tumaḥḥaṣunna ḥattä lâ yabqä minkum illâ al-aqall*" al-Nu'mânî, *Kitâb al-ghayba*, pp. 301–2, num. 13. "Glass" (*al-zujâj*), a noble and transparent material, of course refers to the "true faithful" who, although broken by tests, will be "resuscitated" by the imam; "clay" (*al-fakhkhâr*), a dark and dirty material, represents "nominal Imamites" who, once tested and broken by Evil, will be forever lost. One wonders if perhaps there is also a play on words to be seen here, since the root *zjj* evokes the idea of effort and perseverance, and while the root *fkhr* evokes the idea of pride and vanity.

634. See the studies mentioned in note 526, and especially the work of A. A. Sachedina, *Islamic Messianism . . .*, s.v.; for Imamite sources, see the references in note 628, in particular al-Nu'mânî, *Kitâb al-ghayba*, ch. 14, pp. 356–406.

635. On him, see previous discussion, especially note 316.

636. E.g., al-Nu'mânî, *Kitâb al-ghayba*, pp. 372–73. In reality, things would

have taken place in the opposite way. It was not the imams, and especially not Jaʿfar, who were responsible for the majority of the traditions about "the assassination of the Pure Soul" that placed the coming of the *Qâʾim* just after the revolt of the Shîʿite insurgent. On the contrary, it was the insurgent who seems to have attempted to exploit the facts concerning the "signs of Return" that had been circulating for a long time among the Muslims; he did so in the hope of passing himself off as the precursor of the Mahdî, if not the Mahdî himself. It must also be remembered that, as was pointed out in an old tradition concerning the Mahdî, he was to have the same name as the Prophet, that is, Muḥammad b. ʿAbdAllâh.

637. Cf. e.g., al-Kulaynî, *Uṣûl,* "kitâb al-ḥujja," bâb mawlid al-Ḥusayn b. ʿAlî, vol. 2, pp. 366–67, num. 6 (the *Qâʾim* is not yet born; he is in the pre-existential world of "shadows"; God has the shadow of the *Qâʾim* "rise up" before his angels (*faʾaqâmaʾllâhu lahum ẓill al-qâʾim,* announcing that he will be the avenger of al-Ḥusayn's death); Ibn Bâbûye, *ʿIlal,* vol. 1, ch. 129, p. 160, num. 1. (We are still in the World of Shadows; God shows the angels the shadow of one of the imams who, "standing erect, is praying" *fa-idhâ aḥaduhum qâʾimun yuṣallî*; the *Qâʾim,* "avenger of al-Ḥusayn," is the one standing in prayer. It is notable that in these traditions the word *Qâʾim* means "He Who Stands.") Cf. also Ibn Bâbûye, *Amâlî,* pp. 140, 168; Ibn Rustam al-Ṭabarî, *Dalâʾil al-imâma,* p. 239; al-Ḥurr al-ʿAmilî, *al-Jawâhir al-saniyya,* pp. 244f.; al-Majlisî, *Biḥâr,* vol. 45, p. 221 (citing al-Ṭûsî's *Amâlî*) and vol. 51, pp. 67–68.

638. Cf. al-Khazzâz al-Râzî, *Kifâyat al-athar,* pp. 187–92 (the angel Gabriel adds that the Qâʾim is "the Verb of Truth, the Expression of Veracity, and the Place of manifestation of [or "he who manifests"] the Truth," *kalimat al-ḥaqq wa lisân al-ṣidq wa maẓhar [muẓhir] al-ḥaqq.* In a general way, *al-ḥaqq* (Truth) is one of the appellations of the Qâʾim; cf., e.g., Jaʿfar's commentary on the verse "And we will show them our signs on the horizons and in themselves, so that it will be clear to them that *he* is the Truth," Qurʾan 41:53, in al-Kulaynî, *al-Rawḍa,* vol. 1, p. 244; elsewhere it is said that "the Truth is with and in the Mahdî," *al-ḥaqq maʿahu wa fihi*; *Kamâl al-dîn,* vol. 2, ch. 35, p. 372, num. 5). See also al-Majlisî, *Biḥâr,* vol. 36, pp. 348-50; ʿAlî Akbar al-Nahâwandî (d. 1369/1949), *ʿAbqarî al-ḥassân fî tawârîkh Ṣâḥib al-zamân,* pp. 15–16.

639. Cf. e.g., al-Nuʿmânî, *Kitâb al-ghayba,* pp. 333f. ("[The *Qâʾim*] will do what the Prophet did; he will destroy what will be before him just as the Prophet destroyed the rules of the period of Ignorance, and he will establish Islam again (*yaṣnaʿu kamâ ṣanaʿarasûl Allâh yahdimu mâ kâna qablahu kamâ hadama rasûl Allâh amr al-jâhiliyya wa yastaʾnifu l-islâm jadîdan*"); al-Nuʿmânî, *Kitâb al-ghayba,* ch. 21, pp. 451f. (" . . . [The men of the Qâʾim] will set up their tents in the enclosure of the mosque at Kûfa and will teach people the Qurʾan as it was revealed. Then, our Qâʾim will repair the mosque and reset its *qibla*; . . . *ḍarabû l-fasâṭiṭ bi-masjid al-Kûfa wa yuʿallimûna l-nâs al-Qurʾân kamâ unzila amâ inna qâʾimunâ aqâma kasrahu wa sawwä qiblatahu*). Should we believe that at this time Islam will become so unknown that its reestablishment by the Qâʾim will be perceived as the foundation of a new religion? Is it in this sense that we are supposed to take the several traditions reported by al-Nuʿmânî where the imams declare that the Qâʾim will bring "a new Order, a new Book, a new legislation, a new Sunna" (*yaqûmu l-qâʾim bi-amrin jadîd wa kitâbin jadîd wa qaḍâʾin jadîd wa sunnatin jadîda*) (al-Nuʿmânî, *Kitâb al-ghayba,* ch. 13, p. 336; ch. 14, pp. 368, 378)? Or is it perhaps the case, as some Shîʿite "extremists" main-

tain, that a new religion will abrogate Islam and a new Book will abrogate the Qur'an? Given the series of traditions whose translations were furnished at the beginning of this note, we would opt for the first solution.

640. *"Inna l-islâm bada'a gharîban wa sa-ya'ûdu gharîban fa-ṭûbä li l-ghurabâ' . . . idhâ qâma qâ'imunâ yasta'nifu du'â'an jadîdan kamâ da'â rasûl Allâh,"* al-Nu'mânî, *Kitâb al-ghayba*, pp. 455–57; on this prophetic tradition, cf. previous discussion and note 451.

641. Al-Nu'mânî, *Kitâb al-ghayba*, pp. 342f.; Ibn Bâbûye, *'Ilal*, vol. 1, ch. 129, p. 161; Ibn 'Ayyâsh, *Muqtaḍab*, pp. 181f. (" . . . He will take the Torah and the other holy Books from the cave [according to one version, this cave is located in Antioch/Anṭâkiyya] and will judge the faithful of the Torah from the Torah, and the faithful of the Gospels from the Gospels, the faithful of al-Zabûr [the Book of David] according to al-Zabûr, and the faithful of the Qur'an according to the Qur'an . . . ").

642. Cf., e.g., the *Tafsîr* attributed to imam al-Ḥasan al-'Askarî, lith. ed., p. 186 (prophetic tradition: "The ninth descendent of al-Ḥusayn will be the Qâ'im; he will fill the earth with justice, just as it was filled with tyranny and darkness; and he will fight for the hidden spiritual meaning of Revelation, just as I myself have fought for its literal meaning" . . . *wa innahu yuqâtilu li l-ta'wîl kamâ qâtaltu li l-tanzîl*); al-Nu'mânî, *Kitâb al-ghayba*, ch. 13, p. 345 (" . . . And in his time [that of the Qâ'im], Wisdom will be given to you" *wa tu'tûna al-ḥikma fî zamânihi*; *Nahj al-balâgha*, p. 458 (" . . . [in the time of the Qâ'im] men will have their eyes cleared by literal Revelation and their ears touched by the hidden sense of Revelation; their thirst will constantly be quenched by morning and evening cups of Wisdom" . . . *tujlä bi l-tanzîl abṣâruhum wa yurmä bi l-tafsîr fî masâmi'ihim wa yughbiqûna ka's al-ḥikma ba'd al-ṣabûḥ*).

643. *"Innamâ summiya l-mahdî mahdîyyan liannahu yahdî ilä ḥadîthin khafiyy"*; al-Nu'mânî, *Kitâb al-ghayba*, ch. 13, p. 342. The definition proposed by al-Bâqir would not have won complete approval from grammarians (*mahdî* = "guided"; "guide" = *hâdî*).

644. See, e.g., Ibn Qûlûye, *Kâmil al-ziyârât*, ch. 19, pp. 65f.; ch. 50, pp. 136f.; al-Majlisî, *Biḥâr*, vol. 51, pp. 77-78, and vol. 53, pp. 101–17. Ishmael "faithful to his promises" appears once in the Qur'an (19:54–55): "And mention in the Book, Ishmael; he was faithful to his promises, a messenger and a prophet/He commanded his people to perform prayer and to pay alms; he was pleasing to his Lord." According to Ja'far's commentary reported by Ibn Qûlûye (*Kâmil al-ziyârât*, p. 65, num. 3), Ishmael was the son of the prophet Ezechiel (Ḥizqiyâl); he was himself a prophet and a messenger; he was arrested, dismembered, and killed by his ungrateful people.

645. *"Law qad kharaja l-qâ'im la-naṣarahu'llâhu bi l-malâ'ik at al-musawwimîn wa l-murdifîn wa l-munzalîn wa l-karrûbiyyîn yakûnu jabra'îl amâmahu wa mikâ'îl 'an yamînihi wa isrâfîl 'an yasârih . . . ,"* al-Nu'mânî, *Kitâb al-ghayba*, ch. 13, p. 337.

646. " . . . *Yahbiṭu tis'a âlâf malak wa thalâthumi'a wa thalâtha 'ashar malakan . . . hum alladhîna kânû ma'a Nûḥ fi l-safîna wa lladhîna kânû ma'a Ibrâhîm ḥaythu ulqiya fî l-nâr wa hum alladhîna kânû ma'a Mûsä lammâ fuliqa lahu l-baḥr wa lladhîna kânû ma'a 'Isä lammâ rafa'ahu'llâhu ilayhi wa arba'atu âlâf musawwimîn kânû ma'a rasûl Allâh wa thalâthumi'a wa thalâtha 'ashara malakan kânû ma'ahu yawma badr . . . ,"* al-Nu'mânî, *Kitâb al-ghayba*, ch. 19, pp. 439–40.

647. References to this mysterious force remain vague: "Our Qâ'im is assisted by the Terror" (*al-qâ'im minnâ manṣûr bi l-ruʿb*) (Ibn Bâbûye, *Kamâl al-dîn*, vol. 1, ch. 33, p. 331, num. 16); " . . . And the Terror will march ahead of him [i.e., the Mahdî] at a distance of one month, behind him, on his right and on his left . . . " (. . . *wa l-ruʿb yasîru masîra shahrin amâmahu wa khalfahu wa ʿan yamînihi wa ʿan shimâlihi* . . .) (al-Nuʿmânî, *Kitâb al-ghayba*, p. 337). The Imamite *ruʿb* may be compared with the *emât Jahve* (the Terror of God) of the Old Testament: Exodus 23:27: "I will send before you a Terror of God and I will rout all the peoples before whom you arrive" (or Job 9:34 and 13:21). In the Qur'an, the word *ruʿb* refers simply to the feeling of fear that God casts into the hearts of unbelievers. Early Imamism recognized a number of celestial entities that were different from the angels; we have had occasion to see the cases of al-Rûḥ and al-Rûḥ al-Quds; there are perhaps others, although we have not systematically analyzed the subject.

648. See, e.g., al-Nuʿmânî, *Kitâb al-ghayba*, pp. 285, 378f., 443f.; Ibn Bâbûye, *Kamâl*, vol. 1, pp. 268, 331, and vol. 2, pp. 378, 654, 671f. Let us note the numerical value of the letters of the word *jaysh* ("troops"): (j, 3) + (y, 10) + (sh, 300) = 313. In the Sunni tradition, rather than 313 combattants at the Battle of Badr, there were "310 and a few."

649. In response to the question "How many of those who accompany the Qâ'im are Arabs?" Jaʿfar said, "Very few (*shay'un yasîr*)"; then someone said, "But numerous are the Arabs who profess this Cause," and Jaʿfar replied, "People will inevitably be chosen, separated, sifted through; many are those who will fall through the sifter [*lâbudda li l-nâs min an yumaḥḥaṣû wa yumayyazû wa yugharbalû wa yakhruju min al-ghirbâl khalqun kathîr*]; al-Nuʿmânî, *Kitâb al-ghayba*, ch. 12, pp. 298–99. According to a tradition attributed to al-Bâqir, all 313 Companions of the Qâ'im are the sons of *ʿajam* ("non-Arabs," or "Persians") (*aṣḥâb al-qâ'im thalâthumi'a wa thalâtha ʿashar rajulan awlâd al-ʿajam*), al-Nuʿmânî, *Kitâb al-ghayba*, ch. 20, p. 448.

650. *"Waylun li l-ʿarab," "Waylun li l-ʿarab min sharrin qad iqtarab," "Qâ'imunâ ʿalä l-ʿarab shadîd," "Lam yakun bayna l-qâ'im wa bayna l-ʿarab illâ l-sayf," "Ma baqiya/baynanâ wa bayna l-ʿarab illâ l-dhabḥ"*; see, e.g., al-Nuʿmânî, *Kitâb al-ghayba*, ch. 13, pp. 337f.; see also al-Kulaynî, *Uṣûl*, "bâb al-tamḥîṣ wa ll-imtiḥân, vol. 2, ch. 21, pp. 194–97.

651. Cf. the tradition by al-Bâqir reported in note 649, or this vision of ʿAlî's: "I can see the *ʿajam*, the companions of the Mahdî, set up their tents in the enclosure of the mosque of Kûfa . . . " al-Nuʿmânî, *Kitâb al-ghayba*, ch. 21, p. 452.

652. Al-Nuʿmânî, *Kitâb al-ghayba*, ch. 21, pp. 451–52. Is this an allusion to the fact that the Companions of the Mahdî profess a completely different religion from the exoteric Islam practiced by the Arabs?

653. " . . . *Thalâthumi'a wa thalâtha ʿashara rajulan ʿalayhim suyûf maktûb ʿalayhâ alfu kalimatin kullu kalima miftaḥ alfi kalima*"; al-Nuʿmânî, *Kitâb al-ghayba*, ch. 20, pp. 447f.; Ibn Bâbûye, *Kamâl*, vol. 2, ch. 58, p. 671, num. 19. For the phrase "a thousand words, a thousand chapters or words," see the section corresponding to note 381.

654. *"Idha udhina l-imâm daʿâ'llâha bi'smihi l-ʿibrânî fa-utîḥat lahu-ṣaḥâbatuhu bi-Makka al-thalâthumi'a wa thalâtha ʿashara qazaʿun ka-qazaʿ al-kharîf"*; al-Nuʿmânî, *Kitâb al-ghayba*, ch. 20, p. 445. On the Supreme Name and the fact that it is in Hebrew (or in Syriac), cf. the texts corresponding to notes 473 to 478.

655. Al-Kulaynî, *al-Rawḍa,* vol. 2, p. 145.

656. *"Al-mafqûdûn 'an furushihim thalâthumi'a wa thalâtha 'ashar rajulan 'idda ahl badr fa-yuṣbiḥûn bi-Makka wa huwa qawl Allâh 'azza wa jalla "aynamâ takûnû ya'ti bikum Allâh jamî'an" wa hum aṣḥâb al-qâ'im"*; Ibn Bâbûye, *Kamâl,* vol. 2, ch. 57, p. 654, num. 21.

657. E.g. al-Nu'mânî, *Kitâb al-ghayba,* ch. 20, pp. 445f.; Ibn Bâbûye, *Kamâl al-dîn,* vol. 2, ch. 58, p. 673, num. 24.

658. E.g., al-Nu'mânî, *Kitâb al-ghayba,* ch. 13, pp. 352f. (" . . . *nazalat min al-samâ' suyûf al-qitâl 'alä kulli sayf ism al-rajul wa ism abîhi*").

659. E.g., Ibn Bâbûye, *Kamâl al-dîn,* vol. 2, ch. 58, p. 673, num. 25

660. E.g., al-Nu'mânî, *Kitâb al-ghayba,* ch. 21, p. 453 (" . . . *'ahduka fî kaffika fa-idhâ warada 'alayka amrun lâ tafhamuhu wa lâ ta'rifu l-qaḍâ' fîhi fa'nẓur ilä kaffika wa'mal bimâ fîhâ* . . . ").

661. E.g., al-Nu'mânî, *Kitâb al-ghayba,* p. 454 ("K*atabû 'alä aqdâmihim shay'an wa mashaw 'alä l-mâ'* . . . ").

662. See, e.g., al-Nu'mânî, *Kitâb al-ghayba,* ch. 13, pp. 434f.; Ibn Bâbûye, *Kamâl al-dîn,* vol. 2, ch. 58, p. 673f.

663. According to certain traditions, all the faithful that rejoin the ranks of the Mahdî will be endowed with miraculous powers, particularly that of suprasensible communication with the imam ("At the time of the Rising of our Qâ'im," said Ja'far, "God—may He be exulted and glorified—will develop the ears and eyes of our faithful to such an extent that, even without the presence of a messenger between them and the Qâ'im, the Qâ'im will hear their speech and they will hear him, or they will be able to see him without his leaving the place where he is." *Qâ'imunâ idhâ qâma madda'llâhu 'azza wa jall li-shî'atinâ fî asmâ'ihim wa abṣârihim ḥattä lâ yakûn baynahum wa bayna l-qâ'im barîdun yukallimuhum faysama'ûn wa yanẓurûna ilayhi wa huwa fî makânih*; al-Kulaynî, *al-Rawḍa*, vol. 2, p. 49).

664. Al-Nu'mânî, *Kitâb al-ghayba,* all of chapter 26, pp. 473–75 (the chapter contains four traditions, one of which comes from al-Bâqir and the other three from Ja'far).

665. This comes from the final part of the tradition referred to as *faḍl al-nabî wa l-ḥujaj 'alä l-malâ'ika*; the beginning of this tradition has already been translated. It ends as follows, with the Prophet speaking first:

> And I asked: "O Lord! Are these my Heirs [he is referring to the pre-existential luminous entities of the imams]?" The reply given to me was: "O Muḥammad! These are my Friends [*awliyâ'î*], My pure Chosen ones [*aṣfiyâ'î*] and My Proofs after you for men; they are your Heirs and your vicars and the best of My creatures after you. By My Glory and My Majesty! I will show My religion through them and I will raise up my Verb through them [*la-uẓhiranna bihim dînî wa la-u'liyanna bihim kalimatî*]; by the last of them I will purify the earth of My enemies [*wa lauṭahhiranna l-arḍ bi-âkhirihim min a'dâ'î*]; I will set him up firmly in the Easts and the Wests of the earth [*wa la-umkinannahu mashâriq al-arḍ wa maghâribahâ*]; I will make the winds subject to him [*wa la-usakhkhiranna lahu l-riyâḥ*] and I will make the indocile clouds lie down [*wa la-udhallilanna lahu al-saḥâb al-ṣi'âb*]; I will assist him through My Army, and I will help him through my angels [*wa la-anṣurannahu bijundî wa la-umiddannahu bimalâ'ikatî*] until My Call is

raised up and the creatures are in accord on My Unicity [*ḥattä taʿluwa daʿwatî wa yajtamiʿa al-khalq ʿalä tawḥîdî*], then I will prolong My reign [*thumma la-udîmanna mulkahu*] and I will have My Friends continue in time until the Day of Resurrection [*wa la-udâwilanna l-ayyâm bayna awliyâʾî ilä yawm al-qiyâma*]

Cf. Ibn Bâbûye, *ʿIlal*, ch. 7, pp. 6–7; Ibn Bâbûye, *Kamâl al-dîn*, vol. 1, ch. 23, p. 256, num. 4; Ibn Bâbûye, *ʿUyûn*, vol. 1, ch. 26, p. 263, num. 22.

666. Al-Nuʿmânî, *Kitâb al-ghayba*, p. 474; might this tradition have an arithmomantic reading?

667. See, e.g., al-Kulaynî, *Uṣûl*, "kitâb al-ḥujja," bâb karâhiyyat al-tawqît, vol. 2, pp. 190–94; al-Kulaynî, *al-Rawḍa*, vol. 2, pp. 93f. and 119f.; al-Nuʿmânî, *Kitâb al-ghayba*, ch. 11, pp. 282–93; Ibn Bâbûye, *Kamâl*, vol. 2, ch. 55, pp. 644–47.

668. See, e.g., these words of al-Bâqir: "God, may He be exulted and glorified, had forseen the year 70 for this affair to take place [the Return and the Joy that follows], but when al-Ḥusayn was assassinated, God was angry with the inhabitants of the earth and decided to delay it until the year 140, and we have spoken to you [disciples] about this, but you have divulged our words and taken the veil off the Secret [*fa-adhaʿtum al-ḥadîth fa-kashaftum qinâʿ al-satr*], so God decided to no longer let us know the determination of the time"; al-Kulaynî, *Uṣûl*, "kitâb al-ḥujja," bâb karâhiyyat al-tawqît, vol. 2, p. 190, num. 1.

669. See, e.g., the words of Jaʿfar: "Those who hurry are lost, while those who are submissive are saved, and thus the fortress remains solid on its foundation [i.e., the doctrine is safe, *al-ḥiṣn ʿalä awtâdihâ*]; remain always at home [i.e., do not revolt against the authorities, *kûnû aḥlâs buyûtikum*] for the dust will settle on him who has raised it [*fa-ʾinna al-ghabara ʿalä man athâraha*]; know that each time that they [the "enemies"] wish you harm, God will turn their attention away from you, except when one of you is opposed to them [*innahum lâ yurîdûnakum bijâʾiḥa illâ atâhum Allâhu bi-shâghilin illâ man taʿarraḍa lahum minkum*]; al-Nuʿmânî, *Kitâb al-ghayba*, p. 286. On Imamite apoliticism, see also Part III-1.

670. *"Iʿrif imâmaka faʾinnaka idhâ ʿaraftahu lam yaḍurraka taqaddama hâdhâ al-amr aw taʾakhkhara"*; *"man ʿarafa imâmahu kâna ka-man huwa fî fusṭâṭ al-muntaẓar"*; al-Nuʿmânî, *Kitâb al-ghayba*, ch. 25, pp. 470–73; this probably refers to recognition of the Light of the Imam in the heart, i.e., passing "the test of the heart" (cf. Part II-3). The emphasis placed on "the Imam of each of the faithful" is significant. In a tradition, Jaʿfar mysteriously replaces the word "imam" with the word "Sign": "Try to know the Sign [*al-ʿalâma*], for from that moment on, the advancement or the "delay of this matter will not be able to bring any prejudgment upon you" (al-Nuʿmânî, *Kitâb al-ghayba*, p. 472).

671. *"Man mâta wa laysa lahu imâm [wa lam yaʿrif imâmahu] fa-mîtatuhu mîtatu jâhiliyya),"* cf. e.g., al-Kulaynî, *Uṣûl*, "kitâb al-ḥujja," bâb annahu man ʿarafa imâmahu . . . , vol. 2, pp. 197–99; al-Nuʿmânî, *Kitâb al-ghayba*, pp. 471–72; Ibn Bâbûye, *ʿUyûn*, vol. 1, ch. 6, pp. 54f.; Ibn Bâbûye, *Kamâl al-dîn*, vol. 2, ch. 33, p. 337, num. 9; vol. 2, ch. 38, p. 409, num. 9; vol. 2, ch. 39, pp. 412–14, num. 10; vol. 2, ch. 58, p. 668, num. 11.

CONCLUSIONS

672. *"Al-ḥujja qabla l-khalq wa maʿa l-khalq wa baʿda l-khalq"*; the words of Jaʿfar al-Ṣâdiq, al-Kulaynî, *Uṣûl*, "kitâb al-ḥujja," vol. 1, ch. 5, p. 251, num. 4; Ibn

Bâbûye, *Kamâl al-dîn*, author's introduction, vol. 1, p. 4; ch. 22, p. 221, num. 5, p. 232, num. 36.

673. For the different versions of this sentence so ubiquitous in the teachings of the imams, see, e.g., al-Ṣaffâr, *Baṣâ'ir*, section 10, ch. 10–12, pp. 484–89; al-Kulaynî, *Uṣûl*, vol. 1, ch. 6, pp. 251–53; al-Nu'mânî, *Kitâb al-ghayba*, ch. 8, pp. 194–99; Ibn Bâbûye, *'Uyûn*, vol. 1, ch. 28; Ibn Bâbûye, *'Ilal*, chapter 153; Ibn Bâbûye, *Kamâl al-dîn*, chapters 21, 22.

674. *"Law lam yabqa fî l-'âlam [al-arḍ] illâ rajulân la-kâna aḥaduhumâ l-imâm [al-ḥujja]"*; the words of several imams; cf. e.g., al-Ṣaffâr, *Baṣâ'ir*, section 10, ch. 11; al-Kulaynî, *op. cit.*, ch. 7; al-Nu'mânî, *Kitâb al-ghayba*, chapter 9.

675. *"Binâ qâmat al-samâwât wa l-arḍ"/"Bihum yumsiku 'llâhu l-samâ' an taqaa'alâ l-arḍ . . . bihim yaḥfaẓu' llâhu l-arḍ an tamîda bi-ahlihâ"*; *Kamâl al-dîn*, vol. 2, ch. 37, p. 383, num. 9; vol. 1, ch. 24, p. 259, num. 3.

676. Cf. e.g., al-Barqî, *Kitâb al-maḥâsin*, vol. 1, pp. 80f.; al-Kulaynî, *al-Rawḍa*, vol. 1, p. 154, and vol. 2, pp. 43, 89, 143; al-Nu'mânî, *Kitâb al-ghayba*, pp. 291-92, num. 16; Ibn Bâbûye, *Kamâl al-dîn*, vol. 1, ch. 24, p. 258, num. 3; p. 259, num. 4; p. 261, num. 8; Ibn Bâbûye, *Amâlî*, "majlis" 45, pp. 268-69, nums. 14, 16; "majlis" 54, p. 333, num. 2; p. 339, num. 24; "majlis" 63, p. 409, num. 13; "majlis" 73, pp. 484–85, num. 12; "majlis" 74, pp. 494-95, num. 16; "majlis" 85, pp. 5831–84, num. 28.

677. Nearly all the studies dedicated to Imamism speak of a "theory" or a "doctrine" of the Imamate. W. Madelung goes so far as to attribute the elaboration of this "theory" to Hishâm b. al-Ḥakam (s.v. *EI2*), a complex figure the true nature of whose relationship with the imams and their teachings remains to be determined.

678. These are teachings essentially recorded in compilations like al-Kulaynî's *Furû' min al-kâfî*, Ibn Bâbûye's *Kitâb man lâ yaḥḍuruhu ' l-faqîh*, or the majority of the "Four Hundred Original Books" (*al-Uṣûl al-arba'u mi' a*).

679. Literally, "the dispersion of Knowledge," (*tabdîd al-'ilm*); on its use in the Jâbirian corpus, see P. Kraus, *Jâbir b. Ḥayyân; tome I: le corpus des écrits jâbiriens*, pp. xxvii–xxx; P. Lory, *Dix Traités d'Alchimie*, pp. 53, 242f. In the very beginning of his *Kitâb al-mâjid*, Jâbir gives an idea of this method:

> Know this: when the Master [i.e., Ja'far al-Ṣâdiq], may God be pleased with him, told me to compose these books, he instructed me to arrange them in a certain hierarchical order that I am not at liberty to change. Of course you know what some of his intentions were when he set up the hierarchy of these books, but their ensemble you do not know. . . . Do not be disheartened then, my brother, if you happen to find a speech about esoteric religion in the very middle of which there is a speech about alchemy, a speech whose conclusion is not reached; or perhaps a speech about alchemy that is followed by a speech about religion but where the bases of the speech on religon are never set; or even a speech about devotion or some other subject that belongs to these sciences and arts that we treat of in these books of divine character. For all our developments that are offered to you in the course of these books, our Master . . . had intentions that I am not allowed to disclose to you. If I disclosed what they contain, you would be like Jâbir b. Ḥayyân. But from the moment that you were like him, you would no longer have any more need than does he for these things to be disclosed to you. Understand.

French translation by H. Corbin, "Le Livre du Glorieux," in *Alchimie comme art hiératique*, pp. 183–84 and note 84.

680. *Taqiyya*, literally "abstaining from something out of fear," and *kitmân*, literally "hiding, disguising"; the two words, synonymous in the context they have here, both refer to 1) the faithful believers' hiding their association with the Cause of the imams when being open about it would expose them to real danger; and especially, 2) keeping the occult teachings of the imams secret. Most specialists have only remembered the first of these two aspects, since they have seen nothing more than a political religious movement in Imamism, and perhaps also because the word *taqiyya* is of Khârijite origin (cf. Shahrastânî, *Livre des Religions*, pp. 383, 414). Not only are the two aspects connected, but the second is by far the more important from a doctrinal point of view, since it concerns the initiated, while the first is related to the mass of faithful. We prefer "keeping the Secret," a translation "in the first degree," to "the discipline of the arcane," proposed by H. Corbin. The latter expression, despite its beauty, has the problem of being too charged with a strictly Christian technical meaning. Actually, the *disciplina arcani*, used for the first time in the seventeenth century by J. Daillé (*De usu patrum*, Geneva, 1686), refers to one of the oldest rules of certain early Christian communities, and consisted in the obligatory hiding of the most secret of the aspects of Christ's Teaching; some sacraments were kept secret (Holy Eucharist), as were prayers, symbols (the fish, the symbol for Christ), teachings (transubstantiation, the Trinity) not only vis-à-vis the infidels and the "pagans," but also vis-à-vis the newly initiated believers. Among those considered to be the faithful of the *disciplina arcani* were Clement of Alexandria, Origen, Saint Basil, Saint Cyril of Jerusalem, pseudo-Dionysius the Areopagite (cf. *Dict. de théologie catholique*, A. Vacant and E. Mangenot, ed., Tome 1, ed. Letouzey and Ané, 1937, fasc. 2, col. 1738–158; M. Goguel, "Pneumatisme et eschatologie du christianisme primitif," *RHR*, vol. 132, 1946, and vol. 133, 1947–48; J. Daniélou and H. I. Marrou, *Nouvelle Histoire de l'Eglise*, Paris, 1963, vol. 1, pp. 99f).

681. A tradition of Ja'far; al-Kulaynî, *Uṣûl,* "kitâb al-îmân wa l-kufr," bâb al-taqiyya, vol. 3, p. 307, num. 2.

682. A tradition of al-Bâqir; al-Kulaynî, *Uṣûl*, "kitâb al-îmân wa l-kufr," bâb al-taqiyya, vol. 3, p. 312, num. 12; see the similar tradition of al-Riḍâ, in Ibn Bâbûye, *Kamâl al-dîn*, vol. 2, ch. 35, p. 371, num. 5. Also, al-Barqî, *Kitâb al-Maḥâsin*, vol. 1, pp. 202–3. In some traditions, "Faith" (*îmân*) is replaced by "Religion" (*dîn*).

683. A tradition of Ja'far; al-Kulaynî, *Uṣûl,* "kitâb al-îmân wa l-kufr," bâb al-idhâ'a, vol. 4, p. 77, num. 2.

684. A tradition of Ja'far; Ja'far's *Tafsîr*, ed. P. Nwyia, p. 194; ed. Zay'ûr, p. 136.

685. A tradition of Ja'far; al-Nu'mânî, *Kitâb al-ghayba*, ch. 1, p. 55, num. 3. The faithful Imamite can abandon the practice of *taqiyya* only after the Return of the hidden imam. Before that, abandoning *taqiyya* is like abandoning a canonical duty (Ibn Bâbûye, *I'tiqâdât*, pp. 44f.). For a general overview of the idea, see al-Barqî, *Kitâb al-Maḥâsin,* vol. 1, pp. 255–59; al-Ṣaffâr, *Baṣâ'ir*, section 1, chap. 12; section 8, chap. 3; section 9, chap. 2; section 10, chap. 22; al-Kulaynî, *Uṣûl*, bâb al-taqiyya, vol. 3, pp. 307–14; bâb al-kitmân, vol. 3, pp. 314–21; bâb al-idhâ'a, vol. 4, pp. 76–79; al-Kulaynî, *al-Rawḍa*, vol. 1, pp. 34, 81, 115, 125, 146, 180-83, 231, 233; vol. 2, pp. 14, 112; al-Nu'mânî, *Kitâb al-ghayba*, pp. 54–60; p. 203, num. 3; p. 230, num. 6; Ibn Bâbûye,

Kamâl al-dîn, vol. 1, pp. 253, 288; vol. 2, pp. 312–13, 330, 371, 385, 434, 646–47. Cf. on the subject and its historical and doctrinal evolutions I. Goldziher, "Das Prinzip der Takija im Islam," *ZDMG*, vol. 60, 1906, pp. 213–26; Kâmil M. al-Shaybî, "al-Taqiyya, uṣûluhâ wa taṭawwuruhâ," *Revue de la Faculté des Lettres de l'Université d'Alexandrie*, vol. 16, 1962–63; E. Kohlberg, "Some Imâmî-Shî'î Views on *taqiyya*," *JAOS*, vol. 95, 1975, pp. 395–402; E. Meyer, "Anlass und Anwendungsbereich der *taqiyya*," *Der Islam*, vol. 57, 1980, pp. 246–80.

686. Cf. al-Kulaynî, *al-Rawḍa*, vol. 1, p. 223. See also E. Kohlberg, "Some Shî'î Views on the Antediluvian World," especially pp. 45f.

687. See these sayings of the imams: "Our Teaching [var. "our Cause"] is a Secret, a Secret hidden by a Secret, a Secret made Secret, a Secret about a Secret [*ḥadîthunâ (amrunâ) sirr wa sirrun fî sirr wa sirrun mustasirr wa sirrun 'alä sirr*]"; "Our Teaching [Cause] is the Truth [*al-ḥaqq*], the Truth of the Truth, the exoteric (*al-zâhir*), the esoteric of the exoteric [*bâṭin al-zâhir*], and the esoteric of the esoteric [*bâṭin al-bâṭin*]; it is a Secret, a Secret hidden by a Secret . . . " (*Baṣâ'ir*, section 1, ch. 12, pp. 26–29); "Every thing has a Secret; that of Islam is Shî'ism [lit. "the Shî'ites," i.e., the initiated] (*inna li-kulli shay' sirrun wa sirr al-islam al-shî'a*)" (al-Kulaynî, *al-Rawḍa*, vol. 2, pp. 13–14).

688. On the different groups of *ghulât* and the (probably deformed) fragments of their doctrines, see, e.g., G. Van Vloten, *Recherches*; I. Friedländer, "'Abdallâh b. Sabâ, der Begründer der Shî'a und sein Jüdischer Ursprung," *ZA*, vol. 23, 1909, and vol. 24, 1910; R. Strothmann, "History of Islamic Heresiography," *Islamic Culture*, 1938; Gh. H. Sadighi, *Les Mouvements religieux*; S. Moscati, "Per una storia dell' antica shi'a," *RSO*, vol. 30, 1955; M. G. S. Hodgson, "How Did the Early Shî'a Become Sectarian?" *JAOS*, vol. 75, 1955; M. G. S. Hodgson, "Ghulât" in *EI2*, vol. 2, pp. 1119–21; P. J. Vatikiotis, "The Rise of Extremist Sects and the Dissolutions of the Fatimid Empire of Egypt," *Islamic Culture*, 1957; W. F. Tucker, "Rebels and Gnostics: Al-Mughîra b. Sa'îd and the Mughîriyya," *Arabica*, vol. 22, 1975; W. F. Tucker, "Bayân b. Sam'ân and the Bayâniyya: Shî'ite Extremists of Umayyad Iraq," *MW*, vol. 65, 1975; W. al-Qâdî, "The Development of the Term *ghulât* in Muslim Literature with Special Reference to the Kaysâniyya," *Akten VII Kong. Arabistic*, Göttingen, 1976; H. Halm, *Die islamische Gnosis*; Sayyid M. 'Askarî, *Naqsh-e a' emme*, s.v.; R. Freitag, *Seelenwanderung*. Matti Moosa's book, *Extremist Shiites. The Ghulat Sects* (New York, Syracuse University Press, 1987) deals almost exclusively with contemporary Shî'ite ideological groups.

689. We have already had occasion to see Ja'far's words resembling the *shaṭaḥât* of the mystics (note 277). In the same line of thinking, the following hadith reported by al-Kulaynî might be cited. The Prophet is speaking to 'Alî: "Something in you is like Jesus the son of Mary, and if I were not afraid that certain groups in my Community might say about you what the Christians said about him, I would reveal something about you that would make people collect the dust from under your feet in order to get its blessing [*fîka shibhun min 'Isä ibn Maryam wa law lâ an taqûla fîka ṭawâ' if min ummatî mâ qâlat al-naṣârä fî 'Isä ibn Maryam la-qultu fîka qawlan lâ tamurru bi-mala' min al-nâs illâ akhadhû l-turâb min taḥt qadamayka yaltamisûna bi-dhâlika l-baraka*]," *al-Rawḍa*, vol. 1, p. 81.

690. Cf. e.g., among the disciples of the third imam: Furât b. al-Aḥnaf al-'Abdî

(al-Ṭûsî, Rijâl, p. 99); those of the seventh imam: Md b. Sulaymân al-Baṣrî al-Daylamî (also a disciple of the eighth imam; *ibid.*, p. 359), Md b. Bishr (p. 361); those of the eighth imam: Sa'îd b. Ukht Ṣafwân b. Yaḥyä (p. 377), Ṭâhir b. Ḥâtim (p. 379), 'Umar b. Furât Kâtib Baghdâdî (p. 383), Md b. Jumhûr al-'Ummî (p. 387), Md b. al-Fuḍayl al-Azdî al-Ṣayrafî (who was also a disciple of the sixth and seventh imams; p. 389), Md b. Ṣadaqa al-Baṣrî (p. 391); among those of the ninth imam: al-Ḥasan b. 'Alî b. Abî 'Uthmân (also a disciple of the tenth imam, p. 400); among those of the tenth imam: Aḥmad b. Hilâl al-Baghdâdî (who showed up as a disciple of the eleventh imam, p. 410), Isḥâq b. Md al-Baṣrî (also a disciple of the eleventh imam, p. 411); al-Ḥusayn b. 'UbaydAllâh al-Qummî (p. 413), al-Ḥasan b. Md b. Bâbâ al-Qummî (also a disciple of the eleventh imam, p. 414), 'Alî b. Yaḥyä al-Dihqân (p. 418), 'Urwa al-Nakhkhâs al-Dihqân (p. 420), Fâris b. Ḥâtim al-Qazwînî (p. 420), al-Qâsim al-Sha'rânî al-Yaqṭînî (p. 421), Md b. 'AbdAllâh b. Mihrân al-Karkhî (who was also a disciple of the ninth imam; p. 423), Abû 'AbdAllâh al-Maghâzî (p. 426); among the disciples of the eleventh imam: Md b. Mûsä al-Suray'î (p. 436), Md b. al-Ḥasan al-Baṣrî (also a disciple of the ninth and tenth imams; p. 436). Let us note that, according to al-Ṭûsî's list, the greatest number of "extremist" disciples was in the entourage of the tenth imam, 'Alî al-Naqî al-Hâdî, and then in that of the eighth imam, 'Alî b. Mûsä al-Riḍâ. It was thus not only the entourages of the fifth and sixth imams that nourished and sheltered "extremist" milieux, as the heresiographers would have us believe. Through an injustifiable twisting of the situation, and in contradiction to the texts, Hodgson ("Ghulât," *EI2*) states that it was the imams who were influenced by "extremist" ideas; he thus turns disciples into teachers and teachers into disciples. According to him, and in contrast to what is reported by the Imamite corpus and by heresiographical works, ideas like *raj'a*, the impeccability of the imams, or spiritual *waṣiyya*, were also ideas professed for the first time by the *ghulât*.

691. *"Innî la-uḥaddithu l-rajul al-ḥadîth fa-yanṭaliqu fa-yuḥaddithu bihi 'annî kamâ sami'ahu fa-astaḥillu bihi la'nahu wa l-barâ' a minhu"*; al-Nu'mânî, *Kitâb al-ghayba*, ch. 1, p. 57, num. 7.

692. There are some studies that provide priceless information in this regard, although they are in need of revision or completion, in light of the cosmogonic, occult, and magical information we now know about early Imamism; let us cite, for example, E. Blochet, "Etudes sur le gnosticisme musulman"; E. Blochet, "Etudes sur l'ésotérisme musulman"; T. Andrae, *Die Person Muhammeds*; L. Massignon, "Die Ursprünge und die Bedeutung des Gnostizismus im Islam"; Kâmil M. al-Shaybî, *al-Fikr al-shî'i*; al-Shaybî, *al-Ṣila bayna l-taṣawwuf wa l-tashayyu'*; 'Abd Allâh S. al-Sâmarrâ'î, *al-Ghuluww wa l-firaq al-ghâliya fî l-ḥaḍârat al-islâmiyya*, Baghdad, 1392/1972; J. B. Taylor, "Ja'far al-Ṣâdiq, spiritual forebear of the sûfis"; S. H. Nasr, "Le shî'isme et le soufisme: Leurs relations principielles et historiques"; Y. Marquet, "Le Chiisme au IXe siècle à travers l'Histoire de Ya'qûbî"; Y. Marquet, "Sabéens et Ikhwân al-Ṣafâ"; H. Halm, *Die islamische Gnosis*; and, of course, studies of Imamism in the works of H. Corbin.

NOTES TO APPENDIX

693. Some of the information used here is taken from, and is complementary to, our article "Le shî'isme doctrinal et le fait politique," *Iran, une première république*.

694. The first great systematic compilations of Imamite law were the *Furû' min al-kâfî*, by al-Kulaynî, and Ibn Bâbûye's *Kitâb man lâ yaḥḍuruhu l-faqîh*; there have been numerous editions of both works. On this subject, see H. Löschner, *Die dogmatischen Grundlagen des schi'itischen Rechts*; H. Ma'rûf al-Ḥasanî, *al-Mabâdi' al-'âmma li l-fiqh al-ja'farî*; H. Modarressi Tabâtabâ'î, *An Introduction to Shî'î Law*.

695. Cf. Part I-2.

696. Cf. Part I-1.

696bis. Cf. J. Calmard, "Mudjtahid," *EI2*.

697. E.g., al-Mufîd, *Awâ'il al-maqâlât*, pp. 99f.; al-Murtaḍä 'Alam al-Hudä, *al-Dharî'a*, pp. 270, 605, 623f.

698. Abû Ja'far al-Ṭûsî, *Kitâb 'Uddat al-uṣûl*, pp. 65f.

699. Al-'Allâma al-Ḥillî, *Tahdhîb al-uṣûl*, chapter 4.

700. On this period of Imamite law, see R. Brunschvig, "les *uṣûl al-fiqh* imâmites à leur stade ancien," *Le Shî'isme imâmite*, pp. 201–13.

701. On these points of divergence (e.g., temporary marriage, conditions of inheritance, repudiation) see Y. Linant de Bellefonds, "Le droit imâmite," *Le shî'isme imâmite*, especially pp. 192–99.

702. Cf. Ibn Bâbûye, *Kitâb al-faqîh*, vol. 1, chap. 79, p. 332. Al-Ash'arî (d. 324/935) emphasizes the existence of this for Imamites, cf. *Maqâlât al-islâmiyyin*, ed. 'Abd al-Ḥamîd, p. 130.

703. See Aqâ Bozorg al-Ṭihrânî, *al-Dharî'a*, vol. 15, pp. 62–82.

704. Aqâ Bozorg al-Ṭihrânî, *al-Dharî'a*, vol. 5, pp. 296–98; on this subject, see E. Kohlberg, "The Development of the Imâmi-Shî'î Doctrine of *jihâd*," *ZDMG*, 126, 1976. In the same regard, the treatise entitled *al-Risâlat al-jihâdiyya* by Md Karîm Khân Kirmânî (the great master of the Shaykhiyya school, d. 1288/1870), written during the invasion of southern Iranian port of Bushahr by the British troops in 1273/1856, is quite enlightening. The author looks at the question from all sides (ms. num. 2534 of the Madrasa Sepahsâlâr in Tehran). A mention of al-Ash'arî shows that for the early Imamites, holy war could only be waged under the direction of the imam, or someone specifically named by him; cf. a-Ash'arî, *Maqâlât al-islâmiyyin*, p. 129.

705. Ja'far said: "Beware of exercising jurisdiction, for [the office of judge] belongs to only one guide [who is] wise in his judgment and just among Muslims, [a guide] like a prophet or an heir to a prophet [i.e., an imam]" (*ittaqû l-ḥukûma fa'inna l-ḥukûma innamâ hiya li l-imâm al-'âlim bi l-qaḍâ' al-'âdil fî l-muslimîn ka-nabî aw waṣî nabî*), Ibn Bâbûye, *Kitâb . . . al-faqîh*, vol. 3, ch. 1, p. 4, num. 7. Pointing to a judge's seat, the first imam is said to have stated: " . . . That is a seat that can only be occupied by a prophet, the heir to a prophet, or an unhappy man" (. . . *majlisan mâ jalasahu illâ nabî aw waṣî nabî aw shaqî*), *ibid.*, num. 8. In number 4 of the the following subchapter, the imams ask their faithful to avoid frequenting judges, for judges are constantly susceptible to attracting divine disfavor.

706. On these polemics, see al-Ṭihrânî, *al-Dharî'a*, vol. 6, p. 296, and vol. 17, pp. 136–43.

707. See, e.g., al-Mufîd, *al-I'lâm*, chapter 5, on legal penalties; Faḍl b. al-Ḥasan al-Ṭabarsî, *I'lâm al-warä bi a'lâm al-hudä*, pp. 446f.

708. Al-Murtadä al-Sayyid 'Alam al-Hudä, *Risalât al-ghayba*, in the margins of Mullâ Akhûnd al-Khurâsânî's *Farâ'id al-uṣûl*, n.d. We offer A. Sachedina's English

translation because we have no access to the original text; it is entitled "A Treatise on the Occultation of the Twelfth Imâmite Imam," *SI*, vol. 68, 1978, pp. 109–24. The text is from page 124.

709. For a short history of discussions on this subject, see W. Madelung, "Authority in Twelver Shiism in the Absence of the Imam," in *Religious Schools*, part 10, pp. 163–73. Polemics on the same order take place around another of the collective practices, that of religious taxes; on this subject, again see Madelung, "Shiite Discussions on the Legality of the *kharâj*," *Religious Schools*, part 1, pp. 193–202; N. Calder, "Zakât in Imami Shiʿi Jurisprudence from the Tenth to the Sixteenth century A.D.," *BSOAS*, num. 44, vol. 3, 1981; N. Calder, "Khums in Imami Shiʿi Jurisprudence from the Tenth to the Sixteenth Century A.D.," *BSOAS*, num. 45, vol. 1, 1982; for an overview of the "doctrine of inapplicability" [*suqûṭ*] of duties with collective implications—including "ordering what is good" and "forbidding what is evil" for the power holder—, a doctrine elaborated from as early as the Buyid period, see N. Calder, *The Structure of Authority in Imami Jurisprudence*, doctoral thesis, London, 1979, ch. 3; S. A. Arjomand, *The Shadow of God and the Hidden Imam . . .*, Chicago-London, 1984, pp. 61f.; E. Kohlberg, "The Development of the Imami Shiʿi Doctrine of *Jihâd*," pp. 67–68.

710. *"Wa ammâ l-ukhrä fa-yaṭûlu amaduhâ ḥattä yarjiʿa ʿan hâdhâ l-amr aktharu man yaqûlu bihi falâ yuthbitu ʿalayhi illâ man qawä* [this can also be read in passive voice: *quwwiya*] *yaqînuhu wa ṣaḥḥat* [passive voice: *ṣuḥḥat*] *maʾrifatuhu wa lam yajid fî nafsihi ḥarajan mimmâ qaḍaynâ wa sallama lanâ ahl al-bayt*"; Ibn Bâbûye, *Kamâl al-dîn*, vol. 1, ch. 31, pp. 323–34, num. 8.

711. *"Li l-qâʾim ghaybatân iḥdâhumâ qaṣîra wa l-ukhrä ṭawîla al-ghaybat al-ûlä lâ yaʿlamu bi-makânihi fîhâ illâ khâṣṣa shâʿatihi wa l-ukhrä lâ yaʿlamu bi-makânihi fîhâ illâ khâṣṣa mawâlîhi fî dînihi*"; al-Nuʿmânî, *Kitâb al-ghayba*, ch. 10, pp. 249-50; cf. also al-Kulaynî, *Uṣûl*, "kitâb al-ḥujja," bâb fî l-ghayba, vol. 2, pp. 141–42, num. 19 (= 900) (here, *"fî dînihi"* is missing at the end of the sentence). "The chosen ones among the Shîʿites" are undoubtedly the "representatives" during the minor Occultation; during this period, they alone had the privilege of knowing the "location" of the hidden imam. "The chosen ones among the intimate Friends in his Religion" would be those faithful believers especially initiated to be able to be in contact with the hidden imam during his major Occultation. Note the distinction made between the two kinds of "chosen ones": the first are said to be Shîʿite by confession, a point that does not appear in the second group.

712. *"Inna li-ṣâḥib hâdhâ l-amr ghaybatân iḥdâhumâ taṭûlu ḥattä yaqûlu baʿḍuhum mâta wa baʿḍuhum yaqûlu qutila wa baʿḍuhum yaqûlu dhahaba falâ yabqä ʿalä amrihi min aṣḥâbihi illâ nafarun yasîr lâ yaṭṭaliʿu ʿalä mawḍiʿihi aḥad min walî wa lâ ghayrihi illâ l-mawlä alladhî yalî amrahu,"* al-Nuʿmânî, *Kitâb al-ghayba*, pp. 250–51. An unusual distinction is made between *walî* (that we have translated as "friend") and *mawlä* ("intimate Friend"); normally both words, applied to the faithful, denote the "intimate disciple" of the imam. Here, a hierarchy is undoubtedly established among the faithful; let us bear in mind that *mawlä* also means "leader," "boss" (see also the use of the word *mawâlî*, the plural of *mawlä*, in the words reported in the preceding note).

713. *"Amrunâ [ḥadîthunâ] ṣaʿb mustaṣʿab lâ yaḥmiluhu [lâ yaḥtamiluhu] illâ nabî mursal aw malak muqarrab aw muʾmin imtaḥanaʾllâhu qalbahu li l-îmân*"; the

tradition is from a number of imams; cf. note 283. On the *imtiḥân al-qalb*, see previous discussion. In one tradition, it is specifically stated that "only those whose hearts have been tested by God for faith will remain firm in their belief in the hidden imam" (*Kamâl*, vol. 1, ch. 23, p. 253, num. 3). In one place "the prayer at the time of the Occultation," says: "Lord, show us eternally his Light [that of the hidden imam] without shadow, and through it enliven hearts that have died [*arinâ nûrahu sarmadan lâ ẓulma fîhi wa aḥyî bihi l-qulub al-mayyita*]," (*Kamâl*, vol. 2, ch. 45, p. 515, num. 43). On the hypothesis of the vision of the Imam with (or through) the heart, see Part II-3. It is perhaps while thinking about such a disciple having reached the source of inspiration that Ja'far is said to have stated: "We consider a man to be truly wise only when he is inspired by suprasensible voices" (*"Lâ na'uddu l-faqîh faqîhan ḥattä yakûna muḥaddathan"*; cf. al-Kashshî, *Rijâl*, p. 9), or al-Riḍâ: "I should like each faithful believer [i.e., each initiated Shî'ite] to become one who is inspired by suprasensible voices" (*"Innî uḥibbu an yakûna l-mu'min muḥaddathan"*; cf. Ibn Bâbûye, *Ma'ânî al-akhbâr*, p. 172). In both cases, the word *muḥaddath* is explained as a synonym of *mufahham*—he to whom understanding from "On-High" is given—(on these two terms, see earlier discussion), and thus reading the word as *muḥaddith* ("traditionnist") is not possible.

714. Such is the case for those in Iran called the Uwaysî (Oveysî) Imamites, those to whom the imam appears as a suprasensible spiritual master (not to be confused with sufis from the Oveysî School led by teachers from the 'Anqâ' family); the phenomenon is strictly secret, usually not divulged until after the mystic's death; cf. e.g., Mîrzâ Ḥusayn al-Nûrî al-Ṭabarsî, *al-Najm al-thâqib* (in Persian), Tehran, lith. ed., 1309/1891; N. Modarresî Tchahârdehî, *Seyrî dar taṣawwuf*, Tehran, second ed., 1361 solar/1981, chapter dedicated to the Uwaysî, pp. 428–32. Each imam, not only the hidden imam, can appear to the mystic as a suprasensible teacher.

715. As can be imagined, it is the esoteric texts that furnish the details about the "invisible companions of the Mahdî"; first, there are the Bâṭinite and Ismâ'îli sources that all introduce a spiritual hierarchy with a fixed number of members at each level, since upon a member's death, he is replaced by a new initiate; cf. e.g., *Kitâb al-haft al-sharîf*, attributed to al-Mufaḍḍal b. 'Umar al-Ju'fî, one of Ja'far's disciples, ed. M. Ghâlib, Beirut, 3rd. ed, 1980, chapter 37 (there is an older but less carefully done edition by 'A. Tâmer, entitled *Kitâb al-haft wa l-aẓilla*, Beirut, 1969); "Haft bâb-e Bâbâ Sayyidnâ" in *Two Early Ismaili Treatises*, ed. W. Ivanow, Bombay, 1933, pp. 12f. Among Imamites, the most interesting developments are found in the Shaykhis; cf. e.g., Md Karîm Khân Kirmânî, *Ṭarîq al-najât*, pp. 105f. and 500f.; Md Khân Kirmânî, *Kitâb al-mubîn*, pp. 412f., and especially 'Abd al-Riḍâ Khân Ebrâhîmî Kirmânî, *Dûstî-ye dûstân*. The "men of the Invisible" thus fill a double mission: they help those who are worthy acquire Knowledge through the teaching of the imam, at the same time they hide their identity as companions of the imam from the public eye.

716. For the "rationalist" evolution of early Imamism and the marginalization of the original "esoteric suprarational" tradition, see Part I-2.

716bis. The development of the Imamite theory of *ijtihâd* is due primarily to the "rationalist" thinkers of the Ḥilla School: Ibn Idrîs (d. 596/1201), al-Muḥaqqiq (d. 676/1277), and especially al-'Allâma (d. 726/1325); cf. N. Calder, "Doubt and Prerogative: The Emergence of an Imami Shi'i Theory of *ijtihâd*," *SI*, vol. 70, 1989.

717. On these traditions, see the texts cited in notes 328 to 334; for an overview of the "apoliticalism" of the imams, see Part III-1. In passing, let us remark on the three categories of Imamite attitudes toward power presented by Y. Richard (*Le Shîʿisme en Iran*, pp. 25–29): apoliticalism, government by the doctor-theologian, and the collectivization of the Imamate. This division appears to have some historical truth, but it must be pointed out that the two latter categories are relatively recent and that, from a doctrinal point of view, they have nothing to do with Imamism.

718. See, e.g., J. A. Bill, *The Politics of Iran*, Columbus, 1972, pp. 21f.

719. Cf. J. Aubin, "La politique religieuse des Safavides," in *Le Shîʿisme imâmite*, pp. 235–44, especially 238–41.

720. See, e.g., the powers and the political role of doctor-theologians like al-Muḥaqqiq al-Karakî (d. 941/1534; it is he who had the sovereign name him "representative of the hidden imam" *nâʾib al-imâm*; this is a "first," since the title up to that time was exclusively reserved for the four historical "representatives" of the twelfth imam), or al-Majlisî II (d. 1111/1699); cf. Md ʿAlî Mudarris, *Rayḥânat al-adab*, vol. 5, pp. 191f. and 244f.

721. Cf. e.g., G. Scarcia, "Intorno alle controversia . . . "; H. Modarressi, "Rationalism and Traditionalism in Shîʿi Jurisprudence: A Preliminary Survey," *SI*, vol. 59, 1984; J. R. Cole, "Shiʿi clerics in Irak and Iran: The Akhbari-Usuli Conflict Reconsidered," *Iranian Studies*, vol. 18, 1, 1985; J. A. Newman, *The Development and Political Significance* . . . ; for the *uṣulî/akhbârî* opposition in earlier times, see J. Calmard, "Le chiisme imâmite en Iran à l'époque seldjoukide d'après le *Kitâb al-naqḍ*"; Scarcia Amoretti, "L'Imamismo in Iran nell'epoca selgiuchide . . . "; for the brief and fragile resurgence of the Akhbârî school in the seventeenth and eighteenth centuries, see S. A. Arjomand, *The Shadow of God and the Hidden Imam*, pp. 146f.; E. Kohlberg, "Aspects of Akhbârî Thought in the Seventeenth and Eighteenth Centuries."

722. A whole series of religious technical terms came into being during this period and thereafter; others that already existed were altered; e.g., *al-nâʾib al-khâṣṣ/al-nâʾib al-ʿâmm*, *al-walâyat al-khâṣṣa* (specific *walâya*, that is, the divine selection of the imams)/*al-walâya al-ʿâmma* (general *walâya*, that of the jurist-theologian or of the "just sovereign," that is, his political and charismatic power), *awliyâʾ al-amr* ("the commanders of the Cause," a title up to that time reserved for the imams, but which thereafter meant "directors of affairs" and referred to the "official" judges or the sovereigns who were "guardians of the religion"). Cf. M. Langarûdî, *Termînolozhî-ye ḥuqûq* ("terminology of law" including also that of canon law), Tehran, 1346 solar/1967, s.v.

723. It is interesting to note that the famous tradition *al-ʿulamâʾ warathat al-anbiyâʾ* is no longer understood in the Shîʿite sense that it had in the early compilations, that is, "the initiated sages are the heirs of the prophets" (cf. Part III-2, and especially note 387), but in a completely "Sunnite" sense: "the scholars [i.e., the jurist-theologians] are the heirs of the prophets."

724. This "process of substitution" saw a revival after the "Islamic revolution" in Iran and the revolutionary necessity of emphasizing the ideological nature of the religion; thus, the spiritual "landmarks" of Imamite doctrine saw themselves metamorphosized into political and ideological "slogans"; we limit ourselves to pointing out a few of the most flagrant: *imâm* (traditionally limited to the twelve historical imams, but

today the religious "leader" of the revolution), *shahîd* (traditionally a martyr-witness who suffered the consequences of oppression, today a martyr-combattant who has fallen while attacking oppression), *qiyâm* (traditionally the eschatological rising of the Mahdî at the End of Time, today a popular uprising or a revolution), *ḥizb Allâh* (traditionally the totality of the initiates of the imams, today the partisans of the Islamic revolution). For a sociological analysis of the phenomenon, see F. Khosrokhavar, "Iran, la rupture d'une alliance," *Peuples méditerranéens*, 14, January–March 1981; for a look at the religion in the process of becoming an ideology, see D. Shayegan, *Qu'est-ce qu'une révolution religieuse?*, Paris, 1982.

Bibliography

In order to facilitate the reader's task in locating sources, the bibliography is in alphabetical rather than thematic order. The titles of works in Persian are transcribed according to Iranian pronunciation.

'ABD AL-JABBÂR, *al-Mughnî,* Cairo, 16 vol., 1960–65.

ABEL, A., "Changements politiques et littérature eschatologique dans le monde musulman", *SI,* vol. 2, 1954.

ABÛ MIKHNAF AL-AZDÎ, *Maqtal al-Ḥusayn (= Waq'at al-Ṭaff),* ed. M. H. Yûsufî Gharawî, Qumm, 1367 solar/1988.

ABÛ RIḌÂ, M. 'A, ed., *Zeitschrift für Geschichte der Arabisch-Islamischen Wissenschaften,* vol. 1, Berlin, 1984.

'AFÎFÎ, A. E., *al-Malâmatiyya wa l-ṣûfiyya wa ahl al-futuwwa,* Cairo, 1364/1945.

AICHELE, W., "Biblische Legenden der Schî'iten aus dem Prophetenbuch des Hoseinî," *MSOS,* vol. 18, 1915.

Akhbâr al-dawlat al-'abbâsiyya (anonymous), ed. 'A. 'A. al-Dûrî, Beirut, 1971.

'ALÎ IBN ABÎ ṬÂLIB (1st imam), *Nahj al-balâgha,* compiled by al-sharîf al-Raḍî, text and Persian translation by 'Alî Naqi Fayḍ al-Islâm, Tehran, 1351 solar/1972.

'ALI IBN al-ḤUSAYN (4th imam), *al-Ṣaḥifat al-Sajjâdiyya,* text, Persian translation, and commentaries by 'Alî Naqî Fayḍ al-Islâm, Tehran, 1375/1955 (see also CHITTICK).

al-'ALLÂMA al-ḤILLÎ, *Khulâṣat al-aqwâl (=Rijâl al-'Allâma al-Ḥilli),* Najaf, 1961.

———, *Tahdhîb al-usûl,* Bombay, n.d.

AMALDI, D., "Osservazioni sulle catene di trasmissione in alcuni testi di *rijâl* imamiti," *Cahiers d'Arabe,* 1979.

al-'ÂMILÎ, al-Sayyid Muḥsin, *A'yân al-shî'a,* vols. 1–56, Damascus, 1935–61; vols. 1–17, Beirut, 1960–61.

al-AMÎN, Hassan, *Islamic Shi'ite Encyclopaedia,* Beirut, n. d.

al-AMÎNÎ, 'A. A., *al-Ghadîr fî l-Kitâb wa l-Sunna wa l-adab*, Tehran, 1372/1952.

AMIR-MOEZZI, M. A., "Al-Ṣaffâr al-Qummî (d. 290/902–3) et son *Kitâb Baṣâ'ir al-darajât*," *Journal Asiatique*, vol. 280, num. 3–4, 1992 pp.221–250.

———, "Le shi'isme doctrinal et le fait politique," *Iran, une première république*, Paris, 1983.

ANDRAE, *T., Die Person Muhammeds im Leben und Glauben seiner Gemeinde*, Stockholm, 1918.

ANTES, P., *Zur Theologie der Schi'a*, Freiburg im Brisgau, 1971.

al-ARDABÎLÎ, *Jâmi' al-ruwât*, Qumm, 1331 solar/1953.

ARIOLI, A., "Introduzione allo studio del *'ilm ar-rijal* imâmita: le fonti," *Cahiers d'Onomastique Arabe*, 1979.

ARJOMAND, S. A., *The Shadow of God and the Hidden Imam. Religion, Political Order and Social Change in Iran from the Beginning to 1890*, Chicago, London, 1984.

ARNALDEZ, R., *Jésus dans la pensée musulmane*, Paris, 1988.

ARNOLD, L., "Le crédo du shî'isme duodécimain," *Travaux et Jours*, vol. 17, 1965.

al-ASH'ARÎ, *Maqâlât al-islâmiyyîn*, ed. H. Ritter, 2d ed., Wiesbaden, 1382/1963, and (ed.) 'Abd al-Hamîd, 2d ed., Cairo, 1389/1969.

al-ASH'ARÎ al-QUMMÎ, see al-QUMMÎ, Sa'd b. 'AbdAllah.

al-'ASKARÎ, S. M., *Naqṣḥ-e a'emme dar eḥyâ'-e dîn*, Tehran, 1363 solar/1984.

al-ASTARÂBADÎ, Mîrzâ Md b. 'Alî, *Manhaj al-maqâl fî taḥqîq aḥwâl al-rijâl*, Tehran, 1306/1888.

AUBIN, J., "La politique religieuse des Ṣafavides," see (Le) *Shi'isme imâmite*.

AYOUB, M. M., *Redemptive Suffering in Islam. A Study of the Devotional Aspects of Ashûrâ in Twelver Shi'ism*, The Hague, 1978.

———, "The Speaking Qur'ân and the Silent Qur'ân: A Study of the Principles and Development of Imâmi Shî'i *tafsîr*," *Approaches to the History of the Interpretation of the Qur'ân*, ed. A. Rippin, Oxford, 1988.

———, "Towards an Islamic Christology: An Image of Jesus in Early Shî'î Muslim Literature," *Muslim World*, vol. 66, 1976.

al-'AYYÂSHÎ Md b Mas'ûd, *Tafsîr*, ed. H. al-Rasûlî al-Maḥallâtî, Qumm, 1380/1960.

A'ẒAMÎ, A. M., *Studies in Early Hadith Literature*, 2d ed., Indianapolis, 1978.

al-BAGHDÂDÎ 'Abd al-Qâhir, *al-Farq bayna l-firaq*, Beirut, 1393/1973; Persian trans: *Târikh-e shi'e va ferqehâ-ye eslâmî*, by M. J. Mashkour, Tehran, 1339 solar/1960.

———, *Uṣul al-dîn*, Istanbul, 1928.

al-BAGHDÂDÎ Ismâ'îl Pâshâ, *Hidyat al-'ârifîn wa asmâ' al-mu'allifîn*, Istanbul, 1951–55.

al-BALÂDHURÎ, *Ansâb al-ashrâf*, ed. Schloesinger, Jerusalem, 1938.

al-BÂQILLÂNÎ, *Kitâb al-tamhîd*, ed. Mc Carthy, Beirut, 1957.

BAR-ASHER, M., "Deux traditions hétérodoxes dans les anciens commentaires Imamites du Coran," *Arabica*, vol. 37, 1990.

———, "Variant Readings and Additions of the Imâmî-Shî'a to the Qur'an," *Israel Oriental Studies*, vol. 13, 1993.

al-BARQÎ, Abû Ja'far, *Kitâb al-maḥâsin*, ed. J. Muḥaddith Urmawî, Tehran, 1370/1950, and ed. Baḥr al-'Ulûm, Najaf, 1964.

———, *Kitab al-rijâl*, ed. J. Muḥaddith Urmawî, Tehran, 1342 solar/1964.

al-BAYHAQÎ, *Dalâ'il al-nubuwwa*, ed. Md 'Uthmân, Cairo, 1969.

BILL, J. A., *The Politics of Iran*, Columbus, 1972.

BIRKELAND, H., *The Legend of Opening of Muhammad's Breast*, Oslo, 1955.

BLACHÈRE, R., *Introduction au Coran*, Paris, 1958.

BLICHFELDT, J. O., *Early Mahdism. Politics and Religion in the Formative Period of Islam*, Leiden, 1985.

BLOCHET, E., "Etudes sur le gnosticisme musulman," *RSO*, vol. 2, 1908–9; vol. 3, 1910 ; vol. 4, 1911–12 ; vol. 6, 1914–15.

———, "Etudes sur l'ésotérisme musulman," *Muséon*, special numbers 7 to 10, 1906–1909.

BLOOM, A., "Contemplation et ascèse, contribution orthodoxe," *Etudes Carméli-taines*, 1948.

———, "L'Hésychasme, yoga chrétien?" *Yoga, science de l'Homme Intégral*, Paris, 1953.

BOSWORTH, C. E., "lawḥ," *EI2*, vol. 4, p. 703 (cf. also WENSINCK).

BROCKELMANN, C., *Geschichte der Arabischen Literatur*, Weimar, 1898.

BRUNSCHVIG, R., "Les *uṣûl al-fiqh* imâmites à leur stade ancien (X^{e} et XIe siècles)," see *(le) Shî'isme imâmite*.

BUSSE, H., *Die Buyiden und das Chalifat*, Beirut, 1969.

CABASSUT, A., "Coeur," *Dictionnaire de spiritualité ascétique et mystique*, vol. 2, pp. 1023–51 (see also HAMON, A.).

CAHEN, Cl., "Buwayhides," *EI2*, vol. 1, pp. 1390–97.

CALDER, N., *The Structure of Authority in Imâmî Shîʿî Jurisprudence*, Doctoral thesis, University of London, School of Oriental and African Studies, 1979.

———, "Accommodation and Revolution in Imâmî Shîʿî Jurisprudence: Khumayni and Classical Tradition," *Middle East Studies*, 18, 1, 1982.

———, "Zakat in Imami Shiʿi Jurisprudence from the Tenth to the Sixteenth Century A.D.," *BSOAS*, 44-3, 1981.

———, Khums in Imami Shiʿi Jurisprudence from the Tenth to the Sixteenth Century A.D.," *BSOAS*, 45-1, 1982.

———, "Doubt and Prerogative: The Emergence of an Imami Shiʿi Theory of Ijtihâd," *SI*, 70, 1989.

CALMARD, J., "Le chiisme Imamite en Iran à l'époque seldjoukide d'après le *Kitâb al-naqḍ*"in *Le Monde iranien et l'Islam*, vol. 1, 1971.

———, *Le Culte de l'imâm Husayn. Étude sur la commémoration du drame de Karbalâ dans l'Iran pré-safavide*, Doctoral thesis, Paris, 1975.

———, "Mudjtahid," *EI2*.

CARRINGTON, H., *Hindu Magic*, London, 1909.

CHITTICK, W., "ʿAql," *Encyclopaedia Iranica*, vol. 1, pp. 194f. (see also RAHMAN, F.)

———, *The Psalms of Islam*, English translation of *al-Ṣaḥîfat al-Sajjâdiyya* (cf. ʿALÎ IBN AL-HUSAYN), London, 1988.

CHOKR, M., *Zandaqa et Zindîqs en Islam jusqu'à la fin du II/VIII*[e] siècle, Doctoral thesis, Paris III, 1987–88.

COLE, J. R., "Shiʿi Clerics in Iraq and Iran: The Akhbari-Usuli Conflict Reconsidered," *Iranian Studies*, 18, 1, 1985.

CORBIN, H., "Sur le douzième Imâm," *Table Ronde*, Feb. 1957.

———, "L'Imâm caché et la rénovation de l'homme en théologie shî'ite," *Eranos Jahrbuch*, vol. 28, 1960.

———, *Trilogie ismaélienne*, Tehran-Paris, 1961.

———, "Au Pays de l'Imâm caché," *Eranos Jahrbuch*, vol. 32, 1964.

———, "Le Livre du Tawhîd de Shaykh Sadûq et son commentaire par Qâzî Saʿîd Qommî," *Annuaire de l'EPHE-section des sciences religieuses*, num. 83 to 85, 1965–67.

———, *L'Homme de lumière dans le soufisme iranien*, 2d ed., Paris, 1971.

———, *En Islam iranien: aspects spirituels et philosophiques*, Paris, 1971–72.

———, *Corps spirituel et terre céleste: de l'Iran mazdéen à l'Iran shi'ite,* 2nd. revised edition, Paris, 1979.

———, *Temple et contemplation. Essais sur l'Islam iranien,* Paris, 1980.

———, *Le Paradoxe du monothéisme,* Paris, 1981.

———, *Temps cyclique et gnose ismaélienne,* reedition, Paris, 1982.

———, *Histoire de la philosophie islamique,* 3rd. ed., 2 vols. in 1 book, Paris, 1986.

———, *Alchimie comme art hiératique,* reedition, Paris, 1986.

Dabestân-e madhâhib, see KEY KHOSROW ESFANDIYÂR.

DANIELOU, J., *Nouvelle Histoire de l'église,* Paris, 1963 (see also MARROU, H. I.)

DEDERING, S., "Ein Kommentar der Tradition über die 73 Sekten," *MO,* vol. 25, 1931.

DELLA VIDA, L., "Mu'âwiya," *EI1.*

DERMENGHEM, E., "Techniques d'extase en Islam," *Yoga, science de l'Homme Intégral,* Paris, 1953.

al-DHAHABÎ, *Kitâb duwal al-islâm,* Heyderabad, n.d.

———, *Mîzân al-i'tidâl,* Cairo, 1325/1907–8.

———, *Tadhkirat al-ḥuffâz,* Heyderabad, 1955-1958.

———, *Siyar a'lâm al-nubalâ'* Cairo, 1962.

DONALDSON, M. D., *The Shi'ite Religion: A History of Islam in Persia and Iraq,* London, 1933.

al-DÛRÎ, A. A., *Nash'at al-'ilm al-ta'rîkh 'inda l-'arab,* Beirut, 1960.

EBRÂHÎMÎ 'Abd al-Riḍâ Kirmânî, *Fehrest-e kotob-e mashâyekh-e 'eẓâm va kholâṣ-eye aḥvâl-e îshân,* Kerman, 1957.

———, *Dûstî-ye dûstân,* Kerman, Bibliothèque shaykhî, ms. Z-8, facsimile 1400/1979, EPHE fund, religious sciences section.

ELIASH, J., *'Alî b. Abî Ṭâlib in ithnâ 'asharî shî'î belief,* Doctoral thesis, University of London, 1966.

———, "The Ithnâ 'Asharî Shî'î Juristic Theory of Political and Legal Authority," *SI,* vol. 29, 1969.

———, "The Shî'ite Qur'ân. A Reconsideration of Goldziher's Interpretation," *Arabica,* vol. 16, 1969.

'EMÂDZÂDEH EṢFAHÂNÎ, *zendegânî-ye emâm-e davâzdahom,* Tehran, 1335 solar/1956.

EQBÂL, 'A., *Khândân-e Nawbakhtî,* 2d ed., Tehran, 1966.

———, *(l') Etrange et le Merveilleux dans l'Islam médiéval,* Actes du Colloque held at Collège de France, under the direction of M. Arkoun, J. Le Goff, T. Fahd and M. Rodinson, Paris, 1978.

FAHD, T., "Le monde du sorcier en Islam," *Le Monde du sorcier,* Seuil, coll. "Sources Orientales," Paris, 1966.

———, "Djafr," *EI2,* vol. 2, pp. 386–88.

———, "Ḥurûf," *EI2,* vol. 3, pp. 616–17.

———, *La Divination arabe,* Paris, reedition, 1987.

———, "Gaʿfar aṣ-Ṣâdiq et la tradition scientifique arabe," see *(le) Shîʿisme imâmite.*

FALATURI, A., "Die Zwölfer-Schia aus der Sicht eines Schiiten: Probleme ihrer Untersuchung," *Festschrift Werner Caskel,* ed., E. Gräf, Leiden, 1968.

FAQÎHÎ, ʿA. A., *Âl-e Bûye va owḍâʿ-e zamân-e îshân,* 3- ed., Tehran, 1987.

al-FÂRÂBÎ, *Risâla fî l-ʿaql,* ed. M. Bouyges, Beirut, 1938.

FOUCHECOUR, Ch. -H. de, *Moralia. Les Notions morales dans la littérature persane du 3/9e* au 7/13e siècle, Paris, 1986.

FRANK, R. M., "The Neo-Platonism of Gahm ibn Ṣafwân," *Muséon,* vol. 78, 1965.

FREITAG, R., *Seelenwanderung in der islamischen Häresie,* Berlin, 1985.

FRIEDLAENDER, 1., *Die Messiasidee im Islam,* Frankfurt, 1903.

———, "The Heterodoxies of the Shiites in the Presentation of Ibn Hazm," *JAOS,* 29, 1908.

———, "ʿAbdallâh b. Sabâ, der Begründer der Shîʿa und sein Jüdischer Ursprung," *ZA,* vol. 23, 1909 and vol. 24, 1910.

FRIEDMANN, Y., "Finality of Prophethood in Sunni Islam," *JSAI,* vol. 7, 1986.

FURÂT b. Ibrâhîm al Kûfî, *Tafsîr,* Najaf, 1354/1935 and ed. Md al-Kâẓim, Tehran, 1410/1990.

FYZEE, A. A. A., *Shiʿite Creed,* Oxford, 1942 (see also IBN BÂBÛYE).

———, "Ibn Bâbawayh," *EI2,* vol. 3, pp. 749–50.

GABRIELI, F., *Al-Ma'mûn e gli Alidi,* Leipzig, 1929.

———, "Amîn," *EI2,* vol. 1, p. 449.

———, "Imâmisme et littérature sous les Bûyides," see *(le) Shîʿisme imâmite.*

GARCIN DE TASSY, A., "Chapitre inconnu du Coran," *JA,* vol. 13, May 1842.

GARDET, L., "La mention du nom divin (dhikr) en mystique musulmane," *Revue Thomiste,* 1952 and 1953.

———, "Les Noms et les Statuts, *SI*, vol. 5, 1956.

———, "Fins dernières selon la théologie musulmane," *Revue Thomiste*, 1957.

———, "Kalb," *EI2*, vol. 4, pp. 507–10 (see also VADET).

———, *Dieu et la destinée de l'homme*, Paris, 1967.

GHAZZÂLÎ, *Iḥyâ' 'ulûm al-dîn (+'Awârif al-ma'ârif* d'al-Suhrawardî), Cairo, 1387/1967–68.

GILLIOT, C., "Muqâtil, grand exégète, traditionniste el théologien maudit," *JA*, vol. 279, 1991, num. 1–2.

GIMARET, D., *K Bilawhar wa Bûdhasaf*, Paris-Geneva, 1971.

———, *Les Noms divins en Islam*, Paris, 1988.

———, *La Doctrine d'al-Ash'arî*, Paris, 1990.

See also Shahrastânî, *Livre des religions et des sectes*.

GOGUEL, M., "Pneumatisme et eschatologie du christianisme primitif," *RHR*, vol. 132, 1946, and vol. 133, 1947.

GOLDZIHER, 1., *Beiträge zur Literaturgeschichte der Schî'a und der sunnitischen Polemik*, Vienna (Austria), 1874.

———, "Spottnamen der ersten Chalifen bei den Schî'iten," *WZMG*, vol. 15, 1901.

———, "Das Prinzip der Takija im Islam," *ZDMG*, vol. 60, 1906.

———, "Neuplatonische und gnostische Elemente im Hadit," *ZA*, 1908.

———, *Vorlesungen über den Islam*, Heidelberg, 1910.

———, *Die Richtungen der islamischen Koranauslegung*, Uppsala, 1913 (reedition., Leiden, 1952).

———, *Muslim Studies*, ed. S. M. Stern, London, 1971.

GOLPÂYEGÂNÎ Ṣâfî, *Muntakhab al-athar fî l-imâm al-thânî 'ashar*, Tehran, 1373/1953.

GOUILLARD, J., see *Petite Philocalie de la prière du coeur*.

GRAMLICH, R., *Die schiitischen Derwischorden Persiens*, Wiesbaden, 1981 (3d ed.).

———, *Die Wunder der Freunde Gottes. Teologien und Erscheinungsformen des islamischen Heiligewunders*, Wiesbaden, 1987.

GUILLAUMONT, A., "Les sens du nom du coeur dans l'Antiquité," *Etudes Carméli-taines*, number dedicated to "coeur," 1953.

al-GUJARÂTÎ Abû l-Mu'ayyad (actually, Muḥammad Ghawth Guwâlyârî), *al-Jawâhir al-khamsa,* (by Md Ghawth al-GWÂLYÂRÎ) (India), 1301/1883.

al-Haft wa al-aẓilla (ed. A. Tamer and A. Khalifé; Beirut, 2nd ed., 1970) = *al-Haft al-sharif* (ed. M. Ghâlib, Beirut, 3d ed., 1980), attributed to al-Mufaḍḍal b. 'Umar al-Ju'fî, who reports the sayings of Ja'far al-Ṣâdiq.

al-ḤALABÎ, *al-Sîrat al-Ḥalabiyya,* Beirut, n.d.

HALLAQ, W. B., "On the Origins of the Controversy About the Existence of Mujtahids and the Gate of Ijtihâd," *SI*, vol. 63, 1986.

HALM, H., "Das 'Buch der Schatten'. Die mufaḍḍal Tradition der Gulat und die Ursprünge des Nuṣairiertums," *Der Islam,* vol. 55, 1978, pp. 219–66 and vol. 58, 1981, pp. 15-86.

———, *Die islamische Gnosis. Die extreme Schia und die 'Alawiten,* Zurich-Munich, 1982.

———, *Die Schia,* Darmstadt, 1988.

HAMON, A., "Coeur," *Dictionnaire de spiritualité ascétique et mystique;* cf. CABASSUT, A.

al-ḤASAN al-'ASKARÎ (11th imâm), *Tafsîr,* ed. Lucknow, 1310/1893; litho., Iran, 1316/1898; Qumm, 1407/1987.

al-ḤASANÎ, see MA'RÛF AL-ḤASANÎ.

HAUSHERR, I., "La méthode d'oraison Hésychaste," *Orientalia Christiana,* vol. 9, 1927.

al-ḤILLÎ, see al-'ALLÂMA.

———, IBN DÂWÛD.

———, IBN IDRÎS.

———, al-MUḤAQQIQ.

HODGSON, E. G., "How Did the Early Shî'a Become Sectarian?," *JAOS,* 75, 1955.

———, "Ghulât," *EI2*, vol. 2, pp. 1119–21.

HOLMYARD, E. J., *The Arabic Works of Jâbir b. Ḥayyân,* Paris, 1928.

HOROVITZ, J., "Alter und Ursprung des Isnâd," *Der Islam,* vol. 8, 1918.

al-HUJWÎRÎ, *Kashf al-maḥjûb,* ed. Zhukovskij, reedition, Tehran, 1979.

al-ḤURR al-'ÂMILÎ, *al-Jawâhir al-saniyya fî l-aḥâdîth al-qudsiyya,* Baghdad, 1964.

HUSSAIN, J. M., *The occultution of the twelfth imam. A historical background,* London, 1982.

IBN AL-ATHÎR, *al-Kâmil fi l-ta'rîkh*, ed. Tornberg, Leiden, 14 vol., 1851/1876.

IBN 'AYYÂSH AL-JAWHARÎ, *Muqtaḍab al-athar fî l-naṣṣ 'alä 'adad al-a'immat al-ithnay 'ashar*, Tehran, 1346/1927.

IBN BÂBÛYE al-ṢADÛQ, *'Ilal al-sharâ'i' wa l-aḥkâm*, Najaf, 1385/1966.

———, *Kamâl al-dîn wa tamâm al-ni'ma*, ed. 'A. A. Ghaffârî, Qumm, 1405/1985.

———, *Kitâb al-khiṣâl*, text and Persian translation by M. B. Kamareyî, Tehran, 1329 solar/1950; also the Tehran edition, 1361 solar/1982.

———, *Ṣifât al-shî'a + Faḍâ'il al-shî'a*, texts and Persian translations by Ḥ. Fashâhî, Tehran, 1342 solar/1963–64.

———, *al-Amâlî (= al-Majâlis)*, text and Persian translation by M. B. Kamareyî, Tehran, 1404/1984.

———, *Kitâb al-tawḥîd*, ed. Ḥ. al-Husaynî al-Ṭihrânî, Tehran, 1398/1978; Persian translation: *Asrâr-e tawḥîd*, by Md 'Alî b. Md Ḥasan Ardakânî, Tehran, n.d.

———, *Muṣâdaqat al-ikhwân*, Tehran, n.d. (the introduction by S. Nafîsî is dated 1325 solar/1946).

———, *'Uyûn akhbâr al-Riḍâ*, ed. M. Ḥ. Lâjevardî, Tehran, 1378/1958; Persian translation by 'A. Ḥ. Riḍâ'î et M. B. Ṣâ'idî, Tehran, 1396/1976.

———, *Ma'ânî al-akhbâr*, Tehran, litho. ed., n.d.; and 'A. A. Ghaffârî (ed.), Tehran, 1379/1959.

———, *al-Muqni' + al-Hidâya*, ed. Md Wâ'iẓ Khurâsânî, Tehran, 1377/1957.

———, *Kitâb man lâ yaḥḍuruhu l-faqîh*, ed. al-Mûsawî al-Kharsân, 5th. ed., 1390/1970.

———, *Risâlat al-i'tiqâdât al-imâmiyya*, Tehran, n.d.; English translation by A. A. A. Fyzee, *Shi'ite Creed*, Oxford, 1942.

IBN AL-BIṬRÎQ, *Khaṣâ'iṣ waḥy al-mubîn fî manâqib Amîr al-mu'minîn* (n.d., n.l.).

———, *Kitâb al-'umda fî 'uyûn ṣiḥâḥ al-akhbâr* (n.d., n.l.).

IBN ḌAWÛD AL-ḤILLÎ, *Kitâb al-rijâl*, Tehran 1964; Najaf 1972.

IBN ḤAJAR AL-'ASQALÂNÎ, *Lisân al-mîzân*, Heyderabad, 1329–31/1911–13.

———, *Tahdhîb al-tahdhîb*, Heyderabad, 1325–27/1907–9.

IBN ḤANBAL, *Musnad*, Cairo, 1313/1896.

IBN ḤAZM, *al-Fiṣal fî l-milal wa l-ahwâ' wa l-niḥal*, Cairo, 1321/1903.

IBN HISHÂM, *al-Sîrat al-nabawiyya*, ed. al-Saqâ, al-Abyârî, Shalabî, 3d. ed., Beirut, 1971.

IBN IDRÎS AL-ḤILLÎ, *al-Sarâ'ir al-ḥâwî li taḥrîr al-fatâwî,* Tehran, 1270/1853.

IBN ISḤÂQ, *Sirat Ibn Isḥâq al-musammât bi-kitâb al-mubtada' wa l-mab'ath wa l-maghâzî,* ed. Md Hamidullah, Rabat, 1976.

IBN AL-JAWZÎ, *al-Wafâ bi-aḥwâl al-Muṣṭafä,* Cairo, 1966.

IBN KATHÎR, *al-Bidâya wa l-nihâya,* Cairo, 14 vol., 1932–39.

IBN KHALDÛN, *al-Muqaddima,* ed. Quatremère and English translation by F. Rosenthal, New York, 1958.

IBN MATTÛYE, *al-Majmû' fî l-muḥiṭ bi l-taklîf,* ed. 'U. al-'Azmî, Cairo, 1965.

IBN AL-NADÎM, *al-Fihrist,* ed. Flüegel, 1871; ed. Tajaddod, Tehran, 1971.

IBN QÛLÛYE AL-QUMMÎ, *Kâmil al-ziyârât,* litho. ed., Iran, n.d.

IBN RAJAB, *Kitâb al-dhayl 'alä ṭabaqât al-ḥanâbila,* Cairo, 1953.

IBN RUSTAM AL-ṬABARÎ, *Dalâ'il al-imâma,* Najaf, 1369/1949.

IBN SAB'ÎN, *Rasâ'il,* ed. 'A. R. Badawî, Egypt, n.d.

IBN SA'D, *al-Ṭabaqât al-kubrä,* ed. Sachau, Leyde, 1904–17.

IBN SHAHRÂSHÛB, *Ma'âlim al-'ulamâ* ed. 'A. Eqbâl, Tehran, 1353/1934.

———, *Manâqib âl Abî Ṭâlib,* Najaf, 1956.

———, *Mathâlib al-nawâṣib,* ms. Nâṣiriyya Library, Lucknow.

IBN ṬAQṬAQÂ, *Târîkh-e Fakhrî* ed. Golpâyegânî, Tehran, 1331/1952.

IBN ṬÂWÛS, *Faraj al-mahmûm fî ta'rikh 'ulama' al-nujûm,* Najaf, 1368/1949.

———, *al-Malâḥim wa l-fitan,* Najaf, 1383/1963.

IBN TAYMIYYA, *Kitâb minhâj al-sunnat al-nabawiyya,* Cairo, 1321/1903.

IBRAHIM, L., "The problem of the vision of the God in the theology of az-Zamakhsharî and al-Bayḍâwî," *Die Welt des Orients,* vol. 13, 1982.

al-IṢFAHÂNÎ Abû l-Faraj, *Kitâb al-aghânî,* Cairo, n.d.; reedition. Beirut, 1970.

al-ISFARÂ'INÎ Ṭâhir b. Md, *al-Tabṣîr fî l-dîn,* ed. Kawtharî, Cairo, 1374/1955.

Ithbât al-waṣiyya li l-imâm 'Alî b. Abî Ṭâlib, attributed to al-MAS'ÛDÎ, Najaf, n.d.

IZUTSU, T., *The Concept of Belief in Islamic Theology,* Tokyo, 1965.

———, *Ethico-religious concepts in the Qur'ân,* Montreal, 1966.

JÂBIR IBN ḤAYYÂN, see ABÛ RIḌA, CORBIN *(Alchimie . . .),* HOLMYARD, KRAUS, LORY, RUSKA.

JA'FAR AL-ṢÂDIQ (6th imâm), *Tafsîr*, ed. P. Nwyia, *MUSJ*, vol. 43, 1968, ed. 'A. Zay'ûr, *al-Tafsîr al-ṣûfî li l-Qur'ân 'inda l-Ṣâdiq*, Beirut, 1979; cf. also al-NU'MÂNÎ.

JAFRI, S. H. M., *The Origins and Early Development of Shi'a Islam*, London-New York-Beirut, 1979.

JÂḤIẒ, *Kitmân al-sirr*, ed. Kraus and Ḥâjirî, Cairo, 1941.

JAVAD ALI, "Die beiden ersten Safire des Zwölften Imams," *Der Islam*, vol. 25, 1939.

JEFFERY, A., "The Qur'ânic Readings of Zaid b. 'Alî," *RSO*, vol. 16, 1936.

———, "Materials for the History of the text of the Qur'ân" which comprises the introduction to Ibn Abî Dâwûd's *Kitâb al-Maṣâḥif*, Leiden, 1937.

JOHNSTON, F., *Himalayan Tantric Magic. Theory and Practice*, Bombay, 1949.

JOLIVET, J., "Intellect et intelligence—Note sur la tradition arabo-latine des XIIe et XIIIe siècles," *Mélanges offerts à Henry Corbin*, Tehran, 1977.

al-JU'FÎ al-Mufaḍḍal b. 'Umar, see *al-Haft wa l-aẓilla*.

JUYNBOLL, C. H. A., *Muslim Tradition. Studies in Chronology, Provenance and Authorship of Early Ḥadîth*, Cambridge, 1983–85.

KAHHÂLA 'Umar Riḍâ, *Mu'jam al-mu'allifîn wa âthâr al-muṣannifîn*, Istanbul, 1951–55.

al-KANTÛRÎ, *Kashf al-ḥujub wa l-astâr 'an asmâ' al-kutub wa l-asfâr*, ed. H. Hosain, Calcutta, 1935

al-KARÂJAKÎ Md b. 'Alî, *al-Burhân 'alä Ṣiḥḥa ṭûl 'umr Ṣâḥib al-zamân*, (ed. with the author's *Kanz al-fawâ'id*), Tabriz, n.d.

al-KÂSHÂNÎ, Muḥsin al-Fayḍ, *Tafsîr al-Ṣâfî*, (Iran), 1266/1849.

———, *al-Nawâdir fî jam' al-aḥâdîth*, Tehran, 1960.

al-KASHSHÎ, *Ikhtiyâr ma'rifat al-rijâl* (summarized by al-Ṭûsî), Mashhad, 1970.

———, *Rijâl al-Kashshî*, Bombay, 1317/1899.

KAZEM-BEG, "Observations de Mirzâ Alexandre Kazem-Beg, professeur de langues orientales à l'université de Casan, sur le *Chapitre inconnu du Coran*," *JA*, vol. 14, December 1843.

al-KÂẒIMÎ AsadAllâh b. Ismâ'îl, *Kashf al-qinâ'* Tehran, 1317/1899.

KEY KHOSROW ESFANDIYÂR, *Dabestân-e madhâhib*, ed. R. Reḍâ Zâdeh Malek, Tehran, 1362 solar/1983.

KHALIDI, T., *Islamic historiography: the histories of Mas'ûdî*, Albany, 1975.

KHAZAL, H., *La Notion de l'imâm chez al-Kulaynî,* Doctoral thesis, Paris III, 1972.

al-KHAZZÂZ al-RÂZÎ, *Kifâyat al-athar fî l-naṣṣ 'alä l-a 'immat al-ithnay 'ashar,* Tehran, 1305/1888.

KHOSROKHAVAR, F., "Iran, la rupture d'une alliance," *Peuples Méditerranéens,* vol. 14, Janvier–Mars 1981.

KHOURY, R. G., "L'importance d'Ibn Lahî'a et de son papyrus conservé à Heidelberg dans la tradition musulmane du deuxième siècle de l'Hégire," *Arabica,* vol. 22, fasc. 1, 1975.

———, "Pour une nouvelle compréhension de la transmission des textes dans les trois premiers siècles islamiques," *Arabica,* vol. 34, fasc. 2, 1987.

al-KH(W)ÂNSÂRÎ, *Rawḍât al-jannât,* Tehran, 1307/1889.

al-KH(W)ÂRAZMÎ, *al-Manâqib,* Najaf, 1965.

al-KIRMÂNÎ Md Khân, *Kitâb al-mubîn,* Tabriz, 1324/1906.

al-KIRMÂNÎ Md Karim Khân, *Yâqûtat al-ḥamrâ,* Kirman, n.d.

———, *Ṭarîq al-najât,* Kirman, 1344/1925.

———, *al-Risâla al-jihâdiyya,* ms. 2534, Madrasa Sepahsâlâr of Tehran.

KISTER, M. J., "You Shall Only Set Out for Three Mosques ", *Muséon,* vol. 82, 1969.

———, "Ḥaddithû 'an Banî Isrâ'îl wa lâ ḥaraja," *IOS,* vol. 2, 1972.

———, *Kitâb 'Abbâd al-'Usfurî,* see *Uṣûl arba'u mi'a.*

———, *Kitâb Sulaym b. Qays,* Najaf, n.d.

KLEMM, V., "Die vier *sufarâ'* des Zwölften Imâm. Zur formativen Periode der Zwölferschia," *Die Welt des Orients,* vol. 15, 1984.

KOHLBERG, E., "Some notes on the imâmite attitude to the Qur'an," *Islamic Philosophy and the Classical Traditions: Essays Presented to R. Walzer,* ed. Stern-Hourani-Brown, Oxford, 1972.

———, "Some Imâmî-Shî'î Views on *taqiyya,*" *JAOS,* 95, 1975.

———, "An Unusual Shî'î *isnâd,*" *IOS,* vol. 5, 1975.

———, "The Development of the Imâmî-Shî'î Doctrine of *jihâd,*" *ZDMG,* vol. 126, 1976.

———, "From Imâmiyya to Ithnâ'ashariyya," *BSOAS,* vol. 39, 1976.

———, "Shî'î Ḥadith," *Arabic Literature to the End of the Umayyad Period,* Cambridge, 1983.

———, "Some Imâmî-Shî'î Views on the *Ṣaḥâba,*" *JSAI,* vol. 5, 1984.

———, "Non-Imâmî Muslims in Imâmî *fiqh,*" *JSAI,* vol. 6, 1985.

———, "ʿAlî b. Abî Ṭâlib," *Encyclopaedia Iranica* (see also POONAWALA).

———, "*Barâ'a* in Shîʿî Doctrine," *JSAI*, vol. 7, 1986.

———, "Western Studies of Shiʿa Islam," *Shiʿism: Resistance and Revolution*, M. Kramer ed., London, 1987.

———, "al-Uṣûl al-arbaʿu mi'a," *JSAI*, 10, 1987. See E. Kolberg, *Belief and Law in Imâmî Shîʿism*, Variorum Reprints, England, 1991 (in addition to the articles already cited, we also used V—"The Term *Muḥaddath* in Twelver Shîʿism"; XIII—"Imam and Community in the Pre-Gayba Period," XVI—"Some Shîʿî Views on the Antediluvian World" ; XVII—"Aspects of Akhbârî Thought in the Seventeenth and Eighteenth Centuries").

KOVALENKO, A., *Les Concepts de magie et de sciences occultes en Islam*, Doctoral thesis, Strasbourg, 1979.

KRAUS, P., *Mukhtâr rasâ'il Jâbir b. Ḥayyân*, Paris–Cairo, 1935.

———, *Jâbir ibn Ḥayyân. Contribution à l'histoire des idées scientifiques dans l'Islam*, Cairo, 1943.

al-KULAYNÎ, *al-Uṣûl min al-kâfî*, ed. J. Muṣṭafawi with Persian translation, 4 vol., Tehran, n.d. (the fourth volume translated by H. Rasûlî Maḥallâtî in 1386/1966).

———, *al-Furûʿ min al-kâfî*, 4 vol., Tehran, 1334 solar/1956.

———, *al-Rawḍa min al-kâfî*, text and Persian translation by H. Rasûlî Maḥallâtî, Tehran, 1389/1969.

KUMAYT b. Zayd al-Asadî, *Hâshimiyyât*, Qumm, n.d.

LAMMENS, H., *Études sur le règne du calife omeyyade Moʿawiya Ier*, Beirut, 1908.

———, *Fâtima et les filles de Mahomet. Notes critiques pour l'étude de la Sira*, Rome, 1912.

———, *Le Califat de Yazid Ier*, Beirut, 1921.

LAOUST, H., *Essai sur les doctrines sociales et politiques d'Ibn Taimîya*, Cairo, 1939.

———, *La Profession de foi d'Ibn Baṭṭa*, Damascus, 1958.

———, "Le rôle de ʿAlî dans la sîra shiite," *REI*, vol. 30, 1962.

———, *Les Schismes dans l'islam*, Paris, 2d ed., 1977.

LECOMTE, G., "Aspects de la littérature du *ḥadîth* chez les imâmites," see *(le) Shîʿisme imâmite*.

LINANT DE BELLEFONDS, Y., "Le droit imâmite," see *(le) Shîʿisme imâmite*.

LORY, P., *Dix Traités d'alchimie. Les dix premiers Traités du Livre des Soixante-dix*, Paris, 1983.

———, "La science des lettres en terre d'Islam: le chiffre, la lettre, l'oeuvre," *Cahiers de l'université de St Jean de Jérusalem,* vol. 11, Paris, 1985.

———, *Alchimie et mystique en terre d'Islam,* Verdier, Lagrasse, 1989.

LÖSCHNER, H., *Die Dogmatischen Grundlagen des Shiʿitischen Rechts,* Erlangen-Nürenberg, 1971.

MAC DERMOTT, M. J., *The Theology of Al-Shaikh Al-Mufid (d 413/1022),* Beirut, 1978.

MADELUNG, W., "New Documents Concerning al-Ma'mûn, al-Faḍl b. Sahl, and ʿAlî al-Riḍâ," in *Studia Arabica et Islamica. Festschrift for Iḥsân ʿAbbâs,* ed. W. al-Qâḍî, Beirut, 1981.

———, *Religious Schools and Sects in Medieval Islam,* Variorum Reprints, London, 1985, especially the following articles: I—"Early Sunnî Doctrine Concerning Faith as Reflected in the *Kitâb al-imân* of Abû ʿUbaid al-Qâsim b. Sallâm (d. 224/839)."

———, VI—"Frühe muʿtazilitische Häresiographie: das *Kitâb al-Uṣûl* des Ga'far b. Ḥarb."

———, VII—"Imâmism and Muʿtazilite Theology."

———, VIII—"The Shiite and Khârijite Contribution to Pre-Ashʿarite *Kalâm.*"

———, IX—"A Treatise of the Sharîf al-Murtaḍâ on the Legality of Working for the Government (*Mas'ala fî l-ʿamal maʿa l-sulṭân*)."

———, X—"Authority in Twelver Shiism in the Absence of the Imam."

———, XI—"Shiite Discussions on the Legality of the Kharâj."

———, XV—"Bemerkungen zur imamitischen Firaq-Literatur."

———, *EI2,* the articles: "Ḥishâm b. al-Ḥakam," "Imâma," "al-Kulaynî," "Mahdî."

(la) Magie arabe traditionnelle, Retz, coll. "Bibliotheca Hermetica," Paris, 1976.

al-MAJLISÎ Md Bâqir, *Biḥâr al-anwâr,* litho. ed., Iran, n.d., 35 vol.; edition based on that of Kumpânî, Tehran-Qumm, 110 books in 90 vol., 1376–92/1956–72.

———, *Mir'ât al-ʿuqûl,* Tehran, litho., n.d.

al-MÂMAQÂNÎ, *Tanqîḥ al-maqâl,* Tehran, 1349/1930, 3 vol.

MÂNAKDÎM Aḥmad b. Aḥmad, *Sharḥ al-uṣûl al-khamsa,* ed. ʿA. al-ʿUthmân, Cairo, 1384/1965.

MARQUET, Y., "Le Chiisme au IXe siècle à travers l'Histoire de Yaʿqûbî," *Arabica,* vol. 19, 1972.

———, "Sabéens et Ikhwan al-Ṣafâ," *SI,* vols. 24 and 25, 1976.

MARROU, H. I., *Nouvelle Histoire de l'église,* Paris, 1963 (see also DANIELOU).

MA'RÛF AL-ḤASANÎ, H., *Sîrat al-a'immat al-ithnay 'ashar,* Beirut, 1397/1977.

———, *al-Mabâdi' al-'âmma li l-fiqh al-ja'farî,* Beirut, 1398/1978.

MASSIGNON, L., "Le Jour du Covenant," *Oriens,* vol. 15, 1962.

———, *Essai sur les origines du lexique technique de la mystique musulmane,* Paris, reedition, 1968.

———, "Nûr muḥammadî," *EI1.*

———, *Opera Minora,* Paris, 1969, vol. 1, articles: "Die Ursprünge und die Bedeutung des Gnostizismus im Islam "; "Der Gnostische Kult der Fatima im Shiitischen Islam"; "La Mubâhala de Médine et l'hyperdulie de Fatima"; "La notion du voeu et la dévotion musulmane à Fatima."

———, *La Passion de Hallâj. Martyr mystique de l'Islam,* Paris, 1975.

al-MAS'ÛDÎ, *Murûj al-dhahab,* ed. and French translation by Barbier de Meynard, Paris, 1861–77, see also *Ithbât al-waṣiyya.*

MATÎNÎ, J. "'Elm va 'Olamâ' dar zabân-e Qor'ân va aḥâdîth," *Iran-Nameh,* II-3, 1363 solar/1984.

MEYER, E., "Anlass und Anwendungsbereich der *taqiyya," Der Islam,* vol. 57, 1980.

———, *Mi'râj Nâme-ye Abû'Alî Sînâ be enḍemâm-e taḥrîr-e ân az Shams al-Dîn Ibrâhîm Abarqûhî* ed. N. Mâyel Herawî, Tehran, 1365 solar/1987.

MODARRESSI TABÂTABÂ'I, H., *An Introduction to Shî'î Law; A Bibliographical Study,* London, 1984.

———, "Early Debates on the Integrity of the Qur'ân," *Studia Islamica,* vol. 77, 1993.

———, "Rationalism and Traditionalism in Shî'î Jurisprudence: a Preliminary Survey," *SI,* vol. 59, 1984.

MODARRESSÎ TCHAHÂRDEHÎ, N., *Seyrî dar taṣawwof,* Tehran, 2d ed., 1361 solar/1981.

MODI, J. J., "A Parsee High Priest (Dastûr Azar Kaiwân, 1529–1614 A.D.) with His Zoroastrian Disciples in Patna in the 16th and 17th Century A.C.," *The Journal of the K. R. Cama Oriental Institute,* vol. 20, 1932.

MODÎR SHÂNEHTCHÎ, K., "Kotob-e arba'e-ye ḥadîth-e shî'e," *Nâme-ye Âstân-e Qods,* numbers 1 and 2 of the new series, vol. 38, n.d.

MOELLER, E., *Beiträge zur Mahdilehre des Islams,* Heidelberg, 1901.

MO'ÎN, M., "Âdhar Keyvân va peyrovân-e û," *Majalle-ye Dâneshkade-ye Adabiyyât-e Dâneshgâh-e Tehrân,* num. 3, 4th year, 1336 solar/1958.

MOMEN, M., *An Introduction to Shi'i Islam. The History and Doctrines of Twelver Shi'ism,* New Haven-London, 1985.

MONNOT, G., *Islam et religions,* Paris, 1986, especially the article "La transmigration et l'immortalité " (chapter 12). See also Shahrastânî, *Livre des religions et des sectes.*

MOSCATI, S., "Per una storia dell'antica Shi'a," *RSO,* vol. 30, 1955.

MOTTAHEDEH, R. P., *Loyalty and Leadership in an Early Islamic Society,* Princeton, 1980.

MUDARRIS Md 'Alî, *Rayḥânat al-adab,* Tabriz, n.d., 8 vol.

al-MUFÎD, *Awâ'il al-maqâlât fî l-madhâhib al-mukhtârât,* Tabriz, 1364/1944; French trans. by D. Sourdel, *L'imâmisme vu par le cheikh al-Mufîd, REI,* special edition 7, Paris, 1974.

———, *al-Ikhtiṣâṣ,* ed. 'A. A. Ghaffarî, Tehran, 1379/1959.

———, *al-Irshâd fî ma'rifa ḥujaj Allâh 'alä l-'ibâd,* text and Persian trans. by H. Rasûlî Maḥallâtî, Tehran, 1346 solaire/1968.

———, *al-Fuṣûl al-mukhtâra min al-'uyûn wa l-maḥâsin,* 3d ed., Najaf, 1962.

———, *Kitâb sharḥ 'aqâ'id al-Ṣadûq (= Taṣḥîḥ al-i'tiqâd),* Tabriz, 1371/1951.

———, *al-Fuṣûl al-'ashara fî l-ghayba,* Najaf, 1951.

———, *Khams rasâ'il fî ithbât al-ḥujja,* Najaf, 1951.

———, *al-Muqni'a fî l-fiqh,* Qumm, 1344 solar/1966.

———, *al-I'lâm fî mâ'ttafaqat al-imâmiyya 'alayhi min al-aḥkâm* (Iran), n.d.

———, *al-Radd 'alä aṣḥâb al-'adad,* in 'Alî al-'Âmilî, *al-Durr al-manthûr,* Qumm, 1398/1978.

al-MUḤAQQIQ AL-ḤILLÎ, *al-Mu'tabar,* Tehran, 1318/1900.

———, *Nukat al-nihâya, in al-Jawâmi' al-fiqhiyya,* pp. 373–470, Tehran, 1276/1859.

MULLÂ ṢADRÂ, *Sharḥ Uṣûl al-kâfî,* litho., Tehran, 1283/1865.

al-MURTAḌÂ, *"al-Uṣûl al-i'tiqâdiyya,"* in *Nafâ'is al-makhṭuṭât,* ed. Âl Yâsîn, Baghdad, 1954, vol. 2, pp. 79–92.

———, *Jumal al-'ilm wa l-'amal,* ed. A. al-Ḥusaynî, Najaf, 1387/1967.

———, *Amâlî,* ed. A. Ibrâhîm, Cairo, 1954.

———, *al-Shâfî fî l-imâma,* litho., Tehran, 1301/1884.

———, *"Mas'ala wajîza fî l-ghayba,"* in *Nafâ'is al-makhṭûṭât,* ed. Al Yâsîn, Baghdad, 1955, vol. 4.

———, *al-Muḥkam wa l-mutashâbih* (incorrectly attributed to al-Murtaḍä; see al-NU'MÂNÎ)

———, *Risâlat al-ghayba, see* SACHEDINA.

———, *al-Dharî'a ilä uṣûl al-shî'a,* Tehran, 1967–68.

MUSLIM, *Ṣaḥîḥ,* 2 vol., Cairo, 1349/1930.

al-MUWAḤḤID M. I., *'Alî fî l-aḥâdith al-nabawiyya,* Beirut, 1404/1984.

al-MUẒAFFAR 'Alî, *Dalâ'il al-ṣidq,* Najaf, 1372/1953.

MUẒAFFAR 'ALÎ SHÂH, *Kebrît-e aḥmar (+ Baḥr al-asrâr),* ed. J. Nûrbakhsh, Tehran, 1350 solar/1971.

NAHÂWANDÎ 'Alî Akbar, *'Abqarî al-ḥassân fi tawârîkh Ṣâḥib al-zamân,* Tehran, 1363/1943.

al-NAJÂSHÎ, *Kitâb al-rijâl,* Bombay, 1317/1899.

NAJM AL-DÎN AL-KUBRÂ, ed. F. Meier, *Die Rawâ'iḥ al-jamâl wa fawâtiḥ al-jalâl des Najm ad-Dîn al-Kubrâ,* Wiesbaden, 1957.

NAJM AL-DÎN AL-RÂZÎ, *Mirṣâd al-'ibâd,* ed. Shams al-'urafâ', Tehran, 1312 solar/1933; ed. M. A. Riyâḥî, Tehran, 1352 solar/1973.

NAMÎNIÎ Md Qâdir Bâqirî, *Dîn va del,* Tehran, 1356 solar/1977.

NA'NÂ'A, R., *al-Isrâ'îliyyât wa atharuhâ fî kutub al-tafsîr,* Damascus, 1390/1970.

NANA PRAKASAM, P., *Hindu Occultism,* n.l., 1967.

al-NAQSHBANDÎ Md Amîn al-Kurdî, *Tanwîr al-qulûb,* 6th ed., Cairo, 1348/1929.

NASR, S. H., "Le shî'isme et le soufisme. Leurs relations principielles et historiques," see *(le) Shi'isme imâmite.*

al-NAWBAKHTÎ al-Ḥasan b. Mûsä, *Firaq al-shî'a,* ed. H. Ritter, Istanbul, 1931; French trans. by M. J. Mashkour, *Les Sectes shiites,* Tehran, 2nd ed., 1980.

NEWMAN, A. J., *The Development and Political Significance of the Rationalist (uṣuli) and Traditionalist (akhbari) School in Imami Shi'i History from the Third/Ninth to the Tenth/Sixteen Century* A.D., Doctoral thesis, UCLA, Los Angeles, 1986.

al-NÎSÂBÛRÎ Ḥasan b. Md, *Kitâb 'uqalâ' al-majânîn,* ed. Wajîh b Fâris, Damascus, 2nd ed., 1405/1985.

al-NU'MÂNÎ Ibn Abî Zaynab, *Kitâb al-ghayba,* text and Persian translation by M. J. Ghaffârî, Tehran, 1363 solar/1985; ed. 'A. A. Ghaffârî, Arabic text alone, Tehran, 1397/1977.

———, *al-Muḥkam wa l-mutashâbih,* litho., Tehran, n.d. (placed under the name of al-Murtaḍä 'Alam al-Hudä; this work contains fragments of Ja'far al-Ṣâḍiq's *Tafsîr).*

NÛR 'ALÎ SHÂH GONÂBÂDÎ, *Ṣâliḥiyya,* 2nd ed., Tehran, 1387/1967.

al-NÛRÎ Abû l-Ḥasan, *Maqâmât al-qulûb,* in P. Nwyia, "Textes mystiques inédits d'Abû l-Ḥasan al-Nûrî." *MUSJ,* vol. 44, fasc. 9, 1969.

al-NÛRÎ AL-ṬABARSÎ, *Faṣl al-khiṭâb fî taḥrîf al-Kitâb,* litho., (Tehran), n.d.

———, *al-Najm al-thâqib,* Tehran, litho., 1309/1891.

NWYIA, P., *Exégèse coranique et langage mystique. Nouvel essai sur le lexique technique des mystiques musulmans,* Beirut, 1970. see also JAʿFAR AL-ṢÂDIQ, *Tafsîr. see also* al-NÛRÎ, "Textes mystiques inédits. . . . "

PALÂSÎ SHÎRÂZÎ Ḥasan b. Ḥamza, *Tadhkere-ye sheykh Muḥammad b. Ṣadîq al-Kojojî,* Shiraz, n.d.

PAREJA, F. M., in collaboration with L. Hertling, A. Bausani and Th. Bois, *Islamologie,* Beirut, 1957–63.

PARET, R., *Der Koran, Kommentar und Konkordanz,* ed. 1978, Stuttgart, Berlin, Cologne, Mainz.

———, article "ʿIlliyyûn," *EI2.*

PELLAT, Ch., "Masʿûdî et l'imâmisme," see *(le) Shiʿisme imâmite.*

———, "Ḥilm," *EI2,* vol. 3, pp. 403–4.

———, *(la) Petite Philocalie de la prière du coeur,* introduced and translated by J. Gouillard, Paris, 1979.

PINES, S., "Shîʿite Terms and Conceptions in Judah Halevi's *Kuzari*" *JSAI,* vol. 2, 1980.

POONAWALA, I., "ʿAlî b. Abî Ṭâlib," *Encyclopaedia Iranica* (cf. also KOHLBERG).

PRETZL, O., "Die frühislamische Atomenlehre," *Der Islam,* vol. 19, 1931.

(La) Prière du Coeur, (anonymous), Editions Orthodoxes, Paris, 1952.

PÛRJAVÂDÎ (POORJAVADY), N., "Taḥlîlî az mafâhîm-e ʿaql va jonûn dar ʿuqalâʾ al-majânîn," *Maʿâref,* vol. 4, num. 2, 1366 solar/1987.

———, "Roʾyat-e mâh dar âsmân," *Nashr-i Dânish,* 10th year, nums. 1, 2, 3 . . . 1989, 1990.

al-QÂDÎ, W., "The Development of the Term *ghulât* in Muslim Literature with Special Reference to the Kaysâniyya," *Akten VII. Kong. Arabistic,* Göttingen, 1976.

———, "An early Fâṭimid political document," *SI,* 48,1978.

al-QASṬALLÂNÎ, *Irshâd al-sârî li-sharḥ Ṣaḥîḥ al-Bukhârî,* Beirut, 1323/1905.

al-QAZWÎNÎ ʿAbd al-Jalîl, *Kitâb al-naqḍ,* ed. Muḥaddith Urmawî, Tehran, 1979.

al-QAZWÎNÎ Mullâ Khalîl, *al-Shâfî fî sharḥ al-Kâfî,* Lucknow, 1308/1890.

QUERRY, A., *Recueil des lois concernant les musulmans schyites,* Paris, 1871.

al-QUMMÎ ʿAbbâs, *Hidyat al-aḥbâb fî dhikr al-maʾrûfîn bi l-kunä wa l-alqâb wa l-ansâb,* Najaf, n.d.

———, *Safînat al-Biḥâr,* Tehran, 1355/1936.

al-QUMMÎ ʿAlî b. Ibrâhîm, *Tafsîr,* ed. al-Masawî al-Jazâʾirî, Najaf, 1386–87/1966–68.

al-QUMMÎ Ḥasan b. Md, *Târîkh-e Qomm* (written in 378 A.H. and translated into Persian in 805–6 A.H.), ed. J. Tehrânî, Tehran, 1353 solar/1974.

al-QUMMÎ Jaʿfar b. Md, see IBN QÛLÛYE AL-QUMMÎ.

al-QUMMÎ Saʿd b. ʿAbdAllâh, *Kitâb al-maqâlât wa l-firaq,* ed. M. J. Mashkûr, Tehran, 1963.

al-QUMMÎ al-shaykh al-Ṣaffâr, see ṢAFFÂR AL-QUMMÎ.

al-QUSHAYRÎ, *al-Risâlat al-Qushayriyya,* Cairo, 1379/1959.

RAHBAR, D., "Relation of Shîʿa Theology to the Qurʾân," *MW,* vol. 51, num. 3, July 1961; vol. 52, num. 1, Jan. 1962; num. 2, April 1962.

RAHMAN, F., "ʿAql," *EI2* and *Encyclopaedia Iranica* (with W. CHITTICK).

RÂMYÂR, M., *Târîkh-e Qorʾân,* Tehran, 1346 solar/1968.

———, *Rasâʾil Ikhwân al-ṣafâʾ,* Beirut, 1957.

RASHÎD RIḌÂ, *al-Sunna wa l-shîʿa,* Cairo, 1347/1928.

RAUSCHER, T., *Shariʿa. Islamischen Familienrecht der Sunna und Shiʿa,* Frankfurt, 1987.

RÂZ SHÎRÂZÎ Mîrzâ Bâbâ, *Mirṣâd at-ʿibâd,* Tabriz, n.d.

———, *Resâle-ye hall-e eshkâl-e davâzdah soʾâl-e Râʾiḍ al-Dîn Zanjânî,* Tehran, 1367/1947.

RICHARD, Y., *Le Shiʿisme en Iran. Imam et Révolution,* Paris, 1980.

———, *L'Islam shiʿite,* Paris, 1991.

ROBSON, J., "Ibn Isḥâq's Use of the Isnâd," *The John Rylands Library,* vol. 38, 1955–56.

———, "Ḥadîth," *EI2,* vol. 3, pp. 24 sq.

———, "al-Djarḥ wa al-taʿdîl," *EI2,* vol. 2, pp. 473–74.

ROSENTHAL, F., "The Influence of the Biblical Tradition on Muslim Historiography," *Historians of the Middle East,* B. Lewis and P. M. Holt ed., London, 1962.

———, *Knowledge Triumphant,* reedition., Leiden, 1970.

RUBIN, U. "Pre-Existence and Light: Aspects of the Concept of Nûr Muḥammad," *IOS,* vol. 5, 1975.

———, "Prophets and Progenitors in the Early Shîʿa Tradition," *JSAI,* vol. 1, 1979.

———, "Barâʾa: a study of some Quranic passages," *JSAI,* vol. 5, 1984.

RUSKA, J., *Arabische Alchemisten. II- Gaʿfar al-Ṣâdiq, der sechste Imâm,* Heidelberg, 1924.

SABRI, T., *L'Hagiographie de Fâṭima d'après le Biḥâr al-Anwâr de Muḥammad Bâqir Majlisî (m. 1111/1699),* Doctoral thesis, Paris III, 1969.

SACHEDINA, A., "A Treatise on the Occultation of the Twelfth Imâmite Imâm," *SI,* vol. 68, 1978 (English trans. of al-Murtaḍä's *Risâlat al-ghabya).*

———, *Islamic Messianism: The Idea of the Mahdi in Twelver Shiʿism,* Albany, 1981.

SADIGHI, Gh. H., *Les Mouvements religieux iraniens aux IIe et IIIe siècles de l'Hégire,* Paris, 1938.

al-ṢADR Md, *Taʾrîkh al-ghaybat al-ṣughrä,* vol. 1, Beirut, 1972.

———, *Taʾrîkh al-ghaybat al-kubrä,* vol. 2, Beirut, 1975.

ṢÂFÎ GOLPÂYEGÂNÎ, see GOLPÂYEGÂNÎ.

al-ṢAFFÂR AL-QUMMÎ,, *Baṣâʾir al-darajât,* ed. Mîrzâ Kûtchebâghî, Tabriz, 2d ed., n.d. (the editor's introduction is dated 1380/1960).

SAINT CLAIR TISDALL, "Shiʿah Additions to the Koran," *MW,* vol. 3, July 1913, num. 3.

al-SAMʿÂNÎ, *al-Ansâb,* facsimile ed. with introduction by D. S. Margoliouth, Leiden-London, 1912.

SCARCIA, G., "A proposito del problema della sovranita presso gli Imâmiti," *AIUON,* vol. 7, 1957.

———, "Intorno alle controversie tra Akhbârî e Usûlî presso gli Imâmiti di Persia," *RSO,* vol. 33, 1958.

SCARCIA-AMORETTI, "L'Imamismo in Iran nell'epoca selgiuchide: a proposito del problema delle "communita"" in *La Bissacia dello Sheikh Omaggio ad Alessandro Bausani,* Venice, 1981, pp. 127–40.

SCHIMMEL, A. M., *Islam in the Indian Subcontinent,* Leiden, 1980.

SCHWALLY, F., *Geschichte des Qorans II-Die Sammlung des Qorans,* Leipzig, 1919.

SELLHEIM, R., "Prophet, Chalif und Geschichte," *Oriens,* vol. 18–19, 1965–66.

Sept Upanishads, commentated translation by J. Varenne, Paris, 1981.

SEZGIN, F., *Geschichte des Arabischen Schrifttums,* Leiden, 1967. . . .

SHÂDHÂN IBN JABRÂ'ÎL al-Qummî, *Kitâb al-faḍâ'il,* Najaf, n. d.

SHAFÂ'Î, M., "'Uddat al-uṣûl-e shaykh Ṭûsî va naqsh-e an dar madâr-e târîkh-e 'elm-e uṣûl," *Yâdnâme-ye sheykh al-ṭâ'efe Abû Ja'far Moḥammad b. Ḥasan-e Ṭûsî,* vol. 1, Mashhad, 1348 solar/1970.

al-SHAHÎD al-THÂNÎ Zayn al-Dîn al-'Âmilî, *al-Dirâya,* ed. Âl Ibrâhîm, Najaf, n.d.

al-SHAHRASTÂNÎ, *al-Milal wa l-niḥal,* ed. Cureton, London, 1846; ed. Badrân, Cairo, 1951–52; ed. Kaylânî, Cairo, 1967; French trans, first part, with introd. and notes by D. Gimaret and G. Monnot, *Livre des religions et des sectes (I),* Louvain, 1986.

SHARON, M., "The 'Abbâsid Da'wa Reexamined on the Basis of a New Source," *Arabic and Islamic Studies,* Univers. de Bar Ilan, Israel, 1973.

———, "The Development of the Debate Around the Legitimacy of Authority in Early Islam," *JSAI,* vol. 5, 1984.

al-SHAYBÎ, K. M., "al-Taqiyya, uṣûluhâ wa taṭawwuruhâ," *Revue de la fac. de lettres de l'université d'Alexandrie,*vol. 16, 1962–63.

———, *al-Fikr al-shî'î wa l-naza'ât al-ṣufiyya ḥattä maṭla' l-qarn al-thânî 'ashar al-hijrî,* Baghdad, 1966.

———, *al-Ṣila bayna l-taṣawwuf wa l-tashayyu',* Cairo, 1969.

SHAYEGAN, D., *Qu'est-ce qu'une révolution religieuse?*" Paris, 1982.

SHIHÂB AL-DÎN IBN ḤAJAR, *al-Fatâwâ al-ḥadîthiyya,* Cairo, 1325/1907.

(le) Shi'isme imâmite, Colloque de Strasbourg (6–9 mai 1968), Paris, 1970.

al-SIMNÂNÎ 'Alâ' al-Dawla, *al-'Urwa li-ahl al-khalwa wa l-jalwa,* ed. N. Mâyel Herawî, Tehran, 1362 solar/1985.

SOURDEL, D., "La politique religieuse du calife abbasside al-Ma'mûn," *REI,* vol. 30, 1962.

L'Imâmisme vu par le cheikh al-Mufîd, see al-MUFÎD, *Awâ'il al-maqâlât.*

———, "La politique religieuse des successeurs d'al-Mutawakkil," *SI,* vol. 31, 1973.

———, "Barâmika," *EI2,* vol. 1, p. 1064.

SPITALER, A., "Was bedewtet *baqîja* im Koran ? *Westöstlische Abhandlungen Rudolf Tschudi zum Siebzigsten Geburtstag,* Wiesbaden, 1954.

STROTHMANN, R., *Die Zwölfer-Schî'a: Zwei Religionsgeschichtliche Charakterbilder aus des Mongolenzeit,* Leipzig, 1926.

———, "History of Islamic Heresiography," *IC*, 1938.

———, "Zayd b. 'Alî," *EI1*, vol. 4, p. 1260.

ṢUBḤI AL-ṢÂLIḤ, *'Ulûm al-ḥadîth wa muṣṭalaḥuhu,* Damascus, 1379/1959.

al-SUBKÎ, *Ṭabaqât al-shâfi'iyya,* Cairo, 1324–25/1905–1906.

al-SULAMÎ, *Risâlat al-malâmatiyya,* cf. 'AFÎFÎ.

SULṬÂN 'ALÎ SHÂH GONÂBÂDÎ, *Walâyat Nâmeh,* 2d ed., Tehran, 1385/1965.

al-SUYÛṬÎ, *al-Khaṣâ'iṣ al-kubrä,* ed. Md Kh. Harrâs, Cairo, 1967.

ṬABÂṬABÂ'I Md Ḥusayn, *Shî'e dar Eslâm,* reedition. Qumm, 1966; English trans. by S. H. Nasr, *Shiite Islam,* London, 1975.

al-ṬABARÎ Md b. Jarîr, *Ta'rîkh al-umam wa l-mulûk,* Cairo 1358/1939 (= *Ta'rîkh al-rusul wa l-mulûk,* Cairo, 1960).

———, *Jâmi' al-bayân fî tafsîr al Qur'ân,* reedition., Beirut, 1972.

al-ṬABARÎ Md b. Md, *Bishârat al-Muṣṭafä li-shî'at al-Murtaḍä,* ed. al-Jawâhirî, Najaf, 1383/1963.

al-ṬABARSÎ Faḍl b. al-Ḥasan, *Majma' al-bayân fî tafsîr al-Qur'ân,* Tehran, 1371/1951.

———, *I'lâm al-warä fî a'lam al-hudä,* ed. al-Kharsân, Najaf, 1390/1970.

al-ṬABARSÎ Mîrzâ Ḥusayn, see al-NÛRÎ al-ṬABARSÎ.

al-TAFRISHÎ Sayyid al-Ḥusaynî, *Naqd al-rijâl,* Tehran, 1318/1900.

ṬÂROMÎ, Ḥ. and ṬÂLE'Î, 'A. Ḥ., *Ahâdîth-e qodsî pîrâmûn-e ḥaḍrat-e Mahdî,*

Tehran, 1365 solar/1985.

TAYLOR, J. B., "Ja'far al-Ṣâdiq, Spiritual Forebear of the Sûfis," *IC*, 1966.

al-ṬIHRÂNÎ Aqâ Bozorg, *al-Dharî'a ilä taṣânif al-shî'a,* Tehran-Najaf, 1353–98/1934–78, 25 vol.

al-TIRMIDHÎ Abû 'Îsä Md, *Sunan,* Cairo, 4 vol., 1292/1875.

al-TIRMIDHÎ AL-ḤAKÎM, *al-Farq bayna l-ṣadr wa l-qalb wa l-fu'âd wa l-lubb,* ed. H. Neer, Cairo, 1958.

———, *(Le) Troisième Livre du Dênkart,* trans. J. de Menasce, Paris, 1973.

TUCKER, W. F., "Rebels and Gnostics: al-Mughîra b. Sa'îd and the Mughîriyya," *Arabica,* vol. 22, 1975.

———, "Bayân b. Sam'ân and the Bayâniyya: Shî'ite Extremists of Umayyad Iraq," *MW,* vol. 65, 1975.

al-ṬURAYḤÎ, *Majma' al-baḥrayn wa maṭla' al-nayyirayn,* Tehran, 1321/1903.

al-ṬÛSÎ Abû Ja'far, *Kitâb al-ghayba,* Tabriz, 1322/1905.

———, *Kitâb al-rijâl,* Najaf, 1380/1961.

———, *Fihrist kutub al-shî'a,* ed. Sprenger and 'Abd al-Ḥaqq; reedition. Mashhad, 1972.

———, *al-Istibṣâr,* ed. al-Kharsân, Najaf, 1375–76/1955–56.

———, *Tahdhîb al-aḥkâm,* ed. al-Kharsân, Najaf, 1958–62.

———, *'Uddat al-uṣûl,* Tehran, 1314/1896.

———, *al-Amâlî,* ed. Baḥr al-'ulûm, Najaf, 1384/1964.

Two Early Ismaili Treatises, ed. W. Ivanow, Bombay, 1933 (especially *Haft bâb-e Bâbâ Sayyidnâ).*

Upanishads, English translation, 6 vol., Madras, n.d.

Upanishads du Yoga, translated and annotated by Jean Varenne, Paris, 1971.

al-Uṣûl al-arba'u mi'a, ms. num. 962, University of Tehran.

VADET, J. Cl., "Kalb," *EI2,* vol. 4, pp. 507–10 (cf. also GARDET).

VAJDA, G., "Deux 'Histoires des Prophètes' selon la tradition des shî'ites duodécimains," *Revue d'Etudes Juives,* vol. 106, 1945–46.

———, "Le problème de la vision de Dieu *(ru'ya)* d'après quelques auteurs shî'ites duodécimains," see *(le) Shî'isme imâmite.*

———, "Pour le dossier de *naẓar," Recherches d'islamologie. Recueil d'articles offerts à G. Anawati et L. Gardet par leurs collègues et amis,* Louvain, 1977.

———, "De quelques emprunts d'origine juive dans le ḥadîth shî'ite," *Studies in Judaism and Islam presented to S. D. Goitein,* ed. S. Morag *et. al.*, Jerusalem, 1981.

VAN ESS, J., *Die Gedankenwelt des Ḥârith al-Muḥâsibî,* Bonn, 1961.

———, "Ibn Kullâb und die Miḥna," *Oriens,* 18–19, 1967.

———, "Ḍirar b. 'Amr und die 'Cahmîya,'" *Der Islam,* vol. 43, 1967.

———, *Frühe mu'tazilitische Häresiographie. Zwei Werke des Nâshi' al-akbar,* Beirut, 1971.

———, *Une lecture à rebours de l'histoire du mu'tazilisme, REI,* out of series 14, Paris, 1984.

VAN VLOTEN, G., *Recherches sur la domination arabe, le chiitisme et les croyances messianiques sous le khalifat des Omeyyades,* Amsterdam, 1894.

VARENNE, J. see *Sept Upanishads, Upanishads du Yoga* and *Veda.*

VATIKIOTIS, P. J., "The Rise of Extremist Sects and the Dissolution of the Fatimid Empire in Egypt," *IC*, vol. 31, 1957.

VECCIA VAGLIERI, L. "Sul 'Nahj al-balâghah' et sul suo compilatore ash-Sharîf ar-Raḍî," *AIUON,* special num. 8, 1958.

———, *EI2,* articles: "'Alî b. Abî Ṭâlib"; "al-Ḥusayn b. 'Alî"; "Fâṭima"; "Ghadîr Khumm."

(le) Veda, premier Livre Sacré de l'Inde, trans. J. Varenne, Paris, 1967.

VON ARENDONK, C., *Les Débuts de l'imâmat zaydite du Yémen,* Leiden, 1960.

———, "Yaḥyâ b. Zayd ", *EI1*, vol. 4, pp. 1214–15.

———, "al-Nafs al-Zakiyya," *EI1*, vol. 3, p. 710.

WATT, W. M., "Shi'ism under the Umayyads," *JRAS,* 1960.

———, "The Râfidites: A Preliminary Study," *Oriens,* vol. 16, 1963.

———, "Side Lights on Early Imamite Doctrine," *SI*, vol. 30, 1970.

———, *Formative Period of Islamic Thought,* Edinburgh, 1973.

WELLHAUSEN, J., *Die religiös-politischen Oppositionsparteien im alten Islam,* Berlin, 1901.

WENSINCK, A. J., "Muhammad und die Propheten," *Acta Orientalia,* vol. 2, 1924.

———, *Concordances et indices de la tradition musulmane,* Leiden, 1933–65.

———, "al-Khaḍir," *EI2,* vol. 3, pp. 935–939.

———, "al-Lawḥ," *EI2,* vol. 4, p. 703 (cf. also BOSWORTH).

al-YA'QÛBÎ, *Ta'rîkh,* ed. M. T. Houtsma, Leiden, 1883.

YÂQÛT AL-ḤAMAWÎ, *Mu'jam al-buldân,* Cairo, 10 vol., 1324/1906.

Yek qesmat az târîkh-e ḥayât wa karâmât-e Seyyed Qoṭb al-Dîn Mohammad Shîrâzî, (anonymous), Tabriz, 1309/1891.

Yoga, science de l'Homme Intégral, ed. J. Massin, Paris, 1953.

ZAY'ÛR, 'A., *al-Tafsîr al-ṣûfî li l-Qur'ân 'inda l-Ṣâdiq,* Beirut, 1979 (cf. JA'FAR AL-ṢÂDIQ).

ZIRIKLI Khayr al-Dîn, *al-A'lâm,* Cairo, 1954–59.

al-ZURQÂNÎ, *Sharḥ 'alä l-Mawâhib al-laduniyya li l-Qasṭallânî,* Cairo, 1329/1911.

Index